ESSAYS FROM CONTEMPORARY CULTURE

ESSAYS FROM CONTEMPORARY CULTURE

KATHERINE ANNE ACKLEY

University of Wisconsin
at Stevens Point

Harcourt Brace Jovanovich College Publishers

Fort Worth   Philadelphia   San Diego   New York   Orlando   Austin   San Antonio
Toronto   Montreal   London   Sydney   Tokyo

Acquisitions Editor: Stuart Miller
Manuscript Editor: Karl Yambert
Production Editor: Socorro P. González
Designer: Linda Wooton Miller
Art Editor: Avery Hallowell
Production Manager: David Hough
Permissions Editor: Eleanor Garner

Cover art: Copyright © by Douglas Fraser
Text illustrations: Linda Wooton Miller

ISBN: 0-15-522891-9
Printed in the United States of America

Library of Congress Cataloging Number: 91–65875

Permissions and Acknowledgments begin on page 391 and constitute a continuation of the copyright page.

PREFACE

———————————— • ————————————

T he goals of freshman English are to help you read and think critically, formulate ideas of substance, and write clearly and logically. If you can learn to perform these tasks well in freshman English, you will very likely do better in your other classes, particularly those that require you to write essays or term papers. Hence, freshman English teaches valuable writing skills that you will use over and over again in college — and beyond.

One of the best ways to learn to write well is to read extensively, with care and thought, paying attention to the ways in which professional writers and other intelligent, thinking people express themselves, order their thoughts, and develop and support their ideas. What you read, think, and write about is — or ought to be — inextricably linked with who you are and how you develop as a responsible human being in relation to your classmates, your family, and the community in which you live and work. As an educated adult, you will want to be aware of issues and events that affect you as an individual and as a member of your society.

This textbook is designed to help you express an opinion or observation in an articulate, clearly written form. Its readings come from a variety of sources, including newspapers, magazines, and books. They have been selected to engage your interest and elicit your responses, both in classroom discussion and in essays. Although the readings vary in style, tone, organization, and purpose, all in one way or another respond to particular issues of contemporary culture that concern or touch us all.

While most of the readings come from very recent publications, each chapter concludes with a classic essay that is generally regarded as a model of excellence. The inclusion of a classic essay in each chapter serves several purposes. First, it provides an opportunity for you to read works that have endured on the merits of their readable, clear style and timeless insights into human experience. Further, such enduring essays invite active comparison with more recent works that you will read in this textbook and elsewhere. Finally, the older essays illustrate that some issues are never resolved or do not change significantly. That is, no matter when you were born or where you have lived, certain life experiences remain essentially the same. Growing up, getting along with others, and deciding when to stand on principle, for example, are recurring human concerns.

The majority of the selections in this textbook, however, are contemporary responses not only to abiding social issues but also to more recent phenomena such as AIDS, the alarming rise in the use of hard drugs, and the rampant violent crime. While deadly diseases, substance abuse, and crime have always been part of our society's problems, these problems have grown enormously and demand close attention in the 1990s. The contemporaneity of the readings, which address issues that you may have to face yourself, speaks to the relevance of this textbook to your life beyond the classroom.

You are invited to read these essays, to think about them, and to respond to them. To assist you, each selection is followed by questions about your personal reaction to the reading, as well as by questions for class discussion. You are asked for your personal reaction to the article first because subjective responses usually come before objective analyses of essays. After responding on a subjective level, you are then asked to look back through the essay and answer questions about the author's purpose and meaning and the ways in whose those are achieved.

Following the questions for discussion are topics for writing, suitable for either in-class or out-of-class writing. At the end of each chapter are additional writing suggestions suitable for longer assignments, including research papers.

Katherine Anne Ackley

ACKNOWLEDGMENTS

●

Many people have helped in the preparation of this textbook. I would like to thank Catherine Ligman, freshman English secretary, Christine Ballweg and Debbie Felix, student assistants, at the University of Wisconsin at Stevens Point for their proofreading and typing of the manuscript, and Richard Ackley, my husband. I am especially grateful to Eleanor Ligman, English Department secretary at the University of Wisconsin at Stevens Point, for typing the bulk of the manuscript.

Very special thanks are due to Heather Anne Schilling, who provided helpful suggestions and insightful comments on the text in its early drafts. I am grateful also for the suggestions received from the following reviewers during the manuscript's various stages of completion: Maryann Padget (Tennessee Technological University), Susan Schiller (Sacramento City College), and Nancy Walker (Southwest Missouri State University).

Finally, I am thankful for the wisdom and guidance of the people at Harcourt Brace Jovanovich: Stuart Miller, Karl Yambert, Eleanor Garner, Socorro P. González, Linda Miller, and David Hough. Their help on this project has been immeasurable.

CONTENTS

•4•
SEARCHING FOR A PLACE

•7•
CONFRONTING PREJUDICE

RHETORICAL
TABLE OF CONTENTS

EXEMPLIFICATION

CAUSE-EFFECT ANALYSIS

PROCESS ANALYSIS

COMPARISON/CONTRAST

CLASSIFICATION

DEFINITION

ARGUMENT/PERSUASION

1

TRANSITIONS

"WHO SHALL I BE?"
THE ALLURE OF A FRESH START

●

JENNIFER CRICHTON

*Jennifer Crichton has published articles in a number of national maga-
zines. Her book,* Delivery: A Nurse-Midwife's Story, *is a fictionalized
account of life on the labor and delivery floor of a metropolitan
hospital. In this 1984 article from* Ms. *magazine, Crichton explains,
using both personal experience and the examples of people she knows,
how going away to college offers the opportunity to create an entirely
new identity.*

The student is a soul in transit, coming from one place en route to
someplace else. Moving is the American way, after all. Our guiding
principle is the fresh start, our foundation the big move, and nothing
seduces like the promise of a clean slate.

"Do you realize how many people saw me throw up at Bob Stonehill's party
in tenth grade? A lot of people," says my friend Anne. "How many forgot about
it? Maybe two or three. Do you know how much I wanted to go someplace
where nobody knew I threw up all over Bob Stonehill's living room in tenth
grade? Very much. This may not seem like much of a justification for going away
to college, but it was for me." Going away to college gives us a chance to rinse off
part of our past, to shake off our burdensome reputations.

We've already survived the crises of being known, allowing how American
high schools are as notoriously well-organized as totalitarian regimes, complete
with secret police, punishment without trial, and banishment. High school
society loves a label, cruelly infatuated with pinning down every species of
student. Hilary is a klutz, Julie is a slut, and Michele a gossiping bitch who eats
like a pig.

No wonder so many of us can't wait to be free of our old identities and climb   4
inside a new skin in college. Even flattering reputations can be as confining as a
pair of too-tight shoes. But identity is tricky stuff, constructed with mirrors. How
you see yourself is a composite reflection of how you appear to friends, family,
and lovers. In college, the fact that familiar mirrors aren't throwing back a
familiar picture is both liberating and disorienting (maybe that's why so many
colleges have freshman "orientation week").

"I guess you could call it an identity crisis," Andrea, a junior now, says of her
freshman year. "It was the first time nobody knew who I was. I wasn't even
anybody's daughter any more. I had always been the best and brightest — what
was I going to do now, walk around the dorm with a sign around my neck saying
'Former High School Valedictorian'?"

For most of my college years, I was in hot pursuit of an identity crisis,
especially after a Comparative Literature major informed me that the Chinese

definition of "crisis" was "dangerous opportunity," with the emphasis on opportunity. On college applications, where there were blanks for your nickname, I carefully wrote "Rusty," although none of my friends (despite the fact that I have red hair) had ever, even for a whimsical moment, considered calling me that. I was the high-strung, sensitive, acne-blemished, antiauthoritarian, would-be writer. If I went through a day without some bizarre mood swing, people asked me what was wrong. I didn't even have the leeway to be the cheerful, smiling sort of girl I thought I might have it in me to be. My reputation seemed etched in stone, and I was pretty damn sick of it. As I pictured her, Rusty was the blithe spirit who would laugh everything off, shrug at perils as various as freshman mixers, bad grades, and cafeterias jammed with aloof strangers, and in general pass through a room with all the vitality and appeal of a cool gust of wind.

But when I arrived at college, Rusty had vaporized. She was simply not in the station wagon that drove me up to campus. Much of college had to do with filling in the blanks, but changing myself would not be so easy, so predictable, so clichéd.

My parents, acting as anxious overseers on the hot, humid day I took my new self to college, seemed bound by a demonic ESP to sabotage my scarcely budding new identity. After a summer planning how I would metamorphose into the great American ideal, the normal teenage girl, I heard my mother tell my roommate, "I think you'll like Jenny — she's quite the oddball." Luckily, my roommate was saturated with all kinds of information the first day of college had flung at her, and the last thing she was paying attention to were the off-the-cuff remarks this oddball's mother was making. My unmarked reputation kept its sheen as it waited for me to cautiously build it up according to plan. My parents left without any further blunders, except to brush my bangs from my eyes ("You'll get a headache, Sweetheart") and foist on what had been a blissfully bare dormitory room an excruciatingly ugly lamp from home. As soon as the station wagon became a distant mote of dust on the highway, I pulled my bangs back over my eyes in my New Wave fashion of choice, tossed the ugly lamp in the nearest trash can, and did what I came to college to do. Anonymous, alone, without even a name, I would start over and become the kind of person I was meant to be: like myself, but better, with all my failures, rejections, and sexual indiscretions relegated to a history I hoped none of my new acquaintances would ever hear of.

Why was it, I wondered, when *any* change seemed possible that year, had it been so impossible in high school? For one thing, people know us well enough to see when we're attempting a change, and change can look embarrassingly like a public admission of weakness. Our secret desires, and the fact that we're not entirely pleased with ourselves, are on display. To change in public under the scrutiny of the most hypercritical witnesses in the world — other high school students — is to risk failure ("Look how cool she's trying to be, the jerk!") or succeeding but betraying friends in the process ("I don't understand her any more," they say, hurt and angry) or feeling so much like a fraud that you're forced to back down. And while we live at home, parental expectations, from the lovingly hopeful to the intolerably ambitious, apply the pressure of an invisible but very effective mold.

Jacki dressed in nothing but baggy Levi's and flannel shirts for what seemed to be the endless duration of high school, even though she came to a sort of truce with her developing woman's body in eleventh grade and wasn't averse any longer to looking pretty. Looking good in college was a fantasy she savored because in high school, "I didn't want to make the attempt in public and then fail," she explains now, looking pulled together and chic. "I thought everyone would think I was trying to look good but I only managed to look weird. And I didn't want a certain group of girls who were very image-conscious to think they'd won some kind of victory either, that I was changing to please them.

"So I waited for college, and wore nice, new clothes right off the bat so nobody would know me any other way. I had set my expectations too high, though — I sort of thought that I'd be transformed into a kind of femme fatale or something. When I wasn't measuring up to what I'd imagined, I almost ditched the whole thing until I realized that at least I wasn't sabotaging myself any more. When I ran into a friend from high school, even though I had gotten used to the nice way I looked, I was scared that she could see right through my disguise. That's how I felt for a long time: a slobby girl just pretending to be pulled together."

At first, any change can feel uncomfortably like a pretense, an affectation. 12 Dana had been a punked-out druggy in high school, so worried about being considered a grind that she didn't use a fraction of her considerable vocabulary when she was around her anti-intellectual friends. She promised herself to get serious academically in college, but the first night she spent studying in the science library, she recalls, "I half-expected the other kids to look twice at me, as if my fish-out-of-water feeling was showing. Of course, it wasn't. But it was schizophrenic at first, as if I were an impostor only playing at being smart. But when you do something long enough that thing becomes *you*. It's not playing any more. It's what you are."

Wanting to change yourself finds its source in two wellsprings: self-hatred and self-affirmation. Self-affirmation takes what already exists in your personality (even if slightly stunted or twisted) and encourages its growth. Where self-affirmation is expansive, self-hatred is reductive, negating one's own personality while appropriating qualities external to it and applying them like thick pancake makeup.

Joan's thing was to hang out with rich kids with what can only be described as a vengeance. She dressed in Ralph Lauren, forayed to town for $75 haircuts, and complained about the tackiness of mutual friends. But after a late night of studying, Joan allowed her self-control to slip long enough to tell me of her upbringing. Her mother was a cocktail waitress and Joan had never even found out her father's name. She and her mother had trucked about from one Western trailer park to another, and Joan always went to school dogged by her wrong-side-of-the-tracks background. That Joan had come through her hardscrabble life with such strong intellectual achievement seemed a lot more creditable — not to mention interesting — than the effortless achievements of many of our more privileged classmates. Joan didn't think so, and, I suppose in fear I'd blow her cover (I never did), she cut me dead after her moment's indulgence in self-revelation. Joan was rootless and anxious, alienated not only from her background but, by extension, from herself, and paid a heavy psychic price. This wasn't change: this was lies. She scared me. But we learn a lot about friends from the kinds of masks they choose to wear.

After all, role-playing to some degree is the prerogative of youth. A woman of romance, rigorous academic, trendy New Waver, intense politico, unsentimental jock, by turn — we have the chance to experiment as we decide the kind of person we want to become. And a stereotypical role, adopted temporarily, can offer a refuge from the swirl of confusing choices available to us, by confining us to the limits of a type. Returning to my old self after playing a role, I find I'm slightly different, a little bit more than what I was. To contradict one's self is to transcend it.

As occasional fugitives from our families, we all sometimes do what Joan 16 did. Sometimes you need a radical change in order to form an identity independent of your family, even if that change is a weird but transient reaction. My friend Lisa came from a family of feminists and academics. When she returned home from school for Thanksgiving, dressed as a "ditsy dame" straight out of a beach-blanket-bingo movie, she asked me, "How do you think I look? I've been planning this since tenth grade. Isn't it great?" Well, er, yes, it was great — not because she looked like a Barbie doll incarnate but because nobody would ever automatically connect her life with that of her parents again.

Another friend, Dan, went from a Southern military academy to a Quaker college in the North to execute his scheme of becoming a serious intellectual. The transformation went awry after a few months, partly because his own self was too likably irrepressible. It wouldn't lie down and play dead. "I kept running into myself like a serpent chasing its tail," as he puts it. But his openness to change resulted in a peculiar amalgamation of cultures whose charm lies in his realizing that, while he's of his background, he's not identical to it. Most of our personalities and bodies are just as stubbornly averse to being extinguished, even if the fantasy of a symbolic suicide and a renaissance from the ashes takes its obsessive toll on our thoughts now and again. But a blank slate isn't the same as a blank self, and the point of the blank slate that college provides is not to erase the past, but to sketch out a new history with a revisionist's perspective and an optimist's acts.

And what of my changes? Well, when I was friendly and happy in college, nobody gaped as though I had sprouted a tail. I learned to laugh things off as Rusty might have done, and there was one particular counterman at the corner luncheonette who called me Red, which was the closest I came to being known as Rusty.

What became of Rusty? Senior year, I stared at an announcement stating the dates that banks would be recruiting on campus, and Rusty materialized for the first time since freshman year. Rusty was a Yuppie now, and I pictured her dressed in a navy-blue suit, looking uneasily like Mary Cunningham, setting her sights on Citibank. I was still the high-strung, oversensitive, would-be writer

(I'm happy to report my skin did clear up), but a little better, who left the corporate world to Rusty. For myself, I have the slate of the rest of my life to write on.

● PERSONAL RESPONSE ●

In what ways has college given you the opportunity for a "fresh start"? Have you made any changes in your behavior or appearance from when you were in high school? If so, explain what they are and why you have made them.

● QUESTIONS FOR DISCUSSION ●

1. What do you think Crichton means by the statement that "nothing seduces like the promise of a clean slate" (paragraph 1)?
2. In what sense can the fresh start of college be "both liberating and disorienting" (paragraph 4)?
3. Why is it so difficult to change in high school, according to Crichton?
4. How do the examples of Jacki, Dana, Joan, Lisa, and Dan each work to illustrate why college students want to change themselves and how they go about doing it?
5. What do you think Crichton means in paragraph 15 when she says, "To contradict one's self is to transcend it"?
6. What image of herself did Crichton hope to realize when she went to college?
7. Why do you suppose that Crichton does not seem to mind that she did not essentially alter her personality when she was at college? Has she changed in any way?
8. What major point does Crichton make about the blank slate that college provides?

● WRITING TOPICS ●

1. Tell about an embarrassing experience you had in high school that you would prefer everyone forget.
2. Describe the image of yourself that you hope to have in college. Does it differ significantly from your old self, or is it the same? Have you undergone any changes at college in the way you act or in your appearance?
3. Use your own experience to illustrate concretely Crichton's point that "we learn a lot about friends from the kinds of masks they choose to wear" (paragraph 14).

A TEXTBOOK PREGNANCY

●

Perri Klass

Perri Klass graduated from Harvard Medical School in 1986 and is a pediatrician. She has published articles in The New York Times, Discover, Self, Vogue, Esquire, Mademoiselle, *and* The Boston Globe Magazine. *In addition, she has published two novels,* Recombinations *(1985) and* Other Women's Children *(1990); a collection of short stories,* I Am Having an Adventure *(1986); and a collection of essays,* A Not Entirely Benign Procedure: Four Years as a Medical Student *(1987). In "A Textbook Pregnancy," reprinted from* A Not Entirely Benign Procedure, *Klass explains her decision to have a baby while still in medical school and the conflicts she experienced as a result.*

I learned I was pregnant the afternoon of my anatomy exam. I had spent the morning taking first a written exam and then a practical, centered around fifteen thoroughly dissected cadavers, each ornamented with little paper tags indicating structures to be identified.

My classmates and I were not looking very good, our hair unwashed, our faces pale from too much studying and too little sleep. Two more exams and our first year of medical school would be over. We all knew exactly what we had to do next: go home and study for tomorrow's exam. I could picture my genetics notes lying on my desk, liberally high-lighted with pink marker. But before I went home I had a pregnancy test done.

My period was exactly one day late, hardly worth noticing — but the month before, for the first time in my life, I had been trying to get pregnant. Four hours later I called for the test results.

"It's positive," the woman at the lab told me.   4

With all the confidence of a first-year medical student, I asked, "Positive, what does that mean?"

"It means you're pregnant," she told me. "Congratulations."

Somewhat later that afternoon I settled down to make final review notes for my genetics exam. *Down's syndrome*, I copied carefully onto a clean piece of paper, *most common autosomal disorder, 1 per 700 live births*. I began to feel a little queasy. Over the next twenty-four hours, I was supposed to learn the biological basis, symptoms, diagnosis, and treatment of a long list of genetic disorders. Almost every one was something that could conceivably already be wrong with the embryo growing inside me. I couldn't even think about it; I had to put my notes aside and pass the exam on what I remembered from the lectures.

Over the past months, as I have gone through my pregnancy, and also   8 through my second year of medical school, I have become more and more aware of these two aspects of my life influencing each other, and even sometimes seeming to oppose each other. As a medical student, I was spending my time studying everything that can go wrong with the human body. As a pregnant woman, I was suddenly passionately interested in healthy physiological processes, in my own normal pregnancy and the growth of my baby. And yet pregnancy put me under the care of the medical profession—my own future profession—and I found myself rebelling as a mother and a patient against the attitudes that were being taught to me, particularly the attitude that pregnancy is a perilous, if not pathological, condition. The pregnancy and the decisions I had to make about my own health care changed my feelings about medicine and about the worldview of emergency and intervention which is communicated in medical training. My pregnancy became for me a rebellion against this worldview, a chance to do something healthy and normal with my body, something that would be a joyous event, an important event, a complex event, but not necessarily a medical event.

Medical school lasts four years, followed by internship and residency—three years for medicine, five to seven for surgery. And then maybe a two-year fellowship.

"The fellowship years can be a good time to have a baby," advised one physician. She was just finishing a fellowship in primary care. "Not internship or residency, God knows—that's when everyone's marriage breaks up since you're working eighty hours a week and you're so miserable all the time."

I am twenty-six. After college, I didn't go straight to medical school, but spent two years doing graduate work in biology and one living abroad. I'll probably have reached the fellowship stage by around thirty-three. It seemed like a long time to wait.

The more I thought about it, the more it seemed to me that there was no 12 time in the next seven or so years when it would be as feasible to have a baby as it is now. As a medical student, I have a flexibility that I will not really have further on, a freedom to take a couple of months off or even a year if I decide I need it, and without unduly disrupting the progress of my career. Larry, who is also twenty-six, has just finished his doctoral dissertation on Polish–Vatican relations in the late eighteenth century, and is teaching at Harvard. He also has a great deal of flexibility. Both our lives frequently feel a little frantic, but we don't find ourselves looking ahead to a less complex, less frantic future.

I decided not to take a leave of absence this year. Instead, Larry and I have started on the juggling games which will no doubt be a major feature of the years ahead; I took extra courses last year so I could manage a comparatively light schedule this spring and stay with the baby two days a week while Larry worked at home for the other three. Perfect timing is of course of the essence; happily, we'd already managed to conceive the baby so it would be born between the time I took my exams in December and the time I started work at the hospital in March.

There was one other factor in my decision to have a baby now. All through my first year of medical school, in embryology, in genetics, even in public health, lecturers kept emphasizing that the ideal time to have a baby is around the age of twenty-four. Safest for the mother. Safest for the baby. "Do you think they're trying to tell us something?" grumbled one of my classmates after a particularly pointed lecture. "Like why are we wasting these precious childbearing years in school? It almost makes you feel guilty about waiting to have children."

Ironically, I know no one else my age who is having a baby. The women in my childbirth class were all in their mid-thirties. "Having a baby is a very nineteen-eighties thing to do," said a friend who is a twenty-seven-year-old corporate lawyer in New York. "The only thing is, you and Larry are much too young." In medical school one day last month, a lecturer mentioned the problem of teenage pregnancy, and I imagined that my classmates were turning to look at me.

In theory, medical education teaches first about normal anatomy, normal physiology, and then builds upon this foundation by teaching the processes of pathology and disease. In practice, everyone — student and teacher alike — is eager to get to the material with "clinical relevance" and the whole thrust of the teaching is toward using examples of disease to illustrate normal body functions by showing what happens when such functions break down. This is the way much of medical knowledge is garnered, after all — we understand sugar metabolism partially because of studies on diabetics, who can't metabolize sugar normally. "An experiment of nature" is the phrase often used. 16

Although we had learned a great deal about disease, we had not, in our first year of medical school, learned much about the nitty-gritty of medical practice. As I began to wonder more about what was happening inside me and about what childbirth would be like, I tried to ready my embryology textbook, but again the pictures of the various abnormal fetuses upset me. So I read a couple of books that were written for pregnant women, not medical students, including *Immaculate Deception* by Suzanne Arms, a passionate attack on the American way of childbirth which argues that many routine hospital practices are psychologically damaging and medically hazardous. In particular, Arms protested the "traditional birth," the euphemism used in opposition to "natural birth." Traditional often means giving birth while lying down, a position demonstrated to be less effective and more dangerous than many others, but convenient for the doctor. An intravenous line is often attached to the arm and an electronic fetal heart monitor strapped to the belly. Traditional almost always means a routine episiotomy, a surgical incision in the perineum to allow the baby's head to emerge without tearing the mother.

In our reproductive medicine course this fall, the issue of home birth came up exactly once, in a "case" for discussion. "BB is a 25-year-old married graduate student . . . ," the case began. BB had a completely normal pregnancy. She showed no unusual symptoms and had no relevant past medical problems. When the pregnancy reached full term, the summary concluded, "no factors have been identified to suggest increased risk." Then, the first question: "Do you think she should choose to deliver at home?"

The doctor leading our discussion section read the question aloud and waited. "No," chorused the class.

"Why not?" asked the doctor. 20

"Well, there's always the chance of a complication," said one of the students.

Sure enough, after answering the first set of questions, we went on with BB's case, and it turned out that she went two and a half weeks past her due date, began to show signs of fetal distress, and was ultimately delivered by cesarean after the failure of induced labor. It was clear what the lesson was that BB was supposed to teach us. It was hard to read the case without getting the impression that all of these problems were some kind of divine retribution for even considering a home birth.

In fact, Larry and I eventually decided on a hospital birth with a doctor whose orientation was clearly against intervention except where absolutely necessary; he did not feel that procedures that can help in the event of complications should be applied across the board. It pleased me that he volunteered the cesarean and episiotomy figures for his practice, and also that he regarded the issue of what kind of birth we wanted as an appropriate subject for discussion at our very first meeting. ("A low-tech birth?" he said, sounding amused. "You're at Harvard Medical School and you want a low-tech birth?") He seemed to accept that there were consumer issues involved in choosing a doctor—that expectant parents are entitled to an explanation of the doctor's approach early in the pregnancy, when changing doctors is still a reasonable possibility.

At the beginning of my eighth month, we went to the first meeting of a prepared-childbirth class sponsored by the hospital we had decided to use. I had great hopes of this class; I was tired of feeling like the only pregnant person in the world. My medical school classmates had continued to be extremely kind and considerate, but as I moved around the medical school I was beginning to feel like a lone hippopotamus in a gaggle of geese. I wanted some other people with whom Larry and I could go over the questions we discussed endlessly with each other: how do we know when it's time to leave for the hospital? what is labor going to *feel* like? what can we do to make it go more easily?

The prepared-childbirth class met in the hospital. At the first meeting, it became clear that its major purpose was to prepare people to be good patients. The teacher was exposing us to various procedures so we would cooperate properly when they were performed on us. Asked whether a given procedure was absolutely necessary, the teacher said that was up to the doctor.

I found a childbirth class that met at a local day-care center; we sat on cushions on the floor, surrounded by toys and children's artwork. Many members of the class were fairly hostile toward the medical profession; once again I was greeted with remarks like "A medical student and you think you want a natural birth? Don't you get thrown out of school for that?" This class was, if anything, designed to teach people how to be "bad patients." The teacher explained the pros and cons of the various interventions, and we discussed under what circumstances we might or might not accept them.

The childbirth classes not only prepared me well for labor but also provided that sense of community I wanted. Yet they also left me feeling pulled between two poles, especially if I went to medical school during the day to discuss deliveries going wrong in one catastrophic way after another ("C-section, C-section!" my discussion section once chanted when the teacher asked what we would do next) and then later to childbirth class in the evening to discuss ways to circumvent unwanted medical procedures. As a student of the medical profession, I know I am being trained to rely heavily on technology, to assume that the risk of acting is almost always preferable to the risk of not acting. I consciously had to fight these attitudes when I thought about giving birth.

In our reproductive medicine course, the emphasis was on the abnormal, the pathological. We learned almost nothing about normal pregnancy: the only thing said about nutrition, for example, was said in passing—that nobody knows how much weight a pregnant woman should gain, but "about twenty-four pounds" is considered good. In contrast, I and the other women in my childbirth class were very concerned with what we ate; we were always exchanging suggestions on how to get through those interminable four glasses of milk a day. We learned nothing in medical school about exercise, though exercise books and classes aimed at pregnant women continue to proliferate—will we, as doctors, be able to give valid advice about diet and exercise during pregnancy? We learned nothing about any of the problems encountered in a normal pregnancy; the only thing said about morning sickness was that it could be controlled with a drug—a drug which, as it happens, many pregnant women are reluctant to take because some studies have linked it to birth defects. We learned nothing about the emotional aspects of pregnancy, nothing about helping women prepare for labor and delivery. In other words, none of my medical school classmates, after the course, would have been capable of answering even the most basic questions about pregnancy asked by the people in my childbirth class. The important issues for future doctors simply did not overlap with the important issues for future parents.

I sat with my classmates in our reproductive medicine course in Amphitheater E at Harvard Medical School and listened to the lecture on the disorders of pregnancy. The professor discussed ectopic pregnancy, toxemia, spontaneous abortion, and major birth defects. I was eight months pregnant. I sat there rubbing my belly, telling my baby, don't worry, you're okay, you're healthy. I sat there wishing that this course would tell us more about normal pregnancy, that after memorizing all the possible disasters, we would be allowed to conclude that pregnancy itself is not a state of disease. But I think most of us, including me, came away from the course with a sense that in fact pregnancy is a deeply dangerous medical condition, that one walks a fine line, avoiding one serious problem after another, to reach the statistically unlikely outcome of a healthy baby and a healthy mother.

I mentioned this to my doctor, explaining that I was tormented by fears of every possible abnormality. "Yes," he said, "normal birth is not honored enough in the curriculum. Most of us doctors are going around looking for pathology and feeling good about ourselves when we find it because that's what we were trained to do. We aren't trained to find joy in a normal pregnancy."

I tried to find joy in my own pregnancy. I am sure that the terrors that sometimes visited me in the middle of the night were no more intense than those that visit most expectant mothers: will the labor go well? will the baby be okay? I probably had more specific fears than many, as I lay awake wondering about atrial septal heart defects or placenta previa and hemorrhage. And perhaps I did worry more than I might once have done, because my faith in the normal had been weakened. I, too, in my dark moments, had begun to see healthy development as less than probable, as the highly unlikely avoidance of a million abnormalities. I knew that many of my classmates were worrying with me; I cannot count the number of times I was asked whether I had had an amniocentesis. When I pointed out that we had been taught that amniocentesis is not generally recommended for women under the age of thirty-five, my classmates tended to look worried and mutter something about being *sure*.

The climax came when a young man in my class asked me, "Have you had all those genetic tests? Like for sickle-cell anemia?"

I looked at him. He is white. I am white. "I'm not in the risk group for sickle-cell," I said gently.

"Yeah, I know," he said, "but if there's even a one-in-a-zillion chance —"

I see all of us, including myself, absorbing the idea that when it comes to tests, technology, interventions, more is better. There was no talk in the reproductive medicine course about the negative aspects of intervention, and the one time a student asked in class about the "appropriateness" of fetal monitoring, the question was cut off with a remark that there was no time to discuss issues of "appropriateness." There was also no time really to discuss techniques for attending women in labor — except as they related to labor emergencies.

I see us absorbing the attitude, here as in other courses, that the kinds of decisions that have to be made are absolutely out of the reach of nonphysicians. The risks of devastating catastrophe are so constant — how can we let patients take chances like this with their lives? Those dangers which can actually be controlled by the patients, the pregnant women — cigarettes, alcohol — are deemphasized. Instead, we are taught to think in terms of medical emergencies. And gradually pregnancy itself begins to sound like a medical emergency in which the pregnant woman, referred to as "the patient," must be carefully guided to a safe delivery, almost in spite of herself. And as we spend more and more time absorbing the vocabulary of medicine, it becomes harder to think about communicating our knowledge to those who lack that vocabulary.

There have been very positive aspects of having the baby while in medical school. For one thing, the anatomy and physiology and embryology I have learned deepened my awe of the miracle going on inside me. When I looked ahead to the birth, I thought of what we learned about the incredible changeover that takes place during the first minutes of life, about the details of the switch to breathing air, the changes in circulation. I feel that because of what I have learned I appreciated the pregnancy in a way I never could have before, and I am grateful for that appreciation.

Another wonderful thing about having my baby while in medical school was the support and attention from my classmates. Perhaps because having a baby seems a long way off to many of them, there has been some tendency to regard mine as a "class baby." People asked me all the time to promise that I would bring it to lecture; the person who shows the slides offered to dim the lights for a soothing atmosphere if I wanted to nurse in class. My classmates held a baby shower for Larry and me, and presented us with a fabulous assortment of baby items. At the end of the shower, I lay back on the couch with five medical students feeling my abdomen, finding the baby's bottom, the baby's foot.

Our son, Benjamin Orlando, was born on January 28, 1984. Naturally, I would like to be able to say that all our planning and preparing was rewarded with a perfectly smooth, easy labor and delivery, but of course biology doesn't work that way. The experience did provide me with a rather ironic new wrinkle on the whole idea of interventions. Most of the labor was quite ordinary. "You're demonstrating a perfect Friedman labor curve," the doctor said to me at one point, "you must have been studying!" At the end, however, I had great difficulty pushing the baby out. After the pushing stage had gone on for quite a while, I was absolutely exhausted, though the baby was fine; there were no signs of fetal distress and the head was descending steadily. Still, the pushing had gone on much longer than is usual, and I was aware that there were now two doctors and a number of nurses in the birthing room. Suddenly I heard one of the doctors say something about forceps. At that moment, I found a last extra ounce of strength and pushed my baby out. As I lay back with my son wriggling on my stomach, the birthing room suddenly transformed into the most beautiful place on earth, I heard one of the nurses say to another, "You see this all the time with these birthing-room natural-childbirth mothers — you just mention forceps and they get those babies born."

● PERSONAL RESPONSE ●

Describe your own experiences with physicians. Do they have the attitude toward patients that Klass describes here? How might the training of doctors be changed to avoid the teaching of such attitudes?

● QUESTIONS FOR DISCUSSION ●

1. How do Klass's opening paragraphs illustrate the point she is making about the two aspects of her life that both influence and oppose each other?

2. Why did Klass and her husband decide to have a baby in her second year of medical school instead of waiting?

3. What advantages did having her baby during medical school turn out to have?

4. Summarize the conflict Klass felt between being a medical student and being a pregnant woman.

5. What examples does Klass give to illustrate the contrast between what she was taught about pregnancy in medical school and what she was being told in her childbirth classes?

6. According to Klass, what attitude toward patients does medical school teach? What is the effect of such attitudes on patients?

7. What was the "rather ironic new wrinkle on the whole idea of interventions" (paragraph 39) that Klass experienced when she gave birth?

● WRITING TOPICS ●

1. If you have ever made a decision to do something at a time when other people thought it was inappropriate, write an essay telling what the decision was, why you made it, and whether or not you now think it was the right thing to do.

2. Narrate a specific experience—either positive or negative—you have had with a doctor, dentist, or other health professional. Use vivid, concrete language to convey the experience to your reader.

3. Write a narrative account of a serious illness or accident you have had, making sure to feature only the important points of the event. Provide specific details to describe vividly how you felt at the time.

DEEMS

●

Russell Baker

Russell Baker was born in Virginia and worked as a newspaper reporter in both Baltimore and Washington, D.C., before becoming a columnist for the New York Times. *Since 1962, his Pulitzer Prize–winning syndicated column, the "Observer," has entertained readers with humorous insights into and criticisms of social issues, politics, and culture. Among his eleven books are* A Baker's Dozen *(1964),* So This is Depravity *(1980), and* There's a Country in My Cellar *(1990). He has written two memoirs,* Growing Up *(1982) and* The Good Times *(1989), from which the following is taken. In "Deems," Baker explains how his interest in journalism was sparked by a man he both feared and admired.*

y mother started me in newspaper work in 1937 right after my twelfth birthday. She would have started me younger, but there was a law against working before age twelve. She thought it was a silly law, and said so to Deems.

Deems was boss of a group of boys who worked home delivery routes for the *Baltimore News-Post*. She found out about him a few weeks after we got to Baltimore. She just went out on the street, stopped a paperboy, and asked how he'd got his job.

"There's this man Deems . . ."

Deems was short and plump and had curly brown hair. He owned a car and   4 a light gray suit and always wore a necktie and white shirt. A real businessman, I thought the first time I saw him. My mother was talking to him on the sidewalk in front of the Union Square Methodist Church and I was standing as tall as I could, just out of earshot.

"Now, Buddy, when we get down there keep your shoulders back and stand up real straight," she had cautioned me after making sure my necktie was all right and my shirt clean.

Watching the two of them in conversation, with Deems glancing at me now and then, I kept my shoulders drawn back in the painful military style I'd seen in movies, trying to look a foot taller than I really was.

"Come over here, Russ, and meet Mister Deems," she finally said, and I did, managing to answer his greeting by saying, "The pleasure's all mine," which I'd heard people say in the movies. I probably blushed while saying it, because meeting strangers was painfully embarrassing to me.

"If that's the rule, it's the rule," my mother was telling Deems, "and we'll   8 just have to put up with it, but it still doesn't make any sense to me."

As we walked back to the house she said I couldn't have a paper route until I was twelve. And all because of some foolish rule they had down here in

Baltimore. You'd think if a boy wanted to work they would encourage him instead of making him stay idle so long that laziness got embedded in his bones.

That was April. We had barely finished the birthday cake in August before Deems came by the apartment and gave me the tools of the newspaper trade: an account book for keeping track of the customers' bills and a long, brown web belt. Slung around one shoulder and across the chest, the belt made it easy to balance fifteen or twenty pounds of papers against the hip. I had to buy my own wire cutters for opening the newspaper bundles the trucks dropped at Wisengoff's store on the corner of Stricker and West Lombard streets.

In February my mother had moved us down from New Jersey, where we had been living with her brother Allen ever since my father died in 1930. This move of hers to Baltimore was a step toward fulfilling a dream. More than almost anything else in the world, she wanted "a home of our own." I'd heard her talk of that "home of our own" all through those endless Depression years when we lived as poor relatives dependent on Uncle Allen's goodness. "A home of our own. One of these days, Buddy, we'll have a home of our own."

That winter she had finally saved just enough to make her move, and she 12 came to Baltimore. There were several reasons for Baltimore. For one, there were people she knew in Baltimore, people she could go to if things got desperate. And desperation was possible, because the moving would exhaust her savings, and the apartment rent was twenty-four dollars a month. She would have to find a job quickly. My sister Doris was only nine, but I was old enough for an after-school job that could bring home a few dollars a week. So as soon as it was legal I went into newspaper work.

The romance of it was almost unbearable on my first day as I trudged west along Lombard Street, then south along Gilmor, and east down Pratt Street with the bundle of newspapers strapped to my hip. I imagined people pausing to admire me as I performed this important work, spreading the news of the world, the city, and the racetracks onto doorsteps, through mail slots, and under doorjambs. I had often gazed with envy at paperboys; to be one of them at last was happiness sublime.

Very soon, though, I discovered drawbacks. The worst of these was Deems. Though I had only forty customers, Deems sent papers for forty-five. Since I was billed for every paper left on Wisengoff's corner, I had to pay for the five extra copies out of income or try to hustle them on the street. I hated standing at streetcar stops yelling, "Paper! Paper!" at people getting off trolleys. Usually, if my mother wasn't around to catch me, I stuck the extras in a dark closet and took the loss.

Deems was constantly baiting new traps to dump more papers on me. When I solved the problem of the five extras by getting five new subscribers for home delivery, Deems announced a competition with mouth-watering prizes for the newsboys who got the most new subscribers. Too innocent to cope with this sly master of private enterprise, I took the bait.

"Look at these prizes I can get for signing up new customers," I told my 16 mother. "A balloon-tire bicycle. A free pass to the movies for a whole year."

The temptation was too much. I reported my five new subscribers to help me in the competition.

Whereupon Deems promptly raised my order from forty-five to fifty papers, leaving me again with the choice of hustling to unload the five extras or losing money.

I won a free pass to the movies, though. It was good for a whole year. And to the magnificent Loew's Century located downtown on Lexington Street. The passes were good only for nights in the middle of the week when I usually had too much homework to allow for movies. Still, in the summer with school out, it was thrilling to go all the way downtown at night to sit in the Century's damask and velvet splendor and see MGM's glamorous stars in their latest movies.

To collect my prize I had to go to a banquet the paper gave for its "honor 20 carriers" at the Emerson Hotel. There were fifty of us, and I was sure the other forty-nine would all turn out to be slicksters wised up to the ways of the world, who would laugh at my doltish ignorance of how to eat at a great hotel banquet. My fear of looking foolish at the banquet made me lie awake nights dreading it and imagining all the humiliating mistakes I could make.

I had seen banquets in movies. Every plate was surrounded by a baffling array of knives, forks, and spoons. I knew it would be the same at the Emerson Hotel. The Emerson was one of the swankiest hotels in Baltimore. It was not likely to hold down on the silverware. I talked to my mother.

"How will I know what to eat what with?"

The question did not interest her.

"Just watch what everybody else does, and enjoy yourself," she said. 24

I came back to the problem again and again.

"Do you use the same spoon for your coffee as you do for dessert?"

"Don't worry about it. Everybody isn't going to be staring at you."

"Is it all right to butter your bread with the same knife you use to cut the 28 meat?"

"Just go and have a good time."

Close to panic, I showed up at the Emerson, found my way to the banquet, and was horrified to find that I had to sit beside Deems throughout the meal. We probably talked about something, but I was so busy sweating with terror and rolling my eyeballs sidewise to see what silverware Deems was using to eat with that I didn't hear a word all night. The following week, Deems started sending me another five extras.

Now and then he also provided a treat. One day in 1938 he asked if I would like to join a small group of boys he was taking to visit the *News-Post* newsroom. My mother, in spite of believing that nothing came before homework at night, wasn't cold-hearted enough to deny me a chance to see the city room of a great metropolitan newspaper. I had seen plenty of city rooms in the movies. They were glamorous places full of exciting people like Lee Tracy, Edmund Lowe, and Adolphe Menjou trading wisecracks and making mayors and cops look like saps. To see such a place, to stand, actually stand, in the city room of a great newspaper and look at reporters who were in touch every day with killers and professional baseball players — that was a thrilling prospect.

Because the *News-Post* was an afternoon paper, almost everybody had left 32 for the day when we got there that night. The building, located downtown near the harbor, was disappointing. It looked like a factory, and not a very big factory either. Inside there was a smell compounded of ink, pulp, chemicals, paste, oil, gasoline, greasy rags, and hot metal. We took an elevator up and came into a long room filled with dilapidated desks, battered telephones, and big blocky type-writers. Almost nobody there, just two or three men in shirt-sleeves. It was the first time I'd ever seen Deems look awed.

"Boys, this is the nerve center of the newspaper," he said, his voice heavy and solemn like the voice of Westbrook Van Voorhis, the *March of Time* man, when he said, "Time marches on."

I was confused. I had expected the newsroom to have glamour, but this place had nothing but squalor. The walls hadn't been painted for years. The windows were filthy. Desks were heaped with mounds of crumpled paper, torn sheets of newspaper, overturned paste pots, dog-eared telephone direc-tories. The floor was ankle deep in newsprint, carbon paper, and crushed cigarette packages. Waist-high cans overflowed with trash. Ashtrays were buried under cigarette ashes and butts. Ugly old wooden chairs looked ready for the junk shop.

It looked to me like a place that probably had more cockroaches than we had back home on Lombard Street, but Deems was seeing it through rose-colored glasses. As we stood looking around at the ruins, he started telling us how lucky we were to be newsboys. Lucky to have a foot on the upward ladder so early in life. If we worked hard and kept expanding our paper routes we could make the men who ran this paper sit up and notice us. And when men like that noticed you, great things could happen, because they were important men, the most important of all being the man who owned our paper: Mr. Hearst Himself, William Randolph Hearst, founder of the greatest newspaper organization in America. A great man, Mr. Hearst, but not so great that he didn't appreciate his newsboys, who were the backbone of the business. Many of whom would someday grow up and work at big jobs on this paper. Did we realize that any of us, maybe all of us, could end up one of these days sitting right here in this vitally important room, the newsroom, the nerve center of the newspaper?

Yes, Deems was right. Riding home on the streetcar that night, I realized I was a lucky boy to be getting such an early start up the ladder of journalism. It was childish to feel let down because the city room looked like such a dump instead of like city rooms in the movies. Deems might be a slave driver, but he was doing it for my own good, and I ought to be grateful. In *News Selling*, the four-page special paper Mr. Hearst published just for his newsboys, they'd run a piece that put it almost as beautifully as Deems had.

YOU'RE A MEMBER OF THE FOURTH ESTATE was the headline on it. I was so impressed that I put the paper away in a safe place and often took it out to read when I needed inspiration. It told how "a great English orator" named Edmund Burke "started a new name for a new profession — the Fourth Estate . . . the press . . . NEWSPAPER MEN."

And it went on to say:

"The Fourth Estate was then . . . and IS now . . . a great estate for HE-men . . . workers . . . those who are proud of the business they're in!"

(Mr. Hearst always liked plenty of exclamation marks, dots, and capital 40
letters.)

"Get that kick of pride that comes from knowing you are a newspaper man.
That means something!"

"A newspaper man never ducks a dare. YOU are a newspaper man. A
salesman of newspapers . . . the final cog in the immense machine of newspaper
production — a SERVICE for any man to be proud of."

"So throw back the chest. Hit the route hard each day. Deliver fast and
properly. Sell every day. Add to your route because you add to the NEWS-
PAPER field when you do. And YOU MAKE MONEY DOING IT. It is a great
life — a grand opportunity. Don't boot it — build it up. Leave it better than when
you came into it."

"It is a great life." I kept coming back to that sentence as I read and reread 44
the thing. No matter how awful it got, and it sometimes got terrible, I never quit
believing it was a great life. I kept at it until I was almost sixteen, chest thrown
back, delivering fast and properly, selling every day and adding to my route. At
the end I'd doubled its size and was making as much as four dollars a week from it.

A few months after he took us down to see the city room, Deems quit. My
mother said he'd found a better job. Later, when I thought about him, I
wondered if maybe it wasn't because he hated himself for having to make life
hell for boys. I hoped that wasn't the reason because he was the first newspaper-
man I ever knew, and I wanted him to be the real thing. Hard as nails.

● PERSONAL RESPONSE ●

If you have decided on a career goal, explain how you arrived at your choice. If you have
not yet made a decision, explain what options you are considering.

● QUESTIONS FOR DISCUSSION ●

1. What details are especially effective in conveying a vivid sense of Deems? What was it
   about Deems that Baker admired? How did Deems inspire the young Baker?

2. How does Baker suggest his mother's essential characteristics?

3. In what ways was the young Baker influenced by what he saw in the movies?

4. What part did Baker's mother play in putting him on his career path?

5. Why do you think William Randolph Hearst was such a strong determining influence
   in Baker's life?

6. What contrasts does Baker make between the romanticized images he saw in the
   movies and reality? How did the visit to the *News-Post* newsroom serve both to dispel
   his illusions and inspire Baker to pursue journalism as a career?

7. What conclusions can you draw about Deems's character on the basis of the young
   Baker's perception of him?

● WRITING TOPICS ●

1. Narrate an incident or event that had a strong influence on your choice of career goal.

2. Describe a person who has had a strong influence on your choice of career. Include not only physical details of the person but personality traits or characteristics as well. Be sure to explain in what way the person influenced you.

3. Explain how and why you chose the career goal you now have. If you have not yet selected one, write an essay exploring possible career paths or explaining why you have not yet selected a goal.

THE TEACHER WHO CHANGED MY LIFE

●

NICHOLAS GAGE

Nicholas Gage wrote of the 1948 torture and murder of his mother by Communist guerrillas in Greece in his best-selling book Eleni. *In* A Place For Us, *he tells how he and his sisters adjusted to life in the United States. The essay below, adapted from that book, appeared in* Parade *magazine in December 1989. In this essay, Gage pays stirring tribute to the seventh-grade English teacher who was the inspiration for all he subsequently achieved as a writer.*

T he person who set the course of my life in the new land I entered as a young war refugee — who, in fact, nearly dragged me onto the path that would bring all the blessings I've received in America — was a salty-tongued, no-nonsense schoolteacher named Marjorie Hurd. When I entered her classroom in 1953, I had been to six schools in five years, starting in the Greek village where I was born in 1939.

When I stepped off a ship in New York Harbor on a gray March day in 1949, I was an undersized 9-year-old in short pants who had lost his mother and was coming to live with the father he didn't know. My mother, Eleni Gatzoyiannis, had been imprisoned, tortured and shot by Communist guerrillas for sending me and three of my four sisters to freedom. She died so that her children could go to their father in the United States.

The portly, bald, well-dressed man who met me and my sisters seemed a foreign, authoritarian figure. I secretly resented him for not getting the whole family out of Greece early enough to save my mother. Ultimately, I would grow to love him and appreciate how he dealt with becoming a single parent at the age of 56, but at first our relationship was prickly, full of hostility.

As Father drove us to our new home — a tenement in Worcester, Mass. — and pointed out the huge brick building that would be our first school in America, I clutched my Greek notebooks from the refugee camp, hoping that my few years of schooling would impress my teachers in this cold, crowded country. They didn't. When my father led me and my 11-year-old sister to Greendale Elementary School, the grim-faced Yankee principal put the two of us in a class for the mentally retarded. There was no facility in those days for non-English-speaking children.

By the time I met Marjorie Hurd four years later, I had learned English, been placed in a normal, graded class and had even been chosen for the college preparatory track in the Worcester public school system. I was 13 years old when our father moved us yet again, and I entered Chandler Junior High shortly after the beginning of seventh grade. I found myself surrounded by richer, smarter and better-dressed classmates who looked askance at my strange clothes and heavy accent. Shortly after I arrived, we were told to select a hobby to pursue

4

during "club hour" on Fridays. The idea of hobbies and clubs made no sense to my immigrant ears, but I decided to follow the prettiest girl in my class — the blue-eyed daughter of the local Lutheran minister. She led me through the door marked "Newspaper Club" and into the presence of Miss Hurd, the newspaper adviser and English teacher who would become my mentor and my muse.

A formidable, solidly built woman with salt-and-pepper hair, a steely eye and a flat Boston accent, Miss Hurd had no patience with layabouts. "What are all you goof-offs doing here?" she bellowed at the would-be journalists. "This is the Newspaper Club! We're going to put out a *newspaper*. So if there's anybody in this room who doesn't like work, I suggest you go across to the Glee Club now, because you're going to work your tails off here!"

I was soon under Miss Hurd's spell. She did indeed teach us to put out a newspaper, skills I honed during my next 25 years as a journalist. Soon I asked the principal to transfer me to her English class as well. There, she drilled us on grammar until I finally began to understand the logic and structure of the English language. She assigned stories for us to read and discuss; not tales of heroes, like the Greek myths I knew, but stories of underdogs — poor people, even immigrants, who seemed ordinary until a crisis drove them to do something extraordinary. She also introduced us to the literary wealth of Greece — giving me a new perspective on my war-ravaged, impoverished homeland. I began to be proud of my origins.

One day, after discussing how writers should write about what they know, 8 she assigned us to compose an essay from our own experience. Fixing me with a stern look, she added, "Nick, I want you to write about what happened to your family in Greece." I had been trying to put those painful memories behind me and left the assignment until the last moment. Then, on a warm spring afternoon, I sat in my room with a yellow pad and pencil and stared out the window at the buds on the trees. I wrote that the coming of spring always reminded me of the last time I said goodbye to my mother on a green and gold day in 1948.

I kept writing, one line after another, telling how the Communist guerrillas occupied our village, took our home and food, how my mother started planning our escape when she learned that the children were to be sent to re-education camps behind the Iron Curtain and how, at the last moment, she couldn't escape with us because the guerrillas sent her with a group of women to thresh wheat in a distant village. She promised she would try to get away on her own, she told me to be brave and hung a silver cross around my neck, and then she kissed me. I watched the line of women being led down into the ravine and up the other side, until they disappeared around the bend — my mother a tiny brown figure at the end who stopped for an instant to raise her hand in one last farewell.

I wrote about our nighttime escape down the mountain, across the minefields and into the lines of the Nationalist soldiers, who sent us to a refugee camp. It was there that we learned of our mother's execution. I felt very lucky to have come to America, I concluded, but every year, the coming of spring made me feel sad because it reminded me of the last time I saw my mother.

I handed in the essay, hoping never to see it again, but Miss Hurd had it published in the school paper. This mortified me at first, until I saw that my classmates reacted with sympathy and tact to my family's story. Without telling me, Miss Hurd also submitted the essay to a contest sponsored by the Freedoms Foundation at Valley Forge, Pa., and it won a medal. The Worcester paper wrote about the award and quoted my essay at length. My father, by then a "five-and-dime-store chef," as the paper described him, was ecstatic with pride, and the Worcester Greek community celebrated the honor to one of its own.

For the first time I began to understand the power of the written word. A secret ambition took root in me. One day, I vowed, I would go back to Greece, find out the details of my mother's death and write about her life, so her grandchildren would know of her courage. Perhaps I would even track down the men who killed her and write of their crimes. Fulfilling that ambition would take me 30 years. 12

Meanwhile, I followed the literary path that Miss Hurd had so forcefully set me on. After junior high, I became the editor of my school paper at Classical High School and got a part-time job at the Worcester *Telegram and Gazette*. Although my father could only give me $50 and encouragement toward a college education, I managed to finance four years at Boston University with scholarships and part-time jobs in journalism. During my last year of college, an article I wrote about a friend who had died in the Philippines — the first person to lose his life working for the Peace Corps — led to my winning the Hearst Award for College Journalism. And the plaque was given to me in the White House by President John F. Kennedy.

For a refugee who had never seen a motorized vehicle or indoor plumbing until he was 9, this was an unimaginable honor. When the Worcester paper ran a picture of me standing next to President Kennedy, my father rushed out to buy a new suit in order to be properly dressed to receive the congratulations of the Worcester Greeks. He clipped out the photograph, had it laminated in plastic and carried it in his breast pocket for the rest of his life to show everyone he met. I found the much-worn photo in his pocket on the day he died 20 years later.

In our isolated Greek village, my mother had bribed a cousin to teach her to read, for girls were not supposed to attend school beyond a certain age. She had always dreamed of her children receiving an education. She couldn't be there when I graduated from Boston University, but the person who came with my father and shared our joy was my former teacher, Marjorie Hurd. We celebrated not only my bachelor's degree but also the scholarships that paid my way to Columbia's Graduate School of Journalism. There, I met the woman who would eventually become my wife. At our wedding and at the baptisms of our three children, Marjorie Hurd was always there, dancing alongside the Greeks.

By then, she was Mrs. Rabidou, for she had married a widower when she was in her early 40s. That didn't distract her from her vocation of introducing young minds to English literature, however. She taught for a total of 41 years and continually would make a "project" of some balky student in whom she spied a spark of potential. Often these were students from the most troubled homes, yet she would alternately bully and charm each one with her own special brand of tough love until the spark caught fire. She retired in 1981 at the age of 62 but still 16 avidly follows the lives and careers of former students while overseeing her adult stepchildren and driving her husband on camping trips to New Hampshire.

Miss Hurd was one of the first to call me on Dec. 10, 1987, when President Reagan, in his television address after the summit meeting with Gorbachev, told the nation that Eleni Gatzoyiannis' dying cry, "My children!" had helped inspire him to seek an arms agreement "for all the children of the world."

"I can't imagine a better monument for your mother," Miss Hurd said with an uncharacteristic catch in her voice.

Although a bad hip makes it impossible for her to join in the Greek dancing, Marjorie Hurd Rabidou is still an honored and enthusiastic guest at all family celebrations, including my 50th birthday picnic last summer, where the shish kebab was cooked on spits, clarinets and *bouzoukis* wailed, and costumed dancers led the guests in a serpentine line around our Colonial farmhouse, only 20 minutes from my first home in Worcester.

My sisters and I felt an aching void because my father was not there to lead 20 the line, balancing a glass of wine on his head while he danced, the way he did at every celebration during his 92 years. But Miss Hurd was there, surveying the scene with quiet satisfaction. Although my parents are gone, her presence was a consolation, because I owe her so much.

This is truly the land of opportunity, and I would have enjoyed its bounty even if I hadn't walked into Miss Hurd's classroom in 1953. But she was the one who directed my grief and pain into writing, and if it weren't for her I wouldn't have become an investigative reporter and foreign correspondent, recorded the story of my mother's life and death in *Eleni* and now my father's story in *A Place for Us*, which is also a testament to the country that took us in. She was the catalyst that sent me into journalism and indirectly caused all the good things that came after. But Miss Hurd would probably deny this emphatically.

A few years ago, I answered the telephone and heard my former teacher's voice telling me, in that won't-take-no-for-an-answer tone of hers, that she had decided I was to write and deliver the eulogy at her funeral. I agreed (she didn't leave me any choice), but that's one assignment I never want to do. I hope, Miss Hurd, that you'll accept this remembrance instead.

● PERSONAL RESPONSE ●

Who has been especially influential in helping shape the course of your own life? Explain how that person has influenced you.

● QUESTIONS FOR DISCUSSION ●

1. From the first paragraph when he describes Miss Hurd as a "salty-tongued, no-nonsense schoolteacher," Gage uses vivid details to convey her character. What other details effectively describe Miss Hurd's personality and appearance?

2. Besides Miss Hurd, who else does Gage describe? What image of each does he draw for his readers?

3. In what ways does Gage manage to convey a clear sense of chronology, despite the fact that his narrative covers a number of years in a brief space?

4. What was it about Miss Hurd's teaching that inspired Gage to become a writer?

5. What did Gage learn from his writing assignment that then sparked his determination to write the life story of his mother?

6. What details about his father does Gage's narrative reveal? How, for example, did his father feel about Gage's accomplishments as a writer?

7. What details indicate the closeness between Marjorie Hurd Rabidou and her former pupil?

● WRITING TOPICS ●

1. Write an essay about a person (or persons) who has had a strong effect on your life, either in shaping the way you are now or in helping you determine goals for yourself.

2. Narrate a particular event or incident that changed you in some significant way.

3. Describe someone whom you regard very highly, such as a parent, friend, relative, teacher, or coach. Use vivid, concrete language to convey the characteristics of that person and to explain as precisely as possible why you admire her or him.

ONE MAN'S KIDS

●

Daniel Meier

Daniel Meier earned a master's degree from the Harvard Graduate School of Education in 1984. He taught first grade in Brookline, Massachusetts, from 1985 to 1988, and now teaches in an elementary school in Boston. His thoughts on teaching have been published in a variety of journals and magazines. In the essay reprinted below, which appeared in the "About Men" series of The New York Times Magazine *in 1987, Meier not only explains the benefits for him of teaching first grade but also points out some perceived differences between traditionally male and traditionally female work.*

I teach first graders. I live in a world of skinned knees, double-knotted shoelaces, riddles that I've heard a dozen times, stale birthday cakes, hurt feelings, wandering stories, and one lost shoe ("and if you don't find it my mother'll kill me"). My work is dominated by 6-year-olds.

It's 10:45, the middle of snack, and I'm helping Emily open her milk carton. She has already tried the other end without success, and now there's so much paint and ink on the carton from her fingers that I'm not sure she should drink it at all. But I open it. Then I turn to help Scott clean up some milk he has just spilled onto Rebecca's whale crossword puzzle.

While I wipe my milk- and paint-covered hands, Jenny wants to know if I've seen that funny book about penguins that I read in class. As I hunt for it in a messy pile of books, Jason wants to know if there is a new seating arrangement for lunch tables. I find the book, turn to answer Jason, then face Maya, who is fast approaching with a new knock-knock joke. After what seems like the 10th "Who's there?" I laugh and Maya is pleased.

Then Andrew wants to know how to spell "flukes" for his crossword. As I get to "u," I give a hand signal for Sarah to take away the snack. But just as Sarah is almost out the door, two children complain that "we haven't even had ours yet." I stop the snack mid-flight, complying with their request for graham crackers. I then return to Andrew, noticing that he has put "flu" for 9 Down, rather than 9 Across. It's now 10:50.

My work is not traditional male work. It's not a singular pursuit. There is not a large pile of paper to get through or one deal to transact. I don't have one area of expertise or knowledge. I don't have the singular power over language of a lawyer, the physical force of a construction worker, the command over fellow workers of a surgeon, the wheeling and dealing transactions of a businessman. My energy is not spent in pursuing, climbing, achieving, conquering, or cornering some goal or object.

My energy is spent in encouraging, supporting, consoling, and praising my children. In teaching, the inner rewards come from without. On any given day, quite apart from teaching reading and spelling, I bandage a cut, dry a tear, erase a frown, tape a torn doll, and locate a long-lost boot. The day is really won through matters of the heart. As my students groan, laugh, shudder, cry, exult, and wonder, I do too. I have to be soft around the edges.

A few years ago, when I was interviewing for an elementary-school teaching position, every principal told me with confidence that, as a male, I had an advantage over female applicants because of the lack of male teachers. But in the next breath, they asked with a hint of suspicion why I chose to work with young children. I told them that I wanted to observe and contribute to the intellectual growth of a maturing mind. What I really felt like saying, but didn't, was that I loved helping a child learn to write his name for the first time, finding someone a new friend, or sharing in the hilarity of reading about Winnie the Pooh getting so stuck in a hole that only his head and rear show.

I gave that answer to those principals, who were mostly male, because I thought they wanted a "male" response. This meant talking about intellectual matters. If I had taken a different course and talked about my interest in helping children in their emotional development, it would have been seen as closer to a "female" answer. I even altered my language, not once mentioning the word "love" to describe what I do indeed love about teaching. My answer worked; every principal nodded approvingly. 8

Some of the principals also asked what I saw myself doing later in my career. They wanted to know if I eventually wanted to go into educational administration. Becoming a dean of students or a principal has never been one of my goals, but they seemed to expect me, as a male, to want to climb higher on the career stepladder. So I mentioned that, at some point, I would be interested in working with teachers as a curriculum coordinator. Again, they nodded approvingly.

If those principals had been female instead of male, I wonder whether their questions, and my answers, would have been different. My guess is that they would have been.

At other times, when I'm at a party or a dinner and tell someone that I teach young children, I've found that men and women respond differently. Most men ask about the subjects I teach and the courses I took in my training. Then, unless they bring up an issue such as merit pay, the conversation stops. Most women, on the other hand, begin the conversation on a more immediate and personal level. They say things like "those kids must love having a male teacher" or "that age is just wonderful, you must love it." Then, more often than not, they'll talk about their own kids or ask me specific questions about what I do. We're then off and talking shop.

Possibly, men would have more to say to me, and I to them, if my job had more of the trappings and benefits of more traditional male jobs. But my job has no bonuses or promotions. No complimentary box seats at the ball park. No cab fare home. No drinking buddies after work. No briefcase. No suit. (Ties get stuck in paint jars.) No power lunches. (I eat peanut butter and jelly, chips, milk, and cookies with the kids.) No taking clients out for cocktails. The only place I take my kids is to the playground. 12

Although I could have pursued a career in law or business, as several of my friends did, I chose teaching instead. My job has benefits all its own. I'm able to bake cookies without getting them stuck together as they cool, buy cheap sewing materials, take out splinters, and search just the right trash cans for useful odds and ends. I'm sometimes called "Daddy" and even "Mommy" by my students, and if there's ever a lull in the conversation at a dinner party, I can always ask those assembled if they've heard the latest riddle about why the turkey crossed the road. (He thought he was a chicken.)

● PERSONAL RESPONSE ●

How do you view Meier's decision to teach first grade? Do you think it as reasonable a career choice as any other, or do you feel, as Meier indicates some people do, "a hint of suspicion" about why a man would want to work with young children?

● QUESTIONS FOR DISCUSSION ●

1. What do you think is Meier's purpose for writing this essay? What do you think he hopes to accomplish with it?

2. This essay first appeared in the "About Men" series of the *New York Times Magazine*. Do you think Meier anticipated a sympathetic or a skeptical audience? How can you tell?

3. What is the tone of this essay? Does Meier sound defensive?

4. Meier does not state his central idea until paragraph 5. What function do you think is served by the first four paragraphs? What difference would it have made had Meier put his fifth paragraph first?

5. Why isn't Meier's work "traditional male work" (paragraph 5)? Locate the series of adjectives Meier uses to describe "male work" and the adjectives he uses to describe what he does. What is Meier implying about the difference between "male work" and his work?

6. The central part of Meier's essay contrasts what he says are male activities and attitudes with female activities and attitudes. Summarize what Meier sees as the differences between males and females. Do you agree with him?

7. What benefits does Meier get from being a first-grade teacher? Would those benefits give you the same pleasure that they give Meier?

● WRITING TOPICS ●

1. If you have chosen a career that is often perceived as not typical for your sex, explain why you chose it, what kind of opposition you might expect (or have already had), and the potential benefits you anticipate from it.

2. Support or oppose Meier's contention that people still very much think of certain careers or behaviors as either masculine or feminine. Draw on your own personal experience or observations for your supporting evidence.

3. Contrast the values and long-term benefits of one career path over another. For example, you might consider contrasting a philosophy or art major with one in business or computer science.

I MARRIED AN ACCOUNTANT

●

JOE QUEENAN

Joe Queenan has written for Barron's, The American Spectator, The Wall Street Journal, *and* The New York Times Book Review, *among other publications. This article appeared in 1988 in* Newsweek's *"My Turn" column, a regular series featuring essays by guest writers wishing to express opinions on topics that interest them. Here, Queenan feels called upon to defend accountants from the charge that they are boring.*

At the mature age of 38, a somewhat immature 220-pound friend of mine took up ice hockey. Though he had never before strapped on ice skates and is far from fit, he has spent virtually every Sunday evening for the past two summers barreling up and down the ice in a special hockey league for aging neophytes. He may be strange, but he is not boring.

Another person I know moved to Teheran in the late 1970s, met an Iranian woman, converted to Islam so he could marry her, and had to undergo a circumcision — all of this took place against the backdrop of massive civil unrest in Iran. He, too, may be strange, but he is not boring.

This is equally true of my wife, who for three years wrote video scripts for a man who had previously directed the Gothic soap opera "Dark Shadows." Though the subject of her continuing-education scripts had few ghoulish elements, she can nevertheless claim to have worked closely with a colleague of Jonathan Frid's, the famous TV vampire. It is an honor she will take to her grave. She, like the aging hockey player and the intrepid voyager to Iran, has led a rich, interesting life and has done exciting, unpredictable things. Like them, she is also an accountant.

Accountants have long been the targets of satirists and have been mercilessly lambasted by everyone from Monty Python to the rock group The Kinks. Personally, I hold no brief for accountants as a unit and would be loath to argue that they are, collectively or individually, electrifying fireballs. Yet nothing in my experience would lead me to the conclusion that accountants are quantifiably less interesting than people in other occupations. 4

Thus I have often wondered why these attacks on accountants continue at a time when numerous other professions would make equally suitable targets. Does anyone truly believe that accountants are less fascinating than pension-fund managers? Is there anyone out there ready to argue that people in the precision-tools industry are blessed with personalities of a bodaciously scintillating variety? Breathes there a patent attorney with soul so dead who never to himself has said, "God, this is more boring than accounting"?

There are numerous explanations for the disproportionate amount of heat accountants seem to take. It has even occurred to me that satirists are paid annual retainers by the next most boring profession to keep the public's attention diverted. ("Here's 50 grand, Mr. Keillor, and you're worth every penny. If word ever got out about us systems engineers, we'd be finished.") Judging from my experiences, if a contest for least interesting profession were ever held, public-relations consultants for geothermal-design companies and anyone connected in any way whatsoever with nuclear-magnetic-resonance-imaging technology would be locked in a dead heat. And financial writers wouldn't be far behind.

Several weeks ago I purchased a novel called "Goldenrod." It was written by a young Canadian author who sells his fiction on the sidewalks of New York, where, lamentably, people are allowed to peddle anything, and where, even more lamentably, people like me buy it. The book is the usual onanistic, self-adulating claptrap we have all come to expect from bad young Canadian novelists. But even more irksome was the introduction, in which an obviously close friend of the novelist rips into the current crop of college graduates by declaring, "They're all accountants!"

Today's graduates are not all accountants; they are all investment bankers. 8 Yet the intro writer used the term "accountants" for the same reason that writers always use the word "accountant"; because, with the maniacal indifference to reality that is characteristic of people in the arts, he simply dredged up whatever was handy from the list of obvious targets that bad writers have been blasting for generations. "Businessman." "Politician." "Dentist." "Accountant."

This profession has taken enough abuse. I certainly wouldn't equate all accountants of my acquaintance with such riveting personalities as trapeze artists, gunrunners or foreign correspondents. But it takes chutzpah to move to Teheran and undergo all that mortifying surgery. It takes a little guts to strap on ice skates at the age of 39, especially when you're packing 50 extra pounds. And writing scripts, even if they are continuing-education scripts explaining changes in Financial Accounting Standard Board rules for the guy who used to direct "Dark Shadows," is not the most boring job in the world. Heck, you could be in direct marketing. You could be a young Canadian novelist.

In the fall of 1981, my wife coerced me into attending the first American Writers Congress, which was held at New York's Roosevelt Hotel. Coincidentally, the Association of Chartered Accountants — British accountants working in the United States — happened to be holding a little get-together in the same hotel the day the conference opened. I beat the entrance fee to the writers' conference by going along with my wife — who happens to be a chartered accountant. The room reserved for Britain's equivalent of certified public accountants had loads of booze, canapés and Swedish meatballs. The writers' conference had nothing. The chartered accountants were all talking about British auditing procedures and regulatory nuances. The writers were talking about how unfair it was that a feminist literary magazine from Oregon, publishing work by old women, gay women, working women and politically active women, all in an elegant and uncluttered format, didn't have as many advertisers as *The New Yorker*.

All right, I'll admit it, the chartered accountants' gathering was a bit on the dull side. But when you back me into a corner and ask me which topic I'd rather discuss: British auditing standards or injustices in the treatment of feminist quarterlies from Corvallis, Ore., I've got to side with the accountants every time.

At least they had the Swedish meatballs.   12

● PERSONAL RESPONSE ●

Which profession(s) strike you as particularly dull or boring? Do you agree with those that Queenan names? Would you include or omit "accountant" from your list?

● QUESTIONS FOR DISCUSSION ●

1. Why do you think Queenan feels compelled to defend accountants?

2. What examples does Queenan give of attacks against accountants?

3. Queenan argues against the popular image of accountants as boring by citing several examples of accountants he knows who are not boring. What do those examples have in common?

4. Queenan says in paragraph 6 that "there are numerous explanations for the dispropor-tionate amount of heat accountants seem to take." Does he give any of those explana-tions? Why do you think accounting is perceived as a boring profession?

5. Do you think Queenan believes that particular professions are intrinsically dull and boring, or would he argue that it is the personalities of people themselves that determine their degree of dullness?

6. Why do you think Queenan includes the comparison of the accountants' meeting with the writers' conference? Does he accomplish anything with that particular compari-son, or would any professional meeting have worked just as well to make his point?

● WRITING TOPICS ●

1. Define the characteristics of a career that you would find boring and contrast it with a career that you feel is exciting.

2. Identify a career that many people think is boring and then illustrate how it is not boring by describing people you know in that profession who do not conform to the stereotyped image. Use several examples and give specific details of their personalities or avocations to support your thesis.

3. Instead of writing about people already in the profession, use examples of people you know who are majoring in a field that has a reputation for being boring. Explain why they seem either likely or unlikely to fit the stereotype.

CHINESE PUZZLE

●

GRACE MING-YEE WAI

Grace Ming-Yee Wai is a first-generation Chinese American who grew up in Memphis, Tennessee, and whose father was shot to death when she was ten years old. In the following essay, written for the July 1988 issue of Ms. *magazine, Wai narrates a series of brief stories from her childhood in order to describe her father and to raise the question of how her life might have been different had he lived.*

I am a first generation Chinese-American woman educated in both private and public American schools. I grew up in the mid-South city of Memphis, Tennessee, where there were very few other Asian families. We lived in the South, I realized after my teens, primarily for economic reasons. Although there were more Asians in cities such as New York, Los Angeles, or San Francisco, it would have been very expensive to live in those cities, and our grocery store would have had much more competition. My parents immigrated to the United States from Hong Kong before I was born, for a better life for themselves and their children. Neither had a college education, but both emphasized hard work and the importance of education. Like all parents, they hoped their children would be fortunate enough to receive a quality education that would provide future opportunity and financial security.

My sister, brother, and I have been lucky to receive an education and all of us have reached or are near our goals, but not without pain and sacrifices. When I was 10 years old, my father was shot and killed while being robbed for $26 in change. He was the favorite son of seven living children. He took in one of my cousins from Hong Kong so she could study nursing. My youngest uncle was the only one of their generation to become a professional, primarily because he was lucky enough to have the opportunity to go to dental school at the University of Tennessee in Memphis.

Dad owned a small grocery store in a poor neighborhood. My parents worked more than 12 hours a day, seven days a week. We lived above the store in five rooms and one bathroom. At different times, my grandmother, three uncles, an aunt and her two sons also lived with us. My brother, sister, and I had a maid who came six days a week to take care of us. I became very attached to her and cried on her day off. I still send Willie Christmas cards every year.

My father had a fierce temper. Whenever something upset him a little, he 4 yelled a lot, so my brother, sister, and I shuddered at the thought of angering him. His bark was worse than his bite, however. He was also very fair. He loved us all very much. He and Mom worked hard for us, for the family. Family meant everything.

Since Mom and Dad worked so much, there was not much time for us kids. We occasionally went to Shoney's for a hamburger. It was a big treat to pat the statue of Big Boy on the stomach upon entering and exiting the restaurant. Dad took me to the dog track once because I wanted to go with him. I think I just wanted very much to have him for myself since he was always helping other people and working in the store with Mom.

I was the first to go to school because I was the oldest child. When I was four years old, I went to prekindergarten at a small, private, Episcopal school. On my first day, Dad drove me to the door, but he would not take me to my class. I knew where my class was located because we visited earlier to meet my teachers. My heart was pounding with a force I did not know my little body had when I jumped out of the car, and I know fear was evident on my face, but Dad didn't budge. I asked, "Daddy, aren't you coming with me?" He replied, "No, Grace, you know where your class is and who your teachers are. You can go by yourself." He was teaching me to be self-sufficient at four. Still, it must have been difficult for him to watch his firstborn walk alone into a world of which he would not have a part. It was my first day of independence.

I clearly remember my sixth birthday because Dad was in the hospital with pneumonia. He was working so hard he paid very little attention to his health. As a result, he spent almost the entire summer before I entered first grade in the hospital. Mom visited him nightly. On my birthday I was allowed to see him. I have memories of sitting happily in the lobby of the hospital talking to the nurses, telling them with a big smile that I was going to see my dad because it was my birthday. I couldn't wait to see him because children under 12 were not allowed to visit patients, so I had not seen him in a long time. When I entered his hospital room, I saw tubes inserted into his nose and needles stuck in his arm. He was very, very thin. I was frightened and wanted to cry, but I was determined to have a good visit. So I stayed for a while, and he wished me a happy birthday. When it was time to go, I kissed him good-bye and waited until I left his room to cry.

In first grade, I lived with my grandparents because a public elementary 8 school was just across the street. My father bought the house for my grandparents with plans for us three children to attend Levi Elementary School since it was close and convenient. My brother and sister stayed with my parents because Nancy was only four, and Robert was in kindergarten at my old school which was near the store. I felt very isolated and alone in that great big house away from my immediate family.

I learned from my father while in first grade one valuable lesson that still affects me now: never be afraid to ask questions. I was very self-conscious and timid in school. My grades were falling. My father asked me: "How are you going to learn if you don't ask questions?" Even then, when I was six years of age, he tried to make me realize the importance of taking initiative in school. He made me realize improving in school was up to me because he could not be with me all the time.

In those days, my grandmother took care of me. She had moved to America when I was three years old to be with my youngest uncle when he came to go to college. My grandfather joined us three years later. Every morning my grandmother got me dressed and made my breakfast. While I sat at the dining room table, she combed and brushed my hair to prepare me for school. She spoke no English, so we conversed in Cantonese. Every day after school, I called the store to talk to my mother. I really missed being with my parents, brother, and sister and looked forward to their weekly visits. Of course, only one parent visited at a time because someone had to be at the store. I was very jealous that Robert and Nancy were able to stay with my parents.

After school, my grandfather liked to see what I learned that day. It was always a treat to show him the new words I was taught to write in school. Every night I rewrote all the new words for him. He always smiled with approval. Sometimes he helped me with my mathematics. My grandfather played with numbers a lot and actually had an abacus on his desk, which he used daily.

My grandmother did not read or write English. I was learning material she would never understand. She was my caretaker. She cooked and cleaned the house. She fed and bathed me. Neither of my grandparents worked. At that time, they were in their mid-sixties. They had no desire to learn the culture of the new land. Their livelihood depended upon my father, and they were happy merely to be near their children's families.

In the summer, my sister and brother joined me at our grandparents' house. We played a lot more since we had a yard. At the store, we stayed upstairs mostly. When summer was over, I was alone with my grandparents again. That year, in second grade, I was often chased around by Albert, a little black boy in my class. He would try to kiss me. Other children were fascinated by my straight black hair, and would constantly try to touch it. I was jeered at by other children for being Chinese, for having squinty eyes and a flat nose. I was almost ashamed of being Chinese, and being so young I did not understand it at all. I had grown up around other blacks who had frequented our store. Many were my friends, but in school I was having trouble — with black and white children. There were no other Chinese children in my school.

I refrained from telling my parents about Albert because earlier in the school year, I had been hit on the head during recess by a classmate with a baseball bat and had to have stitches. My father told me I should not have been playing so recklessly in school. But one day, in my attempt to hide from Albert, I fell and scraped both knees badly. The principal found me and told me that I should tell my teacher if he did it again. After the next episode, I told my teacher, but made the mistake of embarrassing myself by telling in front of the class. What hurt even more was the fact that my teacher did not do anything about it. Finally, I decided I must tell my parents. I think I feared they would think I had done something wrong, that it was my fault — that perhaps I provoked the boy. I also feared my father's temper.

First I told my mother, and she encouraged me to tell my dad about it. He would make the final decision. I sighed and then proceeded to creep upstairs where he was taking a nap and sat outside their bedroom. When my father awoke, fearfully, I told him about what was happening to me in school. Dad was so understanding. To my relief, he was calm and collected, not angry. He asked me what I wanted to do. He asked if I would like to go to the private school my brother and sister attended. Would I! I was so happy. Yes! I wanted to go back to school with Robert and Nancy! That meant, also, that I would be moving back to the store to live with my parents.

I realize now that Dad was very angry. Not at me, but angry with the teachers and the principal of my elementary school for ignoring my distress. He took me out of Levi in the middle of the year. I feel for the people Dad dealt with to get me out of school. I imagine he probably went there red-faced and smoking with anger to fill out the necessary paperwork. It is funny, though, how Dad let me feel I made the decision to leave Levi. 16

My father was a loving and devoted son to my grandparents. He made sure they were happy and comfortable. He wanted them with us so he was assured of their well-being. My grandfather had fallen ill when I was around seven years old. The doctors thought he had cancer. Twenty years ago, that meant certain death. The night the diagnosis was given, I was alone with my parents after the store was closed. Dad was crying. I was frightened because I had never before seen him cry. Taking off his glasses and looking at me with red, teary eyes and unmistakable pain, he asked me, "Do you love your Ye-Ye?" It was difficult to speak to him when he seemed so vulnerable, but with all the courage I could muster and tears welling up in my eyes, I answered, "Yes." Mom was behind Dad comforting him. At seven years of age, I was learning what it is to love your parents, and I was learning even Dads cry. Thankfully, my grandfather's cancer went into remission after treatment.

When Dad caught wind of the fact that I was doing poorly on my multiplication tables in third grade, he drilled me nightly in the back of the store where he stood behind the meat counter. I remember sweating and feeling extremely apprehensive and fearful of his wrath if I answered incorrectly. I quickly learned my multiplication tables inside out.

On the day he died, Dad came to my grandparents' house where my brother, sister, and I were staying for Thanksgiving weekend. He planned to go car-shopping with his older brother. I went along with them. We had lunch at Shoney's afterward, at my suggestion, of course. I did not care about car-shopping. I just wanted to spend time with Dad, even if we were with my uncle. I chattered away while we had lunch. When we returned to my grandparents' house, he took a nap in my bedroom before going back to work at the store. I was to wake him in an hour. Upon leaving, he picked me up for a big hug and kiss good-bye. I had my arms around his neck and my head on his shoulder. He told me to be good before putting me down. I did not know it would be the last time I would see him alive.

Later, in the afternoon, I heard my grandfather making dozens of phone calls, saying with grief and shock: "Ah, Davey say joh loh, Davey say joh loh!" meaning, "Davey's dead, Davey's dead!" I couldn't believe his words and rushed to tell my sister and brother, who responded with disbelief and dismay. They thought I was lying to them, playing a cruel trick on them. Later, when we had heard the grown-ups talking and were in fact sure Dad was killed, the three of us went up to our favorite spot in the attic where we cried and cried and hugged one another. We were in the way of the adults. They did not know how to talk to us, nor would they answer our questions. We only had each other for comfort. 20

My aunts and uncles from various parts of the country left their families to rush to Memphis the day Dad was shot. We had a full house of people who came by to bring food, to pay respects. It was very late in the evening before all but family were left in our house. It seemed peaceful once again. My best friend brought a plant the next day. We were both at a loss for words — we did not need them. It was enough just to see her.

The next day, there was an article in the newspaper about what happened. My aunt said it did not do my father justice. The robber was never caught by the police. In fact, the police later found the bag of change lying in an alley nearby. My mom's reaction was calm as she told me, "Even if they find him, it won't bring your daddy back, Grace."

The day of my father's funeral was rainy and cold. There was a long procession of cars on the way to the cemetery. My father was well respected by others in the community and had many friends. My grandmother did not attend the funeral. As long as I knew her, she never once set foot in a hospital, nor did she go to funerals. My grandfather also elected not to attend, but as the hearse passed by their house, he ran out, down the long walkway to the gate with a black raincoat held above his head. He wished to open the coffin to see his son one more time, but it was nailed shut. It was only possible for him to touch the casket.

All my teachers and the principal of our school attended Dad's funeral. Willie was there too. We were all crying when they came to see us. Later, my best friend told me the teachers didn't think we would be returning to school for a while. They were surprised to find us in class the following day. My friends did not know how to react to me, and in homeroom, my teacher asked, in front of everyone, if I was okay. I was not okay. I was in pain, but what could I do? I lost my father. He was never coming back. I tried to be strong, and looking down at my desk, I said, "Yes, I'm okay." 24

We were so young: Robert eight, and Nancy seven. Now we are grown adults. I wonder what it would have been like if Dad were living during our developing years. I suspect I would be a very different person. I am very much a feminist and a professional now. I don't think he would have allowed me to move 1,000 miles from home to live on my own after college. I probably would not have been allowed to participate in many things such as dating, parties, and school activities if he were alive during my adolescence, for he was extremely strict.

We visited his gravesite every year on his birthday, on the anniversary of his death, and on holidays such as New Year's and Christmas. Following my grandmother's Asian traditions, we brought incense to burn at the gravesite, and food: a bowl of rice, fruit, a main dish for his spirit to eat. We also burned special paper, which my grandmother stated represented money for Dad to spend in the afterlife. We did these things for her since she would not go to the cemetery. Following American tradition, we also brought flowers. When the incense was lit, the money burning, and the food set out with chopsticks along with tea and sometimes scotch (he had to have something to drink as well as utensils!), we took turns paying our respects by bowing to the headstone three times and silently told his spirit whatever we wanted to tell him, whatever was on our minds. When done, we bowed again three times to bid farewell until the next time.

I write this now because it is more than 14 years since my father's death. I think about how fast those 14 years have gone by and all the changes and growing that have taken place. I wonder if he is proud of me now. I wonder what I would be like today if he were alive. Even though I only had him in the first 10 years of my life, I know there is much of him in me. I have his temperament, his strictness, and his self-righteous nature. I have his sense of fairness, generosity, and loyalty. He taught me much in those first 10 years. There are also scars from his death because my family did not talk about our loss. We took the blow and went on with life.

In the last four years, I have also lost both grandparents. They are buried ²⁸ with my father. One day, my mother and uncles will join them. Whenever I return to Memphis to visit family and friends, I also go to the cemetery to visit my father and grandparents. I don't follow all the traditions my grandmother so treasured, but I do carry incense and flowers with me. I still bow and have my talk with each. Those are always peaceful and contemplative moments. Sometimes I drive by the old store, the old house, and the private elementary school to relive some of my past.

Death does not get easier. The people I love will not be with me forever. That hurts. Death, however, is a part of life we all face at some point. Nevertheless, it is a comfort to me to believe that after death, those I love go somewhere nice and comfortable. My grandmother always wished to return as a bird — to fly over the earth — soaring and free. I hope she made it.

● PERSONAL RESPONSE ●

In what ways did your mother or father — or both of them — influence the way you are now? Do you think your life might have been significantly different without their influence? Explain why or why not.

● QUESTIONS FOR DISCUSSION ●

1. What is Wai's attitude toward her family in general and her father in particular? How do the various scenes from Wai's childhood help portray her feelings about them?

2. What is the effect of Wai's frequent use of short, simple sentences?

3. What characteristics of her father does Wai portray in the course of her narrative? What makes her portrait vivid and clear to readers?

4. Besides the values of hard work and the importance of education (paragraph 1) that Wai's parents stressed in all of their children, what other lessons did Wai learn from her father?

5. What aspects of growing up in a city with very few other Asian-American families does Wai remember? How do the traditional Asian customs of Wai's family differ from the customs in your family?

6. In paragraph 25, Wai wonders what her life would have been like had her father not been killed when she was ten years old. In what ways does she think she might be different and in what ways the same?

7. Why do you think Wai entitled her essay "Chinese Puzzle"? What is the puzzle?

● WRITING TOPICS ●

1. Characterize your own relationship with one or both of your parents.

2. Following Wai's technique of focusing on selected events or experiences from childhood, write an essay on the values that one or both of your parents instilled in you.

3. If your family has traditions or customs it follows for particular holidays or events, describe the customs associated with that day and explain their importance to you.

THINKING AS A HOBBY

●

WILLIAM GOLDING

William Golding was born in Cornwall, England, and educated at Oxford University. After serving with the Royal Navy, he has spent his life teaching and writing. His most famous work is Lord of the Flies *(1954), but he has written many other novels, including* Pincher Martin *(1950),* The Spire *(1964),* The Pyramid *(1967),* Darkness Visible *(1979), and* Rites of Passage *(1980). He won the Nobel Prize for literature in 1983. In "Thinking as a Hobby," which first appeared in the magazine* Holiday *in 1961, Golding defines three grades of thinking as he recalls his own intellectual growth from childhood to adolescence to adulthood.*

While I was still a boy, I came to the conclusion that there were three grades of thinking; and since I was later to claim thinking as my hobby, I came to an even stranger conclusion—namely, that I myself could not think at all.

I must have been an unsatisfactory child for grownups to deal with. I remember how incomprehensible they appeared to me at first, but not, of course, how I appeared to them. It was the headmaster of my grammar school who first brought the subject of thinking before me—though neither in the way, nor with the result he intended. He had some statuettes in his study. They stood on a high cupboard behind his desk. One was a lady wearing nothing but a bath towel. She seemed frozen in an eternal panic lest the bath towel slip down any farther; and since she had no arms, she was in an unfortunate position to pull the towel up again. Next to her, crouched the statuette of a leopard, ready to spring down at the top drawer of a filing cabinet labeled A–AH. My innocence interpreted this as the victim's last, despairing cry. Beyond the leopard was a naked, muscular gentleman, who sat, looking down, with his chin on his fist and his elbow on his knee. He seemed utterly miserable.

Some time later, I learned about these statuettes. The headmaster had placed them where they would face delinquent children, because they symbolized to him the whole of life. The naked lady was the Venus of Milo. She was Love. She was not worried about the towel. She was just busy being beautiful. The leopard was Nature, and he was being natural. The naked, muscular gentleman was not miserable. He was Rodin's Thinker, an image of pure thought. It is easy to buy small plaster models of what you think life is like.

I had better explain that I was a frequent visitor to the headmaster's study, because of the latest thing I had done or left undone. As we now say, I was not integrated. I was, if anything, disintegrated; and I was puzzled. Grownups never made sense. Whenever I found myself in a penal position before the headmaster's desk, with the statuettes glimmering whitely above him, I would sink my head, clasp my hands behind my back and writhe one shoe over the other.

The headmaster would look opaquely at me through flashing spectacles.

"What are we going to do with you?"

Well, what *were* they going to do with me? I would writhe my shoe some more and stare down at the worn rug.

"Look up, boy! Can't you look up?"   8

Then I would look up at the cupboard, where the naked lady was frozen in her panic and the muscular gentleman contemplated the hindquarters of the leopard in endless gloom. I had nothing to say to the headmaster. His spectacles caught the light so that you could see nothing human behind them. There was no possibility of communication.

"Don't you ever think at all?"

No, I didn't think, wasn't thinking, couldn't think — I was simply waiting in anguish for the interview to stop.

"Then you'd better learn — hadn't you?"   12

On one occasion the headmaster leaped to his feet, reached up and plonked Rodin's masterpiece on the desk before me.

"That's what a man looks like when he's really thinking."

I surveyed the gentleman without interest or comprehension.

"Go back to your class."   16

Clearly there was something missing in me. Nature had endowed the rest of the human race with a sixth sense and left me out. This must be so, I mused, on my way back to the class, since whether I had broken a window, or failed to remember Boyle's Law, or been late for school, my teachers produced me one, adult answer: "Why can't you think?"

As I saw the case, I had broken the window because I had tried to hit Jack Arney with a cricket ball and missed him; I could not remember Boyle's Law because I had never bothered to learn it; and I was late for school because I preferred looking over the bridge into the river. In fact, I was wicked. Were my teachers, perhaps, so good that they could not understand the depths of my depravity? Were they clear, untormented people who could direct their every action by this mysterious business of thinking? The whole thing was incomprehensible. In my earlier years, I found even the statuette of the Thinker confusing. I did not believe any of my teachers were naked, ever. Like someone born deaf, but bitterly determined to find out about sound, I watched my teachers to find out about thought.

There was Mr. Houghton. He was always telling me to think. With a modest satisfaction, he would tell me that he had thought a bit himself. Then why did he spend so much time drinking? Or was there more sense in drinking than there appeared to be? But if not, and if drinking were in fact ruinous to health — and Mr. Houghton was ruined, there was no doubt about that — why was he always talking about the clean life and the virtues of fresh air? He would spread his arms wide with the action of a man who habitually spent his time striding along mountain ridges.

"Open air does me good, boys — I know it!"   20

Sometimes, exalted by his own oratory, he would leap from his desk and hustle us outside into a hideous wind.

"Now boys! Deep breaths! Feel it right down inside you — huge draughts of God's good air!"

He would stand before us, rejoicing in his perfect health, an open-air man. He would put his hands on his waist and take a tremendous breath. You could hear the wind, trapped in the cavern of his chest and struggling with all the unnatural impediments. His body would reel with shock and his ruined face go white at the unaccustomed visitation. He would stagger back to his desk and collapse there, useless for the rest of the morning.

Mr. Houghton was given to high-minded monologues about the good life, sexless and full of duty. Yet in the middle of one of these monologues, if a girl passed the window, tapping along on her neat little feet, he would interrupt his discourse, his neck would turn of itself and he would watch her out of sight. In this instance, he seemed to me ruled not by thought but by an invisible and irresistible spring in his nape.

His neck was an object of great interest to me. Normally it bulged a bit over his collar. But Mr. Houghton had fought in the First World War alongside both Americans and French, and had come — by who knows what illogic? — to a settled detestation of both countries. If either country happened to be prominent in current affairs, no argument could make Mr. Houghton think well of it. He would bang the desk, his neck would bulge still further and go red. "You can say what you like," he would cry, "but I've thought about this — and I know what I think!"

Mr. Houghton thought with his neck.

There was Miss Parsons. She assured us that her dearest wish was our welfare, but I knew even then, with the mysterious clairvoyance of childhood, that what she wanted most was the husband she never got. There was Mr. Hands — and so on.

I have dealt at length with my teachers because this was my introduction to the nature of what is commonly called thought. Through them I discovered that thought is often full of unconscious prejudice, ignorance and hypocrisy. It will lecture on disinterested purity while its neck is being remorselessly twisted toward a skirt. Technically, it is about as proficient as most businessmen's golf, as honest as most politicians' intentions, or — to come near my own preoccupation — as coherent as most books that get written. It is what I came to call grade-three thinking, though more properly, it is feeling, rather than thought.

True, often there is a kind of innocence in prejudices, but in those days I viewed grade-three thinking with an intolerant contempt and an incautious mockery. I delighted to confront a pious lady who hated the Germans with the proposition that we should love our enemies. She taught me a great truth in dealing with grade-three thinkers; because of her, I no longer dismiss lightly a mental process which for nine-tenths of the population is the nearest they will ever get to thought. They have immense solidarity. We had better respect them, for we are outnumbered and surrounded. A crowd of grade-three thinkers, all shouting the same thing, all warming their hands at the fire of their own prejudices, will not thank you for pointing out the contradictions in their beliefs. Man is a gregarious animal, and enjoys agreement as cows will graze all the same way on the side of a hill.

Grade-two thinking is the detection of contradictions. I reached grade two when I trapped the poor, pious lady. Grade-two thinkers do not stampede easily, though often they fall into the other fault and lag behind. Grade-two thinking is a withdrawal, with eyes and ears open. It became my hobby and brought satisfaction and loneliness in either hand. For grade-two thinking destroys without having the power to create. It set me watching the crowds cheering His Majesty the King and asking myself what all the fuss was about, without giving me anything positive to put in the place of that heady patriotism. But there were compensations. To hear people justify their habit of hunting foxes and tearing them to pieces by claiming that the foxes liked it. To hear our Prime Minister talk about the great benefit we conferred on India by jailing people like Pandit Nehru and Gandhi. To hear American politicians talk about peace in one sentence and refuse to join the League of Nations in the next. Yes, there were moments of delight.

But I was growing toward adolescence and had to admit that Mr. Houghton was not the only one with an irresistible spring in his neck. I, too, felt the compulsive hand of nature and began to find that pointing out contradiction could be costly as well as fun. There was Ruth, for example, a serious and attractive girl. I was an atheist at the time. Grade-two thinking is a menace to religion and knocks down sects like skittles. I put myself in a position to be converted by her with an hypocrisy worthy of grade three. She was a Methodist — or at least, her parents were, and Ruth had to follow suit. But, alas, instead of relying on the Holy Spirit to convert me, Ruth was foolish enough to open her pretty mouth in argument. She claimed that the Bible (King James Version) was literally inspired. I countered by saying that the Catholics believed in the literal inspiration of Saint Jerome's *Vulgate*, and the two books were different. Argument flagged.

At last she remarked that there were an awful lot of Methodists, and they couldn't be wrong, could they — not all those millions? That was too easy, said I restively (for the nearer you were to Ruth, the nicer she was to be near to) since there were more Roman Catholics than Methodists anyway; and they couldn't be wrong, could they — not all those hundreds of millions? An awful flicker of doubt appeared in her eyes. I slid my arm round her waist and murmured breathlessly that if we were counting heads, the Buddhists were the boys for my money. But Ruth had *really* wanted to do me good, because I was so nice. She fled. The combination of my arm and those countless Buddhists was too much for her.

That night her father visited my father and left, red-cheeked and indignant. I was given the third degree to find out what had happened. It was lucky we were both of us only fourteen. I lost Ruth and gained an undeserved reputation as a potential libertine.

So grade-two thinking could be dangerous. It was in this knowledge, at the age of fifteen, that I remember making a comment from the heights of grade two, on the limitations of grade three. One evening I found myself alone in the schoolhall, preparing it for a party. The door of the headmaster's study was open. I went in. The headmaster had ceased to thump Rodin's Thinker down on the desk as an example to the young. Perhaps he had not found any more candidates, but the statuettes were still there, glimmering and gathering dust on top of the cupboard. I stood on a chair and rearranged them. I stood Venus in her bath towel on the filing cabinet, so that now the top drawer caught its breath in a gasp of sexy excitement. "A-ah!" The portentous Thinker I placed on the edge of the cupboard so that he looked down at the bath towel and waited for it to slip. Grade-two thinking, though it filled life with fun and excitement, did not make for content. To find out the deficiencies of our elders bolsters the young ego but does not make for personal security. I found that grade two was not only the power to point out contradictions. It took the swimmer some distance from the shore and left him there, out of his depth. I decided that Pontius Pilate was a typical grade-two thinker. "What is truth?" he said, a very common grade-two thought, but one that is used always as the end of an argument instead of the beginning. There is a still higher grade of thought which says, "What is truth?" and sets out to find it.

But these grade-one thinkers were few and far between. They did not visit my grammar school in the flesh though they were there in books. I aspired to them, partly because I was ambitious and partly because I now saw my hobby as an unsatisfactory thing if it went no further. If you set out to climb a mountain, however high you climb, you have failed if you cannot reach the top.

I *did* meet an undeniably grade-one thinker in my first year at Oxford. I was 36 looking over a small bridge in Magdalen Deer Park, and a tiny mustached and hatted figure came and stood by my side. He was a German who had just fled from the Nazis to Oxford as a temporary refuge. His name was Einstein.

But Professor Einstein knew no English at that time and I knew only two words of German. I beamed at him, trying wordlessly to convey by my bearing all the affection and respect that the English felt for him. It is possible — and I have to make the admission — that I felt here were two grade-one thinkers standing side by side; yet I doubt if my face conveyed more than a formless awe. I would have given my Greek and Latin and French and a good slice of my English for enough German to communicate. But we were divided; he was as inscrutable as my headmaster. For perhaps five minutes we stood together on the bridge, undeniable grade-one thinker and breathless aspirant. With true greatness, Professor Einstein realized that any contact was better than none. He pointed to a trout wavering in midstream.

He spoke: "*Fisch.*"

My brain reeled. Here I was, mingling with the great, and yet helpless as the veriest grade-three thinker. Desperately I sought for some sign by which I might convey that I, too, revered pure reason. I nodded vehemently. In a brilliant flash I used up half of my German vocabulary. "*Fisch. Ja. Ja.*"

For perhaps another five minutes we stood side by side. Then Professor 40 Einstein, his whole figure still conveying good will and amiability, drifted away out of sight.

I, too, would be a grade-one thinker. I was irreverent at the best of times. Political and religious systems, social customs, loyalties and traditions, they all came tumbling down like so many rotten apples off a tree. This was a fine hobby and a sensible substitute for cricket, since you could play it all the year round. I came up in the end with what must always remain the justification for grade-one thinking, its sign, seal and charter. I devised a coherent system for living. It was a moral system, which was wholly logical. Of course, as I readily admitted, conversion of the world to my way of thinking might be difficult, since my system did away with a number of trifles, such as big business, centralized government, armies, marriage. . . .

It was Ruth all over again. I had some very good friends who stood by me, and still do. But my acquaintances vanished, taking the girls with them. Young women seemed oddly contented with the world as it was. They valued the meaningless ceremony with a ring. Young men, while willing to concede the chaining sordidness of marriage, were hesitant about abandoning the organizations which they hoped would give them a career. A young man on the first rung of the Royal Navy, while perfectly agreeable to doing away with big business and marriage, got as rednecked as Mr. Houghton when I proposed a world without any battleships in it.

Had the game gone too far? Was it a game any longer? In those prewar days, I stood to lose a great deal, for the sake of a hobby.

Now you are expecting me to describe how I saw the folly of my ways and came back to the warm nest, where prejudices are so often called loyalties, where pointless actions are hallowed into custom by repetition, where we are content to say we think when all we do is feel. 44

But you would be wrong. I dropped my hobby and turned professional.

If I were to go back to the headmaster's study and find the dusty statuettes still there, I would arrange them differently. I would dust Venus and put her aside, for I have come to love her and know her for the fair thing she is. But I would put the Thinker, sunk in his desperate thought, where there were shadows before him — and at his back, I would put the leopard, crouched and ready to spring.

● PERSONAL RESPONSE ●

What is your response to Golding's categories of thinkers? Do you think he is being too judgmental or even unfair when he places nine-tenths of the population in grade three (paragraph 29)?

● QUESTIONS FOR DISCUSSION ●

1. Golding makes liberal use of vivid figurative language in order to make abstract ideas concrete, as when he describes systems, customs, and traditions as "tumbling down like so many rotten apples off a tree" (paragraph 41) or when he defines the three levels of thinkers in familiar terms throughout the essay. Find several other examples of such language.

2. Find passages that you think are particularly vivid in their descriptions of people or scenes.

3. Why do you think Golding devotes so much time to describing his grade-school teachers?

4. What evidence does Golding supply to explain why he reached the conclusion that he could not think at all?

5. Summarize the distinctive features of each of Golding's levels of thinkers. How does grade-three thinking differ from grade-two thinking?

6. Why does Golding say that "grade-two thinking could be dangerous" and why does he call Pontius Pilate "a typical grade-two thinker" (paragraph 34)? What is it about Einstein that makes him a grade-one thinker?

7. In his narrative of his encounter with Einstein, Golding not only describes his example of an undeniable grade-one thinker but also humorously reveals something about himself. In what way is he making fun of himself? Where else does he do that?

8. How does Golding's rearranging the statuettes in the headmaster's office serve to "comment from the heights of grade two, on the limitations of grade three" (paragraph 34)? Why does Golding say in his conclusion that he would rearrange the statuettes differently now?

● WRITING TOPICS ●

1. Categorize teachers or other role models you have known on the basis of Golding's three grades of thinkers.

2. Analyze your own intellectual development in terms of the three levels Golding describes.

3. Explain why some famous person—writer, scientist, politician, or the like—qualifies as a grade-one thinker, by Golding's standards.

TRANSITIONS

●

ADDITIONAL WRITING SUGGESTIONS

1. Write an essay addressed to parents or friends who strongly oppose a decision you have made about your future. Explain why you have made that decision and try to persuade your audience to accept it.

2. Write an essay focusing on one or two specific experiences you have had as a new college student and how your life has changed as a result.

3. Compare and/or contrast high school with college.

4. Explain the ways in which your parents have influenced the goals you have set for yourself.

5. Some of the essays in this chapter address the issue of setting career goals. For instance, Gage's "The Teacher Who Changed My Life," Meier's "One Man's Kids," Baker's "Deems," and Queenan's "I Married an Accountant" all explain what their writers find appealing about their professions or why they chose them. Write an essay in which you explain the career goal you have in mind for yourself, what appeals to you about it, what you would hope to achieve in it, and/or who or what inspired you to consider it.

2

ACQUIRING VALUES

THE DECLINE OF NEATNESS

●

NORMAN COUSINS

Norman Cousins (1915–1990) was editor of the Saturday Review *for 35 years and continued as chair of its editorial board after 1976. A holistic health pioneer, he served on the medical faculty at UCLA from 1978 until his death. Cousins wrote 25 books and numerous essays on a wide range of subjects, including* Talks with Nehru *(1951),* Who Speaks for Man? *(1953), and* Present Tense *(1967). More recently,* The Celebration of Life *(1974) and* The Anatomy of Illness *(1979) describe his experiences with and recovery from an illness that doctors told him was fatal. Cousins received the Albert Schweitzer Prize for Humanitarianism in 1990 for his efforts on behalf of international peace. In the 1990* Time *essay reprinted below, Cousins explains the connections he sees among casual dress, slovenly speech, and insensitivity to brutality.*

Anyone with a passion for hanging labels on people or things should have little difficulty in recognizing that an apt tag for our time is the Unkempt generation. I am not referring solely to college kids. The sloppiness virus has spread to all sectors of society. People go to all sorts of trouble and expense to look uncombed, unshaved, unpressed.

The symbol of the times is blue jeans — not just blue jeans in good condition but jeans that are frayed, torn, discolored. They don't get that way naturally. No one wants blue jeans that are crisply clean or spanking new. Manufacturers recognize a big market when they see it, and they compete with one another to offer jeans that are made to look as though they've just been discarded by clumsy house painters after ten years of wear. The more faded and seemingly ancient the garment, the higher the cost. Disheveled is in fashion; neatness is obsolete.

Nothing is wrong with comfortable clothing. It's just that current usage is more reflective of a slavish conformity than a desire for ease. No generation has strained harder than ours to affect a casual, relaxed, cool look; none has succeeded more spectacularly in looking as though it had been stamped out by cookie cutters. The attempt to avoid any appearance of being well groomed or even neat has a quality of desperation about it and suggests a calculated and phony deprivation. We shun conventionality, but we put on a uniform to do it. An appearance of alienation is the triumphant goal, to be pursued in oversize sweaters and muddy sneakers.

Slovenly speech comes off the same spool. Vocabulary, like blue jeans, is being drained of color and distinction. A complete sentence in everyday speech is as rare as a man's tie in the swank Polo Lounge of the Beverly Hills Hotel. People communicate in chopped-up phrases, relying on grunts and chants of "you know" or "I mean" to cover up a damnable incoherence. Neatness should be no less important in language than it is in dress. But spew and sprawl are taking over. The English language is one of the greatest sources of wealth in the world. In the midst of accessible riches, we are linguistic paupers.

Violence in language has become almost as casual as the possession of handguns. The curious notion has taken hold that emphasis in communicating is impossible without the incessant use of four-letter words. Some screenwriters openly admit that they are careful not to turn in scripts that are devoid of foul language lest the classification office impose the curse of a G (general) rating. Motion-picture exhibitors have a strong preference for the R (restricted) rating, probably on the theory of forbidden fruit. Hence writers and producers have every incentive to employ tasteless language and gory scenes.

The effect is to foster attitudes of casualness toward violence and brutality not just in entertainment but in everyday life. People are not as uncomfortable as they ought to be about the glamorization of human hurt. The ability to react instinctively to suffering seems to be atrophying. Youngsters sit transfixed in front of television or motion-picture screens, munching popcorn while human beings are battered or mutilated. Nothing is more essential in education than respect for the frailty of human beings; nothing is more characteristic of the age than mindless violence.

Everything I have learned about the educational process convinces me that the notion that children can outgrow casual attitudes toward brutality is wrong. Count on it: if you saturate young minds with materials showing that human beings are fit subjects for debasement or dismembering, the result will be desensitization to everything that should produce revulsion or resistance. The first aim of education is to develop respect for life, just as the highest expression of civilization is the supreme tenderness that people are strong enough to feel and manifest toward one another. If society is breaking down, as it too often appears to be, it is not because we lack the brainpower to meet its demands but because our feelings are so dulled that we don't recognize we have a problem.

Untidiness in dress, speech and emotions is readily connected to human 8 relationships. The problem with the casual sex so fashionable in films is not that it arouses lust but that it deadens feelings and annihilates privacy. The danger is not that sexual exploitation will create sex fiends but that it may spawn eunuchs. People who have the habit of seeing everything and doing anything run the risk of feeling nothing.

My purpose here is not to make a case for a Victorian decorum or for namby-pambyism. The argument is directed to bad dress, bad manners, bad speech, bad human relationships. The hope has to be that calculated sloppiness will run its course. Who knows, perhaps some of the hip designers may discover they can make a fortune by creating fashions that are unfrayed and that grace the human form. Similarly, motion-picture and television producers and exhibitors may realize that a substantial audience exists for something more appealing to the human eye and spirit than the sight of a human being hurled through a store-front window or tossed off a penthouse terrace. There might even be a salutary response to films that dare to show people expressing genuine love and respect for one another in more convincing ways than anonymous clutching and thrashing about.

Finally, our schools might encourage the notion that few things are more rewarding than genuine creativity, whether in the clothes we wear, the way we communicate, the nurturing of human relationships, or how we locate the best in ourselves and put it to work.

● PERSONAL RESPONSE ●

Do you think Cousins has a legitimate complaint about the connections between the wearing of unkempt blue jeans and casual attitudes toward violence in speech and human relationships? To what extent do you agree or disagree with his argument?

● QUESTIONS FOR DISCUSSION ●

1. What do you think Cousins means by his statement in paragraph 3 that wearing blue jeans is "reflective of a slavish conformity"?
2. How are the wearing of blue jeans and slovenly speech habits connected, according to Cousins?
3. What characteristics of Cousins' own writing style and word choice reflect his respect for order and neatness?
4. According to Cousins, how are both the wearing of blue jeans and slovenly speech habits connected to portrayals of violence and casual sex in the movies?
5. What values does Cousins hope to see replace the current trends in dress, speech, and films?
6. What part does Cousins believe education ought to play in instilling values into young people?
7. Beyond sloppy dress, careless speech, and violence in everyday life, what ultimate dangers does Cousin fear for our society if the trends he complains of continue?

● WRITING TOPICS ●

1. Either support or argue against Cousins' observation that "nothing is more characteristic of the age than mindless violence" (paragraph 6).
2. Suggest reasons for the widespread popularity of blue jeans and other casual clothing.
3. Using examples other than blue jeans, illustrate Cousins' point that fads and trends are "reflective of a slavish conformity."

RUFFLES AND FLOURISHES

●

Susan Ohanian

Susan Ohanian was a grammar-school teacher for almost twenty years. In this 1987 Atlantic *article, she argues against many of the alterations that have been made in children's books, noting that children "savor the ruffles and flourishes in special writing." In a writing style that exemplifies the language Ohanian believes children love, she makes a strong case for the value of "powerful, florid, and wild" writing and its ability to "keep us reading books."*

Children like a fine word occasionally," Beatrix Potter once told her publisher, when he complained about the use of the word *soporific* in her book *The Tale of Flopsy Bunnies*. I taught grammar-school students for the better part of two decades, and I count myself firmly in Ms. Potter's camp. It follows, of course, that I can muster little enthusiasm for basal readers, those homogenized and bowdlerized grade-school texts, edited according to elaborate readability formulas and syllable schemes, that constitute the bulk of the average child's officially sanctioned reading material in American schools. Basal readers can be criticized on a lot of grounds. Their worst fault, I think, is that for no good reason they squeeze the juice out of some very fine tales. Here is a passage from the Paul Leyssac translation of Hans Christian Andersen's "The Emperor's New Clothes":

> "Magnificent!" "Excellent!" "Prodigious!" went from mouth to mouth, and everyone was exceedingly pleased.

Here is the same passage as rendered in a modern reader:

> "How marvelous," they echoed the emperor. "How beautiful!"

Sure, *prodigious* is a tough word, but it's a word that young readers would be pleased, perhaps exceedingly pleased, to try out, to repeat, to save.

Admittedly, the publishers of basal readers encounter prodigious difficulties in the preparation of their texts. They are under acute and conflicting pressures from educators, from parents, and from organized interest groups of every kind. Too, the sensibility of many old stories may often be at odds with the tenor of our times. In many instances, however, the sense behind the censorship seems impossible to fathom. The difference between many familiar children's stories in their original form and the way they appear in basal readers is, indeed, so striking and the changes, it seems to me, so unnecessary that several years ago I began comparing old and new versions line by line.

A good many of the editorial changes are of a kind that one would never write an angry letter about but that nevertheless give one pause. I have in mind changes like the following:

Original	Basal
Do a tapdance!	Chirp like a bird!
Cook spaghetti!	Cook pancakes!
"Trust me," I said.	"You'll see," I said.
Cóme to my house at eleven.	Come to my house around twelve.
The sea is our enemy.	The sea is not our friend.
wily swindlers, crafty rogues	weavers
cornflakes	potatoes
Rubbish!	Why?

This sort of thing does not, I suppose, amount to extreme literary deprivation, but the average classic children's tale — a work by, say, Andersen, Kipling, or Pearl Buck — in basal form contains hundreds of such alterations. Taken together they suggest a preternatural disposition to tinker, which in turn perhaps reinforces a parallel disposition to cut and trim and simplify, to tame and domesticate what is powerful, florid, and wild in the way that good writers use our language.

The latter disposition is pronounced. Consider how, in Kipling's "How the Camel Got His Hump," "sticks and thorns and tamarisks and milkweed and prickles" becomes, in basal form, "sticks and shrubs"; or how a "great big lolloping humph" turns into a "great big humph." You lose a great big lolloping lot when you lose the humph's gerundive. Consider how, in Walter Blair's "Pecos Bill," "giving a coyote yell of a size to make any state that was less tough than Oklahoma split right down the middle" becomes, in basal versions, "Howling like a coyote." One of the stories my students have most enjoyed over the years is *Flat Stanley*, by Jeff Brown. As the title implies, Stanley has gotten himself flattened, and the story goes on to describe the very special things that a flat boy can do, including travel across the country by mail. Here is a passage from Brown:

> The envelope fit Stanley very well. There was even room left over, Mrs. Lambchop discovered, for an egg-salad sandwich made with thin bread, and a flat cigarette case filled with milk.
> They had to put a great many stamps on the envelope to pay for both airmail and insurance, but it was still much less expensive than a train or airplane ticket to California would have been.

Here is how the passage appears in a basal reader:

> The envelope fit Stanley very well. There was even room left over for a sandwich.

My students always loved the author's mention of thin bread — they knew he was being very deliberate in his choice of words, and they appreciated his nod to their intelligence, his acknowledgment that they would know he was sustaining a joke. They appreciated, too, the humor of egg salad — a much yuckier substance than, for instance, bologna, and one with which you would certainly not choose to be sealed in an envelope. I appreciate the taboo governing allusions to cigarettes, and yet what my students tended to note is not the reference to tobacco but rather Mrs. Lambchop's ingenuity in finding a way to make sure that her son, while in the mail, is able to drink his milk. Eventually, Stanley's friends mail him back from California in

> a beautiful white envelope they had made themselves. It had red-and-blue markings to show that it was air-mail, and Thomas Jeffrey had lettered it "Valuable" and "Fragile" and "This End Up" on both sides.

Basal readers simply stuff the kid in "a beautiful, large white envelope," and get on with the story.

I have compiled notebook after notebook of alterations of just this kind, which probably makes me some kind of nut. I find it hard to believe, though, that the unscrupulous editing of basal readers doesn't matter. Like Bartleby the Scrivener, modern reading textbooks are "pallidly neat, pitiably respectable, incurably forlorn." There is room in our children's literature for silliness, for unpleasantness, and for difficult words that children do not know. Above all, there is a place for detail and nuance and subtlety, which children perhaps admire more than adults do. Young readers are not like the Emperor of Austria, who told Mozart that his music was great but complained that there were too many notes. Perhaps a few of them could be cut?

Mozart was lucky. He succeeded in silencing his critic with the question, "Which few did you have in mind?" The editors of modern basal readers, unfortunately, would have had a reply. There is a book kids love called *Nate the Great*, by Marjorie Weinman Sharmat, and here is a passage that does not appear in any of the basal versions:

> "Fang has sharp teeth and I, Nate the Great, say that we should keep anybody with sharp teeth happy. Very happy."

I never used the basal texts, and so my students could sigh and grin over that phrase "Very happy." They copied the device, as they did other devices, in their own writing. Children notice and savor the ruffles and flourishes in special writing. It is these, in the end, that keep us reading books.

● PERSONAL RESPONSE ●

Were the books you read in grade school the "homogenized and bowdlerized" versions or the original, uncut versions? Do you agree or disagree with Ohanian's criticism of basal readers? Explain your answer.

● QUESTIONS FOR DISCUSSION ●

1. What purpose is served by the quotation from Beatrix Potter that opens this essay?

2. Ohanian makes use of many examples, both brief and extended, to illustrate the kind of rewriting she objects to. She also makes liberal use of the "powerful" and "florid" language that she favors retaining in children's books. Find several passages in which Ohanian is particularly colorful in her word choice.

3. Where in her argument does Ohanian make concessions to those who favor basal readers?

4. What is Ohanian's major criticism against the practice of cutting and rewriting children's books?

5. What does Ohanian's comparison of modern reading textbooks to Bartleby the Scrivener in paragraph 6 add to her argument?

6. What does Ohanian imply is the effect on children of reading the simplified, tame versions of children's books?

7. Explain in detail whether or not you find Ohanian's argument convincing.

● WRITING TOPICS ●

1. Argue for or against the use of basal readers for low achievers, for high achievers, and for average students. Consider whether or not such readers would help or hinder the intellectual development of each level of student.

2. Explain why your favorite books as a child were your favorites.

3. Explain how you were affected or influenced by a book you read as a child.

IT'S FAILURE, NOT SUCCESS

●

ELLEN GOODMAN

Ellen Goodman was born in Boston and began her career as a reporter for Newsweek *after graduating with a bachelor's degree from Radcliffe College. She worked for the* Detroit Free Press *before becoming a columnist for the* Boston Globe *in 1967. Her column, "At Large," has been syndicated by the Washington Post Writers Group since 1976. In 1980 she won a Pulitzer Prize for distinguished commentary. She has published a study of human change,* Turning Points *(1979), and many of her columns have been collected in* Close to Home *(1979),* At Large *(1981),* Keeping in Touch *(1985), and* Making Sense *(1989). In the following essay, Goodman takes exception to a definition of success advanced in a popular self-help book.*

I knew a man who went into therapy about three years ago because, as he put it, he couldn't live with himself any longer. I didn't blame him. The guy was a bigot, a tyrant and a creep.

In any case, I ran into him again after he'd finished therapy. He was still a bigot, a tyrant and a creep, *but* . . . he had learned to live with himself.

Now, I suppose this was an accomplishment of sorts. I mean, nobody else could live with him. But it seems to me that there are an awful lot of people running around and writing around these days encouraging us to feel good about what we should feel terrible about, and to accept in ourselves what we should change.

The only thing they seem to disapprove of is disapproval. The only judgment they make is against being judgmental, and they assure us that we have nothing to feel guilty about except guilt itself. It seems to me that they are all intent on proving that I'm OK and You're OK, when in fact, I may be perfectly dreadful and you may be unforgivably dreary, and it may be — gasp! — *wrong.* 4

What brings on my sudden attack of judgmentitis is success, or rather, *Success!* — the latest in a series of exclamation-point books all concerned with How to Make It.

In this one, Michael Korda is writing a recipe book for success. Like the other authors, he leapfrogs right over the "Shoulds" and into the "Hows." He eliminates value judgments and edits out moral questions as if he were Fanny Farmer and the subject was the making of a blueberry pie.

It's not that I have any reason to doubt Mr. Korda's advice on the way to achieve success. It may very well be that successful men wear handkerchiefs stuffed neatly in their breast pockets, and that successful single women should carry suitcases to the office on Fridays whether or not they are going away for the weekend.

He may be realistic when he says that "successful people generally have 8
very low expectations of others." And he may be only slightly cynical when he
writes: "One of the best ways to ensure success is to develop expensive tastes or
marry someone who has them."

And he may be helpful with his handy hints on how to sit next to someone
you are about to overpower.

But he simply finesses the issues of right and wrong—silly words, embarrassing words that have been excised like warts from the shiny surface of the new
how-to books. To Korda, guilt is not a prod, but an enemy that he slays on page
four. Right off the bat, he tells the would-be successful reader that:

- It's OK to be greedy.
- It's OK to look out for Number One.
- It's OK to be Machiavellian (if you can get away with it).
- It's OK to recognize that honesty is not always the best policy (provided
  you don't go around saying so).
- And it's always OK to be rich.

Well, in fact, it's not OK. It's not OK to be greedy, Machiavellian, dishonest.
It's not always OK to be rich. There is a qualitative difference between succeeding by making napalm or by making penicillin. There is a difference between
climbing the ladder of success, and macheteing a path to the top.

Only someone with the moral perspective of a mushroom could assure us 12
that this was all OK. It seems to me that most Americans harbor ambivalence
toward success, not for neurotic reasons, but out of a realistic perception of what
it demands.

Success is expensive in terms of time and energy and altered behavior—the
sort of behavior he describes in the grossest of terms: "If you can undermine
your boss and replace him, fine, do so, but never express anything but respect
and loyalty for him while you're doing it."

This author—whose *Power!* topped the best-seller list last year—is intent
on helping rid us of that ambivalence which is a signal from our conscience. He
is like the other "Win!" "Me First!" writers, who try to make us comfortable
when we should be uncomfortable.

They are all Doctor Feelgoods, offering us placebo prescriptions instead of
strong medicine. They give us a way to live with ourselves, perhaps, but not a
way to live with each other. They teach us a whole lot more about "Failure!" than
about success.

● PERSONAL RESPONSE ●

What is your reaction to Goodman's statement in paragraph 11 that "it's not always O.K.
to be rich"? Whether you agree or disagree with Goodman, explain your reasons for
feeling as you do.

● QUESTIONS FOR DISCUSSION ●

1. Do you think Goodman anticipated an audience who buys the kind of book she is writing about or an audience already sympathetic to her view? How can you tell? What does Goodman's reference to "Machiavellian" (paragraphs 10 and 11) suggest about how she perceives her audience?

2. Describe the tone of this piece, as indicated by Goodman's word choice. For example, what effect do you think she wants to achieve when she uses figurative language such as "excised like warts" (paragraph 10) and "only someone with the moral perspective of a mushroom" (paragraph 12)? What level of diction is indicated by words like "creep" (paragraph 1) and "gasp!" (paragraph 4)?

3. Because this piece was originally written for a newspaper column, it has very short paragraphs. If you were evaluating Goodman's essay as if she were one of your classmates in freshman English, where would you suggest she combine paragraphs to avoid so many one- or two-sentence paragraphs? Why do you think newspaper writing tends to use very short paragraphs while the kind of writing you do in your college work requires much longer paragraphs?

4. Besides being restricted to short paragraphs, newspaper columnists often do not have the space to fully develop their central ideas. If Goodman were writing this essay for your freshman English class, where would you suggest that she expand or amplify her examples?

5. Summarize the complaints Goodman has about how-to-make-it books and the "me first" attitude they promote. What do you think she means in paragraph 15 when she writes: "They are all Doctor Feelgoods, offering us placebo prescriptions instead of strong medicine"?

6. How does Michael Korda's book *Success!* define "success"? What does Goodman find wrong with that definition and how would she define the word?

● WRITING TOPICS ●

1. Defend or attack the philosophy that any means you have to use to get to the top are justifiable.

2. Define "success" by using the example of a person (or persons) you know personally or have read about. It might be that one person illustrates how you define the term, or it may be that several people represent different kinds of success.

3. Define "failure" by using the example of a person (or persons) you know personally or have read about. Consider whether a person might be a failure in one area of life and a success in another.

LIVING LIKE WEASELS

●

ANNIE DILLARD

Annie Dillard was a contributing editor for Harper's *from 1973 to 1981. In 1974, she published a book of poems,* Tickets for a Prayer Wheel, *and a volume of essays,* Pilgrim at Tinker Creek, *for which she won the Pulitzer Prize. Her other books include* Living with Fiction *(1982),* Encounters with Chinese Writers *(1984), and* An American Childhood *(1987). The selection that follows comes from* Teaching a Stone to Talk *(1982), a collection of her own narrative essays. Here Dillard describes her sudden encounter with a weasel, an experience that prompted her to reflect that she could "very calmly go wild."*

A weasel is wild. Who knows what he thinks? He sleeps in his underground den, his tail draped over his nose. Sometimes he lives in his den for two days without leaving. Outside, he stalks rabbits, mice, muskrats, and birds, killing more bodies than he can eat warm, and often dragging the carcasses home. Obedient to instinct, he bites his prey at the neck, either splitting the jugular vein at the throat or crunching the brain at the base of the skull, and he does not let go. One naturalist refused to kill a weasel who was socketed into his hand deeply as a rattlesnake. The man could in no way pry the tiny weasel off, and he had to walk half a mile to water, the weasel dangling from his palm, and soak him off like a stubborn label.

And once, says Ernest Thompson Seton — once, a man shot an eagle out of the sky. He examined the eagle and found the dry skull of a weasel fixed by the jaws to his throat. The supposition is that the eagle had pounced on the weasel and the weasel swiveled and bit as instinct taught him, tooth to neck, and nearly won. I would like to have seen that eagle from the air a few weeks or months before he was shot: was the whole weasel still attached to his feathered throat, a fur pendant? Or did the eagle eat what he could reach, gutting the living weasel with his talons before his breast, bending his beak, cleaning the beautiful airborne bones?

I have been reading about weasels because I saw one last week. I startled a weasel who startled me, and we exchanged a long glance.

Twenty minutes from my house, through the woods by the quarry and across the highway, is Hollins Pond, a remarkable piece of shallowness, where I like to go at sunset and sit on a tree trunk. Hollins Pond is also called Murray's Pond; it covers two acres of bottomland near Tinker Creek with six inches of water and six thousand lily pads. In winter, brown-and-white steers stand in the middle of it, merely dampening their hooves; from the distant shore they look like miracle itself, complete with miracle's nonchalance. Now, in summer, the steers are gone. The water lilies have blossomed and spread to a green horizontal plane that is terra firma to plodding blackbirds, and tremulous ceiling to black leeches, crayfish, and carp.

4

This is, mind you, suburbia. It is a five-minute walk in three directions to rows of houses, though none is visible here. There's a 55 mph highway at one end of the pond, and a nesting pair of wood ducks at the other. Under every bush is a muskrat hole or a beer can. The far end is an alternating series of fields and woods, fields and woods, threaded everywhere with motorcycle tracks—in whose bare clay wild turtles lay eggs.

So. I had crossed the highway, stepped over two low barbed-wire fences, and traced the motorcycle path in all gratitude through the wild rose and poison ivy of the pond's shoreline up into high grassy fields. Then I cut down through the woods to the mossy fallen tree where I sit. This tree is excellent. It makes a dry, upholstered bench at the upper, marshy end of the pond, a plush jetty raised from the thorny shore between a shallow blue body of water and a deep blue body of sky.

The sun had just set. I was relaxed on the tree trunk, ensconced in the lap of lichen, watching the lily pads at my feet tremble and part dreamily over the thrusting path of a carp. A yellow bird appeared to my right and flew behind me. It caught my eye; I swiveled around—and the next instant, inexplicably, I was looking down at a weasel, who was looking up at me.

Weasel! I'd never seen one wild before. He was ten inches long, thin as a 8 curve, a muscled ribbon, brown as fruitwood, soft-furred, alert. His face was fierce, small and pointed as a lizard's; he would have made a good arrowhead. There was just a dot of chin, maybe two brown hairs' worth, and then the pure white fur began that spread down his underside. He had two black eyes I didn't see, any more than you see a window.

The weasel was stunned into stillness as he was emerging from beneath an enormous shaggy wild rose bush four feet away. I was stunned into stillness twisted backward on the tree trunk. Our eyes locked, and someone threw away the key.

Our look was as if two lovers, or deadly enemies, met unexpectedly on an overgrown path when each had been thinking of something else: a clearing blow to the gut. It was also a bright blow to the brain, or a sudden beating of brains, with all the charge and intimate grate of rubbed balloons. It emptied our lungs. It felled the forest, moved the fields, and drained the pond; the world dismantled and tumbled into that black hole of eyes. If you and I looked at each other that way, our skulls would split and drop to our shoulders. But we don't. We keep our skulls. So.

He disappeared. This was only last week, and already I don't remember what shattered the enchantment. I think I blinked, I think I retrieved my brain from the weasel's brain, and tried to memorize what I was seeing, and the weasel felt the yank of separation, the careening splashdown into real life and the urgent current of instinct. He vanished under the wild rose. I waited motionless, my mind suddenly full of data and my spirit with pleadings, but he didn't return.

Please do not tell me about "approach-avoidance conflicts." I tell you I've 12 been in that weasel's brain for sixty seconds, and he was in mine. Brains are private places, muttering through unique and secret tapes—but the weasel and I both plugged into another tape simultaneously, for a sweet and shocking time. Can I help it if it was a blank?

What goes on in his brain the rest of the time? What does a weasel think about? He won't say. His journal is tracks in clay, a spray of feathers, mouse blood and bone: uncollected, unconnected, loose-leaf, and blown.

I would like to learn, or remember, how to live. I come to Hollins Pond not so much to learn how to live as, frankly, to forget about it. That is, I don't think I can learn from a wild animal how to live in particular — shall I suck warm blood, hold my tail high, walk with my footprints precisely over the prints of my hands? — but I might learn something of mindlessness, something of the purity without bias or motive. The weasel lives in necessity and we live in choice, hating necessity and dying at the last ignobly in its talons. I would like to live as I should, as the weasel lives as he should. And I suspect that for me the way is like the weasel's: open to time and death painlessly, noticing everything, remembering nothing, choosing the given with a fierce and pointed will.

I missed my chance. I should have gone for the throat. I should have lunged for that streak of white under the weasel's chin and held on, held on through mud and into the wild rose, held on for a dearer life. We could live under the wild rose wild as weasels, mute and uncomprehending. I could very calmly go wild. I could live two days in the den, curled, leaning on mouse fur, sniffing bird bones, blinking, licking, breathing musk, my hair tangled in the roots of grasses. Down is a good place to go, where the mind is single. Down is out, out of your ever-loving mind and back to your careless senses. I remember muteness as a prolonged and giddy fast, where every moment is a feast of utterance received. Time and events are merely poured, unremarked, and ingested directly, like blood pulsed into my gut through a jugular vein. Could two live that way? Could two live under the wild rose, and explore by the pond, so that the smooth mind of each is as everywhere present to the other, and as received and as un-challenged, as falling snow?

We could, you know. We can live any way we want. People take vows of ⟨16⟩ poverty, chastity, and obedience — even of silence — by choice. The thing is to stalk your calling in a certain skilled and supple way, to locate the most tender and live spot and plug into that pulse. This is yielding, not fighting. A weasel doesn't "attack" anything; a weasel lives as he's meant to, yielding at every moment to the perfect freedom of single necessity.

I think it would be well, and proper, and obedient, and pure, to grasp your one necessity and not let it go, to dangle from it limp wherever it takes you. Then even death, where you're going no matter how you live, cannot you part. Seize it and let it seize you up aloft even, till your eyes burn out and drop; let your musky flesh fall off in shreds, and let your very bones unhinge and scatter, loosened over fields, over fields and woods, lightly, thoughtless, from any height at all, from as high as eagles.

● **PERSONAL RESPONSE** ●

Describe your own experience with something wild in its natural setting. What other animal(s) besides weasels do you think humans could learn something from?

● QUESTIONS FOR DISCUSSION ●

1. What point about the nature of weasels do the anecdotes in the opening two paragraphs make?

2. Dillard uses details so effectively that readers are able to visualize exactly what she experienced herself. Find passages that you think are especially descriptive of a thing, a place, or a feeling.

3. Dillard frequently uses metaphors and other figurative language to create images and convey sensory experiences. In paragraph 9, for instance, she writes: "Our eyes locked, and someone threw away the key." Here she plays on the language of a common idiom that is metaphoric (not literal) — eyes locking — by suggesting that it is literal (someone throwing away the key). What do you think she means by that sentence?

4. Explain what you think Dillard means by her comparison in paragraph 10 of the weasel and her to "two lovers, or deadly enemies" coming upon one another suddenly. In what way would the emotions of a sudden encounter between lovers and a sudden encounter between enemies be the same?

5. What do you think Dillard means by the last sentence of paragraph 8: "He had two black eyes I didn't see, any more than you see a window"?

6. This essay is not really about weasels but about ways Dillard thinks people could live. What does Dillard find attractive about how weasels live?

7. What does Dillard think humans might learn from weasels?

● WRITING TOPICS ●

1. Write an essay on an animal other than a weasel from whom you think humans could learn something about living. Try using Dillard's technique of telling a story in order to explain your point.

2. Using concrete, specific details, describe a place that has special meaning to you. Include both objective physical characteristics and the subjective emotional meaning the place holds for you.

3. Compare and contrast living in the wild with living in captivity.

ON EXCELLENCE

●

CYNTHIA OZICK

*Cynthia Ozick is a highly acclaimed writer noted for her serious,
meticulous work. She has written three novels,* Trust *(1983),* The
Cannibal Galaxy *(1983), and* The Messiah of Stockholm *(1987), and
her essays have been collected in* Art and Ardor *(1983) and* Metaphor
and Memory *(1989). The essay reprinted below first appeared in* Ms. *in
1985. In it, Ozick defines two contrasting forms of excellence: that of
her colorful mother and that of her own.*

In my Depression childhood, whenever I had a new dress, my cousin
Sarah would get suspicious. The nicer the dress was, and especially the
more expensive it looked, the more suspicious she would get. Finally
she would lift the hem and check the seams. This was to see if the dress had been
bought or if my mother had sewed it. Sarah could always tell. My mother's
sewing had elegant outsides, but there was something catch-as-catch-can about
the insides. Sarah's sewing, by contrast, was as impeccably finished inside as out;
not one stray thread dangled.

My uncle Jake built meticulous grandfather clocks out of rosewood; he was
a perfectionist, and sent to England for the clockworks. My mother built
serviceable radiator covers and a serviceable cabinet, with hinged doors, for the
pantry. She built a pair of bookcases for the living room. Once, after I was grown
and in a house of my own, she fixed the sewer pipe. She painted ceilings, and also
landscapes; she reupholstered chairs. One summer she planted a whole yard of
tall corn. She thought herself capable of doing anything, and did everything she
imagined. But nothing was perfect. There was always some clear flaw, never
visible head-on. You had to look underneath where the seams were. The corn
thrived, though not in rows. The stalks elbowed one another like gossips in a
dense little village.

"Miss Brrrroooobaker," my mother used to mock, rolling her Russian *r*s,
whenever I crossed a *t* she had left uncrossed, or corrected a word she had
misspelled, or became impatient with a *v* that had tangled itself up with a *w* in
her speech. ("V*vv*entriloquist," I would say. "V*vv*entriloquist," she would obe-
diently repeat. And the next time it would come out "wiolinist.") Miss Brubaker
was my high school English teacher, and my mother invoked her name as an
emblem of raging finical obsession. "Miss Brrrroooobaker," my mother's voice
hoots at me down the years, as I go on casting and recasting sentences in a tiny
handwriting on monomaniacally uniform paper. The loops of my mother's
handwriting — it was the Palmer Method — were as big as hoops, spilling gen-
erous splashy ebullience. She could pull off, at five minutes' notice, a satisfying
dinner for 10 concocted out of nothing more than originality and panache. But
the napkin would be folded a little off-center, and the spoon might be on the

wrong side of the knife. She was an optimist who ignored trifles; for her, God was not in the details but in the intent. And all these culinary and agricultural efflorescences were extracurricular, accomplished in the crevices and niches of a 14-hour business day. When she scribbled out her family memoirs, in heaps of dog-eared notebooks, or on the backs of old bills, or on the margins of last year's calendar, I would resist typing them; in the speed of the chase she often omitted words like "the," "and," "will." The same flashing and bountiful hand fashioned and fired ceramic pots, and painted brilliant autumn views and vases of imaginary flowers and ferns, and decorated ordinary Woolworth platters and lavish enameled gardens. But bits of the painted petals would chip away.

Lavish: my mother was as lavish as nature. She woke early and saturated the 4 hours with work and inventiveness, and read late into the night. She was all profusion, abundance, fabrication. Angry at her children, she would run after us whirling the cord of the electric iron, like a lasso or a whip; but she never caught us. When, in the seventh grade, I was afraid of failing the Music Appreciation final exam because I could not tell the difference between "To a Wild Rose" and "Barcarolle," she got the idea of sending me to school with a gauze sling rigged up on my writing arm, and an explanatory note that was purest fiction. But the sling kept slipping off. My mother gave advice like mad — she boiled over with so much passion for the predicaments of strangers that they turned into permanent cronies. She told intimate stories about people I had never heard of.

Despite the gargantuan Palmer loops (or possibly because of them), I have always known that my mother's was a life of — intricately abashing word! — excellence: insofar as excellence means ripe generosity. She burgeoned, she proliferated; she was endlessly leafy and flowering. She wore red hats, and called herself a Gypsy. In her girlhood she marched with the suffragettes and for Margaret Sanger° and called herself a Red. She made me laugh, she was so varied: like a tree on which lemons, pomegranates, and prickly pears absurdly all hang together. She had the comedy of prodigality.

My own way is a thousand times more confined. I am a pinched perfectionist, the ultimate fruition of Miss Brubaker; I attend to crabbed minutiae and am self-trammeled through taking pains. I am a kind of human snail, locked in and condemned by my own nature. The ancients believed that the moist track left by the snail as it crept was the snail's own essence, depleting its body little by little; the farther the snail toiled, the smaller it became, until it finally rubbed itself out. This is how perfectionists are. Say to us Excellence, and we will show you how we use up our substance and wear ourselves away, while making scarcely any progress at all. The fact that I am an exacting perfectionist in a narrow strait only, and nowhere else, is hardly to the point, since nothing matters to me so much as a comely and muscular sentence. It is my narrow strait, this snail's road: the track of the sentence I am writing now; and when I have eked out the wet substance, ink or blood, that is its mark, I will begin the next sentence. Only in reading out sentences am I perfectionist; but then there is nothing else I know

° (1883–1966) Leader in the American birth-control movement.

how to do, or take much interest in. I miter every pair of abutting sentences as scrupulously as Uncle Jake fitted one strip of rosewood against another. My mother's worldly and bountiful hand has escaped me. The sentence I am writing is my cabin and my shell, compact, self-sufficient. It is the burnished horizon — a merciless planet where flawlessness is the single standard, where even the inmost seams, however hidden from a laxer eye, must meet perfection. Here "excellence" is not strewn casually from a tipped cornucopia, here disorder does not account for charm, here trifles rule like tyrants.

I measure my life in sentences, and my sentences are superior to my mother's, pressed out, line by line, like the lustrous ooze on the underside of the snail, the snail's secret open seam, its wound, leaking attar. My mother was too mettlesome to feel the force of a comma. She scorned minutiae. She measured her life according to what poured from the horn of plenty, which was her ample, cascading, elastic, susceptible, inexact heart. My narrower heart rides between the tiny horns of the snail, dwindling as it goes.

And out of this thinnest thread, this ink-wet line of words, must rise a   8 visionary fog, a mist, a smoke, forging cities, histories, sorrows, quagmires, entanglements, lives of sinners, even the life of my furnace-hearted mother: so much wilderness, waywardness, plentitude on the head of the precise and impeccable snail, between the horns.

● PERSONAL RESPONSE ●

Which approach to life does your own resemble, Ozick's or her mother's? Explain your answer.

● QUESTIONS FOR DISCUSSION ●

1. What do you think is Ozick's primary purpose in this essay? Is her goal to define an abstract concept, describe her mother's character, explain her own approach to writing, or combine all of those purposes?

2. Where does Ozick turn the literal example of the dress in the opening paragraph into a metaphor? Explain the metaphor. Where else does Ozick use similes and metaphors that you think are particularly expressive?

3. What does the fact that Ozick's mother marched with the suffragettes and for Margaret Sanger (paragraph 5) in her girlhood indicate about her mother's character?

4. Explain the difference between Ozick's way of doing things and her mother's.

5. How does Ozick define "excellence" in terms of her mother's nature and personality?

6. How does Ozick's approach to writing define another form of "excellence"?

7. What does Ozick mean in paragraph 6 when she says she is "the ultimate fruition of Miss Brubaker"?

8. What seems to be Ozick's attitude toward the differences between herself and her mother?

• WRITING TOPICS •

1. Describe someone whose personality you find colorful or admirable. Use specific, concrete details to make this person vividly real to your readers.

2. Contrast two people close to one another — relatives, spouses, good friends — who are opposites in personalities, approaches to life, or ways of doing things.

3. Write a story about yourself that dramatizes the kind of person you are.

VALUES WHICH ARE SIMPLY THERE

●

SUE HALPERN

Sue Halpern is a journalist who lives in the Adirondack Mountains of New York. In the following essay, which appeared in May 1990 in The New York Times Magazine, *Halpern explains how an assignment to write about a hospice for AIDS victims led her to discover what basic values are and how humans express them.*

A t the Chris Brownlie AIDS hospice in Los Angeles, Maria Cruz has brought soup she made for her 32-year-old son, Jose, who can no longer eat. He lies in bed curled toward the wall, a spindle of a man, nearly blind now. It is black bean soup and, untouched, it has grown cold on the tray beside him. His mother shrugs. In a little while she will put it in the refrigerator next to the paella and somosas she made him the week before, which sit on top of the chicken and rice she made the week before that. If he cannot swallow, at least he can smell.

Maria is holding my hand. I am here as a journalist, to write about the hospice, but I cannot write because she has placed my hand inside hers and regards it as if it were a gift.

"I am very strong," she tells me. She speaks little English, though she has been here for 30 years, up from Guatemala, scrubbing other people's floors, ironing their shirts.

"I am strong in here." She points to her heart. "God is good. He gives me everything I ask for. People expect everything quickly, but God doesn't work that way." She lets go of my hand and drops down to the floor, this squat little woman in a blue housedress and ragged terry-cloth slippers, splays her fingers, and pats the carpet.

"My faith," she says, "is from here. It is deep in the ground." She asks me if I understand what she means. I say that I do, and I do, in a way, the easy way, the same way I understand when she says "I love my son." But I do not have a son, and I do not have God in the same way as she, although it occurs to me that to have one might be to have the other.

"Pray for him," she says, nodding toward the bed when I get up to leave. I say I will. But it is she I pray for late that night, Maria first, and then her son, and what I pray for is that he dies.

The friend's house where I am staying, high in the Hollywood Hills, has a picture window that frames the Los Angeles skyline. For the better part of a week I have come back from the hospice each evening and stood in front of it, watching until the sun has gone down and the city is bathed in the alien orange glow of sodium vapor street lamps. This morning, unable to sleep, I see the sun overtake them.

I also see, on the table by the window, a book called "Vaclav Havel or Living 8 In Truth," with Havel's face on the cover. It is a younger face than the one that has become so familiar these days, a face that does not yet spell precisely the address of every prison he's been in. I pick it up reflexively, as though it were a newspaper left on the seat of a train by the passenger before me, and leaf through it aimlessly.

In fact, the book has been there all week, and I have avoided it. What could a man of ideas have to say about living or truth that wouldn't be an abstraction? In the hospice, in the corridor of death, there is no time for that which is obscure. It is a place where people have no choice but to live in truth.

The essay I read is called "Politics and Conscience." I read it twice and then, compelled, I take out my notebook, and under the heading "Maria Cruz," on the lines where I could not take my notes, I begin to copy it down. I find that in it is a more apt description of her—and of the hospice—than anything I might have written in its place:

"In this world, categories like justice, honor, treason, friendship, infidelity, courage or empathy have a wholly tangible content, relating to actual persons and important for actual life. At the basis of this world are values which are simply there, perennially, before we ever speak of them, before we reflect upon them and inquire about them. It owes its internal coherence to something like a pre-speculative assumption that the world functions and is generally possible at all only because there is something beyond its horizon, something beyond or above it that might escape our understanding and our grasp but, for just that reason, firmly grounds this world, bestows upon it its order and measure, and is the hidden source of all the rules, customs, commandments, prohibitions and norms that hold within it."

Reading this over, I think of Ken at the opposite end of the hall from Jose, 6 12 feet tall, 117 pounds, riddled with lymphoma, losing his sight. "I've come to terms with why I'm here," he told me one afternoon. "My mother and brother haven't. 'You should put your faith in God,' they keep telling me. I do believe in God. I know it's up to each person, how you approach Him. But they still think they can ask Him to make me well."

And I think of Tony, a former Chris Brownlie resident who is well enough now to volunteer at the hospice twice a week, and his conviction that he is the one who is going to beat this disease, that he is the one who will heal himself. And I think of Maria, patiently reading her Bible with one eye, keeping watch over her son with the other.

She is not there when I next return to the hospice. Someone thinks she has gone home for a few hours, to feed her cats and, I imagine, to cook for Jose. It strikes me that it is not some fantasy that inspires her to prepare meals that he will never eat but something born, as Havel might say, of a "pre-speculative" realism. The food, her vigilance—this is what she can give to him. This is what she has always given to him. And he, lying there, though inert, gives back to her in return the dailiness of their lives—that which gives love its openings.

A few years ago, I was enamored of a clever young man who had worked out an entire system to prove that marriage was stupid. I don't think he actually used the word stupid, but that was the gist of it, nor did he use the word marriage. Rather, he called it "the retreat to the kitchen." What is most onerous about the retreat to the kitchen, he argued, is that it preoccupies people with the trivial necessities of life, reduces their concerns to "the buying of bread," which prevents them from devoting their energies to working out the details of, say, unified field theory or literary deconstruction.

I retreated to the kitchen with someone else but haven't bought a loaf of   16 bread since. Instead, I've bought yeast and flour and honey and eggs, and once a week I spend the morning baking. Strictly speaking, I suppose you could say I do this solely for my husband's benefit since, for health reasons, I cannot eat the bread I make. But like Jose, I can smell it. And like his mother, I just do it — a thoughtful act done thoughtlessly — because it is what I do in this life my husband and I are making together, because it is one of the ways in which this life is made.

I left the Chris Brownlie Hospice before Jose's mother got back, so I don't know what she brought him that day. Back home I might have been doing anything — petting the dog, planning our garden, kneading dough — when he died.

● PERSONAL RESPONSE ●

Do you agree with Halpern's viewpoint toward the "retreat to the kitchen," or do you agree with that of the clever young man? Explain your answer.

● QUESTIONS FOR DISCUSSION ●

1. Halpern says in paragraph 2 that she is at the hospice in order to write about it. To what extent is this article about the hospice? What is the real subject of her essay?

2. What purpose is served by the opening narrative of the mother's activities? How do the mother's comments on strength and faith further support that purpose?

3. What does Halpern mean when she says that Havel's face "does not yet spell precisely the address of every prison he's been in" (paragraph 8)?

4. Summarize the point of the quotation from Havel's book that Halpern includes in her essay. How is the quotation from Havel's book an "apt description" of Maria Cruz (paragraph 10)? Why do you think that Halpern is reminded of Ken and Tony when she thinks about what Havel's words mean?

5. Why does Halpern include the comments of the "clever young man" and his views on marriage and the "trivial necessities of life" (paragraph 15)?

6. What connection does Halpern make among the clever young man's views, her own "retreat to the kitchen," and "values which are simply there"?

7. How do Maria Cruz's food preparation and vigilance demonstrate basic values? What does her son give her in return?

8. Comment on the effectiveness of Halpern's conclusion. How does she connect her observations at the hospice with her own life? What is significant about the activities she names in the final paragraph?

● WRITING TOPICS ●

1. Define an abstract quality like justice, honor, friendship, courage, empathy, commitment, honesty, dedication, or achievement by illustrating how a person you know exemplifies it.

2. Argue that taking care of the trivial necessities of life is ultimately more "valuable" than devoting one's energies to intellectual pursuits.

3. If you have ever taken care of or visited regularly someone who was seriously ill, write an account of your experience.

TEACH ETHICS AND VALUES IN SCHOOL

●

ROBERT SCHOLES

Robert Scholes is a professor of humanities and of English at Brown University in Providence, Rhode Island. In the following article, which appeared on the opinion page of The Philadelphia Inquirer *in June 1989, Scholes argues that philosophy should be taught in public schools in order to teach students to think.*

We have a problem in this country with what our President might call "the ethics thing." We have also been made aware in recent years that we have a massive problem in our school systems. Let us call this second problem, just to keep things neat, a matter of "this thinking thing."

The graduates of our schools — even our elite business and professional schools — don't seem to be very good at solving ethical or moral problems. And the graduates of all our schools — but especially our public secondary schools — don't seem to be very good at any kind of thinking.

Let us consider these two problems together. If you were looking for a discipline in which ethics and thinking could be said to be the main objects of study, what would it be? There is, in fact, a time-honored name for just such a study. For more than 2,000 years, it has been called "philosophy."

It also is the case that, for the more than 200 years of our existence as a nation, philosophy has not been taught in our secondary schools. Americans leaving high school rarely have any formal grounding in reasoning about ethics and values. In other nations sharing a similar cultural heritage, philosophy is indeed taught, as in the final year of education in the French *lycee.*

Why, then do we Americans not encourage the study of philosophy in our public schools? There are no doubt many reasons, including the notion that it is not "useful," or that it is too difficult for our students, though it is no more difficult than some of the things we do teach (or claim to teach), such as algebra and foreign languages.

As to its usefulness, the fact that we are beginning to be seriously worried about our weaknesses in ethics and thinking suggests that we do indeed put some practical value on them. We wouldn't miss them if we didn't need them. So why is philosophy not in our public curriculum?

A large part of the reason for this situation lies in our historic separation of church and state. We built this separation into our Constitution and into our public life for very good reasons, and I am not about to say we shouldn't have done this. But one of the unfortunate side effects of this separation has been the impossibility of teaching philosophy in our public schools, even though philosophy is the discipline that has been historically devoted to ethics and to clear, rigorous thinking.

To keep our churches out of politics, we have had to pay the price of keeping 8 public education out of many serious questions of ethics. We have had, in effect, to keep philosophy out of our schools.

Remember that in some parts of the country religious groups claim that the teaching of evolution in biology courses should be subject to their veto. Then imagine how far one would get in teaching David Hume's criticism of belief in miracles or G. W. F. Hegel's view that Protestantism was an improvement on all other religions and the only path to a rational and free society.

My point is not that Hume and Hegel were necessarily right, but that the great philosophers have regularly tackled questions that are matters of concern to religions, and that they have often come up with answers that would not pass the censorship of one religion or another. Socrates, one of philosophy's first notable teachers, was sentenced to death for challenging accepted beliefs.

At present in this country we regularly confuse ethics with moral conditioning. Instead of wanting students to learn to think for themselves about morality, we prefer to have some authority figure tell them what to think. This is why we leave ethics to television evangelists and football coaches rather than bring it into the classroom.

We are afraid of what might happen if students learned to question values 12 instead of doing the "right thing" by reflex. And the result of this is that, when they are faced with a situation where they have to think for themselves, the graduates of our schools are all too ready to take their values from those around them rather than working out the right thing to do with the aid of reason and conscience. I have no quick fix for this problem.

The first step toward a solution, though, is to find a way around or through the separation of church and state that currently keeps philosophy out of our schoolrooms.

● PERSONAL RESPONSE ●

Do you agree or disagree with Scholes's statement that graduates of our schools do not seem to be good at thinking of any kind? Explain your answer. Are you persuaded that philosophy would help students learn to think better? Why or why not?

● QUESTIONS FOR DISCUSSION ●

1. This essay was written for the opinion page of a large newspaper. What audience do you think Scholes had in mind?

2. How much does Scholes assume that audience knows about the problems he mentions in his opening paragraph?

3. What does Scholes imply by his parenthetical remark in paragraph 5, "or claim to teach"?

4. What reasons does Scholes cite for why philosophy is not taught in public schools? Which reason does he think has had the most influence in keeping philosophy out of the curriculum?

5. What does Scholes have to say about each of the reasons he gives for why philosophy is not being taught?

6. Explain what Scholes means in paragraph 11 when he says that we "regularly confuse ethics with moral conditioning." What does Scholes believe is the result of that confusion?

7. Evaluate Scholes's argument. Is it convincing? Explain why or why not.

● WRITING TOPICS ●

1. Explore the advantages and disadvantages of teaching philosophy in secondary schools.

2. Offer other solutions to the problems that Scholes addresses in his essay.

3. Argue that students either are or are not able to think and to solve ethical or moral problems. Cite examples of people you know and specific situations in which they demonstrated their abilities (or lack of them) to think.

THINK ABOUT IT
Ways We Know, and Don't

●

Frank Conroy

Frank Conroy has worked as a jazz pianist and writes often of American music. He currently directs the Iowa Writers' Workshop. His essays and stories have appeared in The New Yorker, Esquire, Harpers, *and* GQ. *Some of his short stories are collected in* Midair. *In the essay below, first published in* Harper's *in 1988, Conroy distinguishes between two ways that education occurs and concludes that, for some problems, not knowing the resolution is "our special fate, our inexpressibly valuable condition."*

When I was sixteen I worked selling hot dogs at a stand in the Fourteenth Street subway station in New York City, one level above the trains and one below the street, where the crowds continually flowed back and forth. I worked with three Puerto Rican men who could not speak English. I had no Spanish, and although we understood each other well with regard to the tasks at hand, sensing and adjusting to each other's body movements in the extremely confined space in which we operated, I felt isolated with no one to talk to. On my break I came out from behind the counter and passed the time with two old black men who ran a shoeshine stand in a dark corner of the corridor. It was a poor location, half hidden by columns, and they didn't have much business. I would sit with my back against the wall while they stood or moved around their ancient elevated stand, talking to each other or to me, but always staring into the distance as they did so.

As the weeks went by I realized that they never looked at anything in their immediate vicinity—not at me or their stand or anybody who might come within ten or fifteen feet. They did not look at approaching customers once they were inside the perimeter. Save for the instant it took to discern the color of the shoes, they did not even look at what they were doing while they worked, but rubbed in polish, brushed, and buffed by feel while looking over their shoulders, into the distance, as if awaiting the arrival of an important person. Of course there wasn't all that much distance in the underground station, but their behavior was so focused and consistent they seemed somehow to transcend the physical. A powerful mood was created, and I came almost to believe that these men could see through walls, through girders, and around corners to whatever hyperspace it was where whoever it was they were waiting and watching for would finally emerge. Their scattered talk was hip, elliptical, and hinted at mysteries beyond my white boy's ken, but it was the staring off, the long, steady staring off, that had me hypnotized. I left for a better job, with handshakes from both of them, without understanding what I had seen.

Save for the instant it took to discern the color of the shoes, they did not even look at what they were doing while they worked, but rubbed in polish, brushed, and buffed by feel while looking over their shoulders, into the distance, as if awaiting the arrival of an important person. Of course there wasn't all that much distance in the underground station, but their behavior was so focused and consistent they seemed somehow to transcend the physical. A powerful mood was created, and I came almost to believe that these men could see through walls, through girders, and around corners to whatever hyperspace it was where whoever it was they were waiting and watching for would finally emerge. Their scattered talk was hip, elliptical, and hinted at mysteries beyond my white boy's ken, but it was the staring off, the long, steady staring off, that had me hypnotized. I left for a better job, with handshakes from both of them, without understanding what I had seen.

Perhaps ten years later, after playing jazz with black musicians in various Harlem clubs, hanging out uptown with a few young artists and intellectuals, I began to learn from them something of the extraordinarily varied and complex riffs and rituals embraced by different people to help themselves get through life in the ghetto. Fantasy of all kinds — from playful to dangerous — was in the very air of Harlem. It was the spice of uptown life.

Only then did I understand the two shoeshine men. They were trapped in a 4 demeaning situation in a dark corner in an underground corridor in a filthy subway system. Their continuous staring off was a kind of statement, a kind of dance. Our bodies are here, went the statement, but our souls are receiving nourishment from distant sources only we can see. They were powerful magic dancers, sorcerers almost, and thirty-five years later I can still feel the pressure of their spell.

The light bulb may appear over your head, is what I'm saying, but it may be a while before it actually goes on. Early in my attempts to learn jazz piano, I used to listen to recordings of a fine player named Red Garland, whose music I admired. I couldn't quite figure out what he was doing with his left hand, however; the chords eluded me. I went uptown to an obscure club where he was playing with his trio, caught him on his break, and simply asked him. "Sixths," he said cheerfully. And then he went away.

I didn't know what to make of it. The basic jazz chord is the seventh, which comes in various configurations, but it is what it is. I was a self-taught pianist, pretty shaky on theory and harmony, and when he said sixths I kept trying to fit the information into what I already knew, and it didn't fit. But it stuck in my mind — a tantalizing mystery.

A couple of years later, when I began playing with a bass player, I discovered more or less by accident that if the bass played the root and I played a sixth based on the fifth note of the scale, a very interesting chord involving both instruments emerged. Ordinarily, I suppose I would have skipped over the matter and not paid much attention, but I remembered Garland's remark and so I stopped and spent a week or two working out the voicings, and greatly strengthened my foundations as a player. I had remembered what I hadn't understood, you might say, until my life caught up with the information and the light bulb went on.

I remember another, more complicated example from my sophomore year 8 at a small liberal-arts college outside Philadelphia. I seemed never to be able to get up in time for breakfast in the dining hall. I would get coffee and a doughnut in the Coop instead — a basement area with about a dozen small tables where students could get something to eat at odd hours. Several mornings in a row I noticed a strange man sitting by himself with a cup of coffee. He was in his sixties, perhaps, and sat straight in his chair with very little extraneous movement. I guessed he was some sort of distinguished visitor to the college who had decided to put in some time at a student hangout. But no one ever sat with him. One morning I approached his table and asked if I could join him.

"Certainly," he said. "Please do." He had perhaps the clearest eyes I had ever seen, like blue ice, and to be held in their steady gaze was not, at first, an entirely comfortable experience. His eyes gave nothing away about himself while at the same time creating in me the eerie impression that he was looking directly into my soul. He asked a few quick questions, as if to put me at my ease, and we fell into conversation. He was William O. Douglas from the Supreme Court, and when he saw how startled I was he said, "Call me Bill. Now tell me what you're studying and why you get up so late in the morning." Thus began a series of talks that stretched over many weeks. The fact that I was an ignorant sophomore with literary pretensions who knew nothing about the law didn't seem to bother him. We talked about everything from Shakespeare to the possibility of life on other planets. One day I mentioned that I was going to have dinner with Judge Learned Hand. I explained that Hand was my girlfriend's grandfather. Douglas nodded, but I could tell he was surprised at the coincidence of my knowing the chief judge of the most important court in the country save the Supreme Court itself. After fifty years on the bench Judge Hand had become a famous man, both in and out of legal circles — a living legend, to his own dismay. "Tell him hello and give him my best regards," Douglas said.

Learned Hand, in his eighties, was a short, barrel-chested man with a large, square head, huge, thick, bristling eyebrows, and soft brown eyes. He radiated energy and would sometimes bark out remarks or questions in the living room as if he were in court. His humor was sharp, but often leavened with a touch of self-mockery. When something caught his funny bone he would burst out with explosive laughter — the laughter of a man who enjoyed laughing. He had a large repertoire of dramatic expressions involving the use of his eyebrows — very useful, he told me conspiratorially, when looking down on things from behind the bench. (The court stenographer could not record the movement of his eyebrows.) When I told him I'd been talking to William O. Douglas, they first shot up in exaggerated surprise, and then lowered and moved forward in a glower.

"*Justice* William O. Douglas, young man," he admonished. "Justice Douglas, if you please." About the Supreme Court in general, Hand insisted on a tone of profound respect. Little did I know that in private correspondence he had referred to the Court as "The Blessed Saints, Cherubim and Seraphim," "The Jolly Boys," "The Nine Tin Jesuses," "The Nine Blameless Ethiopians," and my particular favorite, "The Nine Blessed Chalices of the Sacred Effluvium."

Hand was badly stooped and had a lot of pain in his lower back. Martinis helped, but his strict Yankee wife approved of only one before dinner. It was my job to make the second and somehow slip it to him. If the pain was particularly acute he would get out of his chair and lie flat on the rug, still talking, and finish his point without missing a beat. He flattered me by asking for my impression of Justice Douglas, instructed me to convey his warmest regards, and then began talking about the Dennis case, which he described as a particularly tricky and difficult case involving the prosecution of eleven leaders of the Communist party. He had just started in on the First Amendment and free speech when we were called into dinner. [12]

William O. Douglas loved the outdoors with a passion, and we fell into the habit of having coffee in the Coop and then strolling under the trees down toward the duck pond. About the Dennis case, he said something to this effect:

"Eleven Communists arrested by the government. Up to no good, said the government; dangerous people, violent overthrow, etc., First Amendment, said the defense, freedom of speech, etc." Douglas stopped walking. "Clear and present danger."

"What?" I asked. He often talked in a telegraphic manner, and one was expected to keep up with him. It was sometimes like listening to a man thinking out loud.

"Clear and present danger," he said. "That was the issue. Did they constitute a clear and present danger? I don't think so. I think everybody took the language pretty far in Dennis." He began walking, striding along quickly. Again, one was expected to keep up with him. "The F.B.I. was all over them. Phones tapped, constant surveillance. How could it be clear and present danger with the F.B.I. watching every move they made? That's a ginkgo," he said suddenly, pointing at a tree. "A beauty. You don't see those every day. Ask Hand about clear and present danger."

I was in fact reluctant to do so. Douglas's argument seemed to me to be crushing—the last word, really—and I didn't want to embarrass Judge Hand. But back in the living room, on the second martini, the old man asked about Douglas. I sort of scratched my nose and recapitulated the conversation by the ginkgo tree.

"What?" Hand shouted. "Speak up, sir, for heaven's sake."

"He said the F.B.I. was watching them all the time so there couldn't be a clear and present danger," I blurted out, blushing as I said it.

A terrible silence filled the room. Hand's eyebrows writhed on his face like two huge caterpillars. He leaned forward in the wing chair, his face settling, finally, into a grim expression. "I am astonished," he said softly, his eyes holding mine, "at Justice Douglas's newfound faith in the Federal Bureau of Investigation." His big, granite head moved even closer to mine, until I could smell the martini. "I had understood him to consider it a politically corrupt, incompetent organization, directed by a power-crazed lunatic." I realized I had been holding my breath throughout all of this, and as I relaxed, I saw the faintest trace of a smile cross Hand's face. Things are sometimes more complicated than they first appear, his smile seemed to say. The old man leaned back. "The proximity of the danger is something to think about. Ask him about that. See what he says."

I chewed the matter over as I returned to campus. Hand had pointed out some of Douglas's language about the F.B.I. from other sources that seemed to bear out his point. I thought about the words "clear and present danger," and the fact that if you looked at them closely they might not be as simple as they had first appeared. What degree of danger? Did the word "present" allude to the proximity of the danger, or just the fact that the danger was there at all—that it wasn't an anticipated danger? Were there other hidden factors these great men were weighing of which I was unaware?

But Douglas was gone, back to Washington. (The writer in me is tempted to create a scene here—to invent one for dramatic purposes—but of course I can't do that.) My brief time as a messenger boy was over, and I felt a certain frustration, as if, with a few more exchanges, the matter of Dennis v. United

States might have been resolved to my satisfaction. They'd left me high and dry. But, of course, it is precisely because the matter did not resolve that has caused me to think about it, off and on, all these years. "The Constitution," Hand used to say to me flatly, "is a piece of paper. The Bill of Rights is a piece of paper." It was many years before I understood what he meant. Documents alone do not keep democracy alive, nor maintain the state of law. There is no particular safety in them. Living men and women, generation after generation, must continually remake democracy and the law, and that involves an ongoing state of tension between the past and the present which will never completely resolve.

Education doesn't end until life ends, because you never know when you're going to understand something you hadn't understood before. For me, the magic dance of the shoeshine men was the kind of experience in which understanding came with a kind of click, a resolving kind of click. The same with the experience at the piano. What happened with Justice Douglas and Judge Hand was different, and makes the point that understanding does not always mean resolution. Indeed, in our intellectual lives, our creative lives, it is perhaps those problems that will never resolve that rightly claim the lion's share of our energies. The physical body exists in a constant state of tension as it maintains homeostasis, and so too does the active mind embrace the tension of never being certain, never being absolutely sure, never being done, as it engages the world. That is our special fate, our inexpressibly valuable condition.

● PERSONAL RESPONSE ●

When in your own education have you had the "resolving kind of click" (paragraph 22) Conroy describes?

● QUESTIONS FOR DISCUSSION ●

1. What does Conroy mean by the "magic dance" of the shoeshine men?
2. How did Red Garland's saying the word "sixths" to Conroy later strengthen Conroy's foundation on the piano?
3. How do Conroy's experiences with the shoeshine men and with what happened to him at the piano illustrate one "way of knowing"?
4. Comment on Conroy's effectiveness in describing Justice Douglas and Judge Hand. Do you have a clear image of both of them? Do you think he portrays one of them more vividly than the other? If so, which one?
5. How do the viewpoints of Judge Hand and Justice Douglas differ on the Dennis case?
6. What does Judge Hand mean when he says that the Constitution and the Bill of Rights are pieces of paper (paragraph 21)?
7. What lesson about education — about the "ways of knowing — does Conroy learn from his experience with Justice Douglas and Judge Hand?

● WRITING TOPICS ●

1. Tell about an occasion on which you experienced "the resolving kind of click" Conroy writes of.

2. If you have ever met someone famous, write an essay about the experience. Describe the person and, if possible, use dialogue to convey a sense of the person's personality.

3. Define "education" by using specific examples of your own intellectual growth.

SHOOTING AN ELEPHANT

●

GEORGE ORWELL

George Orwell is the pseudonym of Eric Blair (1903–1950). Born in Bengal, India, he was brought up in England and educated at Eton. He served five years as a British policeman in Burma, with a growing disgust for the goals and values of British imperialism, before returning to England to become a writer. In 1936, he fought with the Loyalists in the Spanish Civil War. Orwell is best known for Animal Farm *(1945) and* 1984 *(1949), novels that reflect his hatred of totalitarianism and his sympathy for the oppressed. In "Shooting an Elephant," Orwell recounts an incident in Burma when he committed an act of unnecessary violence "solely to avoid looking a fool."*

In Moulmein, in lower Burma, I was hated by large numbers of people—the only time in my life that I have been important enough for this to happen to me. I was subdivisional police officer of the town, and in an aimless, petty kind of way anti-European feeling was very bitter. No one had the guts to raise a riot, but if a European woman went through the bazaars alone somebody would probably spit betel juice over her dress. As a police officer I was an obvious target and was baited whenever it seemed safe to do so. When a nimble Burman tripped me up on the football field and the referee (another Burman) looked the other way, the crowd yelled with hideous laughter. This happened more than once. In the end the sneering yellow faces of young men that met me everywhere, the insults hooted after me when I was at a safe distance, got badly on my nerves. The young Buddhist priests were the worst of all. There were several thousands of them in the town and none of them seemed to have anything to do except stand on street corners and jeer at Europeans.

All this was perplexing and upsetting. For at that time I had already made up my mind that imperialism was an evil thing and the sooner I chucked up my job and got out of there the better. Theoretically—and secretly, of course—I was all for the Burmese and all against their oppressors, the British. As for the job I was doing, I hated it more bitterly than I can perhaps make clear. In a job like that you see the dirty work of Empire at close quarters. The wretched prisoners huddling in the stinking cages of the lock-ups, the gray, cowed faces of the long-term convicts, the scarred buttocks of the men who had been flogged with bamboos—all these oppressed me with an intolerable sense of guilt. But I could get nothing into perspective. I was young and ill educated and I had had to think out my problems in the utter silence that is imposed on every Englishman in the east. I did not even know that the British Empire is dying, still less did I know that it is a great deal better than the younger empires that are going to supplant it. All I knew was that I was stuck between my hatred of the empire I served and my rage against the evil-spirited little beasts who tried to make my job impossible. With one part of my mind I thought of the British Raj as an unbreakable tyranny, as something clamped down, in *saecula saeculorum*, upon the will of prostrate peoples; with another part I thought that the greatest joy in the world would be to drive a bayonet into a Buddhist priest's guts. Feelings like these are the normal by-products of imperialism; ask any Anglo-Indian official, if you can catch him off duty.

One day something happened which in a roundabout way was enlightening. It was a tiny incident in itself; but it gave me a better glimpse than I had had before of the real nature of imperialism — the real motives for which despotic governments act. Early one morning the sub-inspector at a police station the other end of the town rang me up on the 'phone and said that an elephant was ravaging the bazaar. Would I please come and do something about it? I did not know what I could do, but I wanted to see what was happening and I got on to a pony and started out. I took my rifle, an old .44 Winchester and much too small to kill an elephant, but I thought the noise might be useful *in terrorem*. Various Burmans stopped me on the way and told me about the elephant's doings. It was not, of course, a wild elephant, but a tame one which had gone "must." It had been chained up, as tame elephants always are when their attack of "must" is due, but on the previous night it had broken its chain and escaped. Its mahout, the only person who could manage it when it was in that state, had set out in pursuit, but had taken the wrong direction and was now twelve hours' journey away, and in the morning the elephant had suddenly reappeared in town. The Burmese population had no weapons and were quite helpless against it. It had already destroyed somebody's bamboo hut, killed a cow and raided some fruit-stalls and devoured the stock; also it had met the municipal rubbish van and, when the driver jumped out and took to his heels, had turned the van over and inflicted violences upon it.

The Burmese sub-inspector and some Indian constables were waiting for me in the quarter where the elephant had been seen. It was a very poor quarter, a labyrinth of squalid bamboo huts, thatched with palm-leaf, winding all over a steep hillside. I remember that it was a cloudy, stuffy morning at the beginning of the rains. We began questioning the people as to where the elephant had gone and, as usual, failed to get any definite information. That is invariably the case in the East; a story always sounds clear enough at a distance, but the nearer you get to the scene of events the vaguer it becomes. Some of the people said that the elephant had gone in one direction, some said that he had gone in another, some professed not even to have heard of any elephant. I had almost made up my mind that the whole story was a pack of lies, when we heard yells a little distance away. There was a loud, scandalized cry of "Go away, child! Go away this instant!" and an old woman with a switch in her hand came round the corner of a hut, violently shooing away a crowd of naked children. Some more women followed, clicking their tongues and exclaiming; evidently there was something that the children ought not to have seen. I rounded the hut and saw a man's dead body sprawling in the mud. He was an Indian, a black Dravidian coolie, almost naked, and he could not have been dead many minutes. The people said that the elephant had come suddenly upon him round the corner of the hut, caught him with its trunk, put its foot on his back and ground him into the earth. This was the rainy season and the ground was soft, and his face had scored a trench a foot deep and a couple of yards long. He was lying on his belly with arms crucified and head sharply twisted to one side. His face was coated with mud, the eyes wide open, the teeth bared and grinning with an expression of unendurable agony. (Never tell me, by the way, that the dead look peaceful. Most of the corpses I have seen looked devilish.) The friction of the great beast's foot had stripped the skin from his back as neatly as one skins a rabbit. As soon as I saw the dead man I sent an orderly to a friend's house nearby to borrow an elephant rifle. I had already sent back the pony, not wanting it to go mad with fright and throw me if it smelt the elephant.

The orderly came back in a few minutes with a rifle and five cartridges, and meanwhile some Burmans had arrived and told us that the elephant was in the paddy fields below, only a few hundred yards away. As I started forward practically the whole population of the quarter flocked out of the houses and followed me. They had seen the rifle and were all shouting excitedly that I was going to shoot the elephant. They had not shown much interest in the elephant when he was merely ravaging their homes, but it was different now that he was going to be shot. It was a bit of fun to them, as it would be to an English crowd; besides they wanted the meat. It made me vaguely uneasy. I had no intention of shooting the elephant — I had merely sent for the rifle to defend myself if necessary — and it is always unnerving to have a crowd following you. I marched down the hill, looking and feeling a fool, with the rifle over my shoulder and an ever-growing army of people jostling at my heels. At the bottom, when you got away from the huts, there was a metalled road and beyond that a miry waste of paddy fields a thousand yards across, not yet ploughed but soggy from the first rains and dotted with coarse grass. The elephant was standing eight yards from the road, his left side toward us. He took not the slightest notice of the crowd's approach. He was tearing up bunches of grass, beating them against his knees to clean them, and stuffing them into his mouth.

I had halted on the road. As soon as I saw the elephant I knew with perfect certainty that I ought not to shoot him. It is a serious matter to shoot a working elephant — it is comparable to destroying a huge and costly piece of machin-ery — and obviously one ought not to do it if it can possibly be avoided. And at that distance, peacefully eating, the elephant looked no more dangerous than a cow. I thought then and I think now that his attack of "must" was already passing off; in which case he would merely wander harmlessly about until the mahout came back and caught him. Moreover, I did not in the least want to shoot him. I decided that I would watch him for a little while to make sure that he did not turn savage again, and then go home.

But at that moment I glanced round at the crowd that had followed me. It was an immense crowd, two thousand at the least and growing every minute. It blocked the road for a long distance on either side. I looked at the sea of yellow faces above the garish clothes — faces all happy and excited over this bit of fun, all certain that the elephant was going to be shot. They were watching me as they would watch a conjurer about to perform a trick. They did not like me, but with the magical rifle in my hands I was momentarily worth watching. And suddenly I realized that I should have to shoot the elephant after all. The people expected it of me and I had got to do it; I could feel their two thousand wills pressing me forward, irresistibly. And it was at this moment, as I stood there with the rifle in my hands, that I first grasped the hollowness, the futility of the white man's dominion in the East. Here was I, the white man with his gun, standing in front of the unarmed native crowd — seemingly the leading actor of the piece; but in reality I was only an absurd puppet pushed to and fro by the will of those yellow faces behind. I perceived in this moment that when the white man turns tyrant it is his own freedom that he destroys. He becomes a sort of hollow, posing dummy, the conventionalized figure of a sahib. For it is the condition of his rule that he shall spend his life in trying to impress the "natives," and so in every crisis he has got to do what the "natives" expect of him. He wears a mask, and his face grows to fit it. I had got to shoot the elephant. I had committed myself to doing it when I sent for the rifle. A sahib has got to act like a sahib; he has got to appear resolute, to know his own mind and do definite things. To come all that way, rifle in hand, with two thousand people marching at my heels, and then to trail feebly away, having done nothing — no, that was impossible. The crowd would laugh at me. And my whole life, every white man's life in the East, was one long struggle not to be laughed at.

But I did not want to shoot the elephant. I watched him beating his bunch of grass against his knees with that preoccupied grandmotherly air that elephants have. It seemed to me that it would be murder to shoot him. At that age I was not squeamish about killing animals, but I had never shot an elephant and never wanted to. (Somehow it always seems worse to kill a *large* animal.) Besides, there was the beast's owner to be considered. Alive, the elephant was worth at least a hundred pounds; dead, he would only be worth the value of his tusks, five pounds, possibly. But I had got to act quickly. I turned to some experienced-looking Burmans who had been there when we arrived, and asked them how the elephant had been behaving. They all said the same thing: he took no notice of you if you left him alone, but he might charge if you went too close to him. 8

It was perfectly clear to me what I ought to do. I ought to walk up to within, say, twenty-five yards of the elephant and test his behavior. If he charged, I could shoot; if he took no notice of me, it would be safe to leave him until the mahout came back. But also I knew that I was going to do no such thing. I was a poor shot with a rifle and the ground was soft mud into which one would sink at every step. If the elephant charged and I missed him, I should have about as much chance as a toad under a steamroller. But even then I was not thinking particularly of my own skin, only of the watchful yellow faces behind. For at that moment, with the crowd watching me, I was not afraid in the ordinary sense, as I would have been if I had been alone. A white man mustn't be frightened in front of "natives"; and so, in general, he isn't frightened. The sole thought in my mind was that if anything went wrong those two thousand Burmans would see me pursued, caught, trampled on, and reduced to a grinning corpse like that Indian up the hill. And if that happened it was quite probable that some of them would laugh. That would never do. There was only one alternative. I shoved the cartridges into the magazine and lay down on the road to get a better aim.

The crowd grew very still, and a deep, low, happy sigh, as of people who see the theater curtain go up at last, breathed from innumerable throats. They were going to have their bit of fun after all. The rifle was a beautiful German thing with cross-hair sights. I did not then know that in shooting an elephant one would shoot to cut an imaginary bar running from ear-hole to ear-hole. I ought, therefore, as the elephant was sideways on, to have aimed straight at his ear-hole; actually I aimed several inches in front of this, thinking the brain would be further forward.

When I pulled the trigger I did not hear the bang or feel the kick — one never does when a shot goes home — but I heard the devilish roar of glee that went up from the crowd. In that instant, in too short a time, one would have thought, even for the bullet to get there, a mysterious, terrible change had come over the elephant. He neither stirred, nor fell, but every line of his body had altered. He looked suddenly stricken, shrunken, immensely old, as though the frightful impact of the bullet had paralyzed him without knocking him down. At last, after what seemed a long time — it might have been five seconds, I dare say — he sagged flabbily to his knees. His mouth slobbered. An enormous senility seemed to have settled upon him. One could have imagined him thousands of years old. I fired again into the same spot. At the second shot he did not collapse but climbed with desperate slowness to his feet and stood weakly upright, with legs sagging and head drooping. I fired a third time. That was the shot that did for him. You could see the agony of it jolt his whole body and knock the last remnant of strength from his legs. But in falling he seemed for a moment to rise, for as his hind legs collapsed beneath him he seemed to tower upward like a huge rock toppling, his trunk reaching skyward like a tree. He trumpeted, for the first and only time. And then down he came, his belly toward me, with a crash that seemed to shake the ground even where I lay.

I got up. The Burmans were already racing past me across the mud. It was 12 obvious that the elephant would never rise again, but he was not dead. He was breathing very rhythmically with long rattling gasps, his great mound of a side painfully rising and falling. His mouth was wide open — I could see far down into caverns of pale pink throat. I waited a long time for him to die, but his breathing did not weaken. Finally I fired my two remaining shots into the spot where I thought his heart must be. The thick blood welled out of him like red velvet, but still he did not die. His body did not even jerk when the shots hit him, the tortured breathing continued without a pause. He was dying, very slowly and in great agony, but in some world remote from me where not even a bullet could damage him further. I felt that I had got to put an end to that dreadful noise. It seemed dreadful to see the great beast lying there, powerless to move and yet powerless to die, and not even to be able to finish him. I sent back for my small rifle and poured shot after shot into his heart and down his throat. They seemed to make no impression. The tortured gasps continued as steadily as the ticking of a clock.

In the end I could not stand it any longer and went away. I heard later that it took him half an hour to die. Burmans were bringing dahs and baskets even before I left, and I was told they had stripped his body almost to the bones by the afternoon.

Afterward, of course, there were endless discussions about the shooting of the elephant. The owner was furious, but he was only an Indian and could do nothing. Besides, legally I had done the right thing, for a mad elephant has to be killed, like a mad dog, if its owner fails to control it. Among the Europeans opinion was divided. The older men said I was right, the younger men said it was a damn shame to shoot an elephant for killing a coolie, because an elephant was worth more than any damn Coringhee coolie. And afterward I was very glad that the coolie had been killed; it put me legally in the right and it gave me a sufficient pretext for shooting the elephant. I often wondered whether any of the others grasped that I had done it solely to avoid looking a fool.

● PERSONAL RESPONSE ●

What do you think of Orwell's shooting the elephant simply to save face? Do you think you would have done the same, under the circumstances?

● QUESTIONS FOR DISCUSSION ●

1. In what way is the shooting of the elephant "enlightening" (paragraph 3) for Orwell?

2. What audience do you think Orwell is writing for, one that understands and sympathizes with his feelings about imperialism, or one that would be surprised at his views? Explain your answer.

3. This essay is written from the perspective of a mature writer looking back on something that happened to him many years before. What is Orwell's attitude toward what he did at age 19? Does he attempt to excuse his behavior? Is he sympathetic toward or critical of his "young and ill educated" self (paragraph 2)?

4. What is the British Raj (paragraph 2)? What does Orwell learn about "the nature of imperialism" (paragraph 3)? What evidence of its evils does Orwell give?

5. In paragraph 2, Orwell says he has mixed feelings toward the Burmese. On the one hand, he "was all for the Burmese and all against their oppressors, the British." On the other hand, he "thought that the greatest joy in the world would be to drive a bayonet into a Buddhist priest's guts." Explain why he has these ambivalent feelings.

6. Orwell's essay contains some graphic descriptions of two deaths, the coolie's and the elephant's. Which death does Orwell devote more attention to? Why?

7. What does Orwell mean in his concluding paragraph when he writes, "And afterward I was very glad that the coolie had been killed"?

8. Orwell says in paragraph 8 that he did not want to shoot the elephant. It seemed to him "that it would be murder to shoot him." Why, then, does Orwell shoot the elephant? Explain as fully as possible the dilemma of the situation Orwell finds himself in.

● WRITING TOPICS ●

1. Describe an event or incident that happened many years ago and about which you have different feelings now. Tell what you did then and explain your view of it now.

2. Write an essay narrating an incident or event that taught you something about yourself, about another person (such as an authority figure, a parent, a relative, or a friend), or about an institution or organization (such as the police, a school, a church, or a club).

3. Narrate an incident in which you did something you thought was wrong because you did not want to look foolish or lose face in front of others. Describe not only what you did but also your feelings after the incident.

ACQUIRING VALUES

●

ADDITIONAL WRITING SUGGESTIONS

1. Explore the moral aspects of success: to what degree might morality be an issue in certain careers or professions? Which businesses or professions are associated with either morality or immorality? Why?

2. Read recent studies about the inability of high-school graduates to think and then write an essay reporting your results.

3. Using specific examples from the media, describe the effects you think the widespread depictions of graphic violence and brutality have on American culture.

4. Explain how a specific book or course in school has had a strong effect on the formation of your own values.

5. Define what success in life means to you personally and what would constitute a failure for you. Against what goals would you measure your own success or failure, and how far would you be willing to go to achieve those goals?

6. Define "excellence" in terms of an activity you know very well, such as a sport, a hobby, a career, or some other pursuit. Using yourself or someone you know very well, explain the details of the activity that qualify it as excellent.

3

INTERPERSONAL
RELATIONSHIPS

DESIGNER GENES
An Immodest Proposal for Sexual Realignment

—————————— ● ——————————

Dave Barry

Dave Barry is a Pulitzer Prize–winning newspaper columnist for the
Miami Herald *and the author of a number of humorous books. His
column, "America's Barryland," is syndicated in over 200 newspapers
nationwide. His books include* Babies and Other Hazards of Sex
(1984), Stay Fit and Healthy Until You're Dead *(1985),* Bad Habits
(1987), and Dave Barry's Greatest Hits *(1989), among others. In the
following essay, written for a special September 1985* Ms. *magazine
issue focusing on men, Barry brings his usual wit and irreverent humor
to the subject of sex, offering "an immodest proposal" for correcting the
"terrible error" Mother Nature made in creating human sexuality.*

What I think happened is, Mother Nature made some kind of terrible error. I am talking about human sexuality.

When you look at other species, you notice they have everything worked out. Take squid. I haven't bothered to research this, but I'm willing to bet you that when two squids want to have sex, they know *exactly* how to go about it. Probably the male waves his tentacles in a certain way, and the female emits some kind of noxious chemical compound, and the next thing you know they have their suckers all over each other.

Now contrast the effortless suavity of the squid with the sexual behavior of human beings, such as the former hairdresser of my friend Mary Anne. Mary Anne is a television producer who swears that this is an absolutely true anecdote:

This hairdresser, whom I will call Jacques, was leaving the area after having done Mary Anne's hair successfully for several years, and he invited her to his house for one last permanent. It was the old "one last permanent" line, and Mary Anne fell for it. 4

Things were fine until Jacques put the traditional foul-smelling permanent chemical on her hair. As you probably know, the next step is to wait for about 20 minutes, during which you're supposed to pick up *Glamour* Magazine and read an article entitled "12 Common Mistakes Involving Eyeliner." But instead, without warning, Jacques hurled himself into Mary Anne's lap. She perceived this almost immediately as his concept of a sexual advance.

"Jacques," she said. "This is a bad idea."

"Submit to me," Jacques replied, "or there will be *no neutralizer.*"

Really, he said that. And it was no idle threat. Jacques claimed that unless he neutralized the permanent chemical, Mary Anne would go bald, which could of course be a real disadvantage to a person working in television, a visual medium. Nevertheless, Mary Anne shoved him off her lap and made it clear by word and 8 gesture that he was being a jerk. Eventually, he apologized and went on with the permanent, and according to Mary Anne it came out very nice.

The point, obviously, is that this would never, ever, have happened elsewhere in the animal kingdom. But this is only one among billions of bizarre activities we human beings engage in because Mother Nature failed to give us a simple, universal, squidlike ritual to perform when we wish to have sex.

What is worse, she made men and women so profoundly different that even if two people do manage somehow to agree that they wish to have sex, they will quickly discover that their purely physical needs differ greatly, in the sense that the amount of time the woman would like to spend in foreplay and lovemaking is roughly equivalent to the amount of time a man would allocate to foreplay, lovemaking, and building a garage. And what is worst of all, even if a man and a woman agree that they want to have sex *and* manage to become comfortable physically, the odds are they will have totally different psychological motivations. Those of you who hate generalizations should leave the room at this time, because I am going to explain briefly how, as I see it, men and women differ in their attitudes toward sex:

- *Women* want sex to be part of a deeper relationship involving commitment, sensitivity to the other's needs, understanding, tenderness, compassion, concern, sharing, and — above all — love.
- *Men* want sex.

"Wait a minute," I hear you women saying. "Not *all* men are like that. What about Paul Newman? What about the Pope? What about *Phil Donahue*?"

Okay. I will give you those three, and a few others, including of course your Significant Other. But this leaves an awful lot of men who basically attach as much emotional significance to the actual sex act as they do to flossing their teeth. Less, in fact, as we are learning more and more every day about the dangers of gum disease. 12

The vast psychological difference between men and women is the most troublesome of all, because it unfortunately tends to make women think that men have the moral standards of restroom bacteria. Talk to a single woman, and she will tell you about how usually when she dates a male for the first time, he makes a little speech wherein he says that at this point in his life he really does not wish to get involved in a relationship in which he is expected to live with the other person or date the other person exclusively or even necessarily remember the other person's name, but he is nevertheless willing to have sex. Single women call this The Speech, and often when they describe it they stick their fingers partway down their throats to indicate how it makes them feel.

And of course they are right. This truly is repulsive behavior. From their perspective. But that is exactly the problem: their perspective is that of what might as well be a different species altogether. It is as if the blue whale, which mates for life, were criticizing the sexual habits of the dragonfly, which goes through the whole sexual process — meeting, courting, Doing It, and breaking up — without even bothering to land.

Clearly something must be done. The human race has stumbled along for too many thousands of years under the present system, and it has resulted in too many misunderstandings, heartbreaks, divorces, homicides, and totally unnecessary hairdresser attacks.

What can be done, you ask? No doubt you have read articles about how 16 biologists are manipulating genes. The problem is, they're always doing this to life forms that already work just fine, such as cows. As far as I know, there are no major sexual problems with cows. It is *people* who need a major redesign.

So I am proposing that we create a committee of reputable biologists, from both sexes, and ask them to see if they can't whip up a sexually compatible version of the human race. We could have a panel of prominent citizens advising the biologists on moral issues, taking care to avoid citizens who had a particular sexual ax to grind, such as Hugh Hefner or Phyllis Schlafly, because you could end up with a very kinky version of the human race that, for example, wanted to have sex all the time, but only with Republicans.

Assuming we take reasonable precautions, I think genetic manipulation is the way to go. I can think of no greater gift to give to future generations than to put both sexes on exactly the same sexual wavelength, so that everybody could tell instantly who wanted to have sex with whom, and it would always last the perfect length of time and be absolutely terrific for both of them. Or all six of them, depending on what the biologists work out. I think we should keep an open mind about this.

The important thing is that we get rid of the sexual hassles that have obsessed the human race since the dawn of civilization, that have totally dominated our music, our art, our literature, our conversations, our thoughts, our dreams, and our very souls, so we can get on with what we were really put on earth to do. Whatever the hell THAT is.

● PERSONAL RESPONSE ●

Aside from "Mother Nature," is there any other way of accounting for the different expectations men and women have about relationships? How accurate do you think Barry's generalizations about the differing attitudes toward sex are?

● QUESTIONS FOR DISCUSSION ●

1. What purpose is served by Barry's examples of the mating practice of squids and his friend Mary Anne's encounter with the hairdresser?

2. What does Barry accomplish by waiting until the closing paragraphs to introduce the idea of designer genes?

3. What is the effect of Barry's use of the first-person pronoun?

4. At what point did you realize that Barry is not writing a serious proposal? What more famous "immodest proposal" does Barry's subtitle allude to?

5. Why do you think Barry occasionally stresses certain words by italicizing them, such as *no neutralizer* (paragraph 7) and *Phil Donahue* (paragraph 11)?

6. Find passages you think are humorous and identify the particular strategies Barry uses to achieve his comic effect, such as exaggeration, surprise, outright absurdity, or comic juxtapositions.

7. What generalizations about relationships between the sexes does Barry use as the basis of his humor?

8. What else besides human sexuality does Barry poke fun at?

● WRITING TOPICS ●

1. Use humor or satire to comment on some aspect of relationships between the sexes, such as meeting someone new, dating, or maintaining a relationship.

2. Based on what you have experienced or observed, contrast the attitudes of men and women on dating, sex, commitment, and marriage.

3. Using the same tone as Barry's, argue for or against his proposal of genetic manipulation to achieve sexual compatibility, supporting your opinion with concrete examples.

HOW WE NAMED OUR BABY

●

Sarah Pattee

*Sarah Pattee was a newspaper reporter for nearly ten years, writing
feature stories for the* Dallas Times Herald, San Antonio Light, *and*
San Diego Tribune. *She is currently a full-time mother and a part-time
freelance writer for the* Los Angeles Times *and several magazines. In
the following essay, excerpted from the spring 1989 issue of* M.O.M., *a
magazine published by Mothers & Others for Midwives in Huntington
Beach, California, Pattee describes the process she and her husband
went through in what turned out to be the highly emotional issue of
naming their first child. Since this essay was written, Pattee has given
birth to a second child, a girl, whom she and her husband have named
Emma Lincoln Pattee.*

It wasn't easy naming Harley Mack Pattee Henigson. Our son isn't even
four months old and there's been enough debate and emotional upheaval about his name to last a lifetime.

When my husband and I married five years ago we hardly talked about
names. We both assumed I'd keep mine and he'd keep his.

Then we had a child. That's when I realized how deeply emotional the issue
of naming can be, when I began asking myself how deep my convictions run,
when I began questioning just how equal my "equal marriage" was.

Naming Harley has involved not only my husband and me, but both our   4
families and, in a sense, society at large. I found out you can't question society's
way of naming without bumping up against deeply embedded sexism under the
guise of "It's always been done this way."

I quickly learned not to ask anyone emotionally attached to us for advice,
especially relatives. This is truly an issue where parents have to look inside
themselves and choose what feels best for them, no matter what child psychologists and mothers-in-law say.

We thought carefully about each of these choices:

- Giving the father's name to the children seems to be the most common
  choice among two-name couples. One friend told me she took this route
  because "The fight with relatives over keeping my own name was bad
  enough; I didn't have enough energy to fight about the children."

    A lot of people told me that giving children different surnames
  would undermine the strength of the family. I always respond by saying
  love, attention, and acceptance make a family, not sharing the same last
  name, especially in this age of blended families.

    I sympathized with my friends who were tired of the struggle and the   8
  criticism from family members. But I asked myself, What was the use of

keeping my own name only to lose it through our children? And because I really believe children learn from what we do, not from what we say, I was afraid he would think his parents were hypocrites. If we say, "Your mom and dad are equal partners" but push aside Mom's name for Dad's, what does that say about our brand of equality?

- We thought about giving our son my last name. At first I liked this idea, but after thinking about it, I wondered if it was fair to favor my name over my husband's. I didn't want to name our son just to make a statement, either.

- We thought about hyphenating the name, but we never felt comfortable with that option. It seemed unfair to give a child something as bulky as Pattee-Henigson. Whose name would come first? That's a serious issue; in 1982 the Nebraska Supreme Court ruled the father's surname has to precede the mother's surname in the case of hyphenating children's names. Putting aside the scary implications of the state telling parents how to name their children, I also wonder what happens when the last name gets dropped in school or off legal documents that only have so much space for names? And can hyphenated names be sustained across generations? It seems, once again, women's names would get lost.

- We thought—very briefly—about making up a new surname or combining our names into "Henigtee" or "Patson." We didn't like the idea at all. I really like my name—first, middle, and last. My husband really likes his name—first, middle, and last. Even as a child, I liked having an unusual surname.

- The last option we considered was giving our children alternate sur-   12 names. Our boys would be named after my husband; girls would be named after me. And boys would get my surname as a middle name; girls would get my husband's surname as their middle name.

I found out there's even a name for this method of naming children. It's called the "bilineal solution," a new way of naming created by Sharon Lebell, author of a newly published book, *Naming Ourselves, Naming Our Children* (The Crossing Press, $6.95). I called Lebell in San Francisco, where she lives with her husband, John Loudon, and two daughters, who both bear her surname. She believes society's way of naming children after their fathers—she calls it "patronomy"—is so entrenched that a simple and solid alternative is needed. Naming boys for their fathers and girls for their mothers is one way of ensuring both parents' names get passed through the generations, she said. And it will change society slowly but surely.

"So much will change when women stop naming themselves in reference to men," she said.

We chose Lebell's solution. So, three months after his birth, Harley Mack Pattee Henigson had his name. I plan to use those four names all the time and to write all four whenever I have to fill out a form; it's already on his passport. And I plan to tell my son why naming him meant so much to us.

We adapted Lebell's idea a little by adding on an extra middle name, Mack, 16
in honor of an uncle who died suddenly two years ago. Some friends added their
own twist: They named their daughters after the father and sons after the
mother. They told me they did it as protection against a "worst-case scenario,"
meaning in case their daughter gives up her name upon marrying.

Through this struggle to name Harley, I've realized how important names
are. Names hold power. Names are your history. Names have spiritual meaning.

And I think I see why this issue makes a lot of people uncomfortable,
because it forces them to confront their own decisions in life. I've tried to
remember that and balance my philosophy with a good dose of humor and
compassion. Of course, some people will never understand our reasons, and I
have to accept that, too.

Of course, we had a boy this first time so what we've decided so far doesn't
seem so radical. When we have a girl, that will be the true test of our commitment to change.

And if we don't have girls? Already, we're considering naming at least one 20
boy after me, although Lebell told me it's best not to do this as it dilutes the
strength of her "bilineal solution." Part of the charm of her solution, she
believes, is the "roll of the dice" aspect. We may still decide to alternate names if
we have boys, though.

Whatever we decide the next time around, this self-searching has been a gift
for my husband and me. Naming Harley encouraged us to re-examine our
marriage partnership (how equal are we?), our reasons for wanting children (to
make a statement to society?), and our ideas about what it means to be a family.
(In the end, love and acceptance of your children count the most.)

We have grown and changed through naming Harley Mack Pattee Henigson. I hope the same happens to him when it's his turn to name his own children.

● PERSONAL RESPONSE ●

What do you think of the solution Pattee and her husband arrived at for naming their
child? How do you think you would feel if your own parents had made the same decision
about naming you?

● QUESTIONS FOR DISCUSSION ●

1. In what way did Pattee and her husband's naming their baby involve society at large?

2. Why did the issue of naming their child create such a controversy?

3. Review the list of choices Pattee and her husband considered before naming their
   child. Which choices seem to you the most practical? Which seem impractical? Why?

4. Why did Pattee and her husband settle on the "'bilineal solution'" (paragraph 13)?

5. Why do you think Pattee included the information about Sharon Lebell and her
   telephone conversation with her?

6. What do you think Lebell means by her remark that "so much will change when women stop naming themselves in reference to men" (paragraph 14)? What will change?

7. What benefits did Pattee and her husband gain from the experience of deciding their son's name?

● WRITING TOPICS ●

1. Explain your position on the subject of what surname to give children, including a discussion of whether or not you would follow (or have followed) the traditional approach of giving children the father's last name.

2. Using your own name as an example, explore the importance of names: in what ways do names hold power, reveal history, and/or have spiritual meaning (paragraph 17 of Pattee's essay)?

3. Explain why surnames are an issue in male–female relationships. You might want to approach this topic by considering Sharon Lebell's remark that "much will change when women stop naming themselves in reference to men."

THE MIRACLE CHICKEN
(GLIMPSES INTO MY FATHER'S SCRAPBOOK)

●

BERNARD COOPER

Bernard Cooper teaches literature at Otis/Parsons School of Art and Design and at the Southern California Institute of Architecture. He has published frequently in Grand Street *and has had essays in* The Georgia Review, Shenandoah, *and* The Western Humanities Review, *among others.* On The Air *(1989) is a collection of some of his prose. The following piece is excerpted from a longer essay, "Beacons Burning Down," which first appeared in 1987 in* The Georgia Review. *In it, Cooper reveals aspects of his father's personality and of the variety of human relationships as he looks at the newspaper clippings in his father's scrapbook.*

O n 30 March 1940, the day he was notified that he had passed the California State Bar examination, my father began a scrapbook with two items: a letter requesting a seven-dollar fee that entitled him to become a legitimate attorney, and a solicitation from a wholesaler of leather-bound law books. After that come a hundred buckled newspaper clippings that betray his taste for handling unorthodox cases.

One article is emblazoned with the headline "CASE OF THE BAKING NEW-LYWED," about Mrs. Beverly Cleveland, a woman who claimed her husband, Jake, kept her cooking from dawn to dusk during the first ten days of marriage — waffles, casseroles, pies from scratch — so that no time was left for affection. But my father subpoenaed witnesses who testified under oath that Jake Cleveland's appetite was notoriously meager. "Never ate what *I* slaved to make," whispered his first wife under her breath. "Just look at the guy — he's built like a broom," said Mr. Luft of the Chow Now lunch truck. In his final argument, my father spoke of his "kissless client" whose "connubial crisis" was exacerbated during a ten-day "hellmoon." Not only was there an annulment, but my father convinced the court to fine the former Mrs. Cleveland fifty dollars in punitive damages for wasting groceries in a ploy to avoid her wifely obligation.

Profiting from the frequency of tumultuous marriages, my father moved his office into wood-paneled quarters on the fifth floor of the elegant Biscott Building. On his door was stenciled "Edward S. Cooper" in large gold letters. "Attorney at Law" was relegated to a smaller, less illustrious print. On the sill behind his desk, he placed a brass statuette of justice: her toga cleaved her figure as though she were walking against the wind; her scales, loaded with candy, bobbed in the slightest breeze.

The office windows overlooked a small park frequented at noon by secre- 4 taries — Caucasian, Asian, Hispanic, Black — wearing cat-eye glasses held in place by chains. Some of them met my father for assignations over the years in a dark downtown hotel. His lust for the opposite sex (in all their ethnic variety), his clandestine romances, his cultivation of a subterfuge my mother didn't suspect until she was in her sixties — these made him all the more adept at drumming up the deceits that made his divorce trials so bathetic they became genuinely sad, reminding everyone who followed them in the papers that, when love sought justice, both were blind.

And yet my father's most publicized trial had nothing to do with the vicissitudes of human love, though the case of The Miracle Chicken would outstrip his previous arbitrations with its sheer theatricality, media appeal, and metaphysical intimations. Filed in Superior Court on 20 April 1950, Mrs. Martha Green's suit against the Society for the Prevention of Cruelty to Animals describes how she purchased a three-and-one-half-pound rooster, with its head cut off, at a San Bernardino market. She placed it in the bottom of her grocery bag and covered it with at least ten pounds of "victuals." Six hours later she lifted oranges, potatoes, and eggs from the bag, and up fluttered the headless rooster. For four days Mrs. Green reverently nurtured her miracle, naming him Lazarus and feeding him a solution of raw egg and warm milk through an eyedropper. Hundreds of people ventured to her home to glimpse the creature. It was even rumored that a famous actress asked to feed the bird personally, squeezing the vital drops with bejeweled fingers as her chauffeur held its wings. Many people prayed at the sight of Lazarus, some claiming to be instantaneously cured of lifelong afflictions, including one woman who flung away her crutches with the remark, "If that bird can get along without a head, I can get along without these crutches."

Then two men from the city humane department intruded with an order that Mrs. Green either put the rooster out of its misery within twelve hours or face imprisonment. Instead, early that night, under cover of darkness, Mrs. Green smuggled Lazarus to a local veterinarian, Dr. Allan Rice, rather than kill him a second time. But Dr. Rice hardly had time to make Lazarus comfortable (in a cage lined with newspapers full of reports about Mrs. Green) before two SPCA men came and forcibly took the bird — deaf and blind to this onslaught of intrigue — to an undisclosed location.

At midnight, in a frenzy of apprehension, Mrs. Green had a vision in which a benevolent, faceless figure in a feathered cloak walked into her bedroom through the southeast wall and implored her to consider chapter nine, verse eight in the Gospel of Matthew: "When the multitude saw it they marveled and glorified God which had given power unto men." That's when she phoned my father.

Photographed beside the brooding Mrs. Green, my father tried to address [8] the issue from a perspective both secular and devout, telling the reporter from *Life* magazine that Lazarus had come to Mrs. Green as an act of Providence for the interest and benefit of science and mankind — adding that she wanted him back, or five thousand bucks. Meanwhile, Father hired a filmmaker to document the incident for posterity, and the scrapbook contains an itemization of the man's expenditures, including pancake makeup for Mrs. Green, extra eggs for Lazarus, gas to San Bernardino and back. But perhaps the most worthwhile expenditure was for the poster that advertised the film. This was inset with snapshots of a lump with wings, a question mark hovering over its head, the layout rampant with boldface captions: **The Miracle Chicken. Not a Hollywood Make-believe Movie. Headless Rooster Hope of Millions. Bird Cures Blind, Lame, and Sick. Humble Home of Mystic Bird a Shrine**.

The public sentiment in favor of Mrs. Green prompted the SPCA to forgo a court battle and return Lazarus only one week after his abduction, with a decorous apology broadcast on radio. Accompanied by the two henchmen, the miracle was wrapped in a blue flannel blanket. After being examined by Dr. Rice, Lazarus was handed over to the beaming Mrs. Green, her eyedropper at the ready.

Little was said when Lazarus died quietly a few months later. Only my father came to pay condolences, as sure as Mrs. Green that the hoopla had killed it, that no one on earth can cope with divinity. While Mrs. Green lowered the large coffee can containing Lazarus into his grave, my father doffed his fedora and shielded his eyes against the sun.

For years after, he collected every reference to the precedent of The Miracle Chicken. The last page of his scrapbook is covered by a column entitled, "Blames Bubble in Mercy Case," in which a physician was accused of injecting an air bubble into the comatose Mrs. Abbie C. Borroto, thus causing a fatal embolism. During his cross-examination, Dr. Robert Biron, an expert witness, was grilled by the attorney for the prosecution regarding the clinical definition of death:

"Dr. Biron, have you ever seen a chicken with its head cut off?"   12

"Yes."

"If a chicken's head is cut off, and the body is still moving, is the chicken dead or alive?"

"There is life in the tissue."

"Just tell me, Dr. Biron, is that chicken still living?"   16

"I can't answer that. There is life in the tissue."

"I repeat, Doctor, is a chicken with his head cut off still living? Just answer yes or no."

"I can't answer that. That is impossible to answer."

Eighty-one years old, retired, my father is just out of the hospital after an   20 operation to drain a pool of water that had formed around his heart. Gaining weight again, he eats lunch with gusto, telling me about echocardiograms as he looks into the mirrored walls of the Crystal Room, his haunt, and catches a glimpse of himself, alive and almost infinite. Then he shifts his gaze to the silver-haired waitress who, all busy reflection, seems to scatter in different directions like a drop of mercury. Assuming that I too find her alluring, he looks at me and cocks an eyebrow.

All afternoon, conversation fluctuates between his brush with death — cold kiss of the stethoscope, bitter breathfuls of ether — and a running commentary on the waitress, responding now to his winks and piling our empty plates on her arm, with her freckled cleavage seeming to stir in him an impulse as strong as the will to survive. His eyes grow moist at the advent of arousal, each brown iris blazing with highlights. When he pivots to track that aproned anatomy, I can see from across the table that his head of white hair, redolent of tonic, is faintly yellow like old pages.

I hand him back his scrapbook before I hug him goodbye, and I hug him goodbye with a fierceness that startles even me. His iridescent suit, within my embrace, displays its shades of dark and light. I tell him I'm just trying to wring the last of the water out of him. It's a miracle, I tell him, that the heart can float.

● PERSONAL RESPONSE ●

Think about times when you have had the strong rush of emotion for a family member that Cooper describes in the final paragraph. What did you feel and what prompted the emotion?

● QUESTIONS FOR DISCUSSION ●

1. What is Cooper's purpose here? Is it primarily to tell about the miracle chicken, or is it primarily to tell about his father?

2. What do the newspaper clippings in the scrapbook reveal about Cooper's father?

3. How is this glimpse at Cooper's father also about "the vicissitudes of human love" (paragraph 5)? For instance, what function does the "Case of the Baking Newlywed" serve?

4. Why do you think Cooper tells us about his father's affairs?

5. What connections does Cooper imply in the last two paragraphs among the scrapbook, the story of the miracle chicken, and his aging father?

6. How do you think Cooper feels about his father? What in particular reveals his attitude toward him?

7. What do you think Cooper means by the last sentence?

● WRITING TOPICS ●

1. Describe a member of your immediate or extended family—a child, a parent, a grandparent, or a close family friend—by telling a story or stories that reveal that person's character.

2. Describe any colorful character you know, using not only physical characteristics but personality and behavior traits as well. Use concrete, specific, vivid details to make this person seem real to your reader.

3. Narrate or describe the circumstances leading up to a moment of insight into your feelings for a loved one.

TRAINING FOR REAL LIFE

●

ELLEN GOODMAN

Ellen Goodman is a columnist for the Boston Globe. *Her column, "At Large," has been syndicated by the Washington Post Writers Group since 1976. In 1980 she won a Pulitzer Prize for distinguished commentary (see her "It's Failure, Not Success" in Chapter 2). In the following 1987 article, written for her newspaper column, Goodman comments on the advantages coed friendships offer today's college students.*

She went to college last fall carrying two family gifts: a sense of humor and an answering machine. By mid-winter she put together these two weapons in a salvo intended for her elders.

This is what her mother heard: A male voice in the machine stuttered, "Um, uh, you called at a bad time. We're, um, in the shower right now. But we'll be out in a few minutes, so just leave a message."

The unsuspecting caller was not freaked out, as her daughter might put it. She waited for the beep and the giggles to subside and left a return message. After all, the mother said to herself, it was only 10 A.M. The bathroom on her daughter's floor was all female in the morning. It only became coed after noon. Or was it the other way around?

Well, never mind, this is dormitory living, 1987. The national fantasy of coed 4 showers and the reality of coed friendships.

What the mother had witnessed when she visited this campus was not a seething caldron of casual sex. It was rather a comfortable atmosphere of casual friendship of young men and women.

In the morning, they lurch past each other, oozing the same unwashed charm they had in their high-school days. Day and night, they walk in and out of each other's rooms dressed in their finest sweatpants and T-shirts, faces dotted with ritual zit cream. They borrow each other's clothes, cut each other's hair, listen to each other's complaints.

Less has been said about the incest taboo that arises on a floor where people live together like brother and sister, where the family dynamic depends on avoiding the storm and stress of romance and breakup. When the mother was in college in the '60s, a male friend was someone who was shorter than you or maybe your boyfriend's roommate.

Even in coed schools like hers, where she studied with men, went to class 8 with men, they did not live together in the real daily sense of that word. Women and men had to venture out to meet each other.

As her classmates went into the work world, it took time for them to develop anything like camaraderie. It isn't easy to learn to be buddies late in life. Like learning a new language, it happens most fluently when you're young.

To this day, men and women of her generation who travel together, work together, have to get through the flack of male-femaleness. When the business literature talks about this, it stresses the woeful lack of experience women have as teammates in their college years. Those who never played team sports, they say, have trouble in the corporate huddle.

But maybe the best turf for learning how to work together isn't a playing field, not in competition but in the easy give and take, the naturalness of living together.

Men and women marry one by one, or at least one after another. But we   12
work together in droves. The value of the coed dorm may be in graduating men and women who are natural with each other in the work world.

As for the young man in the recorded shower? The mother cannot resist asking. The daughter laughs at their recorded prank. "He lives a couple of doors down the hall," she says, "you met him." "Oh yes," says the mother, "he's your friend."

● PERSONAL RESPONSE ●

In what ways does Goodman's description of the "comfortable atmosphere of casual friendship of young men and women" apply (or not apply) to your own experiences? Do you feel comfortable having a member of the other sex as a "buddy"? Explain your answer.

● QUESTIONS FOR DISCUSSION ●

1. Explain the title of this essay. Who is "training for real life"? In what way?

2. How does the opening anecdote about the answering machine help introduce the subject of this article?

3. What audience do you think Goodman had in mind?

4. Where does Goodman use slang and colloquial words? How appropriate do you believe her word choice is?

5. What differences does Goodman see between the mother's and the daughter's generations in terms of male–female relationships?

6. Which generation does Goodman believe has the better male–female relationships? Why?

7. What does Goodman mean by "the flack of male-femaleness" (paragraph 10)?

● WRITING TOPICS ●

1. Interview someone from either an older or younger generation about friendships between males and females when they were growing up. Then compare and/or contrast their experiences with those of your own generation.

2. Explain the advantages and disadvantages of platonic friendships between men and women, using your own experiences or those of people you know to develop your central idea.

3. Using a humorous or satirical approach, describe life in a college coeducational dormitory.

THE ANDROGYNOUS MALE

●

NOEL PERRIN

Noel Perrin teaches American literature at Dartmouth College and raises beef cattle on his farm in Vermont. His books include Vermont: In All Weathers *(1973) and three collections of his essays,* First Person Rural *(1978),* Second Person Rural *(1980), and* Third Person Rural *(1983). The essay reprinted below first appeared in the "On Men" column in the* New York Times Magazine *in 1984. In it, Perrin defines androgyny by explaining what he feels free to do that the traditionally all-male, 100 percent red-blooded American he-man cannot do.*

The summer I was 16, I took a train from New York to Steamboat Springs, Colo., where I was going to be assistant horse wrangler at a camp. The trip took three days, and since I was much too shy to talk to strangers, I had quite a lot of time for reading. I read all of "Gone With the Wind." I read all the interesting articles in a couple of magazines I had, and then I went back and read all the dull stuff. I also took all the quizzes, a thing of which magazines were even fuller then than now.

The one that held my undivided attention was called "How Masculine/Feminine Are You?" It consisted of a large number of inkblots. The reader was supposed to decide which of four objects each blot most resembled. The choices might be a cloud, a steam engine, a caterpillar and a sofa.

When I finished the test, I was shocked to find that I was barely masculine at all. On a scale of 1 to 10, I was about 1.2. Me, the horse wrangler? (And not just wrangler, either. That summer, I had to skin a couple of horses that died—the camp owner wanted the hides.)

The results of that test were so terrifying to me that for the first time in my life I did a piece of original analysis. Having unlimited time on the train, I looked at the "masculine" answers over and over, trying to find what it was that distinguished real men from people like me—and eventually I discovered two very simple patterns. It was "masculine" to think the blots looked like man-made objects, and "feminine" to think they looked like natural objects. It was masculine to think they looked like things capable of causing harm, and feminine to think of innocent things.

Even at 16, I had the sense to see that the compilers of the test were using rather limited criteria—maleness and femaleness are both more complicated than *that*—and I breathed a huge sigh of relief. I wasn't necessarily a wimp, after all.

That the test did reveal something other than the superficiality of its makers I realized only many years later. What it revealed was that there is a large class of men and women both, to which I belong, who are essentially androgynous. That doesn't mean we're gay, or low in the appropriate hormones, or uncomfortable

4

performing the jobs traditionally assigned our sexes. (A few years after that summer, I was leading troops in combat and, unfashionable as it now is to admit this, having a very good time. War is exciting. What a pity the 20th century went and spoiled it with high-tech weapons.)

What it does mean to be spiritually androgynous is a kind of freedom. Men who are all-male, or he-man, or 100 percent red-blooded Americans, have a little biological set that causes them to be attracted to physical power, and probably also to dominance. Maybe even to watching football. I don't say this to criticize them. Completely masculine men are quite often wonderful people: good husbands, good (though sometimes overwhelming) fathers, good members of society. Furthermore, they are often so unself-consciously at ease in the world that other men seek to imitate them. They just aren't as free as us androgynes. They pretty nearly have to be what they are; we have a range of choices open.

The sad part is that many of us never discover that. Men who are not 100 8 percent red-blooded Americans—say, those who are only 75 percent red-blooded—often fail to notice their freedom. They are too busy trying to copy the he-men ever to realize that men, like women, come in a wide variety of acceptable types. Why this frantic imitation? My answer is mere speculation, but not casual. I have speculated on this for a long time.

Partly they're just envious of the he-man's unconscious ease. Mostly they're terrified of finding that there may be something wrong with them deep down, some weakness at the heart. To avoid discovering that, they spend their lives acting out the role that the he-man naturally lives. Sad.

One thing that men owe to the women's movement is that this kind of failure is less common than it used to be. In releasing themselves from the single ideal of the dependent woman, women have more or less incidentally released a lot of men from the single ideal of the dominant male. The one mistake the feminists have made, I think, is in supposing that *all* men need this release, or that the world would be a better place if all men achieved it. It wouldn't. It would just be duller.

So far I have been pretty vague about just what the freedom of the androgynous man is. Obviously, it varies with the case. In the case I know best, my own, I can be quite specific. It has freed me most as a parent. I am, among other things, a fairly good natural mother. I like the nurturing role. It makes me feel good to see a child eat—and it turns me to mush to see a 4-year-old holding a glass with both small hands, in order to drink. I even enjoyed sewing patches on the knees of my daughter Amy's Dr. Dentons when she was at the crawling stage. All that pleasure I would have lost if I had made myself stick to the notion of the paternal role that I started with.

Or take a smaller and rather ridiculous example. I feel free to kiss cats. Until 12 recently it never occurred to me that I would want to, though my daughters have been doing it all their lives. But my elder daughter is now 22, and in London. Of course, I get to look after her cat while she is gone. He's a big, handsome farm cat named Petrushka, very unsentimental, though used from kittenhood to being kissed on the top of the head by Elizabeth. I've gotten very fond of him (he's the adventurous kind of cat who likes to climb hills with you), and one night I simply felt like kissing him on the top of the head, and did. Why did no one tell me sooner how silky cat fur is?

Then there's my relation to cars. I am completely unembarrassed by my inability to diagnose even minor problems in whatever object I happen to be driving, and don't have to make some insider's remark to mechanics to try to establish that I, too, am a "Man With His Machine."

The same ease extends to household maintenance. I do it, of course. Service people are expensive. But for the last decade my house has functioned better than it used to because I've had the aid of a volume called "Home Repairs Any Woman Can Do," which is pitched just right for people at my technical level. As a youth, I'd as soon have touched such a book as I would have become a transvestite. Even though common sense says there is really nothing sexual whatsoever about fixing sinks.

Or take public emotion. All my life I have easily been moved by certain kinds of voices. The actress Siobhan McKenna's, to take a notable case. Give her an emotional scene in a play, and within 10 words my eyes are full of tears. In boyhood, my great dread was that someone might notice. I struggled manfully, you might say, to suppress this weakness. Now, of course, I don't see it as a weakness at all, but as a kind of fulfillment. I even suspect that the true he-men feel the same way, or one kind of them does, at least, and it's only the poor imitators who have to struggle to repress themselves.

Let me come back to the inkblots, with their assumption that masculine   16 equates with machinery and science, and feminine with art and nature. I have no idea whether the right pronoun for God is He, She or It. But this I'm pretty sure of. If God could somehow be induced to take that test, God would not come out macho, and not feminismo, either, but right in the middle. Fellow androgynes, it's a nice thought.

● PERSONAL RESPONSE ●

To what extent are you and your friends "androgynous"? To what extent do you feel limited to or free from traditional sex-role expectations? How do you feel about men who are only "75 percent red-blooded Americans"?

● QUESTIONS FOR DISCUSSION ●

1. Why did the young Perrin not take very seriously the results of the inkblot test he took?

2. What audience do you think Perrin has in mind here: both male and female, largely male, or largely female? Explain your answer.

3. How does Perrin define the purely masculine personality? What does he see as its limitations?

4. Perrin says that men who are not "100 percent red-blooded Americans" fail to notice their freedom because they are too busy trying to copy he-men. How does he account for this "frantic imitation" (paragraph 8)?

5. What examples of his own behavior does Perrin give to define androgyny?

6. Summarize the point Perrin makes in his final paragraph.

7. Perrin makes the statement that "there is a large class of men and women both . . . who are essentially androgynous" (paragraph 6). Given his definition of the androgynous male, how do you think he would define the androgynous female?

● WRITING TOPICS ●

1. Give your own definition of "androgynous male" or "androgynous female." Using either yourself or someone you know, define the term by using examples of behavior and attitudes that illustrate it.

2. Either support or argue against Perrin's contention that androgynous people are freer than those who adhere to traditional sex-role expectations.

3. Perrin says that the world would not necessarily be a better place if all men were androgynous (paragraph 10). Write an essay in which you support his statement that we also need men who are "100 percent red-blooded Americans."

ALONE TOGETHER
The Unromantic Generation

———————————— ● ————————————

BRUCE WEBER

Bruce Weber is an editor of The New York Times Magazine, *for which he has written many articles on a variety of topics. In 1986, he edited* Look Who's Talking: An Anthology of American Short Stories. *In the following article, first published in 1987 in* The New York Times Magazine, *Weber describes a survey he took of 60 recent college graduates about their attitudes toward relationships, romance, and careers. He concludes that this generation of young people is significantly different from his own of just a dozen years earlier.*

Here is a contemporary love story.

Twenty-four-year-old Clark Wolfsberger, a native of St. Louis, and Kim Wright, twenty-five, who is from Chicago, live in Dallas. They've been going together since they met as students at Southern Methodist University three years ago. They are an attractive pair, trim and athletic, she dark and lissome, he broad-shouldered and square-jawed. They have jobs they took immediately after graduating—Clark works at Talent Sports International, a sports marketing and management company; Kim is an assistant account executive at Tracy-Locke, a large advertising agency—and they are in love.

"We're very compatible," she says.

"We don't need much time together to confirm our relationship," he says. 4

When they speak about the future, they hit the two-career family notes that are conventional now in the generations ahead of them. "At thirty, I'll probably be married and planning a family," says Kim. "I'll stay in advertising. I'll be a late parent."

"By thirty, I'll definitely be married; either that or water-skiing naked in Monaco," Clark says, and laughs. "No. I'll be married. Well-established in my line of work. Have the home, have the dog. Maybe not a kid yet, but eventually. I'm definitely in favor of kids."

In the month I spent last winter visiting several cities around the country, interviewing recent college graduates about marriage, relationships, modern romance, I heard a lot of this, life equations already written, doubt banished. I undertook the trip because of the impression so many of us have; that in one wavelike rush to business school and Wall Street, young Americans have succumbed to a culture of immediate gratification and gone deep-down elitist on us. I set out to test the image with an informal survey meant to take the emotional temperature of a generation, not far behind my own, that *seems* so cynical, so full of such "material" girls and boys.

The sixty or so people I interviewed, between the ages of twenty-two and 8 twenty-six, were a diverse group. They spoke in distinct voices, testifying to a range of political and social views. Graduate students, lawyers, teachers, entertainers, business people, they are pursuing a variety of interests. What they have in common is that they graduated from college, are living in or around an urban center, and are heterosexual, mirrors of myself when I graduated from college in 1975. And yet as I moved from place to place, beginning with acquaintances of my friends and then randomly pursuing an expanding network of names and phone numbers, another quality emerged to the degree that I'd call it characteristic: they are planners. It was the one thing that surprised me, this looking ahead with certainty. They have priorities. I'd ask about love; they'd give me a graph.

This isn't how I remember it. Twelve years ago, who knew? I was three years away from my first full-time paycheck, six from anything resembling the job I have now. It was all sort of desultory and hopeful, a time of dabbling and waiting around for some event that would sprout a future. Frankly, I had it in mind that meeting a woman would do it.

My cultural prototype was Benjamin Braddock, the character played by Dustin Hoffman in Mike Nichols's 1967 film *The Graduate*, who, returning home after his college triumphs, finds the prospect of life after campus daunting in the extreme, and so plunges into inertia. His refrain "I'm just a little worried about my future," served me nicely as a sort of wryly understated mantra.

What hauls Benjamin from his torpor is love. Wisely or not, he responds to a force beyond logic and turns the world upside down for Elaine Robinson. And though in the end their future together is undetermined, the message of the movie is that love is meant to triumph, that its passion and promise, however naïve, are its strength, and that if we are lucky it will seize us and transform our lives.

Today I'm still single and, chastened by that, I suppose, a little more rational 12 about what to expect from love. Setting out on my trip, I felt as if I'd be plumbing a little of my past. But the people I spoke with reminded me more of the way I am now than the way I was then. I returned thinking that young people are older than they used to be, *The Graduate* is out of date, and for young people just out of college today, the belief that love is all you need no longer obtains.

"Kim's a great girl; I love her," Clark Wolfsberger says. "But she's very career-oriented. I am, too, and with our schedules the way they are, we haven't put any restrictions on each other. I think that's healthy."

"He might want to go back to St. Louis," Kim Wright says. "I want to go back to Chicago. If it works out, great. If not, that's fine, too. I can handle it either way."

They are not heartless, soulless, cold, or unimaginative. They *are* self-preoccupied, but that's a quality, it seems to me, for which youthful generations have always been known. What distinguishes this generation from mine, I think, is that they're aware of it. News-conscious, media-smart, they are sophisticated in a way I was not.

They have come of age, of course, at a time when American social traditions 16 barely survive. Since 1975, there have been more than a million divorces annually, and it is well publicized that nearly half of all marriages now end in

divorce. Yet the era of condoned casual promiscuity and sexual experimenta-
tion — itself once an undermining of the nation's social fabric — now seems to be
drawing to a close with the ever-spreading plague of sexually transmitted
disease.

The achievements of feminist activism — particularly the infusion of women
into the work force — have altered the expectations that the sexes have for each
other and themselves.

And finally, the new college graduates have been weaned on scarifying
forecasts of economic gloom. They feel housing problems already; according to
American Demographics magazine, the proportion of young people living at
home with their parents was higher in 1985 than in the last three censuses.
They're aware, too, of predictions that however affluent they are themselves,
they're probably better off than their children will be.

With all this in mind, today's graduates seem keenly aware that the future is
bereft of conventional expectations, that what's ahead is more chaotic than
mysterious. I've come to think it ironic that in a youth-minded culture such as
ours, one that ostensibly grants greater freedom of choice to young people than
it ever has before, those I spoke with seem largely restrained. Concerned with, if
not consumed by, narrowing the options down, getting on track, they are aiming
already at a distant comfort and security. I spoke, on my travels, with several
college counselors and administrators, and they concur that the immediate
concerns of today's graduates are more practical than those of their predecessors. "I talk to them about sex," says Gail Short Hanson, dean of students at
George Washington University, in Washington. "I talk about careers. And
marriage, with women, because of the balancing act they have to perform these
days. But love? I can't remember the last conversation I had about love."

Career-minded, fiercely self-reliant, they responded to me, a single man   20
with a good job, with an odd combination of comradeliness and respect. When
the interviews were over, I fielded a lot of questions about what it's like to work
at *The New York Times*. How did I get my job? Occasionally, someone would ask
about my love life. Considering the subject of our discussions, I was surprised it
happened so rarely. When it did, I told them I'd come reasonably close to
marriage once, but it didn't work out. Nobody asked me why. Nobody asked if I
was lonely.

Micah Materre, twenty-five, recently completed an internship at CBS News
in Chicago and is looking for a job in broadcast journalism. Like many of the
young people I talked to, she is farsighted in her romantic outlook: "I went out
with a guy last fall. He had a good job as a stockbroker. He was nice to me. But
then he started telling me about his family. And there were problems. And I
thought, 'What happens if I fall in love and we get married? What then?'"

It may be a memory lapse, but I don't recall thinking about marriage much
at all until I fell in love. I was twenty-nine; late, that's agreed. But the point is
that for me (and for my generation as a whole, I believe, though you hate to
make a statement like that), marriage loomed only as an outgrowth of happen-
stance; you met a person. Today's graduates, however, seem uneasy with that
kind of serendipity. All of the married couples I spoke with are delighted to be

married, but they do say their friends questioned their judgment. "I heard a lot of reasons why I shouldn't do it," one recent bride told me. "Finally, I just said to myself, 'I feel happier than I've ever felt. Why should I give this up just because I'm young?'"

Most of them too young to remember the assassination of *either* Kennedy, they are old enough to have romantic pasts, to have experienced the trauma of failure in love. What surprised me was how easily so many of them accepted it; it seems a little early to be resigned to the idea that things fall apart. In each interview, I asked about past involvements. Were you ever serious about anyone? Any marital close calls? And virtually everyone had a story. But I heard very little about heartbreak or lingering grief. Instead, with an almost uniform equanimity, they spoke of maturity gained, lessons learned. It isn't disillusionment exactly, and they *are* too young to be weary; rather, it sounds like determination.

Twenty-five-year-old Peter Mundy of San Francisco, for example, says that until six months ago he'd had a series of steady girlfriends. "I'm down on romance," he says. "There's too much pain, too much pressure. There are so many variables, and you can't tell until you're in the middle of it whether it'll be positive. It's only in retrospect that you can see how things went wrong. In the meantime, you end up neglecting other things." 24

The prevalent notion is that chemistry is untrustworthy; partners need to be up to snuff according to pretty rigorous standards. Ellen Lubin, twenty-six, of Los Angeles, for example, has just gotten engaged to the man she has been living with for two years. When she met him, she says: "I wasn't that attracted to him right away. But there were things about him that made me say, 'This is what I want in a man.' He's bright. He's a go-getter. He was making tons of money at the age of twenty-five. He's well-connected. He was like my mentor in coming to deal with life in the city."

At the end of *The Graduate*, Benjamin Braddock kidnaps his lady love at the altar, an instant after she has sealed her vows to someone else, and they manage to make their escape because Benjamin bolts the church door from the outside with a cross. That was the 1960s, vehement times. When I graduated, we were less obstreperous. Sacraments we could take or leave. And marriage wasn't much of an issue. If we put it off, it wasn't for the sake of symbolism so much as that it didn't seem necessary. In the last few years, I've been to a number of weddings among my contemporaries, people in their thirties, and that impression of us is still with me. What we did was drift toward marriage, arriving at it eventually, and with some surprise. Some of us are still drifting.

Today's graduates have forged a new attitude entirely. In spite of the high divorce rate, many of those I spoke with have marriage in mind. Overwhelmingly, they see it as not only desirable, but inevitable. Because of the odds, they approach it with wariness and pragmatism. More cautious than their parents (for American men in 1985, the median age at the time of their first marriage was 25.5, the highest since the turn of the century; it was 23.3 for women, a record), they are methodical in comparison with me.

Perhaps that explains why I find the way they speak about marriage so unromantic. Men and women tend to couch their views in different terms, but 28 they seem to share the perception that marriage is necessarily restricting. Nonetheless they trust in its rewards, whatever they are. Overall, it doesn't represent the kind of commitment that seems viable without adequate preparation.

"I've been dating someone for a year and a half," says Tom Grossman, a twenty-four-year-old graduate of the University of Texas. "We don't talk about marriage, and frankly I don't think it'll occur." Currently area sales manager in San Antonio for the John H. Harland Company, a check-printing concern, Grossman says he has professional success in mind first. "I want to be really well-off financially, and I don't want that struggle to interfere with the marriage. There are too many other stress factors involved. I want to be able to enjoy myself right away. And I never want to look back and think that if I hadn't gotten married, I could have accomplished more."

Many young women say they responded with some alarm to last year's *Newsweek* report on the controversial demographic study conducted at Harvard, which concluded that once past thirty, a woman faces rapidly dwindling chances of marrying. At a time when women graduates often feel it incumbent on them to pursue careers, they worry that the possibility of "having it all" is, in fact, remote.

Janie Russell, twenty-five, graduated from the University of North Carolina in 1983, left a serious boyfriend behind, and moved to Los Angeles to pursue a career in the film industry. Working now as a director of production services at New Visions Inc., like many other young women she believes the independence fostered by a career is necessary, not only for her own self-esteem but as a foundation for a future partnership. "I look forward to marriage," she says. "But this is a very selfish time for me. I have to have my career. I have to say to myself, 'I did this on my own.' It makes me feel more interesting than I would otherwise. Of course, what may happen is that I'll look up one day and say, 'O.K., husband, where are you?' And he won't be there."

About halfway through my trip I stopped interviewing married couples 32 because they tended to say similar things. They consider themselves the lucky ones. As twenty-four-year-old Adam Cooper put it, at dinner with his wife, Melanee, also twenty-four, in their Chicago apartment: "The grass is not greener on the other side."

I came away thinking it is as true as ever: all happy families are the same. But the couples I spoke with seemed to me part of a generation other than their own, older even than mine. Calling the Coopers to arrange an interview, I was invited for "a good, home-cooked meal."

The next day, I met Micah Materre, who expressed the prevailing contemporary stance as well as anyone. Outgoing and self-possessed, she gave me a long list of qualities she's looking for in a man: good looks, sense of humor, old-fashioned values, but also professional success, financial promise, and a solid family background. "Why not?" she said. "I deserve the best." But as I was folding up my notebook, she added a plaintive note: "I'll get married, won't I? It's the American way, right?"

Very early on in my sexual experience I was flattered by a woman who told me she ordinarily wouldn't go to bed with men who were under twenty-six.

"Until then," she said, "all they're doing when they're with you is congratulating themselves." For whatever reason, she never returned my calls after that night. Not an untypical encounter, all in all. Congratulations to both of us.

We were a lusty, if callow, bunch, not least because we thought we could 36 afford to be. Encouraged by the expansive social mores spawned by the sexual revolution, fortified by the advent of a widespread availability of birth control, and fundamentally unaware of germs, we interpreted sex, for our convenience, as pure pleasure shared by "consenting parties." If it feels good, do it. Remember that?

It is an attitude that the current generation inherited and put into practice at an early age. Asked about her circle of friends in Los Angeles, Lesley Bracker, twenty-three, puts it nonchalantly: "Oh, yeah, we were all sexually active as teen-agers. When we were younger, it was considered O.K. to sleep around."

Now, however, they are reconsidering. In general, on this topic, I found them shy. They hesitate to speak openly about their sex lives, are prone to euphemism ("I'm not exactly out there, you know, mingling"), and say they worry about promiscuity only because they have friends who still practice it. According to Laura Kavesh and Cheryl Lavin, who write a column about single life, "Tales from the Front," for the *Chicago Tribune* that is syndicated in some sixty other papers around the country, a letter from a reader about the virtues of virginity generated more supportive mail than anything that has appeared in the column in its two years of existence. I'm not about to say there's a new celibacy among the young, but my impression is that even if they're having twice as much sex as they say they're having, it's not as much as you would think.

The AIDS scare, of course, is of primary relevance. "I talk about AIDS on first dates," says Jill Rotenberg, twenty-five, publishing manager of a rare-book company in San Francisco. "I talk about it all the time. I've spoken with the guy I'm dating about taking an AIDS test. Neither one of us is thrilled about condoms. But we use them. The first time we had sex, I was the one who had one in my wallet."

Not everyone is so vehement. But seriously or jokingly, in earnest tête- 40 à-tête or idly at dinner parties, they all talk about it. To some, the new concern is merely a source of disappointment. Several of the young people I spoke with express the sense of having been robbed. It's tough to find sex when you want it, tougher than it used to be, is the lament of many, mostly men. As it was put to me at one point, "I wish I'd been born ten years earlier."

Jill Rotenberg says she feels betrayed: "I've had one long relationship in my life. He was my first lover, and for a long time my only one. So I feel I've had an untainted past. Now I feel I'm being punished anyway, even though I've been a good girl."

"I feel like I'm over the hurdle," says Douglas Ertman, twenty-two, of San Francisco, who got engaged last summer. "I'm really lucky to know that I'll have one sexual partner forever."

Most agree that the solution is monogamy, at least on a temporary basis. "It's a coupled-up society," says Alan Forman, twenty-six, a law student of George Washington University who, for the last several months, has been in a monogamous relationship. "Now more than ever. A lot of people I know are feeling the pressure to get hooked up with somebody."

I ask Forman and his girlfriend, twenty-four-year-old Debra Golden, about 44 their future together. They say they don't know ("I'm too insecure to make a decision like that," she says), and I get the sense they never talk about it. Then she turns to him, genuinely curious. "Say you break up with me and go to New York next year," she says.

"I don't know," he says. "If I meet someone and I like her, what do I have to do, ask her to take a blood test?"

A decade ago, one of the privileges that my contemporaries and I inferred from our sexual freedom was more or less to deny that there might be, in the sexual act, an innately implied emotional exchange. It's no longer feasible, however, to explain away sex as frivolity, inconsequential gratification. And that has complicated things for all of us, of course, whatever age, single or not.

But for young people, it's an issue, like marriage, that has been raised early: what does sex mean, if it doesn't mean nothing?

It's clearly a struggle for them. In one of my first interviews, twenty-five- 48 year-old Karl Wright of Chicago told me: "Maybe there's a silver lining in all this. Maybe AIDS will bring back romance." The more I think about that, the more chilling it gets.

Beverly Caro, a twenty-five-year-old associate in the Dallas law firm of Gardere & Wynne, graduated from Drake University, in Des Moines, in 1983, and attended law school there as well. Her office high above the street looks out on the city's jungle of futuristic skyscrapers. She had offers from firms in Denver and her hometown of Kansas City, Mo., she says, but chose to come to Dallas because "I see upward mobility here; that's what I was looking for."

Ms. Caro has an attractive, thoughtful manner and a soft voice, but like many of her contemporaries, given the chance to discuss her personal goals, she speaks with a certitude that borders on defiance. Currently, she sees two men "somewhat regularly," she says. "I'd like to have a companion. A friend, I guess. But finding a man is not a top priority. I want to travel. I want to establish myself in the community. I don't see any drastic changes in my life by the time I turn thirty. Except that I'll be a property owner."

During my interviews, the theme of getting on track and staying there surfaced again and again. I came to think of it as the currency of self-definition. As a generation, they are not a particularly well-polled group, but certain figures bear out my impression.

According to annual surveys of 300,000 college freshmen conducted by the 52 Higher Education Research Institute at the Graduate School of Education of the University of California at Los Angeles, young people today, by the time they *enter* college, are more inclined to express concrete life objectives than they've been for many years. Of those surveyed last fall, 73.2 percent cited being "very well off financially" as an essential or very important objective. That's up from 63.3 percent in 1980, 49.5 percent in 1975. Other objectives that the survey shows have risen in importance include "obtain recognition from colleagues for contributions to my special field"; "have administrative responsibility for the work of others"; "be successful in my own business"; and "raise a family." At the same time, the percentage of freshmen who consider it important to "develop a meaningful philosophy of life" has declined from 64.2 percent in 1975 to 40.6 percent last year.

Many of the people I spoke to feel the pressure of peer scrutiny. A status thing has evolved, to which many seem to have regretfully succumbed. Several expressed a weariness with meeting someone new and having to present themselves by their credentials. Yet, overwhelmingly, asked what they're looking for in a romantic partner, they responded first with phrases such as "an educated professional" and "someone with direction." They've conceded, more or less consciously, that unenlightened and exclusionary as it is, it's very uncool not to know what you want and not to be already chasing it.

"Seems like everyone in our generation has to be out there achieving," says Scott Birnbaum, twenty-five, who is the chief accountant for TIC United Corp., a holding company in Dallas.

Birnbaum graduated from the University of Texas in 1984, where, he says, "For me, the whole career-oriented thing kicked in." A native Texan with a broad drawl, he lives in the Greenville section of the city, an area populated largely by young singles. His apartment is comfortably roomy, not terribly well appointed. He shakes his head amiably as he points to the television set propped on a beer cooler. "What do I need furniture for?" he says. "Most of my time is taken up going to work."

Confident in himself professionally, Birnbaum was one of very few inter- 56 viewees who spoke frankly about the personal cost of career success. Many speculated that they'll be worried if, in their thirties, they haven't begun to settle their love lives; this was more true of women than men. But Birnbaum confesses a desire to marry now. "It's kind of lonely being single," he says. "I'd hate to find myself successful at thirty without a family. Maybe once I'm married and have children, that might make being successful careerwise less important."

The problem, he goes on, is the collective outlook he's part and parcel of. "Here's how we think," he says. "Get to this point, move on. Get to that point, move on. Acquire, acquire. Career, career. We're all afraid to slow down for fear of missing out on something. That extends to your social life as well. You go out on a date and you're thinking, 'Hell, is there someone better for me?' I know how terrible that sounds but it seems to be my problem. Most of my peers are in the same position. Men and women. I tell you, it's tough out there right now."

When I returned to New York, I called Alex de Gramont, whom I'd been saving to interview last. I've known Alex for a long time, since he was a gawky and curious high school student and I was his teacher. Handsome now, gentle-looking, he's a literary sort, prone to attractive gloom and a certain lack of perspective. He once told me that his paradigm of a romantic, his role model, was Heathcliff, the mad, doomed passion-monger from Emily Brontë's *Wuthering Heights*.

A year out of Wesleyan University in Middletown, Conn., Alex has reasons to be hopeful. His book-length senior thesis about Albert Camus has been accepted for publication, and on the strength of it, he has applied to four graduate programs in comparative literature. But he's unenthusiastic, and he has applied to law schools, too. In the meantime, he is living with his parents in New Jersey.

He tells me that last summer he went to West Germany in pursuit of a 60 woman he'd met when he was in college. He expected to live there with her, but he was back in this country in a couple of weeks. "Camus has a line," Alex says, "'Love can burn or love can last. It can't do both.'" Like Benjamin Braddock, Alex is a little worried about his future.

Dustin Hoffman is forty-nine. I'm thirty-three. Both of us are doing pretty well. Alex, at twenty-three, confesses to considerable unease. "Every minute I'm not accomplishing something, I feel is wasted," he says, sort of miserably. "I feel a lot of pressure to decide what to do with my life. I'm a romantic, but these are very unromantic times."

● PERSONAL RESPONSE ●

How much of what Weber says about today's young people applies to you? Are their attitudes toward relationships, sex, and the future similar to or different from your own? How would you answer the questions on the survey of college freshmen that Weber mentions in paragraph 52?

● QUESTIONS FOR DISCUSSION ●

1. In what way does the movie *The Graduate* illustrate the attitudes held by Weber and others of his generation?

2. What do you think Weber means when he says that he returned from his trip "thinking that young people are older than they used to be" (paragraph 12)?

3. What does Weber mean when he says that today's young people are "self-preoccupied" (paragraph 15)?

4. Summarize Weber's conclusions about the attitudes of young people toward love and relationships. What do they worry about? What do they want in relationships? How do they feel about love?

5. What differences in attitudes toward relationships and the future does Weber see between people of his own age group and those he interviewed? How do they differ in their views on sex? How does Weber account for that difference?

6. In what way are married couples "part of a generation other than their own" (paragraph 33)?

7. Why does Weber call today's young people an "unromantic generation"? How do the "contemporary love story" of Kim and Clark at the beginning of the essay and the closing extended example of Weber's former student Alex illustrate his point?

● WRITING TOPICS ●

1. Conduct your own survey of classmates, friends, and people in your dorm about their attitudes toward careers, relationships, and/or romance, and write an essay reporting your results.

2. Examine the effects that the AIDS epidemic has had on relationships today.

3. Use the example of a recent movie to illustrate the attitudes of your generation toward relationships and the future.

WHY MARRIAGES FAIL

●

ANNE ROIPHE

Anne Roiphe has written several novels, the most recent of which is
Lovingkindness *(1987). She is best known for her novel about relation-*
ships, Up the Sandbox! *(1970), which was later made into a movie. In*
the following essay, written for Family Weekly *in 1983, Roiphe points*
out a number of causes for the high divorce rate and gives her definition
of a successful marriage.

These days so many marriages end in divorce that our most sacred vows
no longer ring with truth. "Happily ever after" and "Till death do us
part" are expressions that seem on the way to becoming obsolete. Why
has it become so hard for couples to stay together? What goes wrong? What has
happened to us that close to one-half of all marriages are destined for the
divorce courts? How could we have created a society in which 42 percent of our
children will grow up in single-parent homes? If statistics could only measure
loneliness, regret, pain, loss of self-confidence and fear of the future, the
numbers would be beyond quantifying.

Even though each broken marriage is unique, we can still find the common
perils, the common causes for marital despair. Each marriage has crisis points
and each marriage tests endurance, the capacity for both intimacy and change.
Outside pressures such as job loss, illness, infertility, trouble with a child, care of
aging parents and all the other plagues of life hit marriage the way hurricanes
blast our shores. Some marriages survive these storms and others don't. Marriages fail, however, not simply because of the outside weather but because the
inner climate becomes too hot or too cold, too turbulent or too stupefying.

When we look at how we choose our partners and what expectations exist at
the tender beginnings of romance, some of the reasons for disaster become
quite clear. We all select with unconscious accuracy a mate who will recreate
with us the emotional patterns of our first homes. Dr. Carl A. Whitaker, a marital
therapist and emeritus professor of psychiatry at the University of Wisconsin,
explains, "From early childhood on, each of us carried models for marriage,
femininity, masculinity, motherhood, fatherhood, and all the other family roles."
Each of us falls in love with a mate who has qualities of our parents, who will
help us rediscover both the psychological happiness and miseries of our past
lives. We may think we have found a man unlike Dad, but then he turns to drink
or drugs, or loses his job over and over again or sits silently in front of the T.V. just
the way Dad did. A man may choose a woman who doesn't like kids just like his
mother or who gambles away the family savings just like his mother. Or he may
choose a slender wife who seems unlike his obese mother but then turns out to
have other addictions that destroy their mutual happiness.

A man and a woman bring to their marriage bed a blended concoction of   4
conscious and unconscious memories of their parents' lives together. The

human way is to compulsively repeat and recreate the patterns of the past. Sigmund Freud so well described the unhappy design that many of us get trapped in: the unmet needs of childhood, the angry feelings left over from frustrations of long ago, the limits of trust and the recurrence of old fears. Once an individual senses this entrapment, there may follow a yearning to escape, and the result could be a broken, splintered marriage.

Of course people can overcome the habits and attitudes that developed in childhood. We all have hidden strengths and amazing capacities for growth and creative change. Change, however, requires work—observing your part in a rotten pattern, bringing difficulties out into the open—and work runs counter to the basic myth of marriage: "When I wed this person all my problems will be over. I will have achieved success and I will become the center of life for this other person and this person will be my center, and we will mean everything to each other forever." This myth, which every marriage relies on, is soon exposed. The coming of children, the pulls and tugs of their demands on affection and time, place a considerable strain on that basic myth of meaning everything to each other, of merging together and solving all of life's problems.

Concern and tension about money take each partner away from the other. Obligations to demanding parents or still-depended-upon parents create further strain. Couples today must also deal with all the cultural changes brought on in recent years by the women's movement and the sexual revolution. The altering of roles and the shifting of responsibilities have been extremely trying for many marriages.

These and other realities of life erode the visions of marital bliss the way sandstorms eat at rock and the ocean nibbles away at the dunes. Those euphoric, grand feelings that accompany romantic love are really self-delusions, self-hypnotic dreams that enable us to forge a relationship. Real life, failure at work, disappointments, exhaustion, bad smells, bad colds and hard times all puncture the dream and leave us stranded with our mate, with our childhood patterns pushing us this way and that, with our unfulfilled expectations.

The struggle to survive in marriage requires adaptability, flexibility, genuine love and kindness and an imagination strong enough to feel what the other is feeling. Many marriages fall apart because either partner cannot imagine what the other wants or cannot communicate what he or she needs or feels. Anger builds until it erupts into a volcanic burst that buries the marriage in ash. 8

It is not hard to see, therefore, how essential communication is for a good marriage. A man and a woman must be able to tell each other how they feel and why they feel the way they do; otherwise they will impose on each other roles and actions that lead to further unhappiness. In some cases, the communication patterns of childhood—of not talking, of talking too much, of not listening, of distrust and anger, of withdrawal—spill into the marriage and prevent a healthy exchange of thoughts and feelings. The answer is to set up new patterns of communication and intimacy.

At the same time, however, we must see each other as individuals. "To achieve a balance between separateness and closeness is one of the major psychological tasks of all human beings at every stage of life," says Dr. Stuart Bartle, a psychiatrist at the New York University Medical Center.

If we sense from our mate a need for too much intimacy, we tend to push him or her away, fearing that we may lose our identities in the merging of marriage. One partner may suffocate the other partner in a childlike dependency.

A good marriage means growing as a couple but also growing as individuals. 12 This isn't easy. Richard gives up his interest in carpentry because his wife, Helen, is jealous of the time he spends away from her. Karen quits her choir group because her husband dislikes the friends she makes there. Each pair clings to each other and is angry with each other as life closes in on them. This kind of marital balance is easily thrown as one or the other pulls away and divorce follows.

Sometimes people pretend that a new partner will solve the old problems. Most often extramarital sex destroys a marriage because it allows an artificial split between the good and the bad — the good is projected on the new partner and the bad is dumped on the head of the old. Dishonesty, hiding and cheating create walls between men and women. Infidelity is just a symptom of trouble. It is a symbolic complaint, a weapon of revenge, as well as an unraveler of closeness. Infidelity is often that proverbial last straw that sinks the camel to the ground.

All right — marriage has always been difficult. Why then are we seeing so many divorces at this time? Yes, our modern social fabric is thin, and yes the permissiveness of society has created unrealistic expectations and thrown the family into chaos. But divorce is so common because people today are unwilling to exercise the self-discipline that marriage requires. They expect easy joy, like the entertainment on TV, the thrill of a good party.

Marriage takes some kind of sacrifice, not dreadful self-sacrifice of the soul, but some level of compromise. Some of one's fantasies, some of one's legitimate desires have to be given up for the value of the marriage itself. "While all marital partners feel shackled at times, it is they who really choose to make the marital ties into confining chains or supporting bonds," says Dr. Whitaker. Marriage requires sexual, financial and emotional discipline. A man and a woman cannot follow every impulse, cannot allow themselves to stop growing or changing.

Divorce is not an evil act. Sometimes it provides salvation for people who 16 have grown hopelessly apart or were frozen in patterns of pain or mutual unhappiness. Divorce can be, despite its initial devastation, like the first cut of the surgeon's knife, a step toward new health and a good life. On the other hand, if the partners can stay past the breaking up of the romantic myths into the development of real love and intimacy, they have achieved a work as amazing as the greatest cathedrals of the world. Marriages that do not fail but improve, that persist despite imperfections, are not only rare these days but offer a wondrous shelter in which the face of our mutual humanity can safely show itself.

● PERSONAL RESPONSE ●

What do you think of Roiphe's suggestion that successful marriages require some kind of sacrifice and compromise? How far would you be willing (or have you been willing) to make sacrifices and to compromise some of your beliefs and desires in order to make your marriage work?

● QUESTIONS FOR DISCUSSION ●

1. What does Roiphe see as the primary cause of failed marriage today? According to her, what view of marriage should people take in order to solve this problem?
2. What other images does the shelter image in Roiphe's conclusion relate to?
3. What is the effect of beginning paragraph 14 with "all right"? Whom is Roiphe addressing?
4. What "cultural changes" is Roiphe referring to in paragraph 6? That is, what changes have occurred because of the women's movement and the sexual revolution?
5. What does Roiphe mean by the "realities of life" (paragraph 7)? What other realities might Roiphe have mentioned? How do these realities affect marriages?
6. How do the examples of Richard, Helen, and Karen in paragraph 12 illustrate Roiphe's point about what it takes to have a successful marriage? What benefits do couples in solid marriages gain from their marriages?
7. In what ways can divorce be beneficial, according to Roiphe?

● WRITING TOPICS ●

1. Define what you believe is a successful marriage. Support your generalizations with specific examples, using a couple or couples you know who have successful marriages to illustrate what you mean.
2. Explain why a marriage or relationship you know of personally—your own, that of a friend, or even your parents'—did not last.
3. Explain the effects of divorce on the two people involved, on their family, and/or on their friends. If appropriate, use personal experience as a source of this essay.

MEN AND WOMEN IN SEARCH OF COMMON GROUND

●

WENDELL BERRY

Wendell Berry is a poet, novelist, essayist, and farmer who has pub-lished over a dozen books. His collections of essays include The Long-Legged Horse *(1969),* The Hidden Wound *(1970),* A Continuous Harmony *(1972),* The Unsettling of America *(1977),* The Gift of Good Land *(1981), and* Standing By Woods *(1985). His latest,* What Are People For? *(1990), was issued on the twentieth anniversary of Earth Day and addresses his on-going concern with the future of the human race and his belief that we must change the way we live in order to avoid destruction. In the following essay from his 1987 collection of essays,* Home Economics, *Berry searches for reasons why human relationships are now so impermanent and offers suggestions for how to make them permanent.*

> The domestic joys, the daily housework
> or business, the building of houses —
> they are not phantasms . . . they have
> weight and form and location.
> WALT WHITMAN, *TO THINK OF TIME*

I am not an authority on men or women or any of the possible connections between them. In sexual matters I am an amateur, in both the ordinary and the literal senses of that word. I speak about them only because I am concerned about them; I am concerned about them only because I am involved in them; I am involved in them, apparently, only because I am a human, a qualification for which I deserve no credit.

I do not believe, moreover, that any individual *can* be an authority on the present subject. The common ground between men and women can only be defined by community authority. Individually, we may desire it and think about it, but we are not going to occupy it if we do not arrive there together.

That we have not arrived there, that we apparently are not very near to doing so, is acknowledged by the title of this symposium ["Men and Women in Search of Common Ground," a symposium at the Jung Institute of San Francisco]. And that a symposium so entitled should be held acknowledges implicitly that we are not happy in our exile. The specific cause of our unhappiness, I assume, is that relationships between men and women are now too often extremely tentative and temporary, whereas we would like them to be sound and permanent.

Apparently, it is in the nature of all human relationships to aspire to be 4 permanent. To propose temporariness as a goal in such relationships is to bring them under the rule of aims and standards that prevent them from beginning.

Neither marriage, nor kinship, nor friendship, nor neighborhood can exist with a life expectancy that is merely convenient.

To see that such connections aspire to permanence, we do not have to look farther than popular songs, in which people still speak of loving each other "forever." We now understand, of course, that in this circumstance the word "forever" is not to be trusted. It may mean only "for a few years" or "for a while" or even "until tomorrow morning." And we should not be surprised to realize that if the word "forever" cannot be trusted in this circumstance, then the word "love" cannot be trusted either.

This, as we know, was often true before our own time, though in our time it seems easier than before to say "I will love you forever" and to mean nothing by it. It is possible for such words to be used cynically—that is, they may be *intended* to mean nothing—but I doubt that they are often used with such simple hypocrisy. People continue to use them, I think, because they continue to try to mean them. They continue to express their sexual feelings with words such as "love" and "forever" because they want those feelings to have a transferable value, like good words or good money. They cannot bear for sex to be "just sex," any more than they can bear for family life to be just reproduction or for friendship to be just a mutually convenient exchange of goods and services.

The questions that I want to address here, then, are: Why are sexual and other human relationships now so impermanent? And under what conditions might they become permanent?

It cannot be without significance that this division is occurring at a time 8 when division has become our characteristic mode of thinking and acting. Everywhere we look now, the axework of division is going on. We see ourselves more and more as divided from each other, from nature, and from what our traditions define as human nature. The world is now full of nations, races, interests, groups, and movements of all sorts, most of them unable to define their relations to each other except in terms of division and opposition. The poor human body itself has been conceptually hacked to pieces and parceled out like a bureaucracy. Brain and brawn, left brain and right brain, stomach, hands, heart, and genitals have all been set up in competition against each other, each supported by its standing army of advocates, press agents, and merchants. In such a time, it is not surprising that the stresses that naturally, and perhaps desirably, occur between the sexes should result in the same sort of division with the same sort of doctrinal justification.

This condition of division is one that we suffer from and complain about, yet it is a condition that we promote by our ambitions and desires and justify by our jargon of "self-fulfillment." Each of us, we say, is supposed to "realize his or her full potential as an individual." It is as if the whole two hundred million of us were saying with Coriolanus:

> I'll never
> Be such a gosling to obey instinct, but stand
> As if a man were author of himself
> And knew no other kin. (V, iii, 34–37)

By "instinct" he means the love of family, community, and country. In Shakespeare's time, this "instinct" was understood to be the human norm—the definition of humanity, or a large part of that definition. When Coriolanus speaks these lines, he identifies himself, not as "odd," but as monstrous, a *danger* to family, community, and country. He identifies himself, that is, as an individual prepared to act alone and without the restraint of reverence, fidelity, or love. Shakespeare is at one with his tradition in understanding that such a person acted inevitably, not as the "author of himself," but as the author of tragic consequences both for himself and for other people.

The problem, of course, is that we are *not* the authors of ourselves. That we are not is a religious perception, but it is also a biological and a social one. Each of us has had many authors, and each of us is engaged, for better or worse, in that same authorship. We could say that the human race is a great coauthorship in which we are collaborating with God and nature in the making of ourselves and one another. From this there is no escape. We may collaborate either well or poorly, or we may refuse to collaborate, but even to refuse to collaborate is to exert an influence and to affect the quality of the product. This is only a way of saying that by ourselves we have no meaning and no dignity; by ourselves we are outside the human definition, outside our identity. "More and more," Mary Catharine Bateson wrote in *With a Daughter's Eye,* "it has seemed to me that the idea of an individual, the idea that there is someone to be known, separate from the relationships, is simply an error."

Some time ago I was with Wes Jackson, wandering among the experimental plots at his home and workplace, the Land Institute in Salina, Kansas. We stopped by one plot that had been planted in various densities of population. Wes pointed to a Maximilian sunflower growing alone, apart from the others, and said, "There is a plant that has 'realized its full potential as an individual.'" And clearly it had: It had grown very tall; it had put out many long branches heavily laden with blossoms—and the branches had broken off, for they had grown too long and too heavy. The plant had indeed realized its full potential as an individual, but it had failed as a Maximilian sunflower. We could say that its full potential as an individual *was* this failure. It had failed because it had lived outside an important part of its definition, which consists of *both* its individuality and its community. A part of its properly realizable potential lay in its community, not in itself.

In making a metaphor of this sunflower, I do not mean to deny the value or the virtue of a *proper* degree of independence in the character and economy of an individual, nor do I mean to deny the conflicts that occur between individuals and communities. Those conflicts belong to our definition, too, and are probably as necessary as they are troublesome. I do mean to say that the conflicts are not everything, and that to make conflict—the so-called "jungle law"—the basis of social or economic doctrine is extremely dangerous. A part of our definition is our common ground, and a part of it is sharing and mutually enjoying our common ground. Undoubtedly, also, since we are humans, a part of our definition is a recurring contest over the common ground: Who shall describe its boundaries, occupy it, use it, or own it? But such contests obviously can be carried too far, so that they become destructive both of the commonality of the common ground and of the ground itself.

The danger of the phrase "common ground" is that it is likely to be meant as no more than a metaphor. I am *not* using it as a metaphor; I mean by it the actual ground that is shared by whatever group we may be talking about — the human race, a nation, a community, or a household. If we use the term only as a metaphor, then our thinking will not be robustly circumstantial and historical, as it needs to be, but only a weak, clear broth of ideas and feelings.

Marriage, for example, is talked about most of the time as if it were only a "human relationship" between a wife and a husband. A good marriage is likely to be explained as the result of mutually satisfactory adjustments of thoughts and feelings — a "deep" and complicated mental condition. That is surely true for some couples some of the time, but, as a general understanding of marriage, it is inadequate and probably unworkable. It is far too much a thing of the mind and, for that reason, is not to be trusted. "God guard me," Yeats wrote, "from those thoughts men think / In the mind alone . . ."

Yeats, who took seriously the principle of incarnation, elaborated this idea in his essay on the Japanese Noh plays, in which he says that "we only believe in those thoughts which have been conceived not in the brain but in the whole body." But we need a broader concept yet, for a marriage involves more than just the bodies and minds of a man and a woman. It involves locality, human circumstance, and duration. There is a strong possibility that the basic human sexual unit is composed of a man and a woman (bodies and minds), plus their history together, plus their kin and descendants, plus their place in the world with its economy and history, plus their natural neighborhood, plus their human community with its memories, satisfactions, expectations, and hopes.

By describing it in such a way, we begin to understand marriage as the insistently practical union that it is. We begin to understand it, that is, as it is represented in the traditional marriage ceremony, those vows being only a more circumstantial and practical way of saying what the popular songs say dreamily and easily: "I will love you forever" — a statement that, in this world, inescapably leads to practical requirements and consequences because it proposes survival as a goal. Indeed, marriage is a union much more than practical, for it looks both to our survival as a species and to the survival of our definition as human beings — that is, as creatures who make promises and keep them, who care devotedly and faithfully for one another, who care properly for the gifts of life in this world.

The business of humanity is undoubtedly survival in this complex sense — a 16 necessary, difficult, and entirely fascinating job of work. We have in us deeply planted instructions — personal, cultural, and natural — to survive, and we do not need much experience to inform us that we cannot survive alone. The smallest possible "survival unit," indeed, appears to be the universe. At any rate, the ability of an organism to survive outside the universe has yet to be demonstrated. Inside it, everything happens *in concert*; not a breath is drawn but by the grace of an inconceivable series of vital connections joining an inconceivable multiplicity of created things in an inconceivable unity. But of course it is preposterous for a mere individual human to espouse the universe—a possibility that is purely mental, and productive of nothing but talk. On the other hand, it may be that our marriages, kinships, friendships, neighborhoods, and all our forms and acts of homemaking are the rites by which we solemnize and enact our union with the universe. These ways are practical, proper, available to everybody, and they can provide for the safekeeping of the small acreages of the universe that have been entrusted to us. Moreover, they give the word "love" its only chance to mean, for only they can give it a history, a community, and a place. Only in such ways can love become flesh and do its worldly work. For example, a marriage without a place, a household, has nothing to show for itself. Without a history of some length, it does not know what it means. Without a community to exert a shaping pressure around it, it may explode because of the pressure inside it.

These ways of marriage, kinship, friendship, and neighborhood surround us with forbiddings; they are forms of bondage, and involved in our humanity is always the wish to escape. We may be obliged to look on this wish as necessary, for, as I have just implied, these unions are partly shaped by internal pressure. But involved in our humanity also is the warning that we can escape only into loneliness and meaninglessness. Our choice may be between a small, human-sized meaning and a vast meaninglessness, or between the freedom of our virtues and the freedom of our vices. It is only in these bonds that our individuality has a use and a worth; it is only to the people who know us, love us, and depend on us that we are indispensable as the persons we uniquely are. In our industrial society, in which people insist so fervently on their value and their freedom "as individuals," individuals are seen more and more as "units" by their governments, employers, and suppliers. They live, that is, under the rule of the interchangeability of parts: What one person can do, another person can do just as well or a newer person can do better. Separate from the relationships, there is nobody to be known; people become, as they say and feel, nobodies.

It is plain that, under the rule of the industrial economy, humans, at least as individuals, are well advanced in a kind of obsolescence. Among those who have achieved even a modest success according to the industrial formula, the human body has been almost entirely replaced by machines and by a shrinking population of manual laborers. For enormous numbers of people now, the only physical activity that they cannot delegate to machines or menials, who will presumably do it more to their satisfaction, is sexual activity. For many, the only necessary physical labor is that of childbirth.

According to the industrial formula, the ideal human residence (from the Latin *residere*, "to sit back" or "remain sitting") is one in which the residers do not work. The house is built, equipped, decorated, and provisioned by other people, by strangers. In it, the married couple practice as few as possible of the disciplines of household or homestead. Their domestic labor consists principally of buying things, putting things away, and throwing things away, but it is understood that it is "best" to have even those jobs done by an "inferior" person, 20 and the ultimate industrial ideal is a "home" in which *everything* would be done by pushing buttons. In such a "home," a married couple are mates, sexually, legally, and socially, but they are not helpmates; they do nothing useful either together or for each other. According to the ideal, work should be done *away* from home. When such spouses say to each other, "I will love you forever," the meaning of their words is seriously impaired by their circumstances; they are speaking in the presence of so little that they have done and made. Their history together is essentially placeless; it has no visible or tangible incarnation. They have only themselves in view.

In such a circumstance, the obsolescence of the body is inevitable, and this is implicitly acknowledged by the existence of the "physical fitness movement." Back in the era of the body, when women and men were physically useful as well as physically attractive to one another, physical fitness was simply a condition. Little conscious attention was given to it; it was a by-product of useful work. Now an obsessive attention has been fixed upon it. Physical fitness has become extremely mental; once free, it has become expensive, an industry — just as sexual attractiveness, once the result of physical vigor and useful work, has now become an industry. The history of "sexual liberation" has been a history of increasing bondage to corporations.

Now the human mind appears to be following the human body into obsolescence. Increasingly, jobs that once were done by the minds of individual humans are done by computers — and by governments and experts. Dr. William C. DeVries, the current superstar of industrial heart replacement, can blithely assure a reporter that "the general society is not very well informed to make those decisions [as to the imposition of restraints on medical experiments on human patients], and that's why the medical society or the government who has a wider range of view comes in to make those decisions" (Louisville *Courier-Journal*, 3 Feb. 1985). Thus we may benefit from the "miracle" of modern medical science on the condition that we delegate all moral and critical authority in such matters to the doctors and the government. We may save our bodies by losing our minds, just as, according to another set of experts, we may save our minds by forsaking our bodies. Computer thought is exactly the sort that Yeats warned us against; it is made possible by the assumption that thought occurs "in the mind alone" and that the mind, therefore, is an excerptable and isolatable human function, which can be set aside from all else that is human, reduced to pure process, and so imitated by a machine. But in fact we know that the *human* mind is not distinguishable from what it knows and that what it knows comes from or is radically conditioned by its embodied life in this world. A machine, therefore, cannot be a mind or be like a mind; it can only *replace* a mind.

We know, too, that these mechanical substitutions are part of a long-established process. The industrial economy has made its way among us by a process of division, degradation, and then replacement. It is only after we have been divided against each other that work and the products of work can be degraded; it is only after work and its products have been degraded that workers can be replaced by machines. Only when thought has been degraded can a mind be replaced by a machine, or a society of experts, or a government.

It is true, furthermore, that, in this process of industrialization, what is free 24 is invariably replaced by a substitute that is costly. Bodily health as the result of useful work, for instance, is or was free, whereas industrial medicine, which has flourished upon the uselessness of the body, is damagingly and heartlessly expensive. In the time of the usefulness of the body, when the body became useless it died, and death was understood as a kind of healing; industrial medicine looks upon death as a disease that calls for increasingly expensive cures.

Similarly, in preindustrial country towns and city neighborhoods, the people who needed each other lived close to each other. This proximity was free, and it provided many benefits that were either free or comparatively cheap. This simple proximity has been destroyed and replaced by communications and transportation industries that are, again, enormously expensive and destructive, as well as extremely vulnerable to disruption.

Insofar as we reside in the industrial economy, our obsolescence, both as individuals and as humankind, is fast growing upon us. But we cannot regret or, indeed, even know that this is true without knowing and naming those never-to-be-official institutions that alone have the power to reestablish us in our true estate and identity: marriage, family, household, friendship, neighborhood, community. For these to have an effective existence, they must be located in the world and in time. So located, they have the power to establish us in our human identity because they are not merely institutions in a public, abstract sense, like the organized institutions but are also private conditions. They are the conditions in which a human is complete, body and mind, because completely necessary and needed.

When we live within these human enclosures, we escape the tyrannical doctrine of the interchangeability of parts; in these enclosures, we live as members, each in its own identity necessary to the others. When our spouse or child, friend or neighbor is in need or in trouble, we do not deal with them by means of a computer, for we know that, with them, we must not think without feeling. We do not help them by sending a machine, for we know that, with them, a machine cannot represent us. We know that, when they need us, we must go and offer ourselves, body and mind, as we are. As members, moreover, we are useless and worse than useless to each other if we do not care properly for the ground that is common to us.

It is only in these trying circumstances that human love is given its chance to 28 have meaning, for it is only in these circumstances that it can be borne out in deeds through time — "even," to quote Shakespeare again, "to the edge of doom" — and thus prove itself true by fulfilling its true term.

In these circumstances, in place and in time, the sexes will find their common ground and be somewhat harmoniously rejoined, not by some resolution of conflict and power, but by proving indispensable to one another, as in fact they are.

● PERSONAL RESPONSE ●

What have been your observations on relationships? Do you believe, as Berry argues, that they are now too often only tentative and temporary, or have the relationships of people you know been permanent and committed?

● QUESTIONS FOR DISCUSSION ●

1. What is the function of the opening quotation from Walt Whitman?
2. In what ways are we not the "authors of ourselves" (paragraph 10)? How does the example of the Maximilian sunflower (paragraph 11) illustrate that statement?
3. Why is Berry critical of the concept of "self-fulfilment" (paragraph 9)?
4. What does Berry mean when he says that "division has become our characteristic mode of thinking and acting" (paragraph 8)? In what ways does he mean that? What examples does he give?
5. How does Berry's definition of marriage differ from the way it is often regarded?
6. Explain what Berry means when he says that "the smallest possible 'survival unit,' indeed, appears to be the universe" (paragraph 17). What is his point here?
7. In what ways are human relationships forms of bondage, according to Berry?
8. Summarize what Berry says about the impact of the industrial economy on humans. What does Berry think of the ideal human residence, according to the industrial formula (paragraph 20)?
9. What does Berry mean when he says in paragraph 21 that "the obsolescence of the body is inevitable"? In what way is the human mind "following the human body into obsolescence" (paragraph 22)?

● WRITING TOPICS ●

1. Describe the kinds of relationships you have with other people: love, friendship, and kinship. What do they have in common? How do they differ?
2. Analyze the messages about love and commitment in the lyrics of selected popular songs.
3. Explore the depiction of love relationships in one or two popular television shows or movies.

IN DEFENSE OF THE EQUALITY OF *MEN*

●

Lorraine Hansberry

Lorraine Hansberry (1930–1965) was a writer who is best known for her play A Raisin in the Sun *(1959), for which she became, at age 29, the first black playwright to receive the New York Drama Critics award for Best Play. In* Raisin, *Hansberry addressed many of the social issues that were brewing in the late 1950s, particularly those that reached full force in the civil rights movement of the 1960s and the women's movement of the 1970s. The essay reprinted below was originally written in 1961 for a magazine that was to be called* The Fair Sex *but that never appeared. In the essay, Hansberry adopts a writing style that is casual and colloquial in order to provoke and challenge the intended audience for what was to have been an outspoken women's magazine.*

There is currently mushrooming in the land a voluminous body of opinion in which scores of magazine writers, television panelists, and conference speakers with weighted eyebrows and ominous sentences allude to a peril in the Republic such as might herald a second coming of the British. Book, speech, and dissertation titles make the matter explicit: "Modern Woman — The Lost Sex"; "Trousered Mothers and Dishwashing Dads"; "American Man in a Woman's World"; etc.

Women, it is said, have ceased being, of all things, *women*. The conclusion has now been drawn in many circles that womanhood's historical insistence on ever-increasing measures of equality has resulted in women becoming "the imitations of men" — and, it is sometimes added, with something of a Calvinist shout: "Very bad imitations!"

The total theme of the alarm is that the "roles of the sexes are disappearing," and according to one analyst: "We are drifting toward a social structure made up of he-women and she-men." Which, all will admit, if it is true, is pretty scary business!

To aid in the terror, some contemporary schools of psychoanalytical thought 4 have been right in there giving leadership, guiding the worried along paths of "explanation" which have to do with their own preoccupations with "phallus envy," "castration complexes," and the rest of it: the inevitable result being that large numbers of people are now inclined to speak of the hardly new quest for universal equality as a neurotic disorder! "A disorder," we are informed, which seems to be sweeping other modern civilizations as well. For what else could be at the root, for example, of the "trouble in Australia," where a study reveals that sixty percent of the husbands in Melbourne reported that they help their wives with the dishes and yet another twenty-two percent get breakfast for the family in the mornings?

It appears that the horrified commentators have taken note of some very real disorders in modern life and deduced, rather automatically, that the causes must lie in the disintegration of our most entrenched traditions. Yet few of these seers, remarkably enough, seem to have seriously considered the alternative: that the problems might in fact lie in the lingering *life* of certain of our traditions.

There are, to be sure, other observers—a counter force holding their own—who suggest that, at best, the alarm is rooted in archaic concepts and, at worst, is in itself presumptuous as the dickens! Striking a note of rationality, they argue that what we are dealing with is the oldest phenomenon of the planet: *change*. The implication being that, contrary to negative legends, the human race possesses an incredible capacity to adapt itself, physically and psychologically, to its own ever-improving technological condition. Thus, modern man—modern urban man in particular—has begun to lose his *reasons* for the retention of formerly rigid notions of occupational, avocational, or even psychic categorizations which were apparently essential to his forebears in their more primitive social systems.

Affairs behind executive or professorial desks have tended to make "brute strength" irrelevant; World War II showed that virtually the same thing was true for the assembly line. And even if there were wild boars and such things still to be hunted for survival, the force required on the trigger of an automatic weapon is hardly the same once needed to pummel something with a stone axe. Increasingly, it is a human being's thinking capacity, not his bulk, which most equips him for modern life; whatever there once was of a realistic reason for physique determining labor is rapidly disappearing. In that light it is not extraordinary to behold the human attitude also changing. If modern trade unionism, white-collar labor, and the eight-hour day have contrived to diminish the laboring hours of the husband, it is to his credit that he has begun of his own volition to apply his new and hard-won leisure to sharing some part of his wife's still often twelve-to-fourteen-hour workday. It suggests that more than being a question for concern, it is one for celebration inasmuch as for the first time in history the family may now be growing toward a circumstantial reality which will allow it to become the truly harmonized, cooperative unit the human dream has always longed for it to be.

The current aspiration for the retention of ancient polarized concepts of strict divisions of labor reflects a social order which has effectively kept womanhood in her well-known second-class situation, but which is less often criticized for imposing *upon males* the most unreasonable and unnecessary burdens of "superiority" and "authority," which, in fact, work only to insult their humanness and *deny the reality of their civilized state*. 8

Most apologists for a male supremacist culture do not dream that they savagely downgrade *men* in their efforts to provide them with a socially guaranteed place of privilege on the human scale. Yet, it was not romanticism alone, but also shimmering human practicality, which led the great humanist thinkers and artists of history to postulate, in poetry and prose, the ideas that, for instance, the rich must be inevitably degraded, in *human* terms, in a world where so many starve; that the educated remain, in large measure, untested for their wisdom when so few can read or write. And, certainly, in our own time, in the United States, it has become increasingly clear that white Americans are among the most compromised people on the face of the earth, because of their steady demonstration of their fear of running a non-handicapped race with their black countrymen.

If modern males are suffering from high percentages of ulcer, heart ailment, and a thousand-and-one nervous disorders, this might well be the burden imposed on their nervous systems from subjecting the reality of present-day life to the totems and taboos of the primeval, medieval, and Victorian past. As in all questions where nonconformity carries heavy penalties, great numbers of males are naturally reticent to articulate their dissent from the "favors" heaped upon them. But, occasionally, usually in the more acceptable guise of "explaining" to women how to give artificially contrived sustenance to the male ego, the plea can be discerned. John Kord Lagemann provides an excellent example in an article in *Redbook* entitled "The Male Sex": "The average male would be happy to drop the he-man pose if he didn't feel it would mean losing face as a man. It isn't because of his male instinct that he shies away from washing dishes, changing diapers, working under a woman boss or enjoying string quartets and modern art. It's because he suspects that other people, including his wife — despite their protestations to the contrary — still look on these chores and pastimes as 'unnatural' for a man."

We have all become so preoccupied with the "usurpation of the male's authority by the female" that we have neglected to analyze the vestigial presumption of that self-awarded authority; in so doing, we have also neglected to be outraged and shocked by the equally widespread assumption that men are in reality inferior human beings who have to be "propped up." The institutional acceptance of woman as a second-class human being carries its own dynamic which inadvertently must, of necessity, present men as flagrantly unintelligent and somewhat dehumanized creatures. In "Making Marriage Work," featured in a widely read woman's magazine, the professor-analyst author tackled what might seem, to the excessively civilized, a resolved question: *Should a Husband Strike His Wife?*" Bending to enlightenment, the writer opined, "It is impossible to condone such behavior." He then went on, however, to modify that bit of radical abandon by advising his readers that the "provocation" by wives was undoubtedly far greater than they realized. He offered the following directions to wives as to how best avoid their partially deserved beatings: "Gauge his mood; avoid arguments; indulge his whims; help him relax; share his burdens; keep love alive."

Now it must be clear that any group of human beings who *could* impose such saintly behavior on themselves at will, presumably after their own fairly exhausting and temper-rousing workdays, would be a superior lot indeed. But rather more outrageous is the assumption that men must be placated, outwitted, humored, and patronized like the family pet of whom we do not expect rationality and emotional control. One wonders how the writer supposes the criminal charge of "assault" ever found its way to the law books (evolved as it was by *male* representatives of social authority who could not apparently find within *themselves* justification for such behavior regardless of the sex of the victim).

Many men have cast wary eyes at the false crutches handed their sex: Shakespeare toyed freely with pompous assumptions of masculine superiority in several of his works; Mark Twain in his witticisms; Zola in his novels; Frederick Douglass from the antislavery podium; August Bebel in his great studies; John Stuart Mill in his essays; Whitman in his poetry; William Godwin in the stuff of his life and his writings; Karl Marx in the development of his economic theories; and, of course, in our own time, George Bernard Shaw in almost every wise and irreverent word he wrote. None of these figures found themselves diminished by an impending "threat" of the equality of women; most of them took the position that its accomplishment bode but another aspect of the liberation of *men*, in all senses of that mighty word.

It required, in fact, the industrial revolution and the winds of *égalité* from the American and French revolutions before history could thrust forward a woman to set down the case for the "Rights of Woman" in 1792. That the brilliant Jacobin Englishwoman Mary Wollstonecraft did so raised all the stormy outrage that the conservative thinkers of her time, male and female, could muster. That the outrage has lingered and all but obscured her name and her book is a revealing indicator of the unfinished character of what is sometimes called, improperly, the "sexual revolution."

It is worth the digression to remark that whole generations have come to maturity believing that "feminists," upper- or lowercase, were strident, ludicrous creatures in incongruous costumes of feathered hats and oversized bloomers, who marched about, mainly through the saloons of the land, conking poor, peaceful, beer-guzzling males over the head. The image successfully erases a truer and more cogent picture. In deed and oratory, in their recognition of direct political action as opposed to parlor and bedroom wheedling of husbands and fathers as the true key to social transformation, American Feminist leaders, in particular, set a path that a grateful society will undoubtedly, in time, celebrate. The scope of their understanding of the evils of their times is summed up magnificently in a portion of a speech by Susan B. Anthony as she addressed the court where she was being sentenced to jail for voting in the state of New York in 1879: "Your denial of my right to vote is the denial of my right of consent as one of the governed, the denial of my right of representation as one of the taxed, the denial of my right to a trial by a jury of my peers. . . . But, yesterday, the same man-made forms of law declared it a crime punishable with a $1,000 fine and six months' imprisonment, for you, or me, or any of us, to give a cup of cold water, a crust of bread, or a night's shelter to a panting fugitive as he was tracking his way to Canada. And every man or woman in whose veins coursed a drop of human sympathy violated that wicked law, reckless of consequences, and was justified in doing so. As then, the slaves who got their freedom must yet take it over, or under, or through the unjust forms of law, precisely so now must women, to get their right to a voice in this Government, take it; I have taken mine, and mean to take it at every possible opportunity."

This thrilling American patriot, not less than the Franklin radicals or the 16 Jeffersonian democrats — and like scores of other Feminists — put her comfort, and in some brutal instances her very life, upon the line in order to do no more and certainly no less than enlarge the Constitutional promises of the American Republic to include the largest numbers of its people of both sexes. As is apparent from the text of her speech she and the other leaders of the Feminist movement (Lucretia Mott, Elizabeth Cady Stanton, Sojourner Truth, and Harriet Tubman, among many) gave equally of their energies to the greatest issue of their time, the antislavery struggle, as their spiritual descendants were to give theirs, in another period, to prison reform, the eradication of illiteracy, conservation, and the crowning achievement of the abolition of child labor. We might well long for the day when the knowledge of the debt all society owes to organized womanhood in bringing the human race closer together, not pushing it farther apart, will still the laughter in the throats of the now uninformed.

Nonetheless, the lingering infamy in which "feminism" is generally held helps to explain the mystery of the widespread notion that the emancipation of the modern American woman is an accomplished fact, despite all evidence that she does not universally get "equal pay for equal work," that she is discouraged flatly in many occupations and government posts, and that her advance into executive positions is held stringently in check. It also helps to explain the eager mythology of the "tyranny of women" who allegedly rule over the home and even the wealth of the nation. In his book *America as a Civilization*, Max Lerner replies to the myth thusly: "The catch is that women hold their purchasing power largely as wives and have acquired their wealth mainly as widows; economically they are disbursing agents, not principals. . . . The real control of the wealth is in the hands of male trustees, lawyers and bankers. Few women are directors of big corporations, just as there are few who form government policies. . . . The minority of women who are powerful in their ownership of wealth are functionless with respect to their wealth, because they lack strategic control of it."

As for the "tyranny of Mom," Mom has been effectively toppled from her pedestal without society taking a second look to discover, if all those dreadful things are really true about her, *how* she got that way. Our culture has been slow to assume responsibility for ordinary women who have been told, starting with the cradle, that home and husband and children will be the sources of all reward in life, the foundations of all true happiness; it has had almost nothing to say about what she should do with herself when the children are grown and her husband is exhausted and bored with excessive attention, preoccupied as he is with other aspects of the world. Mah-jongg and matinees in the city seem to her to lack purpose, and, whether we like it or not, that is the thing that human beings tend to crave: purpose.

The glaring fact is that Mom's life needs liberation as much as everyone else's. To say so is to be thought of as attacking the "bedrock of our way of life" and all of that, but it must be said. Mom must be allowed to think of herself, as Simone de Beauvoir has insisted brilliantly, as a human being first and a mother second. Housewives insist on identifying themselves, to the frustration of the experts, as *"only* housewives" because, apparently, they perceive that housework and care of the family is but humankind's necessity of function: things requisite to existence; essentials which should permit us to . . . something else. We do not live to wash our faces and eat our meals, we wash our faces and eat our meals in order to participate in the world: in the classroom, in the factory, in the office, in the shop, in the national and international halls of government, in the scientific laboratory and in the studios where the arts are created. *The Feminists did not create the housewife's dissatisfaction with her lot — the Feminists came from out of the only place they could have come — the housewives of the world!* Satisfaction for the housewife, then, lies not in a new program of propaganda to exalt what remains, and always will remain, drudgery; but in the continued effort to reduce it to a hardly perceptible (if ever necessary) interruption in the pursuit of productive labors and creative expression. Satisfaction lies in allowing and encouraging men to freely assume more and more equal relationship with their children and their wives. The argument against this is difficult to understand since the more interesting the lives of the parents (both parents), the more interesting we have every right to expect future generations to be.

One area of the national life where the estate of woman is certainly never   20
debated, and may be passed over quickly, is in the newest crop of "For Men Only" magazines where the whole thing has been resolved by reducing the entire relationship between men and women to a long and rather boring (not to add mechanical) tableaux of simple-minded and degrading animal essences. There, Woman the Child, Woman the Animal, Woman Upside-down-and-naked, Woman the Harem Fantasy — is replete with no conflict and no aspiration, the sex-object of men who cannot fathom the nature of their own delusions. The symptomatic fumes of Romanesque decay which exude from the same pages, where some of the world's most established writers are obliged, like musicians in a whorehouse, to appear between "playmates," is stultifying. To say so, however, is not to long for a new wave of "banning": that unfortunate practice always ends up by lynching the brave new thoughts in the world and merely covering up our social filth. It is to long for a deeper appraisal of what we really want for ourselves and our children; to long for a cultural climate where Mrs. Roosevelt's image will be projected to our young men and women with more regularity than the current courtesans.

It is, finally, a longing that another generation of girls will not have to grow up under a certain pragmatism which insists that men do not like "brainy" women. That notion is a terrible cheat to all, and one of the most belittling indictments of men. Girls are better taught to "reach for the stars" even in the matter of seeking or accepting a mate. The grim possibility is that she who "hides her brains" will, more than likely, end up with a mate who is only equal to a woman with "hidden brains" or none at all. That hardly gives the children of such a union a robust start in life. To hide one's mental capacity is a personality disfigurement which is even more grotesque than to flaunt it — which, at least, boasts *pride.*

There *are* men who find love affairs of stature enough. Men who neither desire nor tolerate affected vacuity: who wish mutuality and stimulation. In this writer's experience *those* are the exciting men; they exist. A woman who is willing to be herself and pursue her own potentials — it is time it was said — runs not so much the risk of loneliness as the challenge of exposure to more interesting men — and people in general.

There are, it is true, perhaps larger numbers of men who have mistaken WOMAN herself for the antagonism between the sexes. And, heaven knows, women passionately, often hysterically, feed the delusion. But it *is* a delusion: it is the codified barriers *between* the sexes that cause the trouble. Accordingly, some men are overwhelmed by the pressures upon their "masculinity" as they understand it, and move through life in perpetual states of agitation because, they are certain, of their persecution by women. Some of them, a few, become pathological woman-haters and proceed to hate all women: those in their "place" at home; and those "out of it." They have hatred of the women who will not sleep with them and hatred for those who will. Their hostility should not be met with hostility: they are frightened and pathetic human beings, as much caught in a social trap as their feminine counterparts who, it is true, get more and uglier attention in popular conversation and literature. These people are the most extreme victims of the *inequality* between the sexes; the rest of us are victims in other ways. In their situation, a member of the opposite sex does not have to open his or her mouth, they just have to *be* and they have offended. The weight is put upon our shoulders when we are hardly out of the womb, *all* of us, and it is more than a little tragic, this exaggerated sense of alienation from one another that we are taught. Having paid such terrible prices for it, need we despair for its passing?

With the barriers should go many of the arbitrary definitions structured into 24 our very language from out of the past: the classification of occupations, activities, roles by gender; the built-in assumption of maleness in certain words; the adjectives which still confuse and confine us in our thinking and make it possible for serious sociologists and psychologists to draw conclusions from "masculine-feminine" charts which are based on nothing other than conditioned concepts of what is "natural" (for whom?). Within that scale, male journalists, firemen and policemen have scored "less masculine" than other men, such as laborers, because of their occupational interest in "womanish" concerns like the human condition and saving lives! Among women, domestic servants score the highest "femininity" ratings of all — because of their demonstrated "interest" in cleaning house!

At the heart of this incredible mish-mosh of nonsense is the time-honored but perfectly silly habit of attributing to a given set of universally human capacities a qualification which implies that they are unique to one sex, race, or culture. (It is by that outrage that the people of Europe and their descendants in North America innocently go on speaking of objective adjectives such as "modern" or even "progressive" as if they were virtually synonymous with the geographical noun "the West" — to the wonder (and fury) of at least two-thirds of the world. Modern ideas, one notes, function elsewhere and, in some instances, these days especially, with greater acceleration. It was not "the West," after all, that first punctured space and it is the women of Ghana who vote and the women of Switzerland who do not.) Thus, women who seek objective fulfillment as people are not trying to be "men" (or good or bad "imitations" of them) — they are trying to be successful human beings.

Finally, it is not to be doubted that our clinging to the habits of the past gives all of us some comfort in this thus-far-unexplained universe: it is always reassuring to think that our ancestors "did it" the same way. But in medicine the price of dogged superstition has too often been death, and in all human affairs there comes a time — to let go. With regard to the sexual connotations of words, can we all not think of what a dream will be realized for the race when the noun "soldier," for example, ceases to conjure up romantic notions of masculinity, but will instead have been unsexed and (at long last) put in its true place in history by the more accurate associations it recalls: "tragedy . . . the organized waste of human life and potential"?

None of this, we can rest easy, will dissipate the *true* distinction between the sexes: that will not happen because nobody *desires* for it to happen. The French have remarked on that matter for all time — for which one need only add another *"Vive!"*

● PERSONAL RESPONSE ●

At the time this essay was written, Hansberry was correct in asserting that "feminism" was not highly regarded. How is feminism viewed today? Do you regard yourself as a feminist? Why or why not?

● QUESTIONS FOR DISCUSSION ●

1. What is the "peril" (paragraph 1) that many speakers and writers were addressing at the time Hansberry wrote this essay?

2. In paragraphs 13–16, Hansberry gives examples of both men and women in the past who have championed the equality of the sexes. How many of those people are you familiar with? Are the names of the men she lists in paragraph 13 more familiar to you than the names of the women in the subsequent paragraphs? In class discussion, see how many of the people Hansberry names you can identify.

3. According to Hansberry, what is the effect on relationships between men and women of "For Men Only" magazines (paragraph 20)? Do you agree with her? Explain your answer.

4. Give examples of the language Hansberry refers to in paragraph 24. Is what Hansberry says about language and "masculine-feminine" divisions still true today? Discuss how such language has changed in the past thirty years and how it is still the same. Do the same for definitions of masculinity and femininity.

5. What parallels does Hansberry draw between the burdens of male superiority and those of other "superior" groups (paragraph 25)?

6. According to Hansberry, what stereotyped expectations about their behavior has society imposed on both men and women and how have those stereotypes prevented both men and women from being whole persons?

7. How do stereotyped assumptions about behavior put barriers between the sexes?

8. What important difference between the sexes does Hansberry have no desire to change?

● WRITING TOPICS ●

1. Analyze the extent to which messages about appropriate sex-role behavior—from family, friends, or popular culture—have limited or shaped your own behavior or plans for the future.

2. Based on your own observations, respond to Hansberry's discussion of the widely held view that men do not like "brainy" women by exploring the ways in which each sex views the other. For instance, are the males you know attracted to or threatened by bright women? Do bright females you know ever try to cover up the fact that they have brains? Conversely, are women attracted to or threatened by bright men? Do bright men have to hide their intelligence?

3. Read about any of the following women mentioned in Hansberry's essay and write a report on who she was and what she accomplished: Susan B. Anthony, Lucretia Mott, Eleanor Roosevelt, Elizabeth Cady Stanton, Sojournor Truth, or Harriet Tubman.

INTERPERSONAL RELATIONSHIPS

●

ADDITIONAL WRITING SUGGESTIONS

1. Describe the relationships you have observed among your friends and classmates. You might, for example, compare two couples you know in terms of their length of time together, how committed they are to one another, and the benefits they derive from one another's company. Or, you might construct a general classification of relationships on the basis of those criteria.

2. After interviewing people from a generation other than your own, compare your own generation's attitude toward relationships between the sexes with those of the people you interviewed. How have they changed? How are they the same?

3. Survey the images of both men and women in magazine advertising by comparing ads in "women's magazines" with those in "men's magazines." What products are advertised in each? What images of women and men are projected in the ads?

4. Write an essay on the subject of sex-role stereotyping on the basis of what you have observed of your friends and acquaintances. Consider to what extent sex-role expectations actually do exist and whether or not the men and women you know conform to those expectations.

5. Explain your own attitudes toward relationships, love, marriage, and/or your future.

4

SEARCHING FOR A PLACE

ROOTLESSNESS

●

DAVID MORRIS

David Morris is co-director of the Institute for Local Self-Reliance, located in Washington, D.C., and an editorial columnist for the St. Paul Pioneer Press-Dispatch. *He has written a book,* The New City States *(1983), and is co-author, with Karl Hess, of* Neighborhood Power: The New Localism *(1975). A regular contributor to the* Utne Reader, *he wrote the following essay for the May/June 1990 issue of that magazine. In it, Morris cites the effects on businesses and neighborhoods of the lack of connectedness among Americans and offers suggestions for restoring deeper roots among people.*

Americans are a rootless people. Each year one in six of us changes residences; one in four changes jobs. We see nothing troubling in these statistics. For most of us, they merely reflect the restless energy that made America great. A nation of immigrants, unsurprisingly, celebrates those willing to pick up stakes and move on: the frontiersman, the cowboy, the entrepreneur, the corporate raider.

Rootedness has never been a goal of public policy in the United States. In the 1950s and 1960s local governments bulldozed hundreds of inner city neighborhoods, all in the name of urban renewal. In the 1960s and 1970s court-ordered busing forced tens of thousands of children to abandon their neighborhood schools, all in the interest of racial harmony. In the 1980s a wave of hostile takeovers shuffled hundreds of billions of dollars of corporate assets, all in the pursuit of economic efficiency.

Hundreds of thousands of informal gathering spots that once nurtured community across the country have disappeared. The soda fountain and lunch counter are gone. The branch library is an endangered species. Even the number of neighborhood taverns is declining. In the 1940s, 90 percent of beer and spirits was consumed in public places. Today only 30 percent is.

This privatization of American public life is most apparent to overseas 4 visitors. "After four years here, I still feel more of a foreigner than in any other place in the world I have been," one well-traveled woman told Ray Oldenburg, the author of the marvelous new book about public gathering spots, *The Great Good Place* (1990, Paragon House). "There is no contact between the various households, we rarely see the neighbors and certainly do not know any of them."

The woman contrasts this with her life in Europe. "In Luxembourg, however, we would frequently stroll down to one of the local cafés in the evening and there pass a very congenial few hours in the company of the local fireman, dentist, bank employee, or whoever happened to be there at the time."

In most American cities, zoning laws prohibit mixing commerce and residence. The result is an overreliance on the car. Oldenburg cites the experience of a couple who had lived in a small house in Vienna and a large one in Los Angeles: "In Los Angeles we are hesitant to leave our sheltered home in order to visit friends or to participate in cultural or entertainment events because every such outing involves a major investment of time and nervous strain in driving long distances. In Vienna everything, opera, theaters, shops, cafés, are within easy walking distance."

Shallow roots weaken our ties in the neighborhood and workplace. The average blue-collar worker receives only seven days' notice before losing his or her job, only two days when not backed by a union. The *Whole Earth Review* unthinkingly echoes this lack of connectedness when it advises its readers to "first visit an electronics store near you and get familiar with the features—then compare price and shop mail order via [an] 800 number."

This lack of connectedness breeds a costly instability in American life. In business, when owners have no loyalty to workers, workers have no loyalty to owners. Quality of work suffers. Visiting Japanese management specialists point to our labor turnover rate as a key factor in our relative economic decline. In the pivotal electronics industry, for example, our turnover rate is four times that of Japan's.

American employers respond to declining sales and profit margins by cutting what they regard as their most expendable resource: employees. In Japan, corporate accounting systems consider labor a fixed asset. Japanese companies spend enormous amounts of money training workers. "They view that training as an investment, and they don't want to let the investment slip away," Martin K. Starr of Columbia University recently told *Business Week*. Twenty percent of the work force, the core workers in major industrial companies, have lifetime job security in Japan.

Rootlessness in the neighborhood also costs us dearly. Neighborliness saves money, a fact we often overlook because the transactions of strong, rooted neighborhoods take place outside of the money economy.

- Neighborliness reduces crime. People watch the streets where children play and know who the strangers are.
- Neighborliness saves energy. In the late 1970s Portland, Oregon, discovered it could save 5 percent of its energy consumption simply by reviving the corner grocery store. No longer would residents in need of a carton of milk or a loaf of bread have to drive to a shopping mall.
- Neighborliness lowers the cost of health care. "It is cruel and unusual punishment to send someone to a nursing home when they are not sick," says Dick Ladd, head of Oregon's Senior Services. But when we don't know our neighbors we can't rely on them. Society picks up the tab. In 1987 home-based care cost $230 a month in Oregon compared to $962 per month for nursing home care.

Psychoanalyst and author Erich Fromm saw a direct correlation between the decline in the number of neighborhood bartenders and the rise in the number of psychiatrists. "Sometimes you want to go where everybody knows your name," goes the apt refrain of the popular TV show *Cheers*. Once you poured out your troubles over a nickel beer to someone who knew you and your family. And if you got drunk, well, you could walk home. Now you drive cross town and pay $100 an hour to a stranger for emotional relief.

The breakdown of community life may explain, in part, why the three best-selling drugs in America treat stress: ulcer medication (Tagamet), hypertension (Inderal), tranquilizer (Valium).

American society has evolved into a cultural environment where it is ever   16
harder for deep roots to take hold. What can we do to change this?

- **Rebuild walking communities.**   Teach urban planners that overde-pendence on transportation is a sign of failure in a social system. Impose the true costs of the car on its owners. Recent studies indicate that to do so would raise the cost of gasoline by as much as $2 a gallon. Recently Stockholm declared war on cars by imposing a $50 a month fee for car owners, promising to increase the fee until the city was given back to pedestrians and mass transit.

- **Equip every neighborhood with a library, a coffeehouse, a diver-sified shopping district, and a park.**

- **Make rootedness a goal of public policy.**   In the 1970s a Vermont land use law, for example, required an economic component to environ-mental impact statements. In at least one case, a suburban shopping mall was denied approval because it would undermine existing city businesses. In Berkeley, citizens voted two to one to permit commercial rent con-trol in neighborhoods whose independently owned businesses were threatened by gentrification.

- **Reward stability and continuity.**   Today, if a government seizes prop-   20
erty it pays the owner the market price. Identical homes have identical value, even if one is home to a third-generation family, while the other is occupied by a new tenant. Why not pay a premium, say 50 percent above the current market price, for every 10 years the occupant has lived there? Forty years of residence would be rewarded with compensation four times greater than the market price. The increment above the market price should go not to the owner but to the occupant, if the two are not the same. By favoring occupants over owners, this policy not only rewards neighborliness, but promotes social justice. By raising the overall costs of dislocation, it also discourages development that undermines rootedness.

- **Prohibit hostile takeovers.**   Japanese, German, and Swedish corpo-rations are among the most competitive and innovative in the world. But in these countries hostile takeovers are considered unethical business practices or are outlawed entirely.

- **Encourage local and employee ownership.**   Protecting existing management is not the answer if that management is not locally rooted.

Very few cities have an ongoing economic campaign to promote local ownership despite the obvious advantages to the community. Employee ownership exists in some form in more than 5,000 U.S. companies, but in only a handful is that ownership significant.

● **And above all, correct our history books.** America did not become a wealthy nation because of rootlessness, but in spite of it. A multitude of natural resources across an expansive continent and the arrival of tens of millions of skilled immigrants furnished us enormous advantages. We could overlook the high social costs of rootlessness. This is no longer true.

Instability is not the price we must pay for progress. Loyalty, in the plant 24
and the neighborhood, does not stifle innovation. These are lessons we've ignored too long. More rooted cultures such as Japan and Germany are now out-competing us in the marketplace, and in the neighborhood. We would do well to learn the value of community.

● PERSONAL RESPONSE ●

Discuss your own sense of connectedness to or disconnectedness from your community or neighborhood. Do you feel strong ties to it? Do you plan to return to the place you grew up to establish your career or find a job, or do you intend to move somewhere else? Explain your answer.

● QUESTIONS FOR DISCUSSION ●

1. What examples of rootlessness does Morris give?

2. How does Morris account for Americans' widespread acceptance of rootlessness as a way of life?

3. In what ways does rootlessness undermine the economy, according to Morris?

4. How does rootlessness affect the quality of American lives, according to Morris?

5. What is the effect of the repetition of the word "neighborliness" in paragraphs 10–13?

6. Comment on the suggestions Morris makes for deepening roots and improving American business and community connectedness. Which do you think would be effective? Which do you think would be difficult to carry out?

● WRITING TOPICS ●

1. In his essay, Morris implies that the Japanese way of running factories and businesses is better than the American way. Do you agree with him? Are there businesses in America that nurture employee welfare and build employee loyalty? Write an essay in which you either agree or disagree with Morris's views on this issue.

2. Describe your own neighborhood in terms of the relationships among people who live there and your own ties to or disconnectedness from it.

3. Write an essay about a town you know of that has a strong community spirit. What accounts for that spirit? What activities, events, and/or goals define the character of that community?

KIDS IN THE MALL
GROWING UP CONTROLLED

●

WILLIAM SEVERINI KOWINSKI

William Severini Kowinski has published articles in the New York Times Magazine, American Film, Esquire, *and* West, *among others. The essay reprinted here is from his first book,* The Malling of America: An Inside Look at the Great Consumer Paradise *(1985), an examination of the reasons why teenagers hang out in shopping malls and the effects that doing so might have on them.*

> Butch heaved himself up and loomed over the group. "Like it was different for me," he piped. "My folks used to drop me off at the shopping mall every morning and leave me all day. It was like a big free baby-sitter, you know? One night they never came back for me. Maybe they moved away. Maybe there's some kind of a Bureau of Missing Parents I could check with."
>
> — Richard Peck
> *Secrets of the Shopping Mall,*
> a novel for teenagers

From his sister at Swarthmore, I'd heard about a kid in Florida whose mother picked him up after school every day, drove him straight to the mall, and left him there until it closed—all at his insistence. I'd heard about a boy in Washington who, when his family moved from one suburb to another, pedaled his bicycle five miles every day to get back to his old mall, where he once belonged.

These stories aren't unusual. The mall is a common experience for the majority of American youth; they have probably been going there all their lives. Some ran within their first large open space, saw their first fountain, bought their first toy, and read their first book in a mall. They may have smoked their first cigarette or first joint or turned them down, had their first kiss or lost their virginity in the mall parking lot. Teenagers in America now spend more time in the mall than anywhere else but home and school. Mostly it is their choice, but some of that mall time is put in as the result of two-paycheck and single-parent households, and the lack of other viable alternatives. But are these kids being harmed by the mall?

I wondered first of all what difference it makes for adolescents to experience so many important moments in the mall. They are, after all, at play in the fields of its little world and they learn its ways; they adapt to it and make it adapt to them. It's here that these kids get their street sense, only it's mall sense. They are learning the ways of a large-scale artificial environment: its subtleties and flexibilities, its particular pleasures and resonances, and the attitudes it fosters.

The presence of so many teenagers for so much time was not something 4 mall developers planned on. In fact, it came as a big surprise. But kids became a fact of mall life very early, and the International Council of Shopping Centers found it necessary to commission a study, which they published along with a guide to mall managers on how to handle the teenage incursion.

The study found that "teenagers in suburban centers are bored and come to the shopping centers mainly as a place to go. Teenagers in suburban centers spent more time fighting, drinking, littering, and walking than did their urban counterparts, but presented fewer overall problems." The report observed that "adolescents congregated in groups of two to four and predominantly at locations selected by them rather than management." This probably had something to do with the decision to install game arcades, which allow management to channel these restless adolescents into naturally contained areas away from major traffic points of adult shoppers.

The guide concluded that mall management should tolerate and even encourage the teenage presence because, in the words of the report, "The vast majority support the same set of values as does shopping center management." *The same set of values* means simply that mall kids are already preprogrammed to be consumers and that the mall can put the finishing touches to them as hard-core, lifelong shoppers just like everybody else. That, after all, is what the mall is about. So it shouldn't be surprising that in spending a lot of time there, adolescents find little that challenges the assumption that the goal of life is to make money and buy products, or that just about everything else in life is to be used to serve those ends.

Growing up in a high-consumption society already adds inestimable pressure to kids' lives. Clothes consciousness has invaded the grade schools, and popularity is linked with having the best, newest clothes in the currently acceptable styles. Even what they read has been affected. "Miss [Nancy] Drew wasn't obsessed with her wardrobe," noted *The Wall Street Journal*. "But today the mystery in teen fiction for girls is what outfit the heroine will wear next." Shopping has become a survival skill and there is certainly no better place to learn it than the mall, where its importance is powerfully reinforced and certainly never questioned.

The mall as a university of suburban materialism, where Valley Girls and 8 Boys from coast to coast are educated in consumption, has its other lessons in this era of change in family life and sexual mores and their economic and social ramifications. The plethora of products in the mall, plus the pressure on teens to buy them, may contribute to the phenomenon that psychologist David Elkind calls "the hurried child": kids who are exposed to too much of the adult world too quickly, and must respond with a sophistication that belies their still-tender emotional development. Certainly the adult products marketed for children — form-fitting designer jeans, sexy tops for preteen girls — add to the social pressure to look like an adult, along with the home-grown need to understand adult finances (why mothers must work) and adult emotions (when parents divorce).

Kids spend so much time at the mall partly because their parents allow it and even encourage it. The mall is safe, it doesn't seem to harbor any unsavory activities, and there is adult supervision; it is, after all, a controlled environment. So the temptation, especially for working parents, is to let the mall be their babysitter. At least the kids aren't watching TV. But the mall's role as a surrogate mother may be more extensive and more profound.

Karen Lansky, a writer living in Los Angeles, has looked into the subject and she told me some of her conclusions about the effects on its teenaged denizens of the mall's controlled and controlling environment. "Structure is the dominant idea, since true 'mall rats' lack just that in their home lives," she said, "and adolescents about to make the big leap into growing up crave more structure than our modern society cares to acknowledge." Karen pointed out some of the elements malls supply that kids used to get from their families, like warmth (Strawberry Shortcake dolls and similar cute and cuddly merchandise), old-fashioned mothering ("We do it all for you," the fast-food slogan), and even home cooking (the "homemade" treats at the food court).

The problem in all this, as Karen Lansky sees it, is that while families nurture children by encouraging growth through the assumption of responsibility and then by letting them rest in the bosom of the family from the rigors of growing up, the mall as a structural mother encourages passivity and consumption, as long as the kid doesn't make trouble. Therefore all they learn about becoming adults is how to act and how to consume.

Kids are in the mall not only in the passive role of shoppers — they also work 12 there, especially as fast-food outlets infiltrate the mall's enclosure. There they learn how to hold a job and take responsibility, but still within the same value context. When *CBS Reports* went to Oak Park Mall in suburban Kansas City, Kansas, to tape part of their hour-long consideration of malls, "After the Dream Comes True," they interviewed a teenaged girl who worked in a fast-food outlet there. In a sequence that didn't make the final program, she described the major goal of her present life, which was to perfect the curl on top of the ice-cream cones that were her store's specialty. If she could do that, she would be moved from the lowly soft-drink dispenser to the more prestigious ice-cream division, the curl on top of the status ladder at her restaurant. These are the achievements that are important at the mall.

Other benefits of such jobs may also be overrated, according to Laurence D. Steinberg of the University of California at Irvine's social ecology department, who did a study on teenage employment. Their jobs, he found, are generally simple, mindlessly repetitive, and boring. They don't really learn anything, and the jobs don't lead anywhere. Teenagers also work primarily with other teenagers; even their supervisors are often just a little older than they are. "Kids need to spend time with adults," Steinberg told me. "Although they get benefits from peer relationships, without parents and other adults it's one-sided socialization. They hang out with each other, have age-segregated jobs, and watch TV."

Perhaps much of this is not so terrible or even so terribly different. Now that they have so much more to contend with in their lives, adolescents probably need more time to spend with other adolescents without adult impositions, just to sort things out. Though it is more concentrated in the mall (and therefore perhaps a clearer target), the value system there is really the dominant one of the whole society. Attitudes about curiosity, initiative, self-expression, empathy, and disinterested learning aren't necessarily made in the mall; they are mirrored there, perhaps a bit more intensely—as through a glass brightly.

Besides, the mall is not without its educational opportunities. There are bookstores, where there is at least a short shelf of classics at great prices, and other books from which it is possible to learn more than how to do sit-ups. There are tools, from hammers to VCRs, and products, from clothes to records, that can help the young find and express themselves. There are older people with stories, and places to be alone or to talk one-on-one with a kindred spirit. And there is always the passing show.

The mall itself may very well be an education about the future. I was struck   16 with the realization, as early as my first forays into Greengate [Mall], that the mall is only one of a number of enclosed and controlled environments that are part of the lives of today's young. The mall is just an extension, say of those large suburban schools—only there's Karmelkorn instead of chem lab, the ice rink instead of the gym: It's high school without the impertinence of classes.

Growing up, moving from home to school to the mall—from enclosure to enclosure, transported in cars—is a curiously continuous process, without much in the way of contrast or contact with unenclosed reality. Places must tend to blur into one another. But whatever differences and dangers there are in this, the skills these adolescents are learning may turn out to be useful in their later lives. For we seem to be moving inexorably into an age of preplanned and regulated environments, and this is the world they will inherit.

Still, it might be better if they had more of a choice. One teenaged girl confessed to *CBS Reports* that she sometimes felt she was missing something by hanging out at the mall so much. "But I'm here," she said, "and this is what I have."

● PERSONAL RESPONSE ●

Where did you hang out when you were growing up? Were your reasons for hanging out there the same as those given in the essay? If not, what were your reasons?

● QUESTIONS FOR DISCUSSION ●

1. What purpose does the quotation that opens the essay serve? How is it connected to the article itself?

2. Who is Kowinski's audience: teenagers, the parents of teenagers, or some other general audience?

3. What positive effects of spending so much of their time in shopping malls does Kowinski name?

4. What are the negative effects of spending so much time in shopping malls, according to Kowinski?

5. In addition to the effects of the controlled environment of malls on the teenagers who hang out in them, Kowinski also explores the effects on teens of having jobs in malls. What potential harm does he see in mall jobs?

6. What is Kowinski's opinion of the value system taught and reinforced by the mall? What values do you think Kowinski would rather see instilled in young people?

7. How does Kowinski answer the question he poses at the end of paragraph 2?

● WRITING TOPICS ●

1. Many adults also find shopping malls attractive. Compare and/or contrast the appeal of malls to teenagers and their appeal to adults.

2. Agree or disagree with Kowinski's statement that our high-consumption society adds great pressure to kids' lives. Cite specific effects — good or bad, depending on your position — of consumerism on teenagers.

3. Agree or disagree with Kowinski's statement in paragraph 6 that "the goal of life is to make money and buy products."

SLOW DESCENT INTO HELL

●

Jon D. Hull

Jon D. Hull has worked at Time *magazine as a Los Angeles correspondent and as bureau chief in Jerusalem. To gather material for this essay, which appeared in* Time *in February 1987, Hull spent a week in Philadelphia living with the homeless. His brief profiles of the people he met that week vividly dramatize their bleak existence.*

A smooth bar of soap, wrapped neatly in a white handkerchief and tucked safely in the breast pocket of a faded leather jacket, is all that keeps George from losing himself to the streets. When he wakes each morning from his makeshift bed of newspapers in the subway tunnels of Philadelphia, he heads for the rest room of a nearby bus station or McDonald's and begins an elaborate ritual of washing off the dirt and smells of homelessness: first the hands and forearms, then the face and neck, and finally the fingernails and teeth. Twice a week he takes off his worn Converse high tops and socks and washes his feet in the sink, ignoring the cold stares of well-dressed commuters.

George, twenty-eight, is a stocky, round-faced former high school basketball star who once made a living as a construction worker. But after he lost his job just over a year ago, his wife kicked him out of the house. For a few weeks he lived on the couches of friends, but the friendships soon wore thin. Since then he has been on the street, starting from scratch and looking for a job. "I got to get my life back," George says after rinsing his face for the fourth time. He begins brushing his teeth with his forefinger. "If I don't stay clean," he mutters, "the world ain't even going to look me in the face. I just couldn't take that."

George lives in a world where time is meaningless and it's possible to go months without being touched by anyone but a thug. Lack of sleep, food, or conversation breeds confusion and depression. He feels himself slipping but struggles to remember what he once had and to figure out how to get it back. He rarely drinks alcohol and keeps his light brown corduroy pants and red-checked shirt meticulously clean. Underneath, he wears two other shirts to fight off the cold, and he sleeps with his large hands buried deep within his coat pockets amid old sandwiches and doughnuts from the soup kitchens and garbage cans.

Last fall he held a job for six weeks at a pizza joint, making $3.65 an hour kneading dough and clearing tables. Before work, he would take off two of his three shirts and hide them in an alley. It pleases him that no one knew he was homeless. Says George: "Sure I could have spent that money on some good drink or food, but you gotta suffer to save. You gotta have money to get out of here and I gotta get out of here." Some days he was scolded for eating too much of the food. He often worked without sleep, and with no alarm clock to wake him from the subways or abandoned tenements, he missed several days and was finally fired. He observes, "Can't get no job without a home, and you can't get a home without a job. They take one and you lose both."

George had sixty-four dollars tucked in his pocket on the evening he was beaten senseless in an alley near the Continental Trailways station. "Those damn chumps," he says, gritting his teeth, "took every goddam penny. I'm gonna kill 'em." Violence is a constant threat to the homeless. It's only a matter of time before newcomers are beaten, robbed, or raped. The young prey on the old, the big on the small, and groups attack individuals in the back alleys and subway tunnels. After it's over, there is no one to tell about the pain, nothing to do but walk away.

Behind a dumpster sits a man who calls himself Red enjoying the last drops of a bottle of wine called Wild Irish Rose. It's 1 A.M., and the thermometer hovers around 20 degrees with a biting wind. His nickname comes from a golden retriever his family once had back in Memphis, and a sparkle comes to his eyes as he recalls examples of the dog's loyalty. One day he plans to get another dog, and says, "I'm getting to the point where I can't talk to people. They're always telling me to do something or get out of their way. But a dog is different."

At thirty-five, he looks fifty, and his gaunt face carries discolored scars from the falls and fights of three years on the streets. An upper incisor is missing, and his lower teeth jut outward against his lower lip, giving the impression that he can't close his mouth. His baggy pants are about five inches too long and when he walks, their frayed ends drag on the ground. "You know something?" he asks, holding up the bottle. "I wasn't stuck to this stuff until the cold got to me. Now I'll freeze without it. I could go to Florida or someplace, but I know this town and I know who the creeps are. Besides, it's not too bad in the summer."

Finishing the bottle, and not yet drunk enough to sleep out in the cold, he gathers his blanket around his neck and heads for the subways beneath city hall, where hundreds seek warmth. Once inside, the game of cat-and-mouse begins with the police, who patrol the maze of tunnels and stairways and insist that everybody remain off the floor and keep moving. Sitting can be an invitation to trouble, and the choice between sleep and warmth becomes agonizing as the night wears on.

For the first hour, Red shuffles through the tunnels, stopping occasionally to urinate against the graffiti-covered walls. Then he picks a spot and stands for half an hour, peering out from the large hood of his coat. In the distance, the barking of German shepherds echoes through the tunnels as a canine unit patrols the darker recesses of the underground. Nearby, a young man in a ragged trench coat stands against the wall, slapping his palms against his sides muttering, "I've got to get some paperwork done. I've just got to get some paperwork done!" Red shakes his head. "Home sweet home," he says. Finally exhausted, he curls up on the littered floor, lying on his side with his hands in his pockets and his hood pulled all the way over his face to keep the rats away. He is asleep instantly.

Whack! A police baton slaps his legs and a voice booms, "Get the hell up, you're outta here. Right now!" Another police officer whacks his nightstick against a metal grating as the twelve men sprawled along the tunnel crawl to their feet. Red pulls himself up and walks slowly up the stairs to the street, never looking back.

Pausing at every pay phone to check the coin-return slots, he makes his way to a long steam grate whose warm hiss bears the acrid smell of a dry cleaner's shop. He searches for newspaper and cardboard to block the moisture but retain the heat. With his makeshift bed made, he curls up again, but the rest is short-lived. "This s.o.b. use to give off more heat," he says, staring with disgust at the grate. He gathers the newspapers and moves down the block, all the while muttering about the differences among grates. "Some are good, some are bad. I remember I was getting a beautiful sleep on this one baby and then all this honking starts. I was laying right in a damn driveway and nearly got run over by a garbage truck."

Stopping at a small circular vent shooting jets of steam, Red shakes his head and curses: "This one is too wet, and it'll go off sometimes, leaving you to freeze." Shaking now with the cold, he walks four more blocks and finds another grate, where he curls up and fishes a half-spent cigarette from his pocket. The grate is warm, but soon the moisture from the steam has soaked his newspapers and begins to gather on his clothes. Too tired to find another grate, he sets down more newspapers, throws his blanket over his head, and sprawls across the grate. By morning he is soaked. ¹²

At the St. John's Hospice for Men, close to the red neon marquees of the porno shops near city hall, a crowd begins to gather at 4 P.M. Men and women dressed in ill-fitting clothes stamp their feet to ward off the cold and keep their arms pressed against their sides. Some are drunk; others simply talk aloud to nobody in words that none can understand. Most are loners who stand in silence with the sullen expression of the tired and hungry.

A hospice worker lets in a stream of women and old men. The young men must wait until 5 P.M., and the crowd of more than two hundred are asked to form four rows behind a yellow line and watch their language. It seems an impossible task. A trembling man who goes by the name Carper cries, "What goddam row am I in!" as he pulls his red wool hat down until it covers his eyebrows. Carper has spent five to six years on the streets, and thinks he may be thirty-three. The smell of putrid wine and decaying teeth poisons his breath; the fluid running from his swollen eyes streaks his dirty cheeks before disappearing into his beard. "Am I in a goddam row? Who the hell's running the rows?" he swears. An older man with a thick gray beard informs Carper he is in Row 3 and assures him it is the best of them all. Carper's face softens into a smile; he stuffs his hands under his armpits and begins rocking his shoulders with delight.

Beds at the shelters are scarce, and fill up first with the old, the very young, and women. Young men have little hope of getting a bed, and some have even come to scorn the shelters. Says Michael Brown, twenty-four: "It stinks to high heaven in those places. They're just packed with people and when the lights go out, it's everybody for themselves." Michael, a short, self-described con man, has been living on the streets three years, ever since holding up a convenience store in Little Rock. He fled, fearing capture, but now misses the two young children he left behind. He says he is tired of the streets and plans to turn himself in to serve his time.

Michael refuses to eat at the soup kitchens, preferring to panhandle for a 16 meal: "I don't like to be around those people. It makes you feel like some sort of crazy. Before you know it, you're one of them." He keeps a tear in the left seam of his pants, just below the pocket; when he panhandles among commuters, he tells them that his subway fare fell out of his pants. When that fails, he wanders past fast-food outlets, waiting for a large group eating near the door to get up and leave. Then he snatches the remaining food off the table and heads down the street, smiling all the more if the food is still warm. At night he sleeps in the subway stations, catnapping between police rounds amid the thunder of the trains. "Some of these guys sleep right on the damn floor," he says. "Not me. I always use two newspapers and lay them out neatly. Then I pray the rats don't get me."

It was the last swig of the bottle, and the cheap red wine contained flotsam from the mouths of three men gathered in a vacant lot in northeast Philadelphia. Moments before, a homeless and dying man named Gary had vomited. The stench and nausea were dulled only by exhaustion and the cold. Gary, wheezing noisily, his lips dripping with puke, was the last to drink from the half-gallon jug of Thunderbird before passing it on, but no one seemed to care. There was no way to avoid the honor of downing the last few drops. It was an offer to share extended by those with nothing, and there was no time to think about the sores on the lips of the previous drinkers or the strange things floating in the bottle or the fact that it was daybreak and time for breakfast. It was better to drink and stay warm and forget about everything.

Though he is now dying on the streets, Gary used to be a respectable citizen. His full name is Gary Shaw, forty-eight, and he is a lifelong resident of Philadelphia and a father of three. He once worked as a precision machinist, making metal dies for casting tools. "I could work with my eyes closed," he says. "I was the best there was." But he lost his job and wife to alcohol. Now his home is an old red couch with the springs exposed in a garbage-strewn clearing amid abandoned tenements. Nearby, wood pulled from buildings burns in a fifty-five-gallon metal drum while the Thunderbird is passed around. When evening falls, Gary has trouble standing, and he believes his liver and kidneys are on the verge of failing. His thighs carry deep burn marks from sleeping on grates, and a severe beating the previous night has left bruises on his lower back and a long scab across his nose. The pain is apparent in his eyes, still brilliant blue, and the handsome features of his face are hidden beneath a layer of grime.

By 3 A.M., Gary's back pains are unbearable, and he begins rocking back and forth while the others try to keep him warm. "Ah, please God help me. I'm f---ing dying, man. I'm dying." Two friends try to wave down a patrol car. After forty-five minutes, a suspicious cop rolls up to the curb and listens impatiently to their plea: "It's not drugs, man, I promise. The guy was beat up bad and he's dying. Come on, man, you've got to take us to the hospital." The cop nods and points his thumb toward the car. As Gary screams, his two friends carefully lift him into the back seat for the ride to St. Mary Hospital.

In the emergency room, half an hour passes before a nurse appears with a 20
clipboard. Address: unknown. No insurance. After an X ray, Gary is told that a
bone in his back may be chipped. He is advised to go home, put some ice on it
and get some rest. "I don't have a goddam home!" he cries, his face twisted in
pain. "Don't you know what I am? I'm a goddam bum, that's what, and I'm
dying!" After an awkward moment, he is told to come back tomorrow and see
the radiologist. The hospital pays his cab fare back to the couch.

Gary returns in time to share another bottle of Thunderbird, and the warm
rush brings his spirits up. "What the hell are we doing in the city?" asks Ray
Kelly, thirty-seven, who was once a merchant seaman. "I know a place in
Vermont where the fishing's great and you can build a whole damn house in the
woods. There's nobody to bother you and plenty of food." Gary interrupts to
recall fishing as a boy, and the memories prior to his six years on the street come
back with crystal clarity. "You got it, man, we're all getting out of here tomorrow,"
he says with a grin. In the spirit of celebration, King, a thirty-four-year-old from
Puerto Rico, removes a tube of glue from his pocket with the care of a
sommelier, sniffs it and passes it around.

When the sun rises, Ray and King are fast asleep under a blanket on the
couch. Gary is sitting at the other end, staring straight ahead and breathing
heavily in the cold air. Curling his numb and swollen fingers around the arm of
the couch, he tries to pull himself up but fails. When another try fails, he sits
motionless and closes his eyes. Then the pain hits his back again and he starts to
cry. He won't be getting out of here today, and probably not tomorrow either.

Meanwhile, somewhere across town in the washroom of a McDonald's,
George braces for another day of job hunting, washing the streets from his face
so that nobody knows where he lives.

● PERSONAL RESPONSE ●

What is your emotional response to the plight of the homeless men depicted in this essay?
Do you feel more sympathetic to some than to others? Why?

● QUESTIONS FOR DISCUSSION ●

1. Why do you think Hull focuses on one particular city and several specific people?
   What do you think would be lost if the names, ages, and backgrounds of the homeless
   men were removed from the essay?

2. What is Hull's attitude toward the homeless? Give evidence from the text to support
   your answer.

3. How is George different from the other homeless people? How did he become homeless? How does he feel about the others? What hope does he have for his own
   future?

4. In contrast to George, what aspect of homelessness does Red illustrate? What do
   Carper and Michael (paragraphs 14–16) add to the picture of the homeless? What
   aspects of homelessness do Gary, Ray, and King illustrate (paragraphs 17–22)?

5. What survival tactics do the homeless depicted here use? How are they helped or hindered by the police and social services?

6. What conclusions can you draw about the backgrounds of homeless people in general? That is, does there seem to be a "typical" homeless person, or is virtually anyone a potential candidate for homelessness?

7. Despite their individual backgrounds, what common characteristics do the lives of the homeless have? What do you think Hull implies about the futures of most people who find themselves living on the streets?

8. Why do you think Hull begins and ends with the example of George? How does the way he orders his examples reflect the title of his essay?

● WRITING TOPICS ●

1. If you know someone who is homeless, describe that person. Explain, if possible, the circumstances that led to that person's homelessness and your feelings about him or her.

2. If you do not know anyone who is actually homeless, perhaps you know someone who lives in poverty and has the potential to become homeless. Write an essay that explains that person's circumstances and describe the conditions under which he or she might actually become homeless.

3. Offer a possible solution to the problem of the homeless in America. Or, argue that homeless people are responsible for their own fates and that they should solve their own problems.

FROM OUTSIDE, IN

●

Barbara Mellix

Barbara Mellix grew up in Greeleyville, South Carolina, moved to Pittsburgh as a young adult, and eventually earned an M.F.A. in creative writing. She currently teaches composition and fiction at the University of Pittsburgh at Greensburg. In the following essay, which first appeared in The Georgia Review *in 1987, Mellix describes what she calls the "two distinctly different languages" she grew up speaking and the struggle she had finding her own voice in her college composition classes.*

Two years ago, when I started writing this paper, trying to bring order out of chaos, my ten-year-old daughter was suffering from an acute attack of boredom. She drifted in and out of the room complaining that she had nothing to do, no one to "be with" because none of her friends were at home. Patiently I explained that I was working on something special and needed peace and quiet, and I suggested that she paint, read, or work with her computer. None of these interested her. Finally, she pulled up a chair to my desk and watched me, now and then heaving long, loud sighs. After two or three minutes (nine or ten sighs), I lost my patience. "Looka here, Allie," I said, "you too old for this kinda carryin' on. I done told you this is important. You wronger than dirt to be in here haggin' me like this and you know it. Now git on outta here and leave me off before I put my foot all the way down."

I was at home, alone with my family, and my daughter understood that this way of speaking was appropriate in that context. She knew, as a matter of fact, that it was almost inevitable; when I get angry at home, I speak some of my finest, most cherished black English. Had I been speaking to my daughter in this manner in certain other environments, she would have been shocked and probably worried that I had taken leave of my sense of propriety.

Like my children, I grew up speaking what I considered two distinctly different languages — black English and standard English (or as I thought of them then, the ordinary everyday speech of "country" coloreds and "proper" English) — and in the process of acquiring these languages, I developed an understanding of when, where, and how to use them. But unlike my children, I grew up in a world that was primarily black. My friends, neighbors, minister, teachers — almost everybody I associated with every day — were black. And we spoke to one another in our own special language: *That sho is a pretty dress you got on. If she don' soon leave me off I'm gon tell her head a mess. I was so mad I could'a pissed a blue nail. He all the time trying to low-rate somebody. Ain't that just about the nastiest thing you ever set ears on?*

Then there were the "others," the "proper" blacks, transplanted relatives 4
and one-time friends who came home from the city for weddings, funerals, and

vacations. And the whites. To these we spoke standard English. "Ain't?" my mother would yell at me when I used the term in the presence of "others." "You *know* better than that." And I would hang my head in shame and say the "proper" word.

I remember one summer sitting in my grandmother's house in Greeleyville, South Carolina, when it was full of the chatter of city relatives who were home on vacation. My parents sat quietly, only now and then volunteering a comment or answering a question. My mother's face took on a strained expression when she spoke. I could see that she was being careful to say just the right words in just the right way. Her voice sounded thick, muffled. And when she finished speaking, she would lapse into silence, her proper smile on her face. My father was more articulate, more aggressive. He spoke quickly, his words sharp and clear. But he held his proud head higher, a signal that he, too, was uncomfortable. My sisters and brothers and I stared at our aunts, uncles, and cousins, speaking only when prompted. Even then, we hesitated, formed our sentences in our minds, then spoke softly, shyly.

My parents looked small and anxious during those occasions, and I waited impatiently for our leave-taking when we would mock our relatives the moment we were out of their hearing. "Reeely," we would say to one another, flexing our wrists and rolling our eyes, "how dooo you stan' this heat? Chile, it just tooo hy*ooo*-mid for words." Our relatives had made us feel "country," and this was our way of regaining pride in ourselves while getting a little revenge in the bargain. The words bubbled in our throats and rolled across our tongues, a balming.

As a child I felt this same doubleness in uptown Greeleyville where the whites lived. "Ain't that a pretty dress you're wearing!" Toby, the town policeman, said to me one day when I was fifteen. "Thank you very much," I replied, my voice barely audible in my own ears. The words felt wrong in my mouth, rigid, foreign. It was not that I had never spoken that phrase before—it was common in black English, too—but I was extremely conscious that this was an occasion for proper English. I had taken out my English and put it on as I did my church clothes, and I felt as if I were wearing my Sunday best in the middle of the week. It did not matter that Toby had not spoken grammatically correct English. He was white and could speak as he wished. I had something to prove. Toby did not.

Speaking standard English to whites was our way of demonstrating that we knew their language and could use it. Speaking it to standard-English-speaking blacks was our way of showing them that we, as well as they, could "put on airs." But when we spoke standard English, we acknowledged (to ourselves and to others—but primarily to ourselves) that our customary way of speaking was inferior. We felt foolish, embarrassed, somehow diminished because we were ashamed to be our real selves. We were reserved, shy in the presence of those who owned and/or spoke *the* language.

My parents never set aside time to drill us in standard English. Their forms of instruction were less formal. When my father was feeling particularly expansive, he would regale us with tales of his exploits in the outside world. In almost flawless English, complete with dialogue and flavored with gestures and embellishment, he told us about his attempt to get a haircut at a white barbershop; his refusal to acknowledge one of the town merchants until the man addressed him as "Mister"; the time he refused to step off the sidewalk uptown to let some whites pass; his airplane trip to New York City (to visit a sick relative) during which the stewardesses and porters — recognizing that he was a "gentleman" — addressed him as "Sir." I did not realize then — nor, I think, did my father — that he was teaching us, among other things, standard English and the relationship between language and power.

My mother's approach was different. Often, when one of us said, "I'm gon wash off my feet," she would say, "And what will you walk on if you wash them off!" Everyone would laugh at the victim of my mother's "proper" mood. But it was different when one of us children was in a proper mood. "You think you are so superior," I said to my oldest sister one day when we were arguing and she was winning. "Superior!" my sister mocked. "You mean I am acting 'biggidy'?" My sisters and brothers sniggered, then joined in teasing me. Finally, my mother said, "Leave your sister alone. There's nothing wrong with using proper English." There was a half-smile on her face. I had gotten "uppity," had "put on airs" for no good reason. I was at home, alone with the family, and I hadn't been prompted by one of my mother's proper moods. But there was also a proud light in my mother's eyes; her children were learning English very well.

Not until years later, as a college student, did I begin to understand our ambivalence toward English, our scorn of it, our need to master it, to own and be owned by it — an ambivalence that extended to the public-school classroom. In our school, where there were no whites, my teachers taught standard English but used black English to do it. When my grammar-school teachers wanted us to write, for example, they usually said something like, "I want y'all to write five sentences that make a statement. Anybody git done before the rest can color." It was probably almost those exact words that led me to write these sentences in 1953 when I was in the second grade:

> The white clouds are pretty.
> There are only 15 people in our room.
> We will go to gym.
> We have a new poster.
> We may go out doors.

Second grade came after "Little First" and "Big First," so by then I knew the implied rules that accompanied all writing assignments. Writing was an occasion for proper English. I was not to write in the way we spoke to one another: The white clouds pretty; There ain't but 15 people in our room; We going to gym; We got a new poster; We can go out in the yard. Rather I was to use the language of "other": clouds *are*, there *are*, we *will*, we *have*, we *may*.

My sentences were short, rigid, perfunctory, like the letters my mother 12 wrote to relatives:

Dear Papa,

How are you? How is Mattie? Fine I hope. We are fine. We will come to see you Sunday. Cousin Ned will give us a ride.

Love,

Daughter

The language was not ours. It was something from outside us, something we used for special occasions.

But my coloring on the other side of that second-grade paper is different. I drew three hearts and a sun. The sun has a smiling face that radiates and envelops everything it touches. And although the sun and its world are enclosed in a circle, the colors I used — red, blue, green, purple, orange, yellow, black — indicate that I was less restricted with drawing and coloring than I was with writing standard English. My valentines were not just red. My sun was not just a yellow ball in the sky.

By the time I reached the twelfth grade, speaking and writing standard English had taken on new importance. Each year, about half of the newly graduated seniors of our school moved to large cities — particularly in the North — to live with relatives and find work. Our English teacher constantly corrected our grammar: "Not 'ain't,' but 'isn't.'" We seldom wrote papers, and even those few were usually plot summaries of short stories. When our teacher returned the papers, she usually lectured on the importance of using standard English: "I *am*; you *are*; he, she, or it *is*," she would say, writing on the chalkboard as she spoke. "How you gon git a job talking about 'I is,' or 'I isn't' or 'I ain't'?"

In Pittsburgh, where I moved after graduation, I watched my aunt and uncle — who had always spoken standard English when in Greeleyville — switch from black English to standard English to a mixture of the two, according to where they were or who they were with. At home and with certain close relatives, friends, and neighbors, they spoke black English. With those less close, they spoke a mixture. In public and with strangers, they generally spoke standard English.

In time, I learned to speak standard English with ease and to switch 16 smoothly from black to standard or a mixture, and back again. But no matter where I was, no matter what the situation or occasion, I continued to write as I had in school:

Dear Mommie,

How are you? How is everybody else? Fine I hope. I am fine. So are Aunt and Uncle. Tell everyone I said hello. I will write again soon.

Love,

Barbara

At work, at a health insurance company, I learned to write letters to customers. I studied form letters and letters written by co-workers, memorizing the phrases and the ways in which they were used. I dictated:

> Thank you for your letter of January 5. We have made the changes in your coverage you requested. Your new premium will be $150 every three months. We are pleased to have been of service to you.

In a sense, I was proud of the letters I wrote for the company: they were proof of my ability to survive in the city, the outside world—an indication of my growing mastery of English. But they also indicate that writing was still mechanical for me, something that didn't require much thought.

Reading also became a more significant part of my life during those early years in Pittsburgh. I had always liked reading, but now I devoted more and more of my spare time to it. I read romances, mysteries, popular novels. Looking back, I realize that the books I liked best were simple, unambiguous: good versus bad and right versus wrong with right rewarded and wrong punished, mysteries unraveled and all set right in the end. It was how I remembered life in Greeleyville.

Of course I was romanticizing. Life in Greeleyville had not been so very uncomplicated. Back there I had been—first as a child, then as a young woman with limited experience in the outside world—living in a relatively closed-in society. But there were implicit and explicit principles that guided our way of life and shaped our relationships with one another and the people outside—principles that a newcomer would find elusive and baffling. In Pittsburgh, I had matured, become more experienced: I had worked at three different jobs, associated with a wider range of people, married, had children. This new environment with different prescripts for living required that I speak standard English much of the time, and slowly, imperceptibly, I had ceased seeing a sharp distinction between myself and "others." Reading romances and mysteries, characterized by dichotomy, was a way of shying away from change, from the person I was becoming.

But that other part of me—that part which took great pride in my ability to hold a job writing business letters—was increasingly drawn to the new developments in my life and the attending possibilities, opportunities for even greater change. If I could write letters for a nationally known business, could I not also do something better, more challenging, more important? Could I not, perhaps, go to college and become a school teacher? For years, afraid and a little embarrassed, I did no more than imagine this different me, this possible me. But sixteen years after coming north, when my younger daughter entered kindergarten, I found myself unable—or unwilling—to resist the lure of possibility. I enrolled in my first college course: Basic Writing, at the University of Pittsburgh.

For the first time in my life, I was required to write extensively about 20 myself. Using the most formal English at my command, I wrote these sentences near the beginning of the term:

> One of my duties as a homemaker is simply picking up after others. A day seldom passes that I don't search for a mislaid toy, book, or gym shoe, etc. I change the Ty-D-Bol, fight "ring around the collar," and keep our laundry smelling "April fresh." Occasionally, I settle arguments between my children

and suggest things to do when they're bored. Taking telephone messages for my oldest daughter is my newest (and sometimes most aggravating) chore. Hanging the toilet paper roll is my most insignificant.

My concern was to use "appropriate" language, to sound as if I belonged in a college classroom. But I felt separate from the language — as if it did not and could not belong to me. I couldn't think and feel genuinely in that language, couldn't make it express what I thought and felt about being a housewife. A part of me resented, among other things, being judged by such things as the appearance of my family's laundry and toilet bowl, but in that language I could only imagine and write about a conventional housewife.

For the most part, the remainder of the term was a period of adjustment, a time of trying to find my bearing as a student in college composition class, to learn to shut out my black English whenever I composed, and to prevent it from creeping into my formulations; a time for trying to grasp the language of the classroom and reproduce it in my prose; for trying to talk about myself in that language, reach others through it. Each experience of writing was like standing naked and revealing my imperfection, my "otherness." And each new assignment was another chance to make myself over in language, reshape myself, make myself "better" in my rapidly changing image of a student in a college composition class.

But writing became increasingly unmanageable as the term progressed, and by the end of the semester, my sentences sounded like this:

> My excitement was soon dampened, however, by what seemed like a small voice in the back of my head saying that I should be careful with my long awaited opportunity. I felt frustrated and this seemed to make it difficult to concentrate.

There is a poverty of language in these sentences. By this point, I knew that the clichéd language of my Housewife essay was unacceptable, and I generally recognized trite expressions. At the same time, I hadn't yet mastered the language of the classroom, hadn't yet come to see it as belonging to me. Most notable is the lifelessness of the prose, the apparent absence of a person behind the words. I wanted those sentences — and the rest of the essay — to convey the anguish of yearning to, at once, become something more and yet remain the same. I had the sensation of being split in two, part of me going into a future the other part didn't believe possible. As that person, the student writer at that moment, I was essentially mute. I could not — in the process of composing — use the language of the old me, yet I couldn't imagine myself in the language of "others."

I found this particularly discouraging because at midsemester I had been writing in a much different way. Note the language of this introduction to an essay I had written then, near the middle of the term:

> Pain is a constant companion to the people in "Footwork." Their jobs are physically damaging. Employers are insensitive to their feelings and in many cases add to their problems. The general public wounds them further by

treating them with disgrace because of what they do for a living. Although the workers are as diverse as they are similar, there is a definite link between them. They suffer a great deal of abuse.

The voice here is stronger, more confident, appropriating terms like "physically damaging," "wounds them further," "insensitive," "diverse"—terms I couldn't have imagined using when writing about my own experience—and shaping them into sentences like "Although the workers are as diverse as they are similar, there is a definite link between them." And there is the sense of a personality behind the prose, someone who sympathizes with the workers. "The general public wounds them further by treating them with disgrace because of what they do for a living."

What caused these differences? I was, I believed, explaining other people's 24 thoughts and feelings, and I was free to move about in the language of "others" so long as I was speaking *of* others. I was unaware that I was transforming into my best classroom language my own thoughts and feelings about people whose experiences and ways of speaking were in many ways similar to mine.

The following year, unable to turn back or to let go of what had become something of an obsession with language (and hoping to catch and hold the sense of control that had eluded me in Basic Writing), I enrolled in a research writing course. I spent most of the term learning how to prepare for and write a research paper. I chose sex education as my subject and spent hours in libraries, searching for information, reading, taking notes. Then (not without messiness and often-demoralizing frustration) I organized my information into categories, wrote a thesis statement, and composed my paper—a series of paraphrases and quotations spaced between carefully constructed transitions. The process and results felt artificial, but as I would later come to realize I was passing through a necessary stage. My sentences sounded like this:

> This reserve becomes understandable with examination of who the abusers are. In an overwhelming number of cases, they are people the victims know and trust. Family members, relatives, neighbors and close family friends commit seventy-five percent of all reported sex crimes against children, and parents, parent substitutes and relatives are the offenders in thirty to eighty percent of all reported cases.[12] While assault by strangers does occur, it is less common, and is usually a single episode.[13] But abuse by family members, relatives and acquaintances may continue for an extended period of time. In cases of incest, for example, children are abused repeatedly for an average of eight years.[14] In such cases, "the use of physical force is rarely necessary because of the child's trusting, dependent relationship with the offender. The child's cooperation is often facilitated by the adult's position of dominance, an offer of material goods, a threat of physical violence, or a misrepresentation of moral standards."[15]

The completed paper gave me a sense of profound satisfaction, and I read it often after my professor returned it. I know now that what I was pleased with was the language I used and the professional voice it helped me maintain. "Use better words," my teacher had snapped at me one day after reading the notes I'd begun accumulating from my research, and slowly I began taking on the language of my sources. In my next set of notes, I used the word "vacillating"; my professor applauded. And by the time I composed the final draft, I felt at ease with terms like "overwhelming number of cases," "single episode," and "reserve," and I shaped them into sentences similar to those of my "expert" sources.

If I were writing the paper today, I would of course do some things differently. Rather than open with an anecdote — as my teacher suggested — I would begin simply with a quotation that caught my interest as I was researching my paper (and which I scribbled, without its source, in the margin of my notebook): "Truth does not do so much good in the world as the semblance of truth does evil." The quotation felt right because it captured what was for me the central idea of my paper — and expressed it in a way I would like to have said it. The anecdote, a hypothetical situation I invented to conform to the information in the paper, felt forced and insincere because it represented — to a great degree — my teacher's understanding of the essay, her idea of what in it was most significant. Improving upon my previous experiences with writing, I was beginning to think and feel in the language I used, to find my own voice in it, to sense that how one speaks influences how one means. But I was not yet secure enough, comfortable enough with the language to trust my intuition.

Now that I know that to seek knowledge, freedom, and autonomy means 28 always to be in the concentrated process of becoming — always to be venturing into new territory, feeling one's way at first, then getting one's balance, negotiating, accommodating, discovering one's self in ways that previously defined "others" — I sometimes get tired. And I ask myself why I keep on participating in this highbrow form of violence, this slamming against perplexity. But there is no real futility in the question, no hint of that part of the old me who stood outside standard English, hugging to herself a disabling mistrust of language she thought could not represent a person with her history and experience. Rather, the question represents a person who feels the consequence of her education, the weight of her possibilities as a teacher and writer and human being, a voice in society. And I would not change that person, would not give back the good burden that accompanies my growing expertise, my increasing power to shape myself in language and share that self with "others."

"To speak," says Frantz Fanon, "means to be in a position to use a certain syntax, to grasp the morphology of this or that language, but it means above all to assume a culture, to support the weight of a civilization."[1] To write means to do the same, but in a more profound sense. However, Fanon also says that to achieve mastery means to "get" in a position of power, to "grasp," to "assume." This, I have learned both as a student and subsequently as a teacher, can involve tremendous emotional and psychological conflict for those attempting to master academic discourse. Although as a beginning student writer I had a fairly good

---

[1] *Black Skin, White Masks* (1952; rpt. New York: Grove Press, 1967), pp. 17–18. [Editor's note: Frantz Fanon (1925-1961), a French West Indian psychiatrist and writer, was the intellectual leader of many twentieth-century liberation and resistance movements.]

grasp of ordinary spoken English and was proficient at what Labov calls "code-switching" (and what John Baugh in *Black Street Speech* terms "style shifting"), when I came face to face with the demands of academic writing, I grew increasingly self-conscious, constantly aware of my status as a black and a speaker of one of the many black English vernaculars — a traditional outsider. For the first time, I experienced my sense of doubleness as something menacing, a built-in enemy. Whenever I turned inward for salvation, the balm so available during my childhood, I found instead this new fragmentation which spoke to me in many voices. It was the voice of my desire to prosper, but at the same time it spoke of what I had relinquished and could not regain: a safe way of being, a state of powerlessness which exempted me from responsibility for who I was and might be. And it accused me of betrayal, of turning away from blackness. To recover balance, I had to take on the language of the academy, the language of "others." And to do that, I had to learn to imagine myself a part of the culture of that language, and therefore someone free to manage that language, to take liberties with it. Writing and rewriting, practicing, experimenting, I came to comprehend more fully the generative power of language. I discovered — with the help of some especially sensitive teachers — that through writing one can continually bring new selves into being, each with new responsibilities and difficulties, but also with new possibilities. Remarkable power, indeed. I write and continually give birth to myself.

● PERSONAL RESPONSE ●

When have you had the experience of "doubleness" that Mellix describes, the feeling of being in two different worlds at the same time and having to adjust to a context different from the one you were used to? How did the experience make you feel?

● QUESTIONS FOR DISCUSSION ●

1. Explain the title of this essay. How was Mellix "outside" and how has she moved "in"? In what way is this essay about finding one's place?

2. Summarize the differences between "the two distinctly different languages" that Mellix grew up speaking.

3. What do you think was the source of the feeling of inferiority Mellix had about her "customary way of speaking" (paragraph 8)? Was her customary way of speaking really inferior, or was she being made to feel that way by others?

4. Why do you think Mellix's teachers were so persistent in reminding students to use "proper English," even as they spoke in their own vernacular?

5. What kind of power is Mellix talking about when she writes of her father's lessons about "the relationship between language and power" (paragraph 9) and in her concluding comments on the "remarkable power" that language gives her?

6. What distinctions does Mellix make between the acts of speaking and of writing? How does Mellix apply the quotations from Frantz Fanon in paragraph 29 to her own experiences with speaking and writing?

7. How did the writing classes Mellix took in college make her confront the doubleness she had felt growing up in Greeleyville and later when she moved to Pittsburgh? How was her adjustment to academic writing compounded by her feeling of "otherness"?

8. What important point does Mellix make about language and using her own voice? How, for example, do the changes she would make now in the research paper she wrote in college reflect her understanding that "how one speaks influences how one means" (paragraph 27)?

• WRITING TOPICS •

1. Narrate an experience in which you felt very much out of place because you were in a different cultural or social context from your usual one. Give details about the experience and explain your feelings about being "other" or "outside."

2. Analyze your own writing. What difficulties have you had with composition classes? What strengths and weaknesses does your writing have? How has your writing improved over time? Do you feel comfortable with your own voice or are you still searching for it?

3. Argue for or against the position that Mellix's teachers took on the issue of "correctness." Consider to what extent writing is "an occasion for proper English" for anyone, regardless of skin color. Do you think people of diverse ethnic backgrounds should be required to write in a style that reflects a white middle-class standard?

EASTWARD

●

William Least Heat Moon

William Least Heat Moon earned critical acclaim with the publication of Blue Highways *(1982), a record of his travels throughout the country on America's back roads, the ones colored blue on maps, and of his conversations with the people he met on that journey. Although his legal name is William Trogdon, he writes under the translation of his Sioux tribal name, which he explains in the excerpts from the opening chapters of* Blue Highways *reprinted below. Also included here is a chapter containing one of the many conversations Heat Moon had with local townspeople in the small towns his travels took him to.*

I

Beware thoughts that come in the night. They aren't turned properly; they come in askew, free of sense and restriction, deriving from the most remote of sources. Take the idea of February 17, a day of canceled expectations, the day I learned my job teaching English was finished because of declining enrollment at the college, the day I called my wife from whom I'd been separated for nine months to give her the news, the day she let slip about her "friend" — Rick or Dick or Chick. Something like that.

That morning, before all the news started hitting the fan, Eddie Short Leaf, who worked a bottomland section of the Missouri River and plowed snow off campus sidewalks, told me if the deep cold didn't break soon the trees would freeze straight through and explode. Indeed.

That night, as I lay wondering whether I would get sleep or explosion, I got the idea instead. A man who couldn't make things go right could at least go. He could quit trying to get out of the way of life. Chuck routine. Live the real jeopardy of circumstance. It was a question of dignity.

The result: on March 19, the last night of winter, I again lay awake in the tangled bed, this time doubting the madness of just walking out on things, doubting the whole plan that would begin at daybreak — to set out on a long (equivalent to half the circumference of the earth), circular trip over the back roads of the United States. Following a circle would give a purpose — to come around again — where taking a straight line would not. And I was going to do it by living out of the back end of a truck. But how to begin a beginning?

A strange sound interrupted my tossing. I went to the window, the cold air against my eyes. At first I saw only starlight. Then they were there. Up in the March blackness, two entwined skeins of snow and blue geese honking north, an undulating W-shaped configuration across the deep sky, white bellies glowing eerily with the reflected light from town, necks stretched northward. Then another flock pulled by who knows what out of the south to breed and remake itself. A new season. Answer: begin by following spring as they did — darkly, with neck stuck out.

2

The vernal equinox came on gray and quiet, a curiously still morning not winter and not spring, as if the cycle paused. Because things go their own way, my daybreak departure turned to a morning departure, then to an afternoon departure. Finally, I climbed into the van, rolled down the window, looked a last time at the rented apartment. From a dead elm sparrow hawks used each year came a high *whee* as the nestlings squealed for more grub. I started the engine. When I returned a season from now — if I did return — those squabs would be gone from the nest.

Accompanied only by a small, gray spider crawling the dashboard (kill a spider and it will rain), I drove into the street, around the corner, through the intersection, over the bridge, onto the highway. I was heading toward those little towns that get on the map — if they get on at all — only because some cartographer has a blank space to fill: Remote, Oregon; Simplicity, Virginia; New Freedom, Pennsylvania; New Hope, Tennessee; Why, Arizona; Whynot, Mississippi. Igo, California (just down the road from Ono), here I come.

3

A pledge: I give this chapter to myself. When done with it, I will shut up 8
about *that* topic.

Call me Least Heat Moon. My father calls himself Heat Moon, my elder brother Little Heat Moon. I, coming last, am therefore Least. It has been a long lesson of a name to learn.

To the Siouan peoples, the Moon of Heat is the seventh month, a time also known as the Blood Moon — I think because of its dusky midsummer color.

I have other names: Buck, once a slur — never mind the predominant Anglo features. Also Bill Trogdon. The Christian names come from a grandfather eight generations back, one William Trogdon, an immigrant Lancashireman living in North Carolina, who was killed by the Tories for providing food to rebel patriots and thereby got his name in volume four of *Makers of America*. Yet to the red way of thinking, a man who makes peace with the new by destroying the old is not to be honored. So I hear.

One summer when Heat Moon and I were walking the ancestral grounds of 12
the Osage near the river of that name in western Missouri, we talked about bloodlines. He said, "Each of the people from anywhere, when you see in them far enough, you find red blood and a red heart. There's a hope."

Nevertheless, a mixed-blood — let his heart be where it may — is a contaminated man who will be trusted by neither red nor white. The attitude goes back to a long history of "perfidious" half-breeds, men who, by their nature, had to choose against one of their bloodlines. As for me, I will choose for heart, for spirit, but never will I choose for blood.

One last word about bloodlines. My wife, a woman of striking mixed-blood features, came from the Cherokee. Our battles, my Cherokee and I, we called the "Indian wars."

For these reasons I named my truck Ghost Dancing, a heavy-handed symbol alluding to ceremonies of the 1890s in which the Plains Indians, wearing cloth shirts they believed rendered them indestructible, danced for the return of warriors, bison, and the fervor of the old life that would sweep away the new. Ghost dances, desperate resurrection rituals, were the dying rattles of a people whose last defense was delusion — about all that remained to them in their futility.

A final detail: on the morning of my departure, I had seen thirty-eight Blood Moons, an age that carries its own madness and futility. With a nearly desperate sense of isolation and a growing suspicion that I lived in an alien land, I took to the open road in search of places where change did not mean ruin and where time and men and deeds connected.

16

14

Had it not been raining hard that morning on the Livingston square, I never would have learned of Nameless, Tennessee. Waiting for the rain to ease, I lay on my bunk and read the atlas to pass time rather than to see where I might go. In Kentucky were towns with fine names like Boreing, Bear Wallow, Decoy, Subtle, Mud Lick, Mummie, Neon; Belcher was just down the road from Mouthcard, and Minnie only ten miles from Mousie.

I looked at Tennessee. Turtletown eight miles from Ducktown. And also: Peavine, Wheel, Milky Way, Love Joy, Dull, Weakly, Fly, Spot, Miser Station, Only, McBurg, Peeled Chestnut, Clouds, Topsy, Isoline. And the best of all, Nameless. The logic! I was heading east, and Nameless lay forty-five miles west. I decided to go anyway.

The rain stopped, but things looked saturated, even bricks. In Gainesboro, a hill town with a square of businesses around the Jackson County Courthouse, I stopped for directions and breakfast. There is one almost infallible way to find honest food at just prices in blue-highway America: count the wall calendars in a cafe.

No calendar: Same as an interstate pit stop.

One calendar: Preprocessed food assembled in New Jersey.

Two calendars: Only if fish trophies present.

Three calendars: Can't miss on the farm-boy breakfasts.

Four calendars: Try the ho-made pie too.

Five calendars: Keep it under your hat, or they'll franchise.

One time I found a six-calendar cafe in the Ozarks, which served fried chicken, peach pie, and chocolate malts, that left me searching for another ever since. I've never seen a seven-calendar place. But old-time travelers — road men in a day when cars had running boards and lunchroom windows said AIR COOLED in blue letters with icicles dripping from the tops — those travelers have told me the golden legends of seven-calendar cafes.

To the rider of back roads, nothing shows the tone, the voice of a small town more quickly than the breakfast grill or the five-thirty tavern. Much of what the people do and believe and share is evident then. The City Cafe in Gainesboro had three calendars that I could see from the walk. Inside were no interstate refugees with full bladders and empty tanks, no wild-eyed children just released from the glassy cell of a stationwagon backseat, no longhaul truckers talking in CB numbers. There were only townspeople wearing overalls, or catalog-order suits with five-and-dime ties, or uniforms. That is, here were farmers and mill hands, bank clerks, the dry goods merchant, a policeman, and chiropractor's receptionist. Because it was Saturday, there were also mothers and children.

I ordered my standard on-the-road breakfast: two eggs up, hashbrowns, tomato juice. The waitress, whose pale, almost translucent skin shifted hue in the gray light like a thin slice of mother of pearl, brought the food. Next to the eggs was a biscuit with a little yellow Smiley button stuck in it. She said, "You from the North?"

"I guess I am." A Missourian gets used to Southerners thinking him a Yankee, a Northerner considering him a cracker, a Westerner sneering at his effete Easternness, and the Easterner taking him for a cowhand.

"So whata you doin' in the mountains?"

"Talking to people. Taking some pictures. Looking mostly."

"Lookin' for what?"

"A three-calendar cafe that serves Smiley buttons on the biscuits."

"You needed a smile. Tell me really."

"I don't know. Actually, I'm looking for some jam to put on this biscuit now that you've brought one."

She came back with grape jelly. In a land of quince jelly, apple butter, apricot jam, blueberry preserves, pear conserves, and lemon marmalade, you always get grape jelly.

"Whata you lookin' for?"

Like anyone else, I'm embarrassed to eat in front of a watcher, particularly if I'm getting interviewed. "Why don't you have a cup of coffee?"

"Cain't right now. You gonna tell me?"

"I don't know how to describe it to you. Call it harmony."

She waited for something more. "Is that it?" Someone called her to the kitchen. I had managed almost to finish by the time she came back. She sat on the edge of the booth. "I started out in life not likin' anything, but then it grew on me. Maybe that'll happen to you." She watched me spread the jelly. "Saw your van." She watched me eat the biscuit. "You sleep in there?" I told her I did. "I'd love to do that, but I'd be scared spitless."

"I don't mind being scared spitless. Sometimes."

"I'd love to take off cross country. I like to look at different license plates. But I'd take a dog. You carry a dog?"

"No dogs, no cats, no budgie birds. It's a one-man campaign to show Americans a person can travel alone without a pet."

"Cain't travel without a dog!"

"I like to do things the hard way."

"Shoot! I'd take me a dog to talk to. And for protection."   40

"It isn't traveling to cross the country and talk to your pug instead of people along the way. Besides, being alone on the road makes you ready to meet someone when you stop. You get sociable traveling alone."

She looked out toward the van again. "Time I get the nerve to take a trip, gas'll cost five dollars a gallon."

"Could be. My rig might go the way of the steamboat." I remembered why I'd come to Gainesboro. "You know the way to Nameless?"

"Nameless? I've heard of Nameless. Better ask the amlance driver in the   44 corner booth." She pinned the Smiley on my jacket. "Maybe I'll see you on the road somewhere. His name's Bob, by the way."

"The ambulance driver?"

"The Smiley. I always name my Smileys — otherwise they all look alike. I'd talk to him before you go."

"The Smiley?"

"The amlance driver."   48

And so I went looking for Nameless, Tennessee, with a Smiley button named Bob.

● PERSONAL RESPONSE ●

Have you ever had an urge to pack up and leave everything behind you, as Heat Moon did? Explain your answer.

● QUESTIONS FOR DISCUSSION ●

1. Why did Heat Moon choose a circular trip over back roads for his search? What did he hope to find in his travels?

2. What is the significance for Heat Moon of the geese he sees on the night he makes his decision to travel the country?

3. Besides the geese, what other references does Heat Moon make to things from nature — trees, birds, spiders, seasons? What significance do those things seem to have for Heat Moon?

4. Why do you think Heat Moon includes the information about the correlation between the number of calendars in a cafe and the quality of its food?

5. What does the detailed conversation between Heat Moon and the waitress at the City Cafe reveal about "the voice" (paragraph 20) of Gainesboro?

6. What do we learn about Heat Moon himself from the section in which he tells about his own name? What do you think he means by the statement in paragraph 9 that "it has been a long lesson of a name to learn"?

7. Point out some of the other references to naming things. Why do you think names are so important to Heat Moon? What is the connection between identity (naming) and

finding one's "place"? What connection can you make between "Nameless" and the fact that Heat Moon devotes so much space to explaining his own name?

8. If you have read Jon D. Hall's essay on the homeless, "Slow Descent into Hell," how does Heat Moon's homelessness compare with the lives of the homeless Hall discusses?

● WRITING TOPICS ●

1. Describe life in a small town you are familiar with by detailing its significant features and/or some of its inhabitants.

2. Use dialogue to convey the essence of someone's character, as Heat Moon does the waitress in the City Cafe.

3. Recount a trip you took that in some way helped you find your identity or locate your "place." Or, if you have ever had an urge to pick up and leave everything behind you, as Heat Moon did, explain why you would like to leave, what you would hope to find, and how you think your life would be different.

BORDERS

—————————— ● ——————————

Barry Lopez

*Barry Lopez is a freelance writer and photographer. He writes fre-
quently of natural history and the environment, particularly in connection with the American West. He is a contributing editor to the* North
American Review *and to* Harper's. *His 1978 book* Of Wolves and Men
was a best seller. Crossing Open Ground, *from which the following
essay is taken, was published in 1988. Here Lopez describes the search
for the international border between Alaska and the Yukon Territory
which took him into vast, seemingly endless open spaces.*

In early September, the eastern Arctic coast of Alaska shows several
faces, most of them harsh. But there are days when the wind drops and
the sky is clear, and for reasons too fragile to explain — the overflight of
thousands of migrating ducks, the bright, silent austerity of the Romanzof
Mountains under fresh snow, the glassy stillness of the ocean — these days have
an edge like no others. The dawn of such a clear and windless day is cherished
against memories of late August snow squalls and days of work in rough water
under leaden skies.

One such morning, a few of us on a biological survey in the Beaufort Sea set
that work aside with hardly a word and headed east over the water for the
international border, where the state of Alaska abuts the Yukon Territory. The
fine weather encouraged this bit of adventure.

There are no settlements along this part of the arctic coast. We did not in
fact know if the border we were headed to was even marked. A northeast wind
that had been driving loose pack ice close to shore for several days forced us to
run near the beach in a narrow band of open water. In the lee of larger pieces of
sea ice, the ocean had begun to freeze, in spite of the strong sunlight and a
benign feeling in the air. Signs of winter.

As we drove toward Canada, banking the open, twenty-foot boat in graceful   4
arcs to avoid pieces of drift ice, we hung our heads far back to watch migrating
Canada geese and black brant pass over. Rifling past us and headed west at fifty
miles an hour a foot off the water were flocks of oldsquaw, twenty and thirty
ducks at a time. Occasionally, at the edge of the seaward ice, the charcoal-gray
snout of a ringed seal would break the calm surface of the ocean for breath.

We drew nearer the border, wondering aloud how we would know it. I
remembered a conversation of years before, with a man who had escaped from
Czechoslovakia to come to America and had later paddled a canoe the length of
the Yukon. He described the border where the river crossed into Alaska as
marked by a great swath cut through the spruce forest. In the middle of nowhere, I said ruefully; what a waste of trees, how ugly it must have seemed. He

looked silently across the restaurant table at me and said it was the easiest border crossing of his life.

I thought, as we drove on east, the ice closing in more now, forcing us to run yet closer to the beach, of the geographer Carl Sauer and his concept of biologically distinct regions. The idea of bioregionalism, as it has been developed by his followers, is a political concept that would reshape human life. It would decentralize residents of an area into smaller, more self-sufficient, environmentally responsible units, occupying lands the borders of which would be identical with the borders of natural regions — watersheds, for example. I thought of Sauer because we were headed that day for a great, invisible political dividing line: 141 degrees western longitude. Like the border between Utah and Colorado, this one is arbitrary. If it were not actually marked — staked — it would not be discernible. Sauer's borders are noticeable. Even the birds find them.

On the shore to our right, as we neared the mouth of Demarcation Bay, we saw the fallen remains of an Eskimo sod house, its meat-drying racks, made of driftwood, leaning askew. Someone who had once come this far to hunt had built the house. The house eventually became a dot on U.S. Coast and Geodetic Survey maps. Now its location is vital to the Inuit, for it establishes a politically important right of prior use, predating the establishment of the Arctic National Wildlife Refuge, within whose borders it has been included. I recall all this as we pass, from poring over our detailed maps the night before. Now, with the warmth of sunlight on the side of my face, with boyhood thoughts of the Yukon Territory welling up inside, the nearness of friends, with whom work has been such keen satisfaction these past few weeks, I have no desire to see maps.

Ahead, it is becoming clear that the closing ice is going to force us right up 8 on the beach before long. The wedge of open water is narrowing. What there is is very still, skimmed with fresh slush ice. I think suddenly of my brother, who lives in a house on Block Island, off the coast of Rhode Island. When I visit we walk and drive around the island. Each time I mean to ask him, does he feel any more ordered in his life for being able to see so clearly the boundary between the ocean and the land in every direction? But I am never able to phrase the question right. And the old and dour faces of the resident islanders discourage it.

Far ahead, through a pair of ten-power binoculars, I finally see what appears to be a rampart of logs, weathered gray-white and standing on a bluff where the tundra falls off fifteen or twenty feet to the beach. Is this the border?

We are breaking ice now with the boat. At five miles an hour, the bow wave skitters across the frozen surface of the ocean to either side in a hundred broken fragments. The rumbling that accompanies this shattering of solid ice is like the low-throttled voice of the outboard engines. Three or four hundred yards of this and we stop. The pack ice is within twenty feet of the beach. We cannot go any farther. That we are only a hundred feet from our destination seems a part of the day, divinely fortuitous.

We climb up the bluff. Arctic-fox tracks in the patchy snow are fresh. Here and there on the tundra are bird feathers, remnants of the summer molt of hundreds of thousands of birds that have come this far north to nest, whose feathers blow inland and out to sea for weeks. Although we see no animals but a flock of snow geese in the distance, evidence of their residence and passage is everywhere. Within a few hundred feet I find caribou droppings. On a mossy tundra mound, like one a jaeger might use, I find two small bones that I know to be a ptarmigan's.

We examine the upright, weathered logs and decide on the basis of these 12 and several pieces of carved wood that this is, indeed, the border. No one, we reason, would erect something like this on a coast so unfrequented by humans if it were not. (This coast is ice-free only eight or ten weeks in the year.) Yet we are not sure. The bluff has a certain natural prominence, though the marker's placement seems arbitrary. But the romance of it — this foot in Canada, that one in Alaska — is fetching. The delightful weather and the presence of undisturbed animals has made us almost euphoric. It is, after days of bottom trawls in thirty-one-degree water, of cold hours of patient searching for seals, so clearly a holiday for us.

I will fly over this same spot a week later, under a heavy overcast, forced down to two hundred feet above the water in a search for migrating bowhead whales. That trip, from the small settlement of Inuvik on the East Channel of the Mackenzie River in the Northwest Territories to Deadhorse, Alaska, will make this border both more real and more peculiar than it now appears. We will delay our arrival by circling over Inuvik until a Canadian customs officer can get there from the village of Tuktoyaktuk on the coast, though all we intend to do is to drop off an American scientist and buy gas. On our return trip we are required by law to land at the tiny village of Kaktovik to check through U.S. Customs. The entry through Kaktovik is so tenuous as to not exist at all. One might land, walk the mile to town, and find or not find the customs officer around. Should he not be there, the law requires we fly 250 miles south to Fort Yukon. If no one is there we are to fly on to Fairbanks before returning to Deadhorse on the coast, in order to reenter the country legally. These distances are immense. We could hardly carry the fuel for such a trip. And to fly inland would mean not flying the coast to look for whales, the very purpose of being airborne. We fly straight to Deadhorse, looking for whales. When we land we fill out forms to explain our actions and file them with the government.

Here, standing on the ground, the border seems nearly whimsical. The view over tens of square miles of white, frozen ocean and a vast expanse of tundra which rolls to the foot of snow-covered mountains is unimpeded. Such open space, on such a calm and innocent day as this, gives extraordinary release to the imagination. At such a remove — from horrible images of human death on borders ten thousand miles away, from the press of human anxiety one feels in a crowded city — at such a remove one is lulled nearly to foundering by the simple peace engendered, even at the border between two nations, by a single day of good weather.

As we turn to leave the monument, we see two swans coming toward us. They are immature tundra swans, in steel-gray plumage. Something odd is in their shape. Primary feathers. They have no primary feathers yet. Too young. And their parents, who should be with them, are nowhere to be seen. They are coming from the east, from Canada, paddling in a strip of water a few inches deep right at the edge of the beach. They show no fear of us, although they slow and are cautious. They extend their necks and open their pink bills to make gentle, rattling sounds. As they near the boat they stand up in the water and step ashore. They walk past us and on up the beach. Against the gritty coarseness of beach sand and the tundra-stained ice, their smooth gray feathers and the deep lucidity of their eyes vibrate with beauty. I watch them until they disappear from view. The chance they will be alive in two weeks is very slim. Perhaps it doesn't exist at all.

In two weeks I am thousands of miles south. In among the letters and   16 magazines in six weeks of mail sitting on the table is a thick voter-registration pamphlet. One afternoon I sit down and read it. I try to read it with the conscientiousness of one who wishes to vote wisely. I think of Carl Sauer, whose ideas I admire. And of Wendell Berry, whose integrity and sense of land come to mind when I ponder any vote and the effect it might have. I think of the invisible borders of rural landscapes, of Frost pondering the value of fences. I read in the pamphlet of referendums on statewide zoning and of the annexation of rural lands, on which I am expected to vote. I read of federal legislative reapportionment and the realignment of my county's border with that of an Indian reservation, though these will not require my vote. I must review, again, how the districts of my state representative and state senator overlap and determine if I am included now within the bounds of a newly created county commissioner's territory.

These lines blur and I feel a choking coming up in my neck and my face flushing. I set the pamphlet on the arm of the chair and get up and walk outside. It is going to take weeks, again, to get home.

● PERSONAL RESPONSE ●

In contrast to an active search for people and towns (like that of Heat Moon in "Eastward"), Lopez's search takes him to a vastly open space where few people are seen. Which search appeals to you? Does each kind of search have its own validity? What feelings does the idea of borders or boundaries evoke in you?

● QUESTIONS FOR DISCUSSION ●

1. Beyond describing just the trip to and probable location of the border between the United States and Canada in the Yukon Territory, what other purpose do you think Lopez has in this essay? Before you answer, consider all of the borders Lopez mentions.

2. What details are particularly effective in conveying the harsh life of the arctic coast of Alaska?

3. In several places, Lopez is reminded of other people as he contemplates borders. What contrasting view of borders is represented by the man who escaped from

Czechoslovakia (paragraph 5)? What is Carl Sauer's theory about borders (paragraph 6)? Why is Lopez reminded of his brother (paragraph 8)?

4. How do Lopez and his party determine the probable site of the border? Why can they not be sure if this is really it?

5. What does the account in paragraph 13 of Lopez's flight over this same area the following week add to your understanding of the remoteness of this region?

6. How does the open space of the tundra make Lopez feel? With what does he contrast the border he has just located?

7. What do the many references to birds and other living creatures, particularly in paragraphs 11 and 15, reveal about Lopez himself and about the environment he is describing?

8. Explain Lopez's concluding paragraph: why he feels "a choking coming up," why he goes outside, and why it will "take weeks, again, to get home."

● WRITING TOPICS ●

1. If you have ever been in a place in which space seemed unlimited and boundaries invisible, describe the experience.

2. Describe the difficulty of "getting home again" after being gone for an extended period, such as to school or on vacation.

3. Explain what the appearance and habits of a particular animal or bird indicate about the environment in which it lives.

JUST MARRIED

●

GRETEL EHRLICH

Gretel Ehrlich was born in California and educated at Bennington, the UCLA Film School, and the New School for Social Research. She writes frequently of the wide open spaces of the Wyoming landscape and publishes in such magazines as Harper's, The New York Times, Atlantic Monthly, *and* New Age Journal. *Her first collection of essays,* The Solace of Open Spaces *(1985), won the Harold B. Vurcell Memorial Award. She has also published a collection of short stories,* City Tales, Wyoming Stories *(1986); a novel,* Heart Mountain *(1988); and a second collection of essays,* Islands, Universe, and Home *(1989). In "Just Married," which appears in* The Solace of Open Spaces, *Ehrlich describes not only her engagement and marriage but also her feelings about property ownership and her sense of connectedness to the land.*

I met my husband at a John Wayne film festival in Cody, Wyoming. The film series was a rare midwinter entertainment to which people from all over the state came. A mutual friend, one of the speakers at the festival, introduced us, and the next morning when *The Man Who Shot Liberty Valance* was shown, we sat next to each other by chance. The fact that he cried during sad scenes in the film made me want to talk to him so we stayed in town, had dinner together, and closed down the bar. Here was a man who could talk books as well as ranching, medieval history and the mountains, ideas and mules. Like me he was a culture straddler. Ten months later we were married.

He had planned to propose while we were crossing Cougar Pass — a bald, ten-thousand-foot dome — with twenty-two head of loose horses, but a front was moving through, and in the commotion, he forgot. Another day he loped up to me: "Want to get hitched?" he said. Before I could respond there was horse trouble ahead and he loped away. To make up for the unceremonious interruption, he serenaded that night with the wistful calls sandhill cranes make. A cow elk wandered into the meadow and mingled with the horses. It snowed and in the morning a choir of coyotes howled, "Yes."

After signing for our license at the county courthouse we were given a complimentary "Care package," a Pandora's box of grotesqueries: Midol, Kotex, disposable razors, shaving cream, a bar of soap — a summing up, I suppose, of what in a marriage we could look forward to: blood, pain, unwanted hair, headaches, and dirt. "Hey, where's the champagne and cigars?" I asked.

We had a spur-of-the-moment winter wedding. I called my parents and 4 asked them what they were doing the following Saturday. They had a golf game. I told them to cancel it. "Instead of waiting, we've decided to get married while the bloom is still on," I said.

It was a walk-in wedding. The road crew couldn't get the snow plowed all the way to the isolated log cabin where the ceremony was to be held. We drove as far as we could in my pickup, chaining up on the way.

In the one hushed moment before the ceremony started, Rusty, my dog, walked through the small crowd of well-wishers and lay down at my feet. On his wolfish-wise face was a look that said, "What about me?" So the three of us were married that day. Afterward we skated on the small pond in front of the house and drank from open bottles of champagne stuck in the snow.

"Here's to the end of loneliness," I toasted quietly, not believing such a thing could come true. But it did and nothing prepared me for the sense of peace I felt — of love gone deep into a friendship — so for a while I took it to be a premonition of death — the deathbed calm we're supposed to feel after getting our affairs in order.

A year later while riding off a treeless mountain slope in a rainstorm I was 8 struck by lightning. There was a white flash. It felt as though sequins had been poured down my legs, then an electrical charge thumped me at the base of my skull as if I'd been mugged. Afterward the crown of my head itched and the bottoms of my feet arched up and burned. "I can't believe you're still alive," my husband said. The open spaces had cleansed me before. This was another kind of scouring, as when at the end of a painful appointment with the dentist he polishes your teeth.

Out across the Basin chips of light on waterponds mirrored the storm that passed us. Below was the end-of-the-road ranch my husband and I had just bought, bumped up against a nine-thousand-foot-high rockpile that looks like a Sung Dynasty painting. Set off from a series of narrow rambling hayfields which in summer are cataracts of green is the 1913 poor-man's Victorian house — uninsulated, crudely plumbed — that is now ours.

A Texan, Billy Hunt, homesteaded the place in 1903. Before starting up the almost vertical wagon trail he had to take over the Big Horns to get there, he married the hefty barmaid in the saloon where he stopped for a beer. "She was tough as a piece of rawhide," one old-timer remembered. The ten-by-twenty cabin they built was papered with the editorial and classified pages of the day; the remnants are still visible. With a fresno and a team of horses, Hunt diverted two mountain creeks through a hundred acres of meadows cleared of sagebrush. Across the face of the mountain are the mossed-over stumps of cedar and pine trees cut down and axed into a set of corrals, sheds, gates, and hitchrails. With her first child clasped in front of the saddle, Mrs. Hunt rode over the mountains to the town of Dayton — a trip that must have taken fifteen hours — to buy supplies.

Gradually the whole drainage filled up with homesteaders. Twenty-eight children attended the one-room schoolhouse a mile down the road; there were a sawmill and blacksmith's shop, and once-a-month mail service by saddle horse or sleigh. Now the town of Cloverly is no more; only three families live at the head of the creek. Curiously, our friends in the valley think it's crazy to live in such an isolated place — thirty miles from a grocery store, seventy-five from a movie theater. When I asked one older resident what he thought, he said, "Hell almighty . . . God didn't make ranchers to live close to town. Anyway, it was a better town when you had to ride the thirty miles to it."

We moved here in February: books, tables, and a rack of clothes at one end 12 of the stock truck, our horses tied at the back. There was a week of moonless nights but the Pleiades rose over the ridge like a piece of jewelry. Buying a ranch had sent us into spasms of soul-searching. It went against the bachelor lives we had grown used to: the bunkhouse-bedroll-barroom circuit; it meant our chronic vagrancy would come to an end. The proprietary impulse had dubious beginnings anyway — we had looked all that up before getting married: how ownership translates into possessiveness, protection into xenophobia, power into greed. Our idea was to rescue the ranch from the recent neglect it had seen.

As soon as the ground thawed we reset posts, restrung miles of barbed wire, and made the big ranch gates — hung eighty years ago between cedar posts as big around as my hips — swing again.

Above and around us steep canyons curve down in garlands of red and yellow rimrock: Precambrian, Madison, Chugwater formations, the porous parts of which have eroded into living-room-sized caves where mountain lions lounge and feast on does and snowshoe rabbits. Songbirds fly in and out of towering cottonwoods the way people throng office buildings. Mornings, a breeze fans up from the south; evenings, it reverses directions, so there is a streaming of life, a brushing back and forth like a massage. We go for walks. A friend told us the frosting of limestone that clings to the boulders we climb is all that's left of the surface of the earth a few million years ago. Some kinds of impermanence take a long time.

The seasons are a Jacob's ladder climbed by migrating elk and deer. Our ranch is one of their resting places. If I was leery about being an owner, a possessor of land, now I have to understand the ways in which the place possesses me. Mowing hayfields feels like mowing myself. I wake up mornings expecting to find my hair shorn. The pastures bend into me; the water I ushered over hard ground becomes one drink of grass. Later in the year, feeding the bales of hay we've put up is a regurgitative act: thrown down from a high stack on chill days they break open in front of the horses like loaves of hot bread.

● PERSONAL RESPONSE ●

What do you think of Ehrlich's comparison of settling into marriage with settling down on a piece of land? Does the life Ehrlich depicts appeal to you? Explain why or why not.

● QUESTIONS FOR DISCUSSION ●

1. What does Ehrlich mean when she says that her relationship with her husband was "love gone deep into a friendship" (paragraph 7)?

2. Ehrlich frequently uses vivid descriptive language to evoke images and relate experience. Find passages that you feel are particularly well written and explain why they are effective.

3. Ehrlich also uses figurative language to enliven her writing, as when she describes being struck by lightning as a cleansing, a "kind of scouring" (paragraph 8). What does she mean by that comparison? Find several other examples of figurative language and explain them.

4. What do the many references to the land, to nature, and to animals suggest about Ehrlich's regard for her natural surroundings?

5. What do the details in paragraph 10 about Billy Hunt and his wife, who cleared and homesteaded the "end-of-the-road ranch," contribute to an understanding of what the place meant to Ehrlich and her husband?

6. What does Ehrlich mean when she writes: "Buying a ranch had sent us into spasms of soul-searching" (paragraph 12)? What is it about property ownership that bothered Ehrlich and her husband?

7. Ehrlich makes a somewhat paradoxical statement when she says that "some kinds of impermanence take a long time" (paragraph 14). Explain what you think she means by that remark.

8. What do you think Ehrlich means when she says "the place possesses me" (paragraph 15)? What does her marriage have to do with Ehrlich's feeling of connectedness to the land?

● WRITING TOPICS ●

1. Tell about an experience you have had with some aspect of the natural world — in the wide open spaces, in the forest, at the ocean, or the like. Focus your description on both the physical characteristics of the place and your feelings about being there.

2. Define what you believe is a successful relationship or marriage.

3. Compare what Ehrlich says about property ownership with what E. M. Forster in "My Wood" says about it.

MY WOOD

●

E. M. FORSTER

*E. M. Forster (1879-1970) was a highly respected and critically ac-
claimed British writer. Among his works are the novels* The Longest
Journey *(1907),* A Room With a View *(1908), and* Howards End
(1910), and a book of literary criticism, Aspects of the Novel *(1927). He
also published two collections of essays,* Two Cheers for Democracy
(1951) and Abinger Harvest *(1936), in which "My Wood" appeared.
Here, Forster humorously explores the effects that buying a piece of
property had on him personally. The book he refers to in the first
paragraph is perhaps his best-known novel,* A Passage to India *(1924).*

A few years ago I wrote a book which dealt in part with the difficulties of
the English in India. Feeling that they would have had no difficulties in
India themselves, the Americans read the book freely. The more they
read it the better it made them feel, and a cheque to the author was the result. I
bought a wood with the cheque. It is not a large wood—it contains scarcely any
trees, and it is intersected, blast it, by a public footpath. Still, it is the first
property that I have owned, so it is right that other people should participate in
my shame, and should ask themselves, in accents that will vary in horror, this
very important question: What is the effect of property upon the character? Don't
let's touch economics; the effect of private ownership upon the community as a whole is another question—a more important question, perhaps, but
another one. Let's keep to psychology. If you own things, what's their effect on
you? What's the effect on me of my wood?

In the first place, it makes me feel heavy. Property does have this effect.
Property produces men of weight, and it was a man of weight who failed to get
into the Kingdom of Heaven. He was not wicked, that unfortunate millionaire in
the parable, he was only stout; he stuck out in front, not to mention behind, and
as he wedged himself this way and that in the crystalline entrance and bruised
his well-fed flanks, he saw beneath him a comparatively slim camel passing
through the eye of a needle and being woven into the robe of God. The Gospels
all through couple stoutness and slowness. They point out what is perfectly
obvious, yet seldom realized: that if you have a lot of things you cannot move
about a lot, that furniture requires dusting, dusters require servants, servants
require insurance stamps, and the whole tangle of them makes you think twice
before you accept an invitation to dinner or go for a bathe in the Jordan.
Sometimes the Gospels proceed further and say with Tolstoy that property is
sinful; they approach the difficult ground of asceticism here, where I cannot
follow them. But as to the immediate effects of property on people, they just
show straightforward logic. It produces men of weight. Men of weight cannot,
by definition, move like the lightning from the East unto the West, and the

188

ascent of a fourteen-stone bishop into a pulpit is thus the exact antithesis of the coming of the Son of Man. My wood makes me feel heavy.

In the second place, it makes me feel it ought to be larger.

The other day I heard a twig snap in it. I was annoyed at first, for I thought 4 that someone was blackberrying, and depreciating the value of the undergrowth. On coming nearer, I saw it was not a man who had trodden on the twig and snapped it, but a bird, and I felt pleased. My bird. The bird was not equally pleased. Ignoring the relation between us, it took fright as soon as it saw the shape of my face, and flew straight over the boundary hedge into a field, the property of Mrs. Henessy, where it sat down with a loud squawk. It had become Mrs. Henessy's bird. Something seemed grossly amiss here, something that would not have occurred had the wood been larger. I could not afford to buy Mrs. Henessy out, I dared not murder her, and limitations of this sort beset me on every side. Ahab did not want that vineyard — he only needed it to round off his property, preparatory to plotting a new curve — and all the land around my wood has become necessary to me in order to round off the wood. A boundary protects. But — poor little thing — the boundary ought in its turn to be protected. Noises on the edge of it. Children throw stones. A little more, and then a little more, until we reach the sea. Happy Canute! Happier Alexander! And after all, why should even the world be the limit of possession? A rocket containing a Union Jack, will, it is hoped, be shortly fired at the moon. Mars. Sirius. Beyond which . . . But these immensities ended by saddening me. I could not suppose that my wood was the destined nucleus of universal dominion — it is so very small and contains no mineral wealth beyond the blackberries. Nor was I comforted when Mrs. Henessy's bird took alarm for the second time and flew clean away from us all, under the belief that it belonged to itself.

In the third place, property makes its owner feel that he ought to do something to it. Yet he isn't sure what. A restlessness comes over him, a vague sense that he has a personality to express — the same sense which, without any vagueness, leads the artist to an act of creation. Sometimes I think I will cut down such trees as remain in the wood, at other times I want to fill up the gaps between them with new trees. Both impulses are pretentious and empty. They are not honest movements toward moneymaking or beauty. They spring from a foolish desire to express myself and from an inability to enjoy what I have got. Creation, property, enjoyment form a sinister trinity in the human mind. Creation and enjoyment are both very, very good, yet they are often unattainable without a material basis, and at such moments property pushes itself in as a substitute, saying, "Accept me instead — I'm good enough for all three." It is not enough. It is, as Shakespeare said of lust, "The expense of spirit in a waste of shame": it is "Before, a joy proposed; behind, a dream." Yet we don't know how to shun it. It is forced on us by our economic system as the alternative to starvation. It is also forced on us by an internal defect in the soul, by the feeling that in property may lie the germs of self-development and of exquisite or heroic deeds. Our life on earth is, and ought to be, material and carnal. But we have not yet learned to manage our materialism and carnality properly; they are still entangled with the desire for ownership, where (in the words of Dante) "Possession is one with loss."

And this brings us to our fourth and final point: the blackberries.

Blackberries are not plentiful in this meagre grove, but they are easily seen from the public footpath which traverses it, and all too easily gathered. Foxgloves, too — people will pull up the foxgloves, and ladies of an educational tendency even grub for toadstools to show them on the Monday in class. Other ladies, less educated, roll down the bracken in the arms of their gentlemen friends. There is paper, there are tins. Pray, does my wood belong to me or doesn't it? And, if it does, should I not own it best by allowing no one else to walk there? There is a wood near Lyme Regis, also cursed by a public footpath, where the owner has not hesitated on this point. He had built high stone walls each side of the path, and has spanned it by bridges, so that the public circulate like termites while he gorges on the blackberries unseen. He really does own his wood, this able chap. Dives in Hell did pretty well, but the gulf dividing him from Lazarus could be traversed by vision, and nothing traverses it here. And perhaps I shall come to this in time. I shall wall in and fence out until I really taste the sweets of property. Enormously stout, endlessly avaricious, pseudocreative, intensely selfish, I shall weave upon my forehead the quadruple crown of possession until those nasty Bolshies come and take it off again and thrust me aside into the outer darkness.

● PERSONAL RESPONSE ●

How do you feel about people who fence in their land, put up "no trespassing" signs, and otherwise fiercely attempt to keep anyone from stepping on their property? What legitimate reasons might people have — farmers, for instance — for kicking trespassers off their land? Do you think Forster is being unfair to the public in paragraph 7, or do people in your experience behave this way in parks, woods, and other natural surroundings?

● QUESTIONS FOR DISCUSSION ●

1. Why do you suppose Forster emphasizes so strongly that he is interested only in the psychological, not the economical, effect of owning property (paragraph 1)?

2. How does Forster view himself and his own reaction to becoming a property owner?

3. Forster relies heavily on allusions to literature and the Bible. See how many of the following references you can identify: Tolstoy, paragraph 2; the parable of the camel and the man of weight, paragraph 2; Ahab, Canute, and Alexander in paragraph 4; the quotation from Shakespeare in paragraph 5; Dives and Lazarus in paragraph 7.

4. Forster's wit and humor are evident throughout the essay, as in paragraph 4, when he assumes ownership of a bird that has landed on his property and briefly considers ways of doing away with the neighbor who owns the adjoining property. Point out passages that you find amusing or witty.

5. State each of the four effects that owning property has had on Forster and summarize what he has to say about each one.

● WRITING TOPICS ●

1. Examine the effects that owning something has (or had) on you.

2. If you do not own property yourself, explore the effects of property ownership on someone you know.

3. Recount the effects that a change in fortune, such as coming into money or winning a prize, had on you or someone you know.

SEARCHING FOR A PLACE

●

ADDITIONAL WRITING SUGGESTIONS

1. Define "place" as something other than a physical area. Consider the places that Mellix writes about in "From Outside, In" and that Heat Moon is searching for in "Eastward," in contrast to the physical space in Forster's "My Wood."

2. Examine the effects of hanging out in a favorite spot, such as a shopping mall or a street corner, on your own life or on the lives of your friends.

3. Examine the issue of "latchkey" children whose parents work and are unable to be in the home when the children return from school. Focus on a specific aspect of the topic, such as ways in which parents or community members make that period at home alone easier for children, or potential problems children might have when left alone.

4. Describe a place that has particular meaning to you. Include not only objective, physical details of the place but also your subjective, emotional reaction to it.

5. Explore the issue of people's determination to own, develop, and otherwise dominate nature.

5

RESPONDING
TO
VIOLENCE

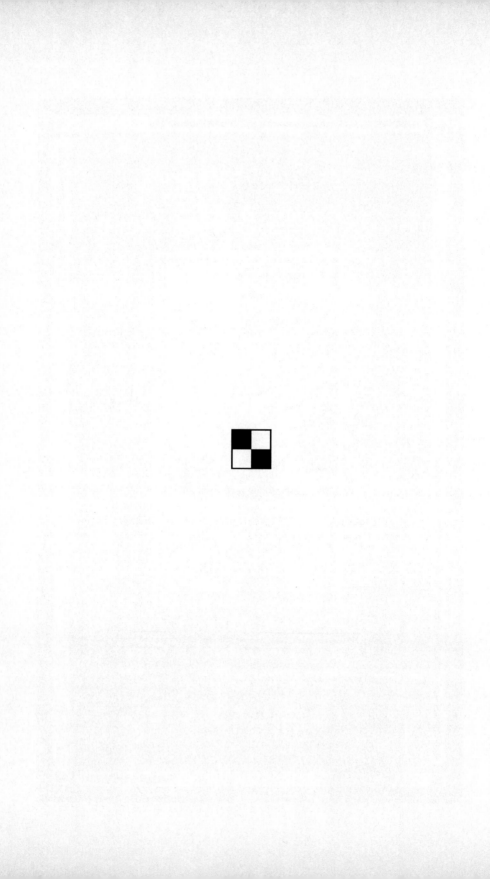

TWO VARIETIES OF KILLERS

●

ELLEN CURRIE

Ellen Currie's articles have appeared in numerous newspapers and magazines. In 1986, she published a novel, Available Light. *In the following article, which first appeared in 1986 in the* New York Times, *Currie contrasts the single murder committed by Madeleine Smith in 1857 with the 1970s serial murders of Theodore Bundy. Currie contends that, in contrast to Smith's crime of passion, Bundy's crimes and the public's reaction to them are pathological.*

Henry James, like many decorous and respectable people, entertained a lively interest in murder. He was a fan of the Scottish solicitor William Roughead, who wrote about real-life crime for the first 40 years of this century; James once told Mr. Roughead he was interested in crime because through it "manners and morals become clearly disclosed." He urged Mr. Roughead to write about "the dear old human and sociable murders and adulteries and forgeries in which we are so agreeably at home. And don't tell me, for charity's sake, that your supply runs short."

Contemporary supplies of murder, adultery and forgery remain abundant. But crime seems to me less sociable these days, if I am right in taking "sociable" to mean human and comprehensible and even sympathetic. The crimes get bigger and more horrible, and yet we are not sufficiently horrified by them; we pay less and less attention to the manners and the morals they disclose.

Look at the difference, for example, between the crimes of Madeleine Smith, who stirred arsenic into her lover's cocoa in 1857, and the convicted killer Theodore R. Bundy, who has been linked with the murders of 36 women he didn't even know.

Madeleine Smith, whose case greatly interested Henry James (he called her a "portentous young person"), was the daughter of a Glasgow architect. In 1855, when she was 19, she crossed paths with a young Frenchman. He was handsome, Mr. Roughead wrote, but "socially impossible." They met in secret and wrote to each other constantly. When they became lovers Miss Smith's letters took on what Mr. Roughead described as "a tropical and abandoned tone." They were indelicate letters, naive and outspoken. Another scholar of crime has pointed out that in a day when sex was supposed to be no more than a woman's bounden duty, Madeleine Smith found it a pagan festival. ·

Her lover kept her letters, 198 of them. When she accepted an older, richer and more settled suitor, she asked for the letters' return. Wild with jealousy, her lover claimed he would return them only to her father. That prospect drove Miss Smith mad with shame and fear. She bought arsenic. Her lover soon died of arsenic poisoning. She was brought to trial and conducted herself with great dignity. The verdict: not proven.

4

These people are not admirable, but they are real. Their awful situation is comprehensible; a blown-up, highly colored version of the kind of dilemma ordinary people face. Madeleine Smith's crime was personal. It was a crime of passion.

The case of Ted Bundy is different. To me, it is not "sociable," not comprehensible on any human scale. It is peculiarly impersonal. He didn't even know his victims; they represented an abstraction — women. His are crimes not of passion but pathology. Our reaction to them seems to me to partake of pathology too.

According to the reports I have read, some law enforcement officials say 8 Mr. Bundy may have killed more than 36 young women in sexual crimes across the country. (Like Madeleine Smith, Ted Bundy says he is innocent of any crime.) He has been convicted of battering to death, early on Super Bowl Sunday 1978 in the Chi Omega sorority house at Florida State University, two young women. He hideously beat two more young women in the same house and, blocks away, savaged another young woman. He didn't know any of them. Captured and charged, Mr. Bundy was also indicted in the kidnapping and murder of a 12-year-old girl. He didn't know her, either. He was convicted of all charges. His execution, scheduled for July 3, was indefinitely postponed to give his lawyers time to frame an appeal.°

The young women Ted Bundy has been convicted of killing, and is suspected of killing, resemble, an investigator said, "everyone's daughter." Their photographs show the sweet faces of their youth, the long hair of their period. Except for those who loved them, their identities overlap now, and blur. These women are not vivid and defined because they did nothing to bring about their deaths. They were not Ted Bundy's angry and discarded lovers. They did not refuse to return his disastrous, impassioned letters. They didn't know him.

At first all these deaths of pretty young women attracted wide public notice. But once Mr. Bundy was apprehended, the attention was all on his antics and not on the innocent dead. Bundy is a 20th century phenomenon. He is mediagenic. He is handsome, usually described as a former law student and witty, brilliant, charming, polished. Oddly, these latter qualities do not come through in any of the several books about him. Mr. Bundy was once active in Republican politics; there are those who profess to believe that he might ultimately have been elected to high public office had he stayed the course. He has twice made dramatic escapes from custody. He has acted as his own counsel in sensational televised trials. He has been the subject of a television movie. Ted Bundy T-shirts, for, against and smart aleck ("Ted Bundy is a one-night stand"), have enjoyed popularity. So have jingles: "Let's salute the mighty Bundy / Here on Friday, gone on Monday / All his roads lead out of town / It's hard to keep a good man down." Bundy Burgers and a Bundy cocktail had some play in a Colorado bar. Groupies have gathered at his trials. He gets a lot of mail.

Theodore Bundy is said by psychiatrists to be an antisocial personality, a man without conscience. In a strange, third-person meditation on the killings, Mr. Bundy described the rapes and murders as "inappropriate acting out."

°[Editor's note: In 1989, Bundy was executed in Florida.]

Perhaps Ted Bundy doesn't labor under a conscience. But how about   12
the rest of us? Shouldn't we feel more revulsion, more grief for those young
lives? Something vile has happened to our ideas of what is valuable and what is
waste. Perhaps we have seen too much evil and on too grand a scale. We are glib
and dismissive of the moral issues. We think Mr. Bundy is good for a laugh. We
made him a celebrity. (Richard Schickel, in his book "Intimate Strangers," about
the nature of celebrity in modern society, contends that multiple murderers
have grasped the essentials of the celebrity system better than normal people.)

Crime does disclose on manners and on morals. If people must kill people, I
have to put my dollar down on wicked Madeleine Smith. With her sexy letters,
poisoned cocoa, caddish lover, she dealt in death. But she is piercingly familiar.
Ted Bundy's unspeakable crimes and our cheap reaction to them reveal us to
ourselves in a strange and deathly light.

● PERSONAL RESPONSE ●

What is your opinion of the way in which the media make a mass murderer like Bundy
into a celebrity?

● QUESTIONS FOR DISCUSSION ●

1. Do you think Currie anticipates an audience who will agree or disagree with her? How
   can you tell?

2. Why do you suppose Currie chose the example of Smith rather than, say, the notorious
   nineteenth-century mass murderer Jack the Ripper? How is her example of Smith
   more directly related to the point she makes about the two murderers?

3. What are the similarities between Smith and Bundy? What are the key differences
   between the two?

4. What does Currie mean by the term "mediagenic" (paragraph 10)? In what sense does
   she mean that "Bundy is a 20th century phenomenon"?

5. What is Currie's attitude toward Smith, toward Bundy, and toward the public's
   reaction to Bundy?

6. What do you think Currie means when she says that "crime seems to me less sociable
   these days" (paragraph 2)? In what way is the Smith murder "comprehensible"
   (paragraph 6)?

7. Why do you think Currie uses the first person plural, as in paragraph 7 when she writes
   "our reaction" and throughout paragraphs 12 and 13?

8. What does Currie mean when she says that "crime does disclose on manners and on
   morals" (paragraph 13)?

● WRITING TOPICS ●

1. Using the example of a crime that received much local or national media coverage,
   exemplify Currie's statement that "crime does disclose on manners and on morals."

2. Try to account for the media's focus on the personality of the criminal rather than on the gravity of the crimes.

3. Either support or argue against Currie's statement that "something vile has happened to our ideas of what is valuable and what is waste" (paragraph 12).

THE WAR AGAINST WOMEN

●

CAROL LYNN MITHERS

Carol Lynn Mithers has written for numerous publications, including The New York Times, Gentlemen's Quarterly, California, and The Village Voice. In the following 1989 essay from Ladies' Home Journal, Mithers surveys the alarming statistics on violent crimes against women and offers reasons and ways to stop the "war against women."

The story was the kind that gives women nightmares. A teenage girl was abducted from a bus station in downtown Los Angeles and repeatedly raped. After several days, she managed to escape into the street, flag down a car and ask the men inside for help. Instead, they raped her. Yet in 1989, it was not the sheer horror of those facts that made reading them so difficult — it was that we had already confronted so many similar cases:

- The infamous gang rape and near-fatal beating of a jogger in New York City's Central Park. The attack on the woman, a Wall Street investment banker, was so savage that it induced brain injury; the victim, who has a graduate degree from Yale, has had to relearn even the simplest reading and math skills.

- The reported hour-long sexual assault on a mentally impaired girl by five teenage boys in the affluent suburb of Glen Ridge, New Jersey, while eight others were present. The girl, who was allegedly raped with a miniature baseball bat and a broomstick, was said to have known most of the youths since childhood.

- The killing of a respected judge in Grand Rapids, Michigan, by her estranged husband, a police officer, who was convicted only of manslaughter. "Everybody," said a male juror, "felt that he was provoked by his wife to do this."

- And for every rape and assault reported by the news media, there were thousands that were not. "He started to come on to me, and when I refused, he pulled a knife and made me strip," recalls Bonnie, twenty-eight, an Iowa student who was raped by the relative of a friend. "When I went to the hospital to report it," she says, starting to cry at the memory, "the doctor was so rough I felt I'd been raped a second time."

Like physical violence, cultural violence against women suddenly seemed to be everywhere this year — in misogynistic rock-music videos; in sadomasochistic comic books and men's magazines; in "slasher" films; in sick and ugly jokes by popular comedians; and even on the computer screen, with an obscene software program.

The more one saw and read in 1989, the more it seemed that, despite decades of crusades against rape and other assaults, sexual rage was not only not abating, it was getting worse. Many women felt a higher level of hostility, a thickening miasma of menace that ranged from degrading imagery to casual insults to overt attacks.

Says Nancy Biele, past president of the National Coalition Against Sexual 4 Assault, in Minneapolis, "I've been doing this kind of work for fifteen years, and it feels more dangerous out there to me now."

"We're seeing a culture in which it has become a little more okay to hate women," says Jennie Balise, of the Los Angeles Commission on Assaults Against Women.

Even President Bush, hardly a radical feminist, was moved to give a name to the growing problem. "We must," he declared, "halt this war against women."

A NEW LEVEL OF VIOLENCE

And a war it often seems to be, fought on every front. It is raging on the streets. According to the FBI, a woman is raped every six minutes, and one in ten will be raped in her lifetime. Since many attacks are not reported, the true figures may be considerably higher; Nancy Biele believes that as many as one woman in three may become a rape victim.

Nor is home a safe harbor. A woman is beaten every fifteen seconds, and 8 each day at least four women are killed by their batterers, according to federal statistics. "Battery," says former Surgeon General C. Everett Koop, "is the single most significant cause of injury to women in this country."

Most troubling of all, perhaps, is the reported rise in levels of sexual hostility among our young. Some rape counselors fear that overexposure to violently anti-female images is creating a kind of emotional numbness. Mary Beth Roden, of the rape treatment center at Santa Monica Hospital, in Santa Monica, California, says, "A few years ago, we'd show high school students a taped interview with a rape victim, and kids would be saying, 'Wow, that was terrible.' Now many of them are less shocked. I don't know any other word to use but *desensitization*."

Male college students, in particular, seem to have become more abusive. "Between 75 and 90 percent of campus women have experienced at least one incident with campus men that made them feel insulted or degraded," says Bernice R. Sandler, of the Association of American Colleges, in Washington, D. C. "When one university held an anti-pornography march, for instance, the women marching were taunted with cries of 'gang rape, gang rape' and 'I'll take that one.'"

Far too often, male students do not confine themselves to verbal assaults: According to a survey of six thousand students at thirty-two campuses by Mary Koss, Ph.D., a professor in the psychiatry department at the University of Arizona, one in twelve men admitted to having forced, or tried to force, a woman to have intercourse.

Incredibly, many men see nothing out of the ordinary about such attacks. "A 12 'nice' guy I was seeing decided he was tired of me saying no to sex," says Kelly, a musician from Seattle. "He had forcible, very painful intercourse with me. I fought, but he was a very large man. Afterward, he seemed to have no idea that he'd done anything wrong." .

More shocking still are statistics on mere boys provided by Elizabeth Holtzman, district attorney for the borough of Brooklyn, in New York City. In the last two years, there has been an astounding increase of 200 percent in rape arrests of boys under thirteen in New York City, she says, while rape arrests of boys under eighteen went up 27 percent.

The comments of one of those youths provide a chilling insight into an attacker's motives. "She was weak. She couldn't do nothing," the boy says of his victim. "I was a dominant force over her."

Certainly, that need for power is a factor in sexual violence, and the current wave of sexual rage may be caused at least in part by a backlash against the challenges to traditional male power that have been posed by the women's movement. "[Some men] may be uncomfortable dealing with strong women," say Bernice Sandler and Jean O'Gorman Hughes in a report on campus harassment. "Lashing out at these and other women by harassing them is a way to alleviate their discomfort."

Many men have been deeply shaken by the social upheaval in the years 16 since the women's movement became mainstream, according to J. William Gibson, Ph.D., an assistant professor of sociology at Southern Methodist University, in Dallas. "From the mid-sixties through the late seventies, many traditional social relationships for men were significantly altered," Gibson says. "A lot of the culture that has emerged in the eighties, such as the increased popularity of movies and novels that present men as warriors, has been a symbolic attempt to restore a more traditional world."

The Heart of the Matter

Then again, some cultural traditions do stand — especially the definition of a "real" man. "Unfortunately," says Holtzman, "we have the idea that men prove themselves by being physically stronger than someone else or even harming that person physically."

Since many boys are also taught that manhood can only be conferred on them by other men, women are seen primarily as "the other" — and the appropriate victims on whom to prove oneself.

And these days, such time-dishonored stereotypes are more widely disseminated than ever. The misogynistic images appear everywhere:

- *Computer software* MacPlaymate, a program that has found its way into both college dorms and executive suites, has graphics that display a nude, spread-eagled woman who is, according to a personal computing magazine, "ready to entertain your wildest electronic fantasies." The author of the program, Mike Saenz, a twenty-nine-year-old from Chicago, cheerfully admits that the program is "sexist as hell." Prudence

Baird, a Los Angeles executive who is conducting an informal campaign against the program, says "I call it 'MacRape.'"

- *Comic books*   Many titles in the $300-million-per-year industry focus with disturbing frequency on the theme of sexual violence. One comic, "Black Orchid," begins with a woman being tied up and set afire; another, "Displaced Paranormals," shows an attractive female "mutant" being suspended from the ceiling and tortured.

- *Men's magazines*   Violent sexual themes such as rape and bondage are often depicted in mainstream publications, says Neil Malamuth, Ph.D., professor of communications at UCLA. In the book *Pornography and Sexual Aggression* (Academic Press, 1984), Malamuth writes of the negative effects of the "coupling of sex and aggression in these portrayals."

- *"Slasher" films*   Box-office attractions like *The Tool Box Murders* and the *Friday the 13th* series customarily show "independent women" being killed "in a sadistic, highly sexualized way," says Pauline Bart, Ph.D., a sociology professor at the University of Illinois, Chicago.

- *Popular music*   An uncomfortably high percentage of the music bought by teenagers emphasizes violence, especially sexual violence against women. Examples: A song by the band Guns 'n' Roses that contains the line *I used to love her, but I had to kill her*; and one by the group Poison, "I Want Action," that contains the lyric *If I can't have her I'll take her and make her*. Still another performer, the rapper Slick Rick, has released a record called "Treat Her Like a Prostitute."

- *Comedy*   Some of the most unabashed contempt for women can be found in the routines of popular performers like Eddie Murphy ("Remember the good old days, when you could beat up on women?"), Sam Kinison ("I don't condone wife beating . . . I *understand* it"), and Andrew Dice Clay, who, said one reviewer, portrays women as "a series of pliant orifices accompanied by a plaintive nagging voice."

Such cracks are no joke. One Los Angeles woman who saw Clay's show 20 called it "forty of the most upsetting minutes I've ever experienced." Routines like Clay's clearly reflect how common some ugly attitudes are; his shows habitually draw raucous approval from hundreds of male fans.

A DREADFUL PRICE

The toll taken by the war against women is clear and devastating. For the millions who've been the victims of sexual assault, life will never be the same. According to a study co-authored by Susan Sorenson, Ph.D., a clinical psychologist at UCLA, victims of rape and other sexual assaults are much more likely than nonvictims to suffer from major depression, alcohol or drug dependence, or anxiety disorders such as phobias and panic attacks. "The rape rules my life; I couldn't stop thinking about it," says Bonnie, the Iowa student. She was unable to work for eight months after the attack, and even today, she speaks haltingly of her ordeal. "It's taken a long time for me to come to terms with it, and I still don't trust men at all."

Kelly, the Seattle woman who was raped by her date, says, "I completely stopped going out with men for a while. But even after I started dating again, I wouldn't go to a man's apartment alone for any reason. I was sure that something awful would happen."

The same kind of fear often grips women even if they have escaped an attack. "I'm completely afraid of being alone anywhere for more than a few minutes," says Alice, thirty-two, a nurse who fought off an attacker on a deserted Northern California beach. "And I'm still furious at the guy, whoever he was. How could he believe he had the right to do that to me?"

For women who have become accustomed to independence, the loss of 24 control they experience after an attack can be almost as frightening as the incident itself: Bonnie had been living on her own at the time she was raped, but she moved back to her parents' home the day of the attack. "I felt terrified," she explains.

Nora, a thirty-five-year-old computer executive from Dallas, was raped in an underground parking lot. Now, she thinks, she will be looking fearfully behind her for the rest of her life. "I had gotten careless," she says. "But you can't ever let your guard down."

And one New York City woman, who was verbally harassed four times in the space of a block late one night, says the incidents have made her more wary of traveling by herself. "I used to think I could go pretty much anywhere at any time," she says. "Now I'm not so sure. I have to start thinking like a victim. No woman should have to do it, but that's reality."

FIGHTING THE VIOLENCE

Although the war against women may seem unwinnable, there are some specific defensive steps that can be taken. "We need to have more effective enforcement of existing laws, and in some cases, strengthening of them," says Elizabeth Holtzman. "We also need to have counseling and training programs *within* the criminal justice system — we still find judges who reflect attitudes that women who are raped are responsible for it."

Unquestionably, though, the most important changes to be made are 28 cultural. "This isn't a problem that can be fixed with a little psychotherapy and a few more prisons," says Diana Russell, Ph.D., professor of sociology at Mills College, in Oakland, California. "The real issue is the way men are brought up to view women and to see manhood."

At home, parents should be aware of the messages their children may be getting from the music they listen to and the videos they see. If those messages are exploitative, parents should reasonably discuss the issue with their kids: It is of the utmost importance that children not think of sexual violence as entertainment.

Holtzman says, "Speaking out against violence in media and particularly violence against women is crucial. I also think we need to address issues of discrimination against women, so we can strengthen the notion of the humanity of women."

It's essential, too, for men to understand that sexual harassment, even if it is not violent, is part of the spectrum that has rape and murder at its farthest end. "Sexual harassment is not a lunchtime sport," says Bonnie Lynn, forty-eight, an insurance claims adjuster from New York City. Lynn was outraged by a humorous *New York Times* article that appeared last April, one week after the Central Park rape, on "good-natured" men in the Wall Street area who volubly judged passing women on their appearance. "In its extreme, the idea that women are fair game leads to the kind of animal violence that was demonstrated against the woman in Central Park.

Most important of all, perhaps, is teaching boys that being a real man does not have to mean being violent or aggressive. It is here, says Jane Hood, associate professor of sociology at the University of New Mexico at Albuquerque, that parents can play an especially significant role. "We need to encourage children of both sexes to play together so that by the time they're teenagers, boys will learn to see girls as friends and not just sex objects," she says. "We don't need to encourage them to fight all their battles physically. I know these are hard changes to make, but they are ones we must think about." 32

Nancy Biele agrees. "If we can stop at a generational level and teach boys and girls differently, we can break through this. A world that is truly equal," she says, "would be a world without sexual violence."

● PERSONAL RESPONSE ●

Does your own experience bear out the grim reality Mithers describes? Do you agree or disagree with the reasons Mithers cites for the high frequency of violent crimes against women? Explain your answer.

● QUESTIONS FOR DISCUSSION ●

1. Where does Mithers get the title of her essay? Do you think it an appropriate metaphor for the social problem Mithers describes?

2. Why do you think Mithers begins with five extended examples of violent crimes against women? Do you think that strategy is more effective than if she had begun with the federal statistics she cites in paragraphs 7 and 8?

3. Why do you suppose Mithers quotes the reactions of some of the victims of violent crimes (paragraphs 21–25)?

4. Besides rape and murder, what other behaviors does Mithers include as evidence of the "war against women"?

5. What seems to be a key factor in sexual violence?

6. What does Mithers suggest is the effect of the kinds of misogynistic images she lists in paragraph 19?

7. What does Mithers suggest as possible ways to end this "war against women"?

● WRITING TOPICS ●

1. If you or someone you know has been the victim of a crime, narrate what happened and describe the effects of the crime.

2. Argue for or against Mithers' contention that misogynistic images in popular culture have a causal relationship to the high rate of violent crimes against women.

3. Offer your own solution to the problem of violence against women.

ROCK LYRICS AND VIOLENCE AGAINST WOMEN

●

CARYL RIVERS

Caryl Rivers is a professor of journalism at Boston University and has written many newspaper and magazine articles. Her novels include Virgins *(1984) and* Intimate Enemies *(1987). The essay below first appeared in* The Boston Globe *and has been widely reprinted. In it, Rivers registers a strong protest against rock lyrics that depict violence against women on the grounds that they legitimize such behavior.*

After a grisly series of murders in California, possibly inspired by the lyrics of a rock song, we are hearing a familiar chorus: Don't blame rock and roll. Kids will be kids. They love to rebel, and the more shocking the stuff, the better they like it.

There's some truth in this, of course. I loved to watch Elvis shake his torso when I was a teenager, and it was even more fun when Ed Sullivan wouldn't let the cameras show him below the waist. I snickered at the forbidden "Rock with Me, Annie" lyrics by a black Rhythm and Blues group, which were deliciously naughty. But I am sorry, rock fans, that is not the same thing as hearing lyrics about how a man is going to force a woman to perform oral sex on him at gunpoint in a little number called "Eat Me Alive." It is not in the same league with a song about the delights of slipping into a woman's room while she is sleeping and murdering her, the theme of an AC/DC ballad that allegedly inspired the California slayer.

Make no mistake, it is not sex we are talking about here, but violence. Violence against women. Most rock songs are not violent—they are funky, sexy, rebellious, and sometimes witty. Please do not mistake me for a Mrs. Grundy. If Prince wants to leap about wearing only a purple jock strap, fine. Let Mick Jagger unzip his fly as he gyrates, if he wants to. But when either one of them starts garroting, beating, or sodomizing a woman in their number, that is another story.

I always find myself annoyed when "intellectual" men dismiss violence 4 against women with a yawn, as if it were beneath their dignity to notice. I wonder if the reaction would be the same if the violence were directed against someone other than women. How many people would yawn and say, "Oh, kids will be kids," if a rock group did a nifty little number called "Lynchin," in which stringing up and stomping on black people were set to music? Who would chuckle and say, "Oh, just a little adolescent rebellion" if a group of rockers went on MTV dressed as Nazis, desecrating synagogues and beating up Jews to the beat of twanging guitars?

I'll tell you what would happen. Prestigious dailies would thunder on editorial pages; senators would fall over each other to get denunciations into the Congressional Record. The president would appoint a commission to clean up the music business.

But violence against women is greeted by silence. It shouldn't be.

This does not mean censorship, or book (or record) burning. In a society that protects free expression, we understand a lot of stuff will float up out of the sewer. Usually, we recognize the ugly stuff that advocates violence against any group as the garbage it is, and we consider its purveyors as moral lepers. We hold our nose and tolerate it, but we speak out against the values it proffers.

But images of violence against women are not staying on the fringes of 8 society. No longer are they found only in tattered, paper-covered books or in movie houses where winos snooze and the scent of urine fills the air. They are entering the mainstream at a rapid rate. This is happening at a time when the media, more and more, set the agenda for the public debate. It is a powerful legitimizing force — especially television. Many people regard what they see on TV as the truth; Walter Cronkite once topped a poll as the most trusted man in America.

Now, with the advent of rock videos and all-music channels, rock music has grabbed a big chunk of legitimacy. American teenagers have instant access, in their living rooms, to the messages of rock, on the same vehicle that brought them Sesame Street. Who can blame them if they believe that the images they see are accurate reflections of adult reality, approved by adults? After all, Big Bird used to give them lessons on the same little box. Adults, by their silence, sanction the images. Do we really want our kids to think that rape and violence are what sexuality is all about?

This is not a trivial issue. Violence against women is a major social problem, one that's more than a cerebral issue to me. I teach at Boston University, and one of my most promising young journalism students was raped and murdered. Two others told me of being raped. Recently, one female student was assaulted and beaten so badly she had $5,000 worth of medical bills and permanent damage to her back and eyes.

It's nearly impossible, of course, to make a cause-and-effect link between lyrics and images and acts of violence. But images have a tremendous power to create an atmosphere in which violence against certain people is sanctioned. Nazi propagandists knew that full well when they portrayed Jews as ugly, greedy, and powerful.

The outcry over violence against women, particularly in a sexual context, is 12 being legitimized in two ways: by the increasing movement of these images into the mainstream of the media in TV, films, magazines, albums, videos, and by the silence about it.

Violence, of course, is rampant in the media. But it is usually set in some kind of moral context. It's usually only the bad guys who commit violent acts against the innocent. When the good guys get violent, it's against those who deserve it. Dirty Harry blows away the scum, he doesn't walk up to a toddler and say, "Make my day." The A Team does not shoot up suburban shopping malls.

But in some rock songs, it's the "heroes" who commit the acts. The people we are programmed to identify with are the ones being violent, with women on the receiving end. In a society where rape and assaults on women are endemic, this is no small problem, with millions of young boys watching on their TV screens and listening on their Walkmans.

I think something needs to be done. I'd like to see people in the industry respond to the problem. I'd love to see some women rock stars speak out against violence against women. I would like to see disc jockeys refuse air play to records and videos that contain such violence. At the very least, I want to see the end of the silence. I want journalists and parents and critics and performing artists to keep this issue alive in the public forum. I don't want people who are concerned about this issue labeled as bluenoses and bookburners and ignored.

And I wish it wasn't always just women who were speaking out. Men have as   16
large a stake in the quality of our civilization as women do in the long run. Violence is a contagion that infects at random. Let's hear something, please, from the men.

● PERSONAL RESPONSE ●

Do you agree or disagree with the argument Rivers makes about rock lyrics? Explain your answer.

● QUESTIONS FOR DISCUSSION ●

1. What distinction does Rivers draw between the lyrics of music she enjoyed when she was younger and the lyrics she is opposed to now? What distinction does Rivers draw in *any* music between what she finds tolerable and intolerable in lyrics?

2. How would you characterize the tone of this essay? Explain your answer.

3. What examples does Rivers use to back up her argument about sexual violence in today's rock music?

4. Where does Rivers present the views of those opposed to her own?

5. According to Rivers, what is the difference between depictions of violence in movies and the news media and depictions of violence in some rock lyrics and rock videos?

6. In what two ways does Rivers believe that violence against women is legitimized?

7. What action does Rivers call for in addressing the problem of violent rock lyrics?

8. Comment on Rivers' closing paragraph. Do you think it is effective? Explain why or why not.

● WRITING TOPICS ●

1. Drawing from the lyrics of selected popular rock songs, support or argue against Rivers' contention that such lyrics legitimize and even promote violence against women. Make sure you use specific examples. Your essay may focus on one, two, or several artists or groups.

2. Analyze the content of several MTV videos that contain depictions of violence against women. What messages do they send? Consider whether what you observe supports Rivers' argument or not.

3. Write an opinion essay on whether or not people are influenced by the music they listen to. Could listening to music about love and peace, for instance, alter a person's feelings about war? Do violent lyrics make people want to commit violence?

SOME REASONS FOR "WILDING"

●

SUSAN BAKER AND TIPPER GORE

Susan Baker and Tipper Gore are cofounders of Parents' Music Re-
source Center, located in Arlington, Virginia. PMRC was founded in
1985 to address the issue of popular-music lyrics that glorify sex and
violence and glamorize the use of drugs and alcohol. The following
article, which appeared in Newsweek *magazine in May 1989, is one of*
many the two women have written in their attempt to educate the
public about what they see as the dangers of certain media and music
messages.

Wilding." It's a new word in the vocabulary of teenage violence. The crime
that made it the stuff of headlines is so heinous, the details so lurid as to
make them almost beyond the understanding of any sane human being.

When it was over, a 28-year-old woman, an investment banker out for a jog,
was left brutally beaten, knifed and raped by teenagers. She was found near an
isolated road in New York's Central Park, covered with mud, almost dead from
brain damage, loss of blood and exposure.

"It was fun," one of her suspected teenage attackers, all between 14 and 17
years old, told the Manhattan district attorney's office. In the lockup, they were
nonchalantly whistling at a policewoman and singing a high-on-the-charts rap
song about casual sex: "Wild Thing."

Maybe it's the savagery, the remorseless brutality that brought the national 4
attention to this crime. We all heard about this one, either directly or from a
friend or family member who would end the story with an "I can't believe it."

Believe it. Because it's happening elsewhere too.

In 1987, in Brooklyn, N.Y., three teenagers methodically set fire to a
homeless couple. When at first rubbing alcohol wouldn't ignite the couple, they
went to a local service station for gasoline. It worked.

In 1988, in rural Missouri, three teenagers killed a friend—partly out of
curiosity! They just wanted to know what it would feel like to kill someone. One
of the teenagers claimed the fascination with death began with heavy-metal
music. When the victim asked "Why?" over and over as his friends brutally
attacked with baseball bats, the answer was "Because it's fun."

In 1988 a record 406 people died in the county of Los Angeles alone in teen- 8
gang-related attacks. One victim who survived was a pregnant woman who was
shot, allegedly by a 16-year-old as a gang initiation rite.

This is truly a "generation at risk." Indeed, the statistics reflect its pain and
confusion:

- The three leading causes of death among adolescents are drug- and
  alcohol-related accidents, suicide and homicide.

- Every year 1 million teenagers run away from home.
- Every year 1 million teenagers get pregnant.
- Every year over half a million—600,000 teenagers—attempt suicide; 5,000 succeed.
- Alcohol and drug abuse are so prevalent among the young that a *Weekly Reader* survey recently reported that 10-year-olds often feel pressure to try alcohol and crack.
- According to the Department of Education, 81 percent of the victims of violent crime are preteens and teenagers, 19 or younger. For the first time, teenagers have topped adults in the percentages of serious crimes committed per capita.

There are many complex reasons for this sad litany. Divorce and working parents strain the family's ability to cope. Latchkey kids are the rule more than the exception. Our schools and neighborhoods have become open-air drug markets. But it is not enough to excuse these children as products of a bad environment.

As a society, we must take full responsibility. Our music, movies and television are filled with images of sexual violence and killing. The message to our kids is: it's OK to enjoy brutality and suffering: "It's fun."

The American Academy of Pediatrics released a national policy statement 12 on the impact of rock lyrics and music videos on adolescents last November. In it, they noted that some lyrics communicate potentially harmful health messages in a culture beset with drug abuse, teenage pregnancy, AIDS and other sexually transmitted diseases.

The No. 2 album in the country this week is "GN'R Lies" from the very popular group, Guns N' Roses. This band is a favorite of sixth through 12th graders. It contains the following lyrics: "I used to love her but I had to kill her, I had to put her six feet under, and I can still hear her complain."

Teen "slasher" films, featuring scenes of graphic, sadistic violence against women are so popular that characters like Jason from "Friday the 13th" and Freddie from "Nightmare on Elm Street" are considered cult heroes, and now there are spinoff television shows.

As parents, it is our responsibility to teach our children to make wise decisions. This responsibility is not only to feed and clothe their bodies, but also to feed and nurture their spirits, their minds, their values. The moral crisis facing our nation's youth requires that we *all* share the responsibility, parents and the entertainment industry.

Too often, those who produce this violence evade any discussion of their 16 own responsibility by pretending the entire debate begins and ends with the First Amendment. We are strong advocates of its protections of free speech and free expression. We do not and have not advocated or supported restrictions on those rights; we have never proposed government action. What we are advocating, and what we have worked hard to encourage, is responsibility.

For example, producers and songwriters don't consider putting out songs, movies or videos that would portray racism in a positive way. They could. The

First Amendment provides that freedom. But they don't. In part, perhaps it's because they think those products wouldn't sell. But in part, they recognize it would be irresponsible. Why is there no similar reticence when the issue is glorifying violence, generally against women?

The same sense of responsibility should be brought to a marketplace so saturated with violence that it legitimizes it for our children. It's time to stop the spilling of blood both as "entertainment" and in real life.

● PERSONAL RESPONSE ●

Do you think that Baker and Gore are overreacting to the dangers they see in certain rock music and teenage slasher films, or do they have a legitimate basis for complaint? Explain your answer.

● QUESTIONS FOR DISCUSSION ●

1. What connection do Baker and Gore make between "wilding" and media and music images of sexual violence?
2. Besides the example of the brutal crime against the Central Park jogger, what other examples do Baker and Gore offer to illustrate the brutality of crimes committed by young people? How effective are their illustrations?
3. How convincing is the evidence Baker and Gore present to substantiate their claim that today's youth are "truly a 'generation at risk'" (paragraph 9)?
4. What actions do Baker and Gore call for in order to address what they see as "the moral crisis facing our nation's youth" (paragraph 15)?
5. What reasons or excuses do song writers and filmmakers give to defend the violence in their products?
6. Do you think Baker and Gore make a convincing argument against violence in music? If not, what would make it more effective?

● WRITING TOPICS ●

1. Argue for or against extending the First Amendment's freedom of speech to violent lyrics in rock music. Consider how far you think the First Amendment's protection of free speech should be allowed to go.
2. Focusing on teenage "slasher" films, argue for or against Baker and Gore's position that such movies send morally wrong messages to children. Use specific examples of scenes in one or two movies to support your argument.
3. Explain one possible cause for the widespread social problems among teenagers that Baker and Gore cite in their article.

OLD ENOUGH TO KILL?

●

Anna Quindlen

Anna Quindlen was born in Philadelphia, Pennsylvania, and educated
at Barnard College. She began her journalism career at the New York
Post *and then became deputy metropolitan editor of the* New York
Times. *In 1986, she began her syndicated column, "Life in the Thir-*
ties," some of which essays were collected in Living Out Loud *(1988).*
Also a frequent contributor to magazines, Quindlen often addresses
difficult moral and ethical issues. In the Times *syndicated article*
reprinted below, Quindlen expresses her dismay at the increasingly
lower ages at which children commit violent crimes.

Later this year, when the forsythia on the mountain slopes here has turned from yellow to green, Cameron Kocher will stand trial for killing Jessica Carr. Late May or early June, his lawyer says, unless there is some kind of plea bargain. The timing is fortunate; the defendant will not miss much of fifth grade.

He was 9 years old when the shooting of the little girl took place, and Cameron Kocher, Cub Scout and only child, could well become the youngest person in this century tried as an adult in a homicide case. The defense has entered a plea of not guilty. The prosecutor has not asked for the death penalty. He says a primary goal in this prosecution is psychiatric, not punitive, and that the decision to try Cameron as an adult was influenced by the seriousness of the crime. You have to wonder how it was influenced by an atmosphere of frustration and disillusionment, an atmosphere in which we have had it with criminals and we no longer believe in childhood.

In our big cities and our little burgs, people have become enraged by a criminal justice system they think favors the bad guys. The rehabilitative prison model is dead; mention it to legal experts and they laugh, a mirthless chuckle. "Lock 'em up and throw away the key" is a constant refrain, and the death penalty is the Big Daddy of solutions. When crack gangs are populated by 12-year-olds, and rapists are high-school sophomores, the rage is keener, and tinged with something more personal. It's 10 o'clock; do you know where your children are?

They're living in a fearsome world. It's become a truism that they are too early 4 adult, that they learn about abortion and AIDS at the same time that they're learning to read. The bright line between child and adult, drawn in the past by knowledge and privilege, has faded. We judge them grown up by the things they do, and unkindest cut of all, by things that are done to them.

"I'd like information on the 7-year-old who was raped," I said to a sergeant in the Bronx sex crimes unit recently. "Which one?" he replied. It is self-protection for adults to think of children growing up in such a world as more mature than they truly are.

Oh, the children themselves have provided ample evidence of corruption. When the infamous Willie Bosket, New York State's most incorrigible inmate, said he had committed 2 murders and 25 stabbings by the time he was 15, it seemed incredible. No more. Age down, severity up.

The National Center for Juvenile Justice reports that in the last decade more than two-thirds of the states have got tougher with juveniles. Some make younger kids more culpable; some pick out certain crimes as outside any possible boundary of childhood. If you are 13 in New York, you are a juvenile unless you commit murder. Murder is a grown-up crime.

Prosecutors say Cameron Kocher acted in a grown-up fashion a year ago. They 8 say he got the key to his father's gun cabinet from the base of a lamp, unlocked the cabinet and the ammunition drawer, loaded the gun, and removed a screen before he fired from a second-story window, hitting the 7-year-old in the back as she rode on a snowmobile. There is speculation that he did so because she boasted of being better at Nintendo.

Is that horrible scenario an answer, or a question? At what age does a child realize that death is not a video game, that only on television do people get up after they are shot, that actions have permanent consequences? Nine? Eleven? Fourteen? Are we past the point where we care? A witness says that after the shooting, Cameron said to his playmates, "If you don't think about it, you won't be sad."

Kids who commit crimes rob adults of illusions. We enshrine the years when our children are young, at least until we first read "Lord of the Flies." The easiest way to respond to child criminals is to say that they are somehow not children at all. We think of them as children without childhood, growing up on streets crunchy with hypodermic needles and crack vials.

Not Cameron Kocher. He will go on trial in a town with a Main Street and a courthouse square, a neighborly place that might as well be the Bedford Falls of "It's a Wonderful Life." He made the honor roll, has no history of behavioral problems, and can't go to jail. He's even too young for a juvenile facility; if he were convicted and given a custodial sentence, he would have to be sent initially to some private institution.

This prosecution is essentially an exercise. The defense attorney says it is an 12 exercise in futility. He hints at a tragic accident and says this is not the way to proceed if his client needs help. The prosecutor talks of diagnosis, and rehabilitation. Let's hope so. If we stick with rehabilitation for anyone, it should be for the young, if not out of compassion, then out of pragmatism. They'll be around for a long, long time.

This is also an exercise in self-definition. On the day this trial begins in the Monroe County courthouse, we will be a nation that believes it is right to try a fifth-grader for murder.

● PERSONAL RESPONSE ●

What was your reaction to the news that a 9-year-old had killed someone, apparently deliberately? Do you agree with the explanations Quindlen gives for how such a thing could happen? Why or why not?

● QUESTIONS FOR DISCUSSION ●

1. How does the prosecutor's description of the Cameron Kocher case as an "exercise in futility" (paragraph 12) reinforce Quindlen's central point?

2. What effect do you suppose Quindlen wanted to achieve in the opening paragraph? That is, why does she start with references to forsythia on mountain slopes and the timing of Cameron Kocher's trial?

3. Quindlen reports that the prosecution in the Kocher case wants to try the boy as an adult because of the seriousness of the crime. What other possible reasons does Quindlen offer for the decision to prosecute Kocher as an adult?

4. Explain Quindlen's statement in paragraph 4 that "the bright line between child and adult, drawn in the past by knowledge and privilege, has faded."

5. What does Quindlen mean in paragraph 10 when she writes: "Kids who commit crimes rob adults of illusions."

6. What is the purpose of the allusions to *Lord of the Flies* (paragraph 10) and *It's a Wonderful Life* (paragraph 11)?

7. In what way, according to Quindlen, is this case "an exercise in self-definition" (paragraph 13)?

● WRITING TOPICS ●

1. Quindlen says that children are living in "a fearsome world" (paragraph 4). Define what you think this "fearsome world" is.

2. Explore the ways in which certain everyday realities of our world push children into adulthood too early. If possible, use children you know as examples to support your observations.

3. Argue for or against trying Cameron Kocher as an adult.

GUNS 'Я' US

•

MATTHEW MARANZ

*Matthew Maranz is a student at the Columbia School of Journalism.
The following essay, which appeared in* The New Republic *in 1989,
explains how an American citizen can purchase an automatic submachine gun. The occasional ironic tone of Maranz's essay reveals his
astonishment at how simple the process really is.*

I am over 21 years of age. I am a citizen of the United States. I have not
been convicted of a felony. And I have not been treated or confined for
drug addiction, drunkenness, or mental illness. According to the National Firearms Act of 1934, I thus qualify to purchase a fully automatic machine
gun capable of firing hundreds of bullets with a single squeeze of the trigger. A
few months ago, I decided to try.

As far as the federal government is concerned, private citizens have always
had the right to purchase machine guns — at a price. The Firearms Act, passed
by Congress to curb mob warfare, added a $500 manufacturers tax and $200
transfer tax to the cost. And in May 1986, Congress effectively doubled the price
by banning the future manufacture of machine guns for private sale, making
them an increasingly scarce commodity. Also, prospective machine-gun buyers
must go through a lengthy (one to three months) licensing process, including
fingerprinting, that helps the FBI do a background check. But provided I pass
muster on the federal (and state) level, a MAC-10 or Uzi can be mine.

In order to apply for a machine-gun permit, I have to specify exactly what
make of machine gun I want. So I walked down to my local newsstand to consult
the machine-gunners equivalent of *Consumer Reports. Assault Rifles* carried
the definitive work on the .223 controversy — "Can it Measure up to the 7.62 on
the Battlefield?" (rest easy, it can). *Firepower* ran a full-page color ad for "Rock
n' Roll #3: Sexy Girls and Sexy Guns," a mail-order home video. It starred
Dottie/Uzi, Tani Jo/MAC-10, Rosie/MP-5, and Lillian/MP-K and sold for $59.95
plus $3 shipping. Then I came upon an article referring to the Ingram M-11
LISP. The M-11 is a tiny machine pistol that fires 1,200 rounds per minute and
fits neatly in a single hand. The CIA used to favor it as a weapon for operations
behind enemy lines. That sounded like the gun for me.

Taking names from the advertisers' index, I started calling some of the 4
nation's 3,530 licensed machine-gun dealers. My first call reached an answering
machine: "Hello. This is SWD Incorporated. Our offices are closed for the
holidays. M-11-9 semi-auto pistols and carbines are in stock. M-11-9, M-11-380,
and M-10-45 submachine-guns are also in stock in limited quantities. All SMG
[submachine-gun] orders must be prepaid to ensure you receive yours. We will
ship semi-autos on a c.o.d. basis. Have a joyous holiday season."

The first dealer I actually contacted told me that federal law requires machine-gun purchases to be in-state transactions. He suggested I locate a local machine-gun shop. If it didn't have the gun I wanted, an out-of-state dealer would then sell the M-11 to the in-state dealer, who would sell it to me. Turning to "Guns" in the Yellow Pages, I found a local machine-gun salesman. I called and asked about the M-11.

"I won't sell it to you," he insisted.

I understood. Surely the Second Amendment wasn't meant to cover weapons used to mow down hundreds of innocent bystanders in the streets of our inner cities.

"It's a piece of junk," he continued. "Try the MAC-10." 8

The MAC-10 is capable of firing 900 rounds every 60 seconds. The .45 version is a mere 10½ inches long and weighs 6.25 pounds. With telescope and silencer, it grows to 22 inches. Critics frown on its unreliability past 30 yards, but the MAC-10 remains an immensely popular weapon. One reason is that buyers don't just get a gun; they get a piece of history. The MAC-10 was one of the ancestors of the Uzi, arguably today's hippest machine gun. The CIA, FBI, DEA, and Special Forces endorse the MAC-10. So do the Crips and Bloods of Los Angeles gang war fame. And so did Tani Jo in "Rock n' Roll #3: Sexy Girls and Sexy Guns." Good enough for Tani Jo, good enough for me. I became a MAC-10 convert.

Now I was ready to apply for a state and federal machine-gun permit. How difficult that is depends on where you live. Some 14 states prohibit private ownership of machine guns; others like Texas, Virginia, and Ohio are notorious for their loose gun laws. In Massachusetts, gun laws are tight. Before going through the cumbersome federal process, I had to think of a subtle way to ask a boss and a friend to provide letters of reference certifying my ability to be a responsible owner of a machine gun. I had to obtain three 1.5 by 1.5 pictures of myself to attach to the handgun application that's required for a machine-gun license. I also had to deal with a policy sergeant manning the licensing table who was understandably hostile to civilians seeking machine guns. I persevered.

But the eternally curious federal bureaucracy almost stopped me in my tracks. They sent me a slew of white Form 4's and yellow Form 7's required by the Bureau of Alcohol, Tobacco, and Firearms, which keeps track of the number of machine guns in private circulation (191,857 as of December 1988). No one, not the National Rifle Association, the local gun dealer, my friends at work, my mother, even the people I called at the Bureau of Alcohol, Tobacco, and Firearms, could decipher them. Paperwork is America's tightest means of gun control.

There had to be an easier, yet legal, way to evade the bureaucracy. I went 12 back to my magazines and found Automatic Weaponry of Brentwood, Tennessee, "America's Foremost Supplier of Title II Firearms [machine guns and silencers]."

The man at Automatic Weaponry said they specialized in simplifying the federal licensing process. I give Automatic Weaponry basic biographical information over the phone. I send them a 50 percent deposit that's refundable except for a $100 processing fee. They mail me an order form, the already completed white Form 4 and two FBI Fingerprint Applicant Cards. I sign the forms, affix a recent 2 by 2 photograph, and declare a purpose for purchasing a machine gun ("don't put down 'to kill human beings,'" he suggested). I take them to my local chief law enforcement officer, who fingerprints me and verifies my identity and age. He also conducts a National Crime Information Center search for felony convictions (misdemeanors OK). He signs the forms. I mail the paperwork back to Automatic Weaponry. I pay the balance. (Automatic Weaponry accepts personal and business checks, and all major credit cards.) They ship the weapon to an in-state gun dealer via United Parcel Service. Seventy to 90 days after I first contact Automatic Weaponry, I pick up my machine gun. A MAC-10 .45 caliber in mint condition costs $1,295 plus the $200 federal machine-gun transfer tax (Tani Jo not included).

For those with less time, money, and respect for the law, there's an easier way. A semi-automatic MAC-10 retails for as little as $350 and is sold under the same federal regulatory guidelines as a rifle—no fingerprinting or background check required, just proof that you are a U.S. citizen over 18, are not a convicted felon, and have never been confined or incarcerated for drunkenness, drug addiction, or mental illness. In some states I could walk into a gun shop, fill out a few forms, plunk down some cash, and leave with gun in hand. True, like all semi-automatics it would fire only one bullet with each squeeze of the trigger. But if I wanted to risk a 20-year jail term and $20,000 fine, I could convert my semi- into a fully-automatic 900-round-a-minute weapon. A matchstick is all that's needed to convert some guns. The MAC-10 is more sophisticated: one gun dealer I spoke with said he's used a nickel. A guy at the NRA boasted it would take him 15 minutes. But what about someone like me, with zero mechanical ability? He asked if I could change a spark plug. Probably, I replied. Don't worry, he said, you could do it in an hour.

● PERSONAL RESPONSE ●

Are you surprised at the relative ease with which anyone can buy a machine gun? Why do you think so many people want to own such weapons?

● QUESTIONS FOR DISCUSSION ●

1. Point out passages that indicate Maranz's point of view toward his subject. Does he approve or disapprove of the ease with which Americans can purchase submachine guns?

2. Why do you suppose Maranz included the information about requirements for purchasing a machine gun according to the National Firearms Act of 1934 and the restrictions or changes that were added to that act by Congress in 1986 (paragraphs 1 and 2)?

3. What resources are available to assist the potential machine-gun buyer in selecting a model for purchase?

4. Why do you think Maranz names agencies and groups that favor the MAC-10 (paragraph 9)?

5. Maranz says that at one stage of this process he almost quit. What stage was that and how did he solve the problem? How long does the process of becoming a machine-gun owner ordinarily take?

6. In his conclusion, Maranz explains the ways people can illegally convert their semi-automatic machine guns into automatic weapons. What point do you think Maranz wants to make with that information?

7. What is the implication of the closing sentences?

● WRITING TOPICS ●

1. Argue for or against the position that the Second Amendment right to bear arms extends to the right of citizens to own semi-automatic machine guns.

2. Both this essay and the following one, Gail Buchalter's "Why I Bought a Gun," touch on the issue of gun control. Taking into consideration Maranz's success at purchasing an automatic machine gun and Buchalter's reasons for buying a hand gun, argue for or against stricter gun control laws.

3. Examine reasons why people desire to own such powerful weapons as the MAC-10. Is there a "typical" machine-gun owner? Do you or someone you know own one? Would you want to own such a weapon?

WHY I BOUGHT A GUN

●

GAIL BUCHALTER

Gail Buchalter attended Hunter College, was a staff writer for People *magazine in the mid-1980s, and is now a freelance writer living in Los Angeles. A regular contributor to* Forbes, Parade, *and* Entertainment Weekly, *she is currently writing a mystery book. The article reprinted below was first published in* Parade *magazine in 1988. In it, Buchalter explains why, despite her ardent pacifism, she decided to purchase a handgun.*

I was raised to wear black and cultured pearls in one of Manhattan's more desirable neighborhoods. My upper-middle-class background never involved guns. If my parents felt threatened, they simply put another lock on the door.

By high school, I had traded in my cashmere sweaters for a black arm band. I marched for Civil Rights, shunned Civil Defense drills and protested the Vietnam war. It was easy being 18 and a peacenik. I wasn't raising an 11-year-old child then.

Today, I am typical of the women whom gun manufacturers have been aiming at as potential buyers — and one of the millions who have succumbed: Between 1983 and 1986, there was a 53 percent increase in female gun-owners in the U.S. — from 7.9 million to 12.1 million, according to a Gallup Poll paid for by Smith & Wesson, the gun manufacturer.

Gun enthusiasts have created ad campaigns with such snappy slogans as 4 "You Can't Rape a .38" or "Should You Shoot a Rapist Before He Cuts Your Throat?" While I was trying to come to a rational decision, I disliked these manipulative scare tactics. They only inflamed an issue that I never even dreamed would touch me.

I began questioning my beliefs one Halloween night in Phoenix, where I had moved when I married. I was almost home when another car nearly hit mine head-on. With the speed of a New York cabbie, I rolled down my window and screamed curses as the driver passed me. He instantly made a U-turn, almost climbing on my back bumper. By now, he and his two friends were hanging out of the car windows, yelling that they were going to rape, cut and kill me.

I already had turned into our driveway when I realized my husband wasn't home. I was trapped. The car had pulled in behind me. I drove up to the back porch and got into the kitchen, where our dogs stood waiting for me. The three men spilled out of their car and into our yard.

My adrenaline was pumping faster than Edwin Moses' legs clearing a hurdle. I grabbed the collars of Jack, our 200-pound Irish wolfhound, and his 140-pound malamute buddy, Slush. Then I kicked open the back door — I was so scared that I became aggressive — and actually dared the three creeps to keep coming. With the dogs, the odds had changed in my favor, and the men ran back to the safety of their car, yelling that they'd be back the next day to blow me away. Fortunately, they never returned.

A few years and one divorce later, I headed for Los Angeles with my 3-year-old son, Jordan (the dogs had since departed). When I put him in preschool a few weeks later, the headmistress noted that I was a single parent and immediately warned me that there was a rapist in my new neighborhood. 8

I called the police, who confirmed this fact. The rapist had no *modus operandi*. Sometimes he would be waiting in his victim's house; other times he would break in while the person was asleep. Although it was summer, I would carefully lock my windows at night and then lie there and sweat in fear. Thankfully, the rapist was caught, but not before he had attacked two more women.

Over some time, at first imperceptibly, my suburban neighborhood became less secure. A street gang took over the apartment building across from my house, and flowers and compact cars gave way to graffiti and low-riders.

Daytime was quiet, but these gang members crawled out like cockroaches after dark. Several nights in a row they woke me up. It was one of the most terrifying times in my life. I could hear them talking and laughing as they leaned against our fence, tossing their empty beer cans into our front yard. I knew that they were drinking, but were they also using violence-inducing drugs such as PCP and crack? And if they broke in, could I get to the police before they got to me?

I found myself, to my surprise, wishing that I had a loaded pistol under my pillow. In the clear light of day, I found this reaction shocking and simply decided to move to a safer neighborhood, although it cost thousands of dollars more. Luckily, I was able to afford it. 12

Soon the papers were telling yet another tale of senseless horror. Richard Ramirez, who became known as "The Walk-In Killer," spent months crippling and killing before he was caught. His alleged crimes were so brutal and bizarre, his desire to inflict pain so intense, that I began to question my beliefs about the sanctity of human life — his, in particular. The thought of taking a human life is repugnant to me, but the idea of being someone's victim is worse. And how, I began to ask myself, do you talk pacifism to a murderer or a rapist?

Finally, I decided that I would defend myself, even if it meant killing another person. I realized that the one-sided pacifism I once so strongly had advocated could backfire on me and, worse, on my son. Reluctantly, I concluded that I had to insure the best option for our survival. My choices: to count on a cop or to own a pistol.

But still I didn't go out and buy a gun. Everything about guns is threatening. My only exposure to them had been in movies; owning one, I feared, would bring all that violence off of the screen and into my home.

So, instead, I called up my girlfriend (who has begged to remain nameless) and told her I had decided to buy a gun. We were both surprised that I didn't know she already had one. She was held up at gunpoint several years ago and bought what she said was a .37. We figured out it must be either a .38 or a .357. I was horrified when she admitted that not only had she no idea what type of gun 16 she owned, but she also had never even shot it. It remains in her drawer, loaded and unused.

Upset, I hung up and called another friend. He was going to the National Rifle Association convention that was being held in Reno and suggested I tag along. My son's godmother lives there, so I figured I could visit her and kill two birds with one stone.

My first night in Reno, I attended the Handgun Hunters' Awards dinner and sat next to a contributing editor for one of the gun magazines. He bitterly complained that killing elephants had been outlawed, although there were thousands still running around Africa. Their legs, he explained, made wonderful trash baskets. I felt like Thumper on opening day of the hunting season, and my foot kept twitching under the table.

The next day at the convention center, I saw a sign announcing a seminar for women on handguns and safety. I met pistol-packing grandmas, kids who were into competitive shooting and law-enforcement agents. I listened to a few of them speak and then watched a video, "A Woman's Guide to Firearms." It explained everything from how guns worked to an individual's responsibilities as a gun owner.

It was my kind of movie, since everything about guns scares me — especially 20 owning one. Statistics on children who are victims of their parents' handguns are overwhelming: About 300 children a year — almost a child a day — are killed by guns in this country, according to Handgun Control, Inc., which bases its numbers on data from the National Safety Council. Most of these killings are accidental.

As soon as I returned to Los Angeles, I called a man I had met a while ago who, I remembered, owned several guns. He told me he had a Smith & Wesson .38 Special for sale and recommended it, since it was small enough for me to handle yet had the necessary stopping power.

I bought the gun. That same day, I got six rounds of special ammunition with plastic tips that explode on impact. These are not for target practice; these are for protection.

For about $50, I also picked up the metal safety box that I had learned about in the video. Its push-button lock opens with a touch if you know the proper combination, possibly taking only a second or two longer than it does to reach into a night-table drawer. Now I knew that my son, Jordan, couldn't get his hands on it while I still could.

When I brought the gun home, Jordan was fascinated by it. He kept picking 24 it up, while I nervously watched. But knowledge, I believe, is still our greatest defense. And since I'm in favor of education for sex, AIDS and learning to drive, I couldn't draw the line at teaching my son about guns.

Next, I took the pistol and my son to the target range. I rented a .22 caliber pistol for Jordan. (A .38 was too much gun for him to handle.) I was relieved when he put it down after 10 minutes — he didn't like the feel of it.

But that didn't prevent him from asking me if he should use the gun if someone broke into our house while I wasn't home. I shrieked "no!" so loud, we both jumped. I explained that, if someone ever broke in, he's young and agile enough to leap out the window and run for his life.

Today he couldn't care less about the gun. Every so often, when we're watching television in my room, I practice opening the safety box, and Jordan times me. I'm down to three seconds. I'll ask him what's the first thing you do when you handle a gun, and he looks at me like I'm a moron, saying for the umpteenth time: "Make sure it's unloaded. But I know I'm not to touch it or tell my friends about it." Jordan's already bored with it all.

I, on the other hand, look forward to Mondays—"Ladies' Night" at the 28 target range—when I get to shoot for free. I buy a box of bullets and some targets from the guy behind the counter, put on the protective eye and ear coverings and walk through the double doors to the firing lines.

Once there, I load my gun, look down the sights of the barrel and adjust my aim. I fire six rounds into the chest of a life-sized target hanging 25 feet away. As each bullet rips a hole through the figure drawn there, I realize I'm getting used to owning a gun and no longer feeling faint when I pick it up. The weight of it has become comfortable in my hand. And I am keeping my promise to practice. Too many people are killed by their own guns because they don't know how to use them.

It took me years to decide to buy a gun, and then weeks before I could load it. It gave me nightmares.

One night I dreamed I woke up when someone broke into our house. I grabbed my gun and sat waiting at the foot of my bed. Finally, I saw him turn the corner as he headed toward me. He was big and filled the hallway—an impossible target to miss. I aimed the gun and froze, visualizing the bullet blowing a hole through his chest and spraying his flesh all over the walls and floor. I didn't want to shoot, but I knew my survival was on the line. I wrapped my finger around the trigger and finally squeezed it, simultaneously accepting the intruder's death at my own hand and the relief of not being a victim. I woke up as soon as I decided to shoot.

I was tearfully relieved that it had only been a dream. 32

I never have weighed the consequences of an act as strongly as I have that of buying a gun—but, then again, I never have done anything with such deadly repercussions. Most of my friends refuse even to discuss it with me. They believe that violence begets violence.

They're probably right.

● PERSONAL RESPONSE ●

How do you feel about Buchalter's decision to buy a handgun? Would you buy one if you were in her place? Could you shoot another human being?

● QUESTIONS FOR DISCUSSION ●

1. Do you think Buchalter is worried about whether or not her audience will agree with her decision? Explain your answer.

2. How convincingly does Buchalter dramatize the series of events that led to her decision to buy a gun?

3. How does Buchalter's decision to buy a handgun contrast with her upbringing and her beliefs as a young woman?

4. What does Buchalter imply about her unnamed woman friend's ignorance of her own gun? How does her own attitude toward gun ownership and her frankness with her son contrast with the attitude of her friend?

5. How did Buchalter's experiences at the National Rifle Association convention help in her decision to buy a gun?

6. Why do you think Buchalter includes the information about her conversation with the man sitting next to her at the Handgun Hunters' Awards dinner (paragraph 18)? Explain what she means when she says she felt like "Thumper on opening day of hunting season."

7. Why do you think Buchalter ends her essay as she does? Do you think she still doubts her reasons for buying a gun, despite her many reasons for doing so?

● WRITING TOPICS ●

1. If you own a handgun, explain your reasons for purchasing it and how you feel about owning it. Or, if you do not own a gun but know someone who does, explain that person's reasons for and feelings about owning one.

2. If you have ever made a decision to do something that conflicted with beliefs you held, explain what led you to the decision and describe how you felt about it once you had made it.

3. Both George Orwell in "Shooting an Elephant" (Chapter 2) and Gail Buchalter in "Why I Bought a Gun" narrate a series of events that led to their doing something they were deeply opposed to doing. Compare the two essays. How do the motives of the two writers differ? Does what they did have the same effect on each of them?

PILGRIMAGE TO NONVIOLENCE

●

MARTIN LUTHER KING, JR.

Martin Luther King, Jr., was born in Atlanta, Georgia, in 1929. At age 18 he was ordained a Baptist minister in his father's church, the same year that he earned his undergraduate degree from Morehouse College. He earned his B.D. from Crozer Theological Seminary in 1951 and his Ph.D. from Boston University in 1954. In 1955, King organized a successful boycott of the Montgomery, Alabama, bus system and became the leader of the civil rights movement. By the time he founded the Southern Christian Leadership Conference in 1957, he had become internationally known for his philosophy of nonviolent resistance. King was Time *magazine's Man of the Year in 1963, and in 1964, he won the Nobel Peace Prize. He was assassinated in Memphis, Tennessee, in 1968. The following excerpt from a chapter of his book* Stride Toward Freedom *(1958) defines King's concept of nonviolent resistance.*

When I went to Montgomery as a pastor, I had not the slightest idea that I would later become involved in a crisis in which nonviolent resistance would be applicable. I neither started the protest nor suggested it. I simply responded to the call of the people for a spokesman. When the protest began, my mind, consciously or unconsciously, was driven back to the Sermon on the Mount, with its sublime teachings on love, and the Gandhian method of nonviolent resistance. As the days unfolded, I came to see the power of nonviolence more and more. Living through the actual experience of the protest, nonviolence became more than a method to which I gave intellectual assent; it became a commitment to a way of life. Many of the things that I had not cleared up intellectually concerning nonviolence were now solved in the sphere of practical action.

Since the philosophy of nonviolence played such a positive role in the Montgomery Movement, it may be wise to turn to a brief discussion of some basic aspects of this philosophy.

First, it must be emphasized that nonviolent resistance is not a method for cowards; it does resist. If one uses this method because he is afraid or merely because he lacks the instruments of violence, he is not truly nonviolent. This is why Gandhi often said that if cowardice is the only alternative to violence, it is better to fight. He made this statement conscious of the fact that there is always another alternative: no individual or group need submit to any wrong, nor need they use violence to right the wrong; there is the way of nonviolent resistance. This is ultimately the way of the strong man. It is not a method of stagnant passivity. The phrase "passive resistance" often gives the false impression that this is a sort of "do-nothing method" in which the resister quietly and passively accepts evil. But nothing is further from the truth. For while the nonviolent resister is passive in the sense that he is not physically aggressive toward his opponent, his mind and emotions are always active, constantly seeking to persuade his opponent that he is wrong. The method is passive physically, but strongly active spiritually. It is not passive nonresistance to evil, it is active nonviolent resistance to evil.

A second basic fact that characterizes nonviolence is that it does not seek to 4 defeat or humiliate the opponent, but to win his friendship and understanding. The nonviolent resister must often express his protest through noncoöperation or boycotts, but he realizes that these are not ends themselves; they are merely means to awaken a sense of moral shame in the opponent. The end is redemption and reconciliation. The aftermath of nonviolence is the creation of the beloved community, while the aftermath of violence is tragic bitterness.

A third characteristic of this method is that the attack is directed against forces of evil rather than against persons who happen to be doing the evil. It is evil that the nonviolent resister seeks to defeat, not the persons victimized by evil. If he is opposing racial injustice, the nonviolent resister has the vision to see that the basic tension is not between races. As I like to say to the people in Montgomery: "The tension in this city is not between white people and Negro people. The tension is, at bottom, between justice and injustice, between the forces of light and the forces of darkness. And if there is a victory, it will be a victory not merely for fifty thousand Negroes, but a victory for justice and the forces of light. We are out to defeat injustice and not white persons who may be unjust."

A fourth point that characterizes nonviolent resistance is a willingness to accept suffering without retaliation, to accept blows from the opponent without striking back. "Rivers of blood may have to flow before we gain our freedom, but it must be our blood," Gandhi said to his countrymen. The nonviolent resister is willing to accept violence if necessary, but never to inflict it. He does not seek to dodge jail. If going to jail is necessary, he enters it "as a bridegroom enters the bride's chamber."

One may well ask: "What is the nonviolent resister's justification for this ordeal to which he invites men, for this mass political application of the ancient doctrine of turning the other cheek?" The answer is found in the realization that unearned suffering is redemptive. Suffering, the nonviolent resister realizes, has tremendous educational and transforming possibilities. "Things of fundamental importance to people are not secured by reason alone, but have to be purchased with their suffering," said Gandhi. He continues: "Suffering is infinitely more powerful than the law of the jungle for converting the opponent and opening his ears which are otherwise shut to the voice of reason."

A fifth point concerning nonviolent resistance is that it avoids not only 8 external physical violence but also internal violence of spirit. The nonviolent resister not only refuses to shoot his opponent but he also refuses to hate him. At the center of nonviolence stands the principle of love. The nonviolent resister would contend that in the struggle for human dignity, the oppressed people of the world must not succumb to the temptation of becoming bitter or indulging in hate campaigns. To retaliate in kind would do nothing but intensify the existence of hate in the universe. Along the way of life, someone must have sense enough and morality enough to cut off the chain of hate. This can only be done by projecting the ethic of love to the center of our lives.

In speaking of love at this point, we are not referring to some sentimental or affectionate emotion. It would be nonsense to urge men to love their oppressors in an affectionate sense. Love in this connection means understanding, redemptive good will. Here the Greek language comes to our aid. There are three words for love in the Greek New Testament. First, there is *eros*. In Platonic philosophy *eros* meant the yearning of the soul for the realm of the divine. It has come now to mean a sort of aesthetic or romantic love. Second, there is *philia* which means intimate affection between personal friends. *Philia* denotes a sort of reciprocal love; the person loves because he is loved. When we speak of loving those who oppose us, we refer to neither *eros* nor *philia*; we speak of love which is expressed in the Greek word *agape*. *Agape* means understanding, redeeming good will for all men. It is an overflowing love which is purely spontaneous, unmotivated, groundless, and creative. It is not set in motion by any quality or function of its object. It is the love of God operating in the human heart.

Agape is disinterested love. It is a love in which the individual seeks not his own good, but the good of his neighbor (I Cor. 10:24). *Agape* does not begin by discriminating between worthy and unworthy people, or any qualities people possess. It begins by loving others *for their sakes*. It is an entirely "neighbor-regarding concern for others," which discovers the neighbor in every man it meets. There, *agape* makes no distinction between friend and enemy; it is directed toward both. If one loves an individual merely on account of his friendliness, he loves him for the sake of the benefits to be gained from the friendship, rather than for the friend's own sake. Consequently, the best way to assure oneself that love is disinterested is to have love for the enemy-neighbor from whom you can expect no good in return, but only hostility and persecution.

Another basic point about *agape* is that it springs from the *need* of the other person — his need for belonging to the best in the human family. The Samaritan who helped the Jew on the Jericho road was "good" because he responded to the human need that he was presented with. God's love is eternal and fails not because man needs his love. St. Paul assures us that the loving act of redemption was done "while we were yet sinners" — that is, at the point of our greatest need for love. Since the white man's personality is greatly distorted by segregation, and his soul is greatly scarred, he needs the love of the Negro. The Negro must love the white man, because the white man needs his love to remove his tensions, insecurities, and fears.

Agape is not a weak, passive love. It is love in action. *Agape* is love seeking to preserve and create community. It is insistence on community even when one seeks to break it. *Agape* is a willingness to sacrifice in the interest of mutuality. *Agape* is a willingness to go to any length to restore community. It doesn't stop at the first mile, but it goes the second mile to restore community. It is a willingness to forgive, not seven times, but seventy times seven to restore community. The cross is the eternal expression of the length to which God will go in order to restore broken community. The resurrection is a symbol of God's triumph over all the forces that seek to block community. The Holy Spirit is the continuing community creating reality that moves through history. He who works against community is working against the whole of creation. Therefore, if I respond to hate with a reciprocal hate I do nothing but intensify the cleavage in broken community. I can only close the gap in broken community by meeting hate with love. If I meet hate with hate, I become depersonalized, because creation is so designed that my personality can only be fulfilled in the context of community. Booker T. Washington was right: "Let no man pull you so low as to make you hate him." When he pulls you that low he brings you to the point of working against community; he drags you to the point of defying creation, and thereby becoming depersonalized.

In the final analysis, *agape* means a recognition of the fact that all life is interrelated. All humanity is involved in a single process, and all men are brothers. To the degree that I harm my brother, no matter what he is doing to me, to that extent I am harming myself. For example, white men often refuse federal aid to education in order to avoid giving the Negro his rights; but because all men are brothers they cannot deny Negro children without harming their own. They end, all efforts to the contrary, by hurting themselves. Why is this? Because men are brothers. If you harm me, you harm yourself.

Love, *agape*, is the only cement that can hold this broken community together. When I am commanded to love, I am commanded to restore community, to resist injustice, and to meet the needs of my brothers.

A sixth basic fact about nonviolent resistance is that it is based on the conviction that the universe is on the side of justice. Consequently, the believer in nonviolence has deep faith in the future. This faith is another reason why the nonviolent resister can accept suffering without retaliation. For he knows that in his struggle for justice he has cosmic companionship. It is true that there are devout believers in nonviolence who find it difficult to believe in a personal God. But even these persons believe in the existence of some creative force that works for universal wholeness. Whether we call it an unconscious process, an impersonal Brahman, or a Personal Being of matchless power and infinite love, there is a creative force in this universe that works to bring the disconnected aspects of reality into a harmonious whole.

● PERSONAL RESPONSE ●

How appropriate do you think King's philosophy of nonviolent resistance is to today's social problems? Under what circumstances would it work? Under what circumstances would it be fruitless?

● QUESTIONS FOR DISCUSSION ●

1. Comment on King's opening paragraph. How well does it introduce his subject?
2. Do you think King has in mind an audience opposed to or in favor of his philosophy? Explain your answer.

3. What characteristics of King's style reflect the fact that he was a minister?

4. King frequently alludes to other people and events. Who was Gandhi (paragraph 1)? What was the Sermon on the Mount (paragraph 1)? Who was the Samaritan (paragraph 11)? Who was Booker T. Washington (paragraph 12)?

5. Find passages in which King says what nonviolent resistance and *agape* are *not* (as opposed to those in which he says what they *are*). Why do you suppose King used that strategy to define nonviolent resistance? Would such an approach work for all definitions? Explain your answer.

6. Explain in your own words what King means by both nonviolent resistance and *agape*.

● WRITING TOPICS ●

1. Write an essay addressed to Martin Luther King, Jr., in which you either support or argue against the practicality of his philosophy of nonviolent resistance.

2. Illustrate the concept of *agape* by showing how it is practiced by community groups, organizations, or individuals you know.

3. Read about the Montgomery bus boycott and explain what its goal was, how it was carried out, and what role King played in it.

RESPONDING TO VIOLENCE
●
ADDITIONAL WRITING SUGGESTIONS

1. Using the *Reader's Guide to Periodicals,* find and read articles about a mass murderer such as Ted Bundy. Summarize public reaction to the criminal and his crimes at the time of his arrest and/or execution. Does your research support or refute the contention of Ellen Currie in "Two Varieties of Killers" that public reaction to such a criminal is "cheap" and that attention focuses more on the criminal than on the heinous nature of the crimes?

2. Compare and contrast crimes against women and crimes against men. Consider the following questions: What do all violent crimes have in common, whether committed against men or women? How do the crimes committed against women differ from the crimes committed against men? Are the reasons for those crimes the same as or different from those that Carol Lynn Mithers in "The War Against Women" and other writers cite for violence against women?

3. Examine a specific social problem that is often accompanied by or leads to violence, such as teenage drug abuse, teenage run-aways, or teenage pregnancy. Limit yourself to one aspect of the problem, such as describing its seriousness or offering one or two possible causes or solutions.

4. Write an essay on violence in children, that is, children who murder, rape, or commit other violent crimes. Focus on one aspect of that subject, such as how widespread it is, how to account for its increase, possible explanations for it, or possible solutions to it.

5. If you (or someone close to you) have ever been the victim of a crime, narrate the experience. What were the circumstances? How did you react? How did you feel afterwards?

6

LIVING
ON THE
OUTSIDE

BEAUTY
WHEN THE OTHER DANCER IS THE SELF

•

ALICE WALKER

Alice Walker, born in Georgia, the youngest of eight children, is a writer and teacher. She attended Spelman College and graduated from Sarah Lawrence. She has taught at Jackson State College, Brandeis University, Wellesley College, and, most recently, the University of California at Berkeley. Walker is perhaps best known for her novel The Color Purple (1982), *which won both the Pulitzer Prize and the American Book Award and was made into a popular film. Her other works include* Revolutionary Petunias and Other Poems (1973); In Love & Trouble (1973), *a collection of short stories;* Meridian (1976) *and* In the Temple of My Familiar (1989), *both novels; and* In Search of Our Mothers' Gardens (1983), *a collection of essays. In the personal narrative below, Walker recounts through a series of brief scenes how a childhood accident resulted in years of feeling different from others, ashamed of how she looked, and insecure of herself.*

It is a bright summer day in 1947. My father, a fat, funny man with beautiful eyes and a subversive wit, is trying to decide which of his eight children he will take with him to the county fair. My mother, of course, will not go. She is knocked out from getting most of us ready: I hold my neck stiff against the pressure of her knuckles as she hastily completes the braiding and then beribboning of my hair.

My father is the driver for the rich old white lady up the road. Her name is Miss Mey. She owns all the land for miles around, as well as the house in which we live. All I remember about her is that she once offered to pay my mother thirty-five cents for cleaning her house, raking up piles of her magnolia leaves, and washing her family's clothes, and that my mother — she of no money, eight children, and a chronic earache — refused it. But I do not think of this in 1947. I am two and a half years old. I want to go everywhere my daddy goes. I am excited at the prospect of riding in a car. Someone has told me fairs are fun. That there is room in the car for only three of us doesn't faze me at all. Whirling happily in my starchy frock, showing off my biscuit-polished patent-leather shoes and lavender socks, tossing my head in a way that makes my ribbons bounce, I stand, hands on hips, before my father. "Take me, Daddy," I say with assurance, "I'm the prettiest!"

Later, it does not surprise me to find myself in Miss Mey's shiny black car, sharing the back seat with the other lucky ones. Does not surprise me that I thoroughly enjoy the fair. At home that night I tell the unlucky ones all I can remember about the merry-go-round, the man who eats live chickens, and the teddy bears, until they say: that's enough, baby Alice. Shut up now, and go to sleep.

It is Easter Sunday, 1950. I am dressed in a green, flocked, scalloped-hem dress   4
(handmade by my adoring sister, Ruth) that has its own smooth satin petticoat
and tiny hot-pink roses tucked into each scallop. My shoes, new T-strap patent
leather, again highly biscuit-polished. I am six years old and have learned one of
the longest Easter speeches to be heard that day, totally unlike the speech I said
when I was two: "Easter lilies / pure and white / blossom in / the morning light."
When I rise to give my speech I do so on a great wave of love and pride and
expectation. People in the church stop rustling their new crinolines. They seem
to hold their breath. I can tell they admire my dress, but it is my spirit, bordering
on sassiness (womanishness), they secretly applaud.

    "That girl's a little *mess*," they whisper to each other, pleased.

    Naturally I say my speech without stammer or pause, unlike those who
stutter, stammer, or, worst of all, forget. This is before the word "beautiful"
exists in people's vocabulary, but "Oh, isn't she the *cutest* thing!" frequently
floats my way. "And got so much sense!" they gratefully add . . . for which
thoughtful addition I thank them to this day.

It was great fun being cute. But then, one day, it ended.

I am eight years old and a tomboy. I have a cowboy hat, cowboy boots, checkered   8
shirt and pants, all red. My playmates are my brothers, two and four years older
than I. Their colors are black and green, the only difference in the way we are
dressed. On Saturday nights we all go to the picture show, even my mother;
Westerns are her favorite kind of movie. Back home, "on the ranch," we pretend
we are Tom Mix, Hopalong Cassidy, Lash LaRue (we've even named one of our
dogs Lash LaRue); we chase each other for hours rustling cattle, being outlaws,
delivering damsels from distress. Then my parents decide to buy my brothers
guns. These are not "real" guns. They shoot "BBs," copper pellets my brothers
say will kill birds. Because I am a girl, I do not get a gun. Instantly I am relegated
to the position of Indian. Now there appears a great distance between us. They
shoot and shoot at everything with their new guns. I try to keep up with my bow
and arrows.

    One day while I am standing on top of our makeshift "garage" — pieces of
tin nailed across some poles — holding my bow and arrow and looking out
toward the fields, I feel an incredible blow in my right eye. I look down just in
time to see my brother lower his gun.

    Both brothers rush to my side. My eye stings, and I cover it with my hand.
"If you tell," they say, "we will get a whipping. You don't want that to happen, do
you?" I do not. "Here is a piece of wire," says the older brother, picking it up
from the roof; "say you stepped on one end of it and the other flew up and hit
you." The pain is beginning to start. "Yes," I say. "Yes, I will say that is what
happened." If I do not say this is what happened, I know my brothers will find
ways to make me wish I had. But now I will say anything that gets me to my
mother.

    Confronted by our parents we stick to the lie agreed upon. They place me
on a bench on the porch and I close my left eye while they examine the right.

There is a tree growing from underneath the porch that climbs past the railing to the roof. It is the last thing my right eye sees. I watch as its trunk, its branches, and then its leaves are blotted out by the rising blood.

I am in shock. First there is intense fever, which my father tries to break 12 using lily leaves bound around my head. Then there are chills: my mother tries to get me to eat soup. Eventually, I do not know how, my parents learn what has happened. A week after the "accident" they take me to see a doctor. "Why did you wait so long to come?" he asks, looking into my eye and shaking his head. "Eyes are sympathetic," he says. "If one is blind, the other will likely become blind too."

This comment of the doctor's terrifies me. But it is really how I look that bothers me most. Where the BB pellet struck there is a glob of whitish scar tissue, a hideous cataract, on my eye. Now when I stare at people — a favorite pastime, up to now — they will stare back. Not at the "cute" little girl, but at her scar. For six years I do not stare at anyone, because I do not raise my head.

Years later, in the throes of a mid-life crisis, I ask my mother and sister whether I changed after the "accident." "No," they say, puzzled. "What do you mean?"

What do I mean?

I am eight, and, for the first time, doing poorly in school, where I have been 16 something of a whiz since I was four. We have just moved to the place where the "accident" occurred. We do not know any of the people around us because this is a different county. The only time I see the friends I knew is when we go back to our old church. The new school is the former state penitentiary. It is a large stone building, cold and drafty, crammed to overflowing with boisterous, ill-disciplined children. On the third floor there is a huge circular imprint of some partition that has been torn out.

"What used to be here?" I ask a sullen girl next to me on our way past it to lunch.

"The electric chair," says she.

At night I have nightmares about the electric chair, and about all the people reputedly "fried" in it. I am afraid of the school, where all the students seem to be budding criminals.

"What's the matter with your eye?" they ask, critically. 20

When I don't answer (I cannot decide whether it was an "accident" or not), they shove me, insist on a fight.

My brother, the one who created the story about the wire, comes to my rescue. But then brags so much about "protecting" me, I become sick.

After months of torture at the school, my parents decide to send me back to our old community, to my old school. I live with my grandparents and the teacher they board. But there is no room for Phoebe, my cat. By the time my grandparents decide there *is* room, and I ask for my cat, she cannot be found. Miss Yarborough, the boarding teacher, takes me under her wing, and begins to teach me to play the piano. But soon she marries an African — a "prince," she says — and is whisked away to his continent.

At my old school there is at least one teacher who loves me. She is the 24
teacher who "knew me before I was born" and bought my first baby clothes. It is
she who makes life bearable. It is her presence that finally helps me turn on the
one child at the school who continually calls me "one-eyed bitch." One day I
simply grab him by his coat and beat him until I am satisfied. It is my teacher
who tells me my mother is ill.

My mother is lying in bed in the middle of the day, something I have never seen.
She is in too much pain to speak. She has an abscess in her ear. I stand looking
down on her, knowing that if she dies, I cannot live. She is being treated with
warm oils and hot bricks held against her cheek. Finally a doctor comes. But I
must go back to my grandparents' house. The weeks pass but I am hardly aware
of it. All I know is that my mother might die, my father is not so jolly, my
brothers still have their guns, and I am the one sent away from home.
    "You did not change," they say.
    Did I imagine the anguish of never looking up?

I am twelve. When relatives come to visit I hide in my room. My cousin Brenda, 28
just my age, whose father works in the post office and whose mother is a nurse,
comes to find me. "Hello," she says. And then she asks, looking at my recent
school picture, which I did not want taken, and on which the "glob," as I think of
it, is clearly visible, "You still can't see out of that eye?"
    "No," I say, and flop back on the bed over my book.
    That night, as I do almost every night, I abuse my eye. I rant and rave at it, in
front of the mirror. I plead with it to clear up before morning. I tell it I hate and
despise it. I do not pray for sight. I pray for beauty.
    "You did not change," they say.

I am fourteen and baby-sitting for my brother Bill, who lives in Boston. He is my 32
favorite brother and there is a strong bond between us. Understanding my
feelings of shame and ugliness he and his wife take me to a local hospital, where
the "glob" is removed by a doctor named O. Henry. There is still a small bluish
crater where the scar tissue was, but the ugly white stuff is gone. Almost
immediately I become a different person from the girl who does not raise her
head. Or so I think. Now that I've raised my head I win the boyfriend of my
dreams. Now that I've raised my head I have plenty of friends. Now that I've
raised my head classwork comes from my lips as faultlessly as Easter speeches
did, and I leave high school as valedictorian, most popular student, and *queen*,
hardly believing my luck. Ironically, the girl who was voted most beautiful in our
class (and was) was later shot twice through the chest by a male companion,
using a "real" gun, while she was pregnant. But that's another story in itself. Or
is it?
    "You did not change," they say.

It is now thirty years since the "accident." A beautiful journalist comes to visit and to interview me. She is going to write a cover story for her magazine that focuses on my latest book. "Decide how you want to look on the cover," she says. "Glamorous, or whatever."

Never mind "glamorous," it is the "whatever" that I hear. Suddenly all I can think of is whether I will get enough sleep the night before the photography session: if I don't, my eye will be tired and wander, as blind eyes will.

At night in bed with my lover I think up reasons why I should not appear on 36 the cover of a magazine. "My meanest critics will say I've sold out," I say. "My family will not realize I write scandalous books."

"But what's the real reason you don't want to do this?" he asks.

"Because in all probability," I say in a rush, "my eye won't be straight."

"It will be straight enough," he says. Then, "Besides, I thought you'd made your peace with that."

And I suddenly remember that I have. 40

I remember:

I am talking to my brother Jimmy, asking if he remembers anything unusual about the day I was shot. He does not know I consider that day the last time my father, with his sweet home remedy of cool lily leaves, chose me, and that I suffered and raged inside because of this. "Well," he says, "all I remember is standing by the side of the highway with Daddy, trying to flag down a car. A white man stopped, but when Daddy said he needed somebody to take his little girl to the doctor, he drove off."

I remember:

I am in the desert for the first time. I fall totally in love with it. I am so 44 overwhelmed by its beauty, I confront for the first time, consciously, the meaning of the doctor's words years ago: "Eyes are sympathetic. If one is blind, the other will likely become blind too." I realize I have dashed about the world madly, looking at this, looking at that, storing up images against the fading of the light. *But I might have missed seeing the desert!* The shock of that possibility — and gratitude for over twenty-five years of sight — sends me literally to my knees. Poem after poem comes — which is perhaps how poets pray.

On Sight

I am so thankful I have seen
The Desert
And the creatures in the desert
And the desert Itself.

The desert has its own moon
Which I have seen
With my own eye.
There is no flag on it.

Trees of the desert have arms
All of which are always up

That is because the moon is up
The sun is up
Also the sky
The stars
Clouds
None with flags.

If there *were* flags, I doubt
the trees would point.
Would you?

But mostly, I remember this:

I am twenty-seven, and my baby daughter is almost three. Since her birth I have worried about her discovery that her mother's eyes are different from other people's. Will she be embarrassed? I think. What will she say? Every day she watches a television program called "Big Blue Marble." It begins with a picture of the earth as it appears from the moon. It is bluish, a little battered-looking, but full of light, with whitish clouds swirling around it. Every time I see it I weep with love, as if it is a picture of Grandma's house. One day when I am putting Rebecca down for her nap, she suddenly focuses on my eye. Something inside me cringes, gets ready to try to protect myself. All children are cruel about physical differences, I know from experience, and that they don't always mean to be is another matter. I assume Rebecca will be the same.

But no-o-o-o. She studies my face intently as we stand, her inside and me outside her crib. She even holds my face maternally between her dimpled little hands. Then, looking every bit as serious and lawyerlike as her father, she says, as if it may just possibly have slipped my attention: "Mommy, there's a *world* in your eye." (As in, "Don't be alarmed, or do anything crazy.") And then, gently, but with great interest: "Mommy, where did you *get* that world in your eye?"

For the most part, the pain left then. (So what, if my brothers grew up to 48 buy even more powerful pellet guns for their sons and to carry real guns themselves. So what, if a young "Morehouse man" once nearly fell off the steps of Trevor Arnett Library because he thought my eyes were blue.) Crying and laughing I ran to the bathroom, while Rebecca mumbled and sang herself off to sleep. Yes indeed, I realized, looking into the mirror. There *was* a world in my eye. And I saw that it was possible to love it: that in fact, for all it had taught me of shame and anger and inner vision, I *did* love it. Even to see it drifting out of orbit in boredom, or rolling up out of fatigue, not to mention floating back at attention in excitement (bearing witness, a friend has called it), deeply suitable to my personality, and even characteristic of me.

That night I dream I am dancing to Stevie Wonder's song "Always" (the name of the song is really "As," but I hear it as "Always"). As I dance, whirling and joyous, happier than I've ever been in my life, another bright-faced dancer joins me. We dance and kiss each other and hold each other through the night. The other dancer has obviously come through all right, as I have done. She is beautiful, whole and free. And she is also me.

● PERSONAL RESPONSE ●

What was your reaction to Walker's account of the shooting "accident" and her subsequent recollection that a white man refused to drive her to the hospital?

● QUESTIONS FOR DISCUSSION ●

1. Walker narrates her growth toward self-acceptance through a series of scenes that jump backward and forward in time. Were you able to follow the sequence of events? Explain your answer.

2. Why do you think Walker repeats certain phrases, such as "'You did not change,' they say" and "*I remember*"?

3. Characterize Walker's mother and father on the basis of the information she gives about them. What are they like and how does Walker feel about them?

4. Besides her parents, who else is important to Walker?

5. In paragraph 32, Walker mentions that the girl voted the most beautiful in her high school was later shot through the chest, adding, "But that's another story in itself. Or is it?" Explain what Walker means by that question. How might the story of that girl's life be like Walker's own story?

6. Explain what you think Walker's daughter Rebecca means when she says, "'Mommy, there's a *world* in your eye'" (paragraph 47). How does Walker interpret what she means? How is that incident the key to Walker's acceptance of herself?

7. In what ways is Walker's blind eye a symbol?

8. Explain what you think Walker's title means.

● WRITING TOPICS ●

1. Narrate an experience you had that changed the way you felt about yourself, including your efforts to deal with your feelings and your success or failure in coming to terms with yourself.

2. Narrate an event from your childhood that frightened you.

3. Define the abstract term "beauty" by describing a specific thing or person who best exemplifies it, in your opinion.

ON BEING A CRIPPLE

●

NANCY MAIRS

*Nancy Mairs was born in California, grew up in New England, and
now lives in Tucson, Arizona. A teacher and writer, she has a Ph.D. in
English from the University of Arizona and has published an award-
winning collection of poems,* In All the Rooms of the Yellow House, *and
two collections of essays,* Carnal Acts *(1990) and* Plaintext *(1986), from
which "On Being a Cripple" is taken. In this intensely personal essay,
Mairs illustrates that physical handicaps need not deprive people of
living ordinary lives. Her essay is an articulate testimony to the fact
that people who have often been pushed to the outside of society can
take their places squarely in the center of it.*

> *To escape is nothing. Not to escape is nothing.*
> — Louise Bogan

The other day I was thinking of writing an essay on being a cripple. I was
thinking hard in one of the stalls of the women's room in my office
building, as I was shoving my shirt into my jeans and tugging up my
zipper. Preoccupied, I flushed, picked up my book bag, took my cane down from
the hook, and unlatched the door. So many movements unbalanced me, and as I
pulled the door open I fell over backward, landing fully clothed on the toilet seat
with my legs splayed in front of me: the old beetle-on-its-back routine. Saturday
afternoon, the building deserted, I was free to laugh aloud as I wriggled back to
my feet, my voice bouncing off the yellowish tiles from all directions. Had
anyone been there with me, I'd have been still and faint and hot with chagrin. I
decided that it was high time to write the essay.

First, the matter of semantics. I am a cripple. I choose this word to name
me. I choose from among several possibilities, the most common of which are
"handicapped" and "disabled." I made the choice a number of years ago,
without thinking, unaware of my motives for doing so. Even now, I'm not sure
what those motives are, but I recognize that they are complex and not entirely
flattering. People — crippled or not — wince at the word "cripple," as they do not
at "handicapped" or "disabled." Perhaps I want them to wince. I want them to
see me as a tough customer, one to whom the fates/gods/viruses have not been
kind, but who can face the brutal truth of her existence squarely. As a cripple, I
swagger.

But, to be fair to myself, a certain amount of honesty underlies my choice.
"Cripple" seems to me a clean word, straightforward and precise. It has an
honorable history, having made its first appearance in the Lindisfarne Gospel in
the tenth century. As a lover of words, I like the accuracy with which it describes

my condition: I have lost the full use of my limbs. "Disabled," by contrast, suggests any incapacity, physical or mental. And I certainly don't like "handicapped," which implies that I have deliberately been put at a disadvantage, by whom I can't imagine (my God is not a Handicapper General), in order to equalize chances in the great race of life. These words seem to me to be moving away from my condition, to be widening the gap between word and reality. Most remote is the recently coined euphemism "differently abled," which partakes of the same semantic hopefulness that transformed countries from "undeveloped" to "underdeveloped," then to "less developed," and finally to "developing" nations. People have continued to starve in those countries during the shift. Some realities do not obey the dictates of language.

Mine is one of them. Whatever you call me, I remain crippled. But I don't 4 care what you call me, so long as it isn't "differently abled," which strikes me as pure verbal garbage designed, by its ability to describe anyone, to describe no one. I subscribe to George Orwell's thesis that "the slovenliness of our language makes it easier for us to have foolish thoughts." And I refuse to participate in the degeneration of the language to the extent that I deny that I have lost anything in the course of this calamitous disease; I refuse to pretend that the only differences between you and me are the various ordinary ones that distinguish any one person from another. But call me "disabled" or "handicapped" if you like. I have long since grown accustomed to them; and if they are vague, at least they hint at the truth. Moreover, I use them myself. Society is no readier to accept crippledness than to accept death, war, sex, sweat, or wrinkles. I would never refer to another person as a cripple. It is the word I use to name only myself.

I haven't always been crippled, a fact for which I am soundly grateful. To be whole of limb is, I know from experience, infinitely more pleasant and useful than to be crippled; and if that knowledge leaves me open to bitterness at my loss, the physical soundness I once enjoyed (though I did not enjoy it half enough) is well worth the occasional stab of regret. Though never any good at sports, I was a normally active child and young adult. I climbed trees, played hopscotch, jumped rope, skated, swam, rode my bicycle, sailed. I despised team sports, spending some of the wretchedest afternoons of my life, sweaty and humiliated, behind a field-hockey stick and under a basketball hoop. I tramped alone for miles along the bridle paths that webbed the woods behind the house I grew up in. I swayed through countless dim hours in the arms of one man or another under the scattered shot of light from mirrored balls, and gyrated through countless more as Tab Hunter and Johnny Mathis gave way to the Rolling Stones, Creedence Clearwater Revival, Cream. I walked down the aisle. I pushed baby carriages, changed tires in the rain, marched for peace.

When I was twenty-eight I started to trip and drop things. What at first seemed my natural clumsiness soon became too pronounced to shrug off. I consulted a neurologist, who told me that I had a brain tumor. A battery of tests, increasingly disagreeable, revealed no tumor. About a year and a half later I developed a blurred spot in one eye. I had, at last, the episodes "disseminated in space and time" requisite for a diagnosis: multiple sclerosis. I have never been sorry for the doctor's initial misdiagnosis, however. For almost a week, until the negative results of the tests were in, I thought that I was going to die right away. Every day for the past nearly ten years, then, has been a kind of gift. I accept all gifts.

Multiple sclerosis is a chronic degenerative disease of the central nervous system, in which the myelin that sheathes the nerves is somehow eaten away and scar tissue forms in its place, interrupting the nerves' signals. During its course, which is unpredictable and uncontrollable, one may lose vision, hearing, speech, the ability to walk, control of bladder and/or bowels, strength in any or all extremities, sensitivity to touch, vibration, and/or pain, potency, coordination of movements — the list of possibilities is lengthy and, yes, horrifying. One may also lose one's sense of humor. That's the easiest to lose and the hardest to survive without.

In the past ten years, I have sustained some of these losses. Characteristic of 8 MS are sudden attacks, called exacerbations, followed by remissions, and these I have not had. Instead, my disease has been slowly progressive. My left leg is now so weak that I walk with the aid of a brace and a cane; and for distances I use an Amigo, a variation on the electric wheelchair that looks rather like an electrified kiddie car. I no longer have much use of my left hand. Now my right side is weakening as well. I still have the blurred spot in my right eye. Overall, though, I've been lucky so far. My world has, of necessity, been circumscribed by my losses, but the terrain left me has been ample enough for me to continue many of the activities that absorb me: writing, teaching, raising children and cats and plants and snakes, reading, speaking publicly about MS and depression, even playing bridge with people patient and honorable enough to let me scatter cards every which way without sneaking a peek.

Lest I begin to sound like Pollyanna, however, let me say that I don't like having MS. I hate it. My life holds realities — harsh ones, some of them — that no right-minded human being ought to accept without grumbling. One of them is fatigue. I know of no one with MS who does not complain of bone-weariness; in a disease that presents an astonishing variety of symptoms, fatigue seems to be a common factor. I wake up in the morning feeling the way most people do at the end of a bad day, and I take it from there. As a result, I spend a lot of time *in extremis* and, impatient with limitation, I tend to ignore my fatigue until my body breaks down in some way and forces rest. Then I miss picnics, dinner parties, poetry readings, the brief visits of old friends from out of town. The offspring of a puritanical tradition of exceptional venerability, I cannot view these lapses without shame. My life often seems a series of small failures to do as I ought.

I lead, on the whole, an ordinary life, probably rather like the one I would have led had I not had MS. I am lucky that my predilections were already solitary, sedentary, and bookish — unlike the world-famous French cellist I have read about, or the young woman I talked with one long afternoon who wanted only to be a jockey. I had just begun graduate school when I found out something was wrong with me, and I have remained, interminably, a graduate student. Perhaps I would not have if I'd thought I had the stamina to return to a full-time job as a technical editor; but I've enjoyed my studies.

In addition to studying, I teach writing courses. I also teach medical students how to give neurological examinations. I pick up freelance editing jobs here and there. I have raised a foster son and sent him into the world, where he has made me two grandbabies, and I am still escorting my daughter and son through adolescence. I go to Mass every Saturday. I am a superb, if messy, cook. I am also an enthusiastic laundress, capable of sorting a hamper full of clothes into five subtly differentiated piles, but a terrible housekeeper. I can do italic writing and, in an emergency, bathe an oil-soaked cat. I play a fiendish game of Scrabble. When I have the time and the money, I like to sit on my front steps with my husband, drinking Amaretto and smoking a cigar, as we imagine our counterparts in Leningrad and make sure that the sun gets down once more behind the sharp childish scrawl of the Tucson Mountains.

This lively plenty has its bleak complement, of course, in all the things I can no longer do. I will never run again, except in dreams, and one day I may have to write that I will never walk again. I like to go camping, but I can't follow George and the children along the trails that wander out of a campsite through the desert or into the mountains. In fact, even on the level I've learned never to check the weather or try to hold a coherent conversation: I need all my attention for my wayward feet. Of late, I have begun to catch myself wondering how people can propel themselves without canes. With only one usable hand, I have to select my clothing with care not so much for style as for ease of ingress and egress, and even so, dressing can be laborious. I can no longer do fine stitchery, pick up babies, play the piano, braid my hair. I am immobilized by acute attacks of depression, which may or may not be physiologically related to MS but are certainly its logical concomitant.

These two elements, the plenty and the privation, are never pure, nor are the delight and wretchedness that accompany them. Almost every pickle that I get into as a result of my weakness and clumsiness—and I get into plenty—is funny as well as maddening and sometimes painful. I recall one May afternoon when a friend and I were going out for a drink after finishing up at school. As we were climbing into opposite sides of my car, chatting, I tripped and fell, flat and hard, onto the asphalt parking lot, my abrupt departure interrupting him in midsentence. "Where'd you go?" he called as he came around the back of the car to find me hauling myself up by the door frame. "Are you all right?" Yes, I told him, I was fine, just a bit rattly, and we drove off to find a shady patio and some beer. When I got home an hour or so later, my daughter greeted me with "What have you done to yourself?" I looked down. One elbow of my white turtleneck with the green froggies, one knee of my white trousers, one white kneesock were blood-soaked. We peeled off the clothes and inspected the damage, which was nasty enough but not alarming. That part wasn't funny: The abrasions took a long time to heal, and one got a little infected. Even so, when I think of my friend talking earnestly, suddenly, to the hot thin air while I dropped from his view as though through a trap door, I find the image as silly as something from a Marx Brothers movie.

I may find it easier than other cripples to amuse myself because I live propped by the acceptance and the assistance and, sometimes, the amusement of those around me. Grocery clerks tear my checks out of my checkbook for me, and sales clerks find chairs to put into dressing rooms when I want to try on clothes. The people I work with make sure I teach at times when I am least likely to be fatigued, in places I can get to, with the materials I need. My students, with one anonymous exception (in an end-of-the-semester evaluation), have been unperturbed by my disability. Some even like it. One was immensely cheered by the information that I paint my own fingernails; she decided, she told me, that if I could go to such trouble over fine details, she could keep on writing essays. I suppose I became some sort of bright-fingered muse. She wrote good essays, too.

The most important struts in the framework of my existence, of course, are my husband and children. Dismayingly few marriages survive the MS test, and why should they? Most twenty-two- and nineteen-year-olds, like George and me, can vow in clear conscience, after a childhood of chickenpox and summer colds, to keep one another in sickness and in health so long as they both shall live. Not many are equipped for catastrophe: the dismay, the depression, the extra work, the boredom that a degenerative disease can insinuate into a relationship. And our society, with its emphasis on fun and its association of fun with physical performance, offers little encouragement for a whole spouse to stay with a crippled partner. Children experience similar stresses when faced with a crippled parent, and they are more helpless, since parents and children can't usually get divorced. They hate, of course, to be different from their peers, and the child whose mother is tacking down the aisle of a school auditorium packed with proud parents like a Cape Cod dinghy in a stiff breeze jolly well stands out in a crowd. Deprived of legal divorce, the child can at least deny the mother's disability, even her existence, forgetting to tell her about recitals and PTA meetings, refusing to accompany her to stores or church or the movies, never inviting friends to the house. Many do.

But I've been limping along for ten years now, and so far George and the   16 children are still at my left elbow, holding tight. Anne and Matthew vacuum floors and dust furniture and haul trash and rake up dog droppings and button my cuffs and bake lasagne and Toll House cookies with just enough grumbling so I know that they don't have brain fever. And far from hiding me, they're forever dragging me by racks of fancy clothes or through teeming school corridors, or welcoming gaggles of friends while I'm wandering through the house in Anne's filmy pink babydoll pajamas. George generally calls before he brings someone home, but he does just as many dumb thankless chores as the children. And they all yell at me, laugh at some of my jokes, write me funny letters when we're apart — in short, treat me as an ordinary human being for whom they have some use. I think they like me. Unless they're faking. . . .

Faking. There's the rub. Tugging at the fringes of my consciousness always is the terror that people are kind to me only because I'm a cripple. My mother almost shattered me once, with that instinct mothers have — blind, I think, in this case, but unerring nonetheless — for striking blows along the fault-lines of their children's hearts, by telling me, in an attack on my selfishness, "We all have to make allowances for you, of course, because of the way you are." From the distance of a couple of years, I have to admit that I haven't any idea just what she meant, and I'm not sure that she knew either. She was awfully angry. But at the time, as the words thudded home, I felt my worst fear, suddenly realized. I could bear being called selfish: I am. But I couldn't bear the corroboration that those around me were doing in fact what I'd always suspected them of doing, professing fondness while silently putting up with me because of the way I am. A cripple. I've been a little cracked ever since.

Along with this fear that people are secretly accepting shoddy goods comes a relentless pressure to please — to prove myself worth the burdens I impose, I guess, or to build a substantial account of goodwill against which I may write drafts in times of need. Part of the pressure arises from social expectations. In our society, anyone who deviates from the norm had better find some way to compensate. Like fat people, who are expected to be jolly, cripples must bear their lot meekly and cheerfully. A grumpy cripple isn't playing by the rules. And much of the pressure is self-generated. Early on I vowed that, if I had to have MS, by God I was going to do it well. This is a class act, ladies and gentlemen. No tears, no recriminations, no faint-heartedness.

One way and another, then, I wind up feeling like Tiny Tim, peering over the edge of the table at the Christmas goose, waving my crutch, piping down God's blessing on us all. Only sometimes I don't want to play Tiny Tim. I'd rather be Caliban, a most scurvy monster. Fortunately, at home no one much cares whether I'm a good cripple or a bad cripple as long as I make vichyssoise with fair regularity. One evening several years ago, Anne was reading at the dining-room table while I cooked dinner. As I opened a can of tomatoes, the can slipped in my left hand and juice spattered me and the counter with bloody spots. Fatigued and infuriated, I bellowed, "I'm so sick of being crippled!" Anne glanced at me over the top of her book. "There now," she said, "do you feel better?" "Yes," I said, "yes, I do." She went back to her reading. I felt better. That's about all the attention my scurviness ever gets.

Because I hate being crippled, I sometimes hate myself for being a cripple. 20 Over the years I have come to expect — even accept — attacks of violent self-loathing. Luckily, in general our society no longer connects deformity and disease directly with evil (though a charismatic once told me that I have MS because a devil is in me) and so I'm allowed to move largely at will, even among small children. But I'm not sure that this revision of attitude has been particularly helpful. Physical imperfection, even freed of moral disapprobation, still defies and violates the ideal, especially for women, whose confinement in their bodies as objects of desire is far from over. Each age, of course, has its ideal, and I doubt that ours is any better or worse than any other. Today's ideal woman, who lives on the glossy pages of dozens of magazines, seems to be between the ages of eighteen and twenty-five; her hair has body, her teeth flash white, her breath smells minty, her underarms are dry; she has a career but is still a fabulous cook, especially of meals that take less than twenty minutes to prepare; she does not ordinarily appear to have a husband or children; she is trim and deeply tanned; she jogs, swims, plays tennis, rides a bicycle, sails, but does not bowl; she travels widely, even to out-of-the-way places like Finland and Samoa, always in the company of the ideal man, who possesses a nearly identical set of characteristics. There are a few exceptions. Though usually white and often blonde, she may be black, Hispanic, Asian, or Native American, so long as she is unusually sleek. She may be old, provided she is selling a laxative or is Lauren Bacall. If she is selling a detergent, she may be married and have a flock of strikingly messy children. But she is never a cripple.

Like many women I know, I have always had an uneasy relationship with my body. I was not a popular child, largely, I think now, because I was peculiar: intelligent, intense, moody, shy, given to unexpected actions and inexplicable notions and emotions. But as I entered adolescence, I believed myself unpopular because I was homely: my breasts too flat, my mouth too wide, my hips too narrow, my clothing never quite right in fit or style. I was not, in fact, particularly ugly, old photographs inform me, though I was well off the ideal; but I carried this sense of self-alienation with me into adulthood, where it regenerated in response to the depredations of MS. Even with my brace I walk with a limp so pronounced that, seeing myself on the videotape of a television program on the disabled, I couldn't believe that anything but an inchworm could make progress humping along like that. My shoulders droop and my pelvis thrusts forward as I try to balance myself upright, throwing my frame into a bony **S**. As a result of contractures, one shoulder is higher than the other and I carry one arm bent in front of me, the fingers curled into a claw. My left arm and leg have wasted into pipe-stems, and I try always to keep them covered. When I think about how my body must look to others, especially to men, to whom I have been trained to display myself, I feel ludicrous, even loathsome.

At my age, however, I don't spend much time thinking about my appearance. The burning egocentricity of adolescence, which assures one that all the world is looking all the time, has passed, thank God, and I'm generally too caught up in what I'm doing to step back, as I used to, and watch myself as though upon a stage. I'm also too old to believe in the accuracy of self-image. I know that I'm not a hideous crone, that in fact, when I'm rested, well dressed, and well made up, I look fine. The self-loathing I feel is neither physically nor intellectually substantial. What I hate is not me but a disease.

I am not a disease.

And a disease is not — at least not singlehandedly — going to determine who I am, though at first it seemed to be going to. Adjusting to a chronic incurable illness, I have moved through a process similar to that outlined by Elizabeth Kübler-Ross in *On Death and Dying*. The major difference — and it is far more significant than most people recognize — is that I can't be sure of the outcome, as the terminally ill cancer patient can. Research studies indicate that, with proper medical care, I may achieve a "normal" life span. And in our society, with its vision of death as the ultimate evil, worse even than decrepitude, the response to such news is, "Oh well, at least you're not going to *die*." Are there worse things than dying? I think that there may be.

I think of two women I know, both with MS, both enough older than I to have served me as models. One took to her bed several years ago and has been there ever since. Although she can sit in a high-backed wheelchair, because she is incontinent she refuses to go out at all, even though incontinence pants, which are readily available at any pharmacy, could protect her from embarrassment. Instead, she stays at home and insists that her husband, a small quiet man, a retired civil servant, stay there with her except for a quick weekly foray to the supermarket. The other woman, whose illness was diagnosed when she was eighteen, a nursing student engaged to a young doctor, finished her training, married her doctor, accompanied him to Germany when he was in the service, bore three sons and a daughter, now grown and gone. When she can, she travels with her husband; she plays bridge, embroiders, swims regularly; she works, like me, as a symptomatic-patient instructor of medical students in neurology. Guess which woman I hope to be.

At the beginning, I thought about having MS almost incessantly. And because of the unpredictable course of the disease, my thoughts were always terrified. Each night I'd get into bed wondering whether I'd get out again the next morning, whether I'd be able to see, to speak, to hold a pen between my fingers. Knowing that the day might come when I'd be physically incapable of killing myself, I thought perhaps I ought to do so right away, while I still had the strength. Gradually I came to understand that the Nancy who might one day lie inert under a bedsheet, arms and legs paralyzed, unable to feed or bathe herself, unable to reach out for a gun, a bottle of pills, was not the Nancy I was at present, and that I could not presume to make decisions for that future Nancy, who might well not want in the least to die. Now the only provision I've made for the future Nancy is that when the time comes — and it is likely to come in the form of pneumonia, friend to the weak and the old — I am not to be treated with machines and medications. If she is unable to communicate by then, I hope she will be satisfied with these terms.

Thinking all the time about having MS grew tiresome and intrusive, especially in the large and tragic mode in which I was accustomed to considering my plight. Months and even years went by without catastrophe (at least without one related to MS), and really I was awfully busy, what with George and children and snakes and students and poems, and I hadn't the time, let alone the inclination, to devote myself to being a disease. Too, the richer my life became, the funnier it seemed, as though there were some connection between largesse and laughter, and so my tragic stance began to waver until, even with the aid of a brace and a cane, I couldn't hold it for very long at a time.

After several years I was satisfied with my adjustment. I had suffered my grief and fury and terror, I thought, but now I was at ease with my lot. Then one summer day I set out with George and the children across the desert for a vacation in California. Part way to Yuma I became aware that my right leg felt funny. "I think I've had an exacerbation," I told George. "What shall we do?" he asked. "I think we'd better get the hell to California," I said, "because I don't know whether I'll ever make it again." So we went on to San Diego and then to Orange, up the Pacific Coast Highway to Santa Cruz, across to Yosemite, down to Sequoia and Joshua Tree, and so back over the desert to home. It was a fine 28 two-week trip, filled with friends and fair weather, and I wouldn't have missed it for the world, though I did in fact make it back to California two years later. Nor would there have been any point in missing it, since in MS, once the symptoms have appeared, the neurological damage has been done, and there's no way to predict or prevent that damage.

The incident spoiled my self-satisfaction, however. It renewed my grief and fury and terror, and I learned that one never finishes adjusting to MS. I don't know now why I thought one would. One does not, after all, finish adjusting to life, and MS is simply a fact of my life — not my favorite fact, of course — but as ordinary as my nose and my tropical fish and my yellow Mazda station wagon. It may at any time get worse, but no amount of worry or anticipation can prepare me for a new loss. My life is a lesson in losses. I learn one at a time.

And I had best be patient in the learning, since I'll have to do it like it or not. As any rock fan knows, you can't always get what you want. Particularly when you have MS. You can't for example, get cured. In recent years researchers and the organizations that fund research have started to pay MS some attention even though it isn't fatal; perhaps they have begun to see that life is something other than a quantitative phenomenon, that one may be very much alive for a very long time in a life that isn't worth living. The researchers have made some progress toward understanding the mechanism of the disease: It may well be an autoimmune reaction triggered by a slow-acting virus. But they are nowhere near its prevention, control, or cure. And most of us want to be cured. Some, unable to accept incurability, grasp at one treatment after another, no matter how bizarre: megavitamin therapy, gluten-free diet, injections of cobra venom, hypothermal suits, lymphocytopharesis, hyperbaric chambers. Many treatments are probably harmless enough, but none are curative.

The absence of a cure often makes MS patients bitter toward their doctors. Doctors are, after all, the priests of modern society, the new shamans, whose business is to heal, and many an MS patient roves from one to another, searching for the "good" doctor who will make him well. Doctors too think of themselves as healers, and for this reason many have trouble dealing with MS patients, whose disease in its intransigence defeats their aims and mocks their skills. Too few doctors, it is true, treat their patients as whole human beings, but the reverse is also true. I have always tried to be gentle with my doctors, who often have more at stake in terms of ego than I do. I may be frustrated, maddened, depressed by the incurability of my disease, but I am not diminished by it, and they are. When I push myself up from my seat in the waiting room and stumble toward them, I incarnate the limitation of their powers. The least I can do is refuse to press on their tenderest spots.

This gentleness is part of the reason that I'm not sorry to be a cripple. I didn't have it before. Perhaps I'd have developed it anyway — how could I know such a thing? — and I wish I had more of it, but I'm glad of what I have. It has opened and enriched my life enormously, this sense that my frailty and need must be mirrored in others, that in searching for and shaping a stable core in a life wrenched by change and loss, change and loss, I must recognize the same process, under individual conditions, in the lives around me. I do not deprecate such knowledge, however I've come by it.

All the same, if a cure were found, would I take it? In a minute. I may be a cripple, but I'm only occasionally a loony and never a saint. Anyway, in my brand of theology God doesn't give bonus points for a limp. I'd take a cure; I just don't need one. A friend who also has MS startled me once by asking, "Do you ever say to yourself, 'Why me, Lord?'" "No, Michael, I don't," I told him, "because whenever I try, the only response I can think of is 'Why not?'" If I could make a cosmic deal, who would I put in my place? What in my life would I give up in exchange for sound limbs and a thrilling rush of energy? No one. Nothing. I might as well do the job myself. Now that I'm getting the hang of it.

● PERSONAL RESPONSE ●

What do you think your response would be if you were faced with the kind of chronic debilitating illness that Mairs has?

● QUESTIONS FOR DISCUSSION ●

1. Mairs begins by stating her purpose: to write an essay "on being a cripple." But why did she want to write such an essay? What do you think she hoped to accomplish?

2. How does the opening scene, which takes place in a public toilet, lead Mairs to decide "it was high time to write the essay" (paragraph 1)? How is that setting—both a very private and a public space—appropriate for introducing her essay?

3. Look at paragraph 7, in which Mairs defines multiple sclerosis. Why do you think she uses medical terminology? What is the effect of the last sentence in that paragraph? What evidence is there that Mairs has not lost her sense of humor?

4. Mairs has a flair for vivid images, such as when she writes "the sharp childish scrawl of the Tucson mountains" (paragraph 11) and "like a Cape Cod dinghy in a stiff breeze" (paragraph 15). Where else do you find images that are especially vivid?

5. Why do you think Mairs prefers to identify with Caliban rather than Tiny Tim (paragraph 19)?

6. Why do you think Mairs goes into such detail about "today's ideal woman" (paragraph 20)? What connection is she making between that image and her own self concept?

7. In what ways are women "trained to display [themselves]" (paragraph 21)? Are men trained similarly to display themselves to others?

8. Summarize the effects, both positive and negative, that Mairs's illness has had on her.

● WRITING TOPICS ●

1. Write an essay on the use of euphemisms, such as those for dying, bodily functions, or certain occupations, citing examples and exploring possible reasons why people often prefer to use euphemisms.

2. If you have undergone a change in self-image, contrast your image of yourself before with your image of yourself now. How do you account for the change?

3. Describe a person you know who has overcome or adjusted to a disability. Use very specific details to convey fully a sense of that person and the difficulties of the disability.

THE QUALITY OF MERCY KILLING

●

ROGER ROSENBLATT

Roger Rosenblatt is a writer and television commentator. In the follow-ing essay, published in the August 1985 issue of Time, *Rosenblatt discusses a controversial case of mercy killing that received widespread news coverage and provoked lively public debate. Rosenblatt makes a powerful case for compassion and understanding in such tragic cases, while at the same time acknowledging the wrenching moral dilemmas they pose.*

If it were only a matter of law, the public would not feel stranded. He killed her, after all. Roswell Gilbert, a 76-year-old retired electronics engineer living in a seaside condominium in Fort Lauderdale, Fla., considered murdering his wife Emily for at least a month before shooting her through the head with a Luger as she sat on their couch. The Gilberts had been husband and wife for 51 years. They were married in 1934, the year after Calvin Coolidge died, the year after Prohibition was lifted, the year that Hank Aaron was born. At 73, Emily had Alzheimer's disease and osteoporosis; her spinal column was gradually collapsing. Roswell would not allow her to continue life as "a suffering animal," so he committed what is called a mercy killing. The jury saw only the killing; they felt Gilbert had mercy on himself. He was sentenced to 25 years with no chance of parole, which would make him 101 by the time he got out. The Governor has been asked to grant clemency. Most Floridians polled hope that Gilbert will go free.

Not that there ever was much of a legal or practical question involved. Imagine the precedent set by freeing a killer simply because he killed for love. Othello killed for love, though his passion was loaded with a different motive. Does any feeling count, or is kindness alone an excuse for murder? Or age: maybe someone has to be 76 and married 51 years to establish his sincerity. There are an awful lot of old people and long marriages in Florida. A lot of Alzheimer's disease and osteoporosis as well. Let Gilbert loose, the fear is, and watch the run on Lugers.

Besides, the matter of mercy killing is getting rough and out of hand. Nobody seems to use poison anymore. In Fort Lauderdale two years ago, a 79-year-old man shot his 62-year-old wife in the stairwell of a hospital; like Emily Gilbert, she was suffering from Alzheimer's disease. In San Antonio four years ago, a 69-year-old man shot his 72-year-old brother to death in a nursing home. Last June a man in Miami put two bullets in the heart of his three-year-old daughter who lay comatose after a freak accident. An organization that studies mercy killings says that nine have occurred this year alone. You cannot have a murder every time someone feels sorry for a loved one in pain. Any fool knows that.

Yet you also feel foolish watching a case like Gilbert's (if any case can be said 4
to be like another) because, while both feet are planted firmly on the side of the
law and common sense, both are firmly planted on Gilbert's side as well. The
place the public really stands is nowhere: How can an act be equally destructive
of society and wholly human? The reason anyone would consider going easy on
Gilbert is that we can put ourselves in his shoes, can sit at his wife's bedside day
after day, watching the Florida sun gild the furniture and listening to the
Atlantic lick the beach like a cat. Emily dozes. He looks at her in a rare peaceful
pose and is grateful for the quiet.

Or he dreams back to when such a scene would have been unimaginable:
she, sharp as a tack, getting the better of him in an argument; he, strong as a bull,
showing off by swinging her into the air — on a beach, perhaps, like the one in
front of the condominium where old couples like themselves walk in careful
slow motion at the water's edge. Since the case became a cause, photographs of
the Gilberts have appeared on television, she in a formal gown, he in tails; they,
older, in a restaurant posing deadpan for a picture for no reason, the way people
do in restaurants. In a way the issue here *is* age: mind and body falling away like
slabs of sand off a beach cliff. If biology declares war, have people no right to a
pre-emptive strike? In the apartment he continues to stare at her who, from
time to time, still believes they are traveling together in Spain.

Now he wonders about love. He loves his wife; he tells her so; he has told
her so for 51 years. And he thinks of what he meant by that: her understanding of
him, her understanding of others, her sense of fun. Illness has replaced those
qualities in her with screams and a face of panic. Does he love her still? Of
course, he says; he hates the disease, but he loves his wife. Or — and this seems
hard — does he only love what he remembers of Emily? Is the frail doll in the
bed an imposter? But no; this is Emily too, the same old Emily hidden
somewhere under the decaying cells and in the folds of the painkillers. It is
Emily and she is suffering and he swore he would always look after her.

He considers an irony: you always hurt the one you love. By what act or
nonact would he be hurting his wife more? He remembers news stories he has
read of distraught people in similar positions, pulling the plugs on sons and
husbands or assisting in the suicides of desperate friends. He sympathizes, but
with a purpose; he too is interested in precedents. Surely, he concludes,
morality swings both ways here. What is moral for the group cannot always be
moral for the individual, or there would be no individuality, no exceptions,
even if the exceptions only prove the rule. Let the people have their rules. What
harm would it do history to relieve Emily's pain? A little harm, perhaps, no more
than that.

This is what we see in the Gilbert case, the fusion of our lives with theirs in 8
one grand and pathetic cliché in which all lives look pretty much alike. We go
round and round with Gilbert: Gilbert suddenly wondering if Emily might get
better, if one of those white-coated geniuses will come up with a cure. Gilbert
realizing that once Emily is gone, he will go too, since her way of life, however
wretched, was their way of life. He is afraid for them both. In *The Merchant of
Venice* Portia says that mercy is "twice blessed; / It blesses him that gives and

him that takes." The murder committed, Gilbert does not feel blessed. At best, he feels he did right, which the outer world agrees with and denies.

Laws are unlikely to be changed by such cases: for every modification one can think of, there are too many loopholes and snares. What Gilbert did in fact erodes the whole basis of law, which is to keep people humane and civilized. Yet Gilbert was humane, civilized and wrong: a riddle. In the end we want the law intact and Gilbert free, so that society wins on both counts. What the case proves, however, is that society is helpless to do anything for Gilbert, for Emily or for itself. All we can do is recognize a real tragedy when we see one, and wonder, perhaps, if one bright morning in 1934 Gilbert read of a mercy killing in the papers, leaned earnestly across the breakfast table and told his new bride: "I couldn't do that. I could never do that."

● PERSONAL RESPONSE ●

What is your reaction to the jury's finding Roswell Gilbert guilty of murder? How do you feel about the issue of mercy killing?

● QUESTIONS FOR DISCUSSION ●

1. What is the dilemma posed by cases such as Gilbert's?

2. Where does Rosenblatt state the views of those opposed to leniency in cases such as Gilbert's?

3. In paragraph 8, Rosenblatt quotes from the play alluded to in his title, Shakespeare's *The Merchant of Venice*. The lines immediately before those he quotes are as follows: "The quality of mercy is not strained, / It droppeth as the gentle rain from heaven / Upon the place beneath." Explain the function of the allusion in the title and the lines Rosenblatt quotes in paragraph 8.

4. Explain Rosenblatt's reference to Othello (pargraph 2). What purpose does that reference serve?

5. Do you think Rosenblatt's emotional appeal is too sentimental? Does the strong emotional appeal undercut his argument? What function do the closing sentences serve?

6. Rosenblatt writes in paragraph 5 that "in a way the issue here *is* age." In what sense might age be the issue?

7. Does Rosenblatt condone mercy killing? Does he imply that exceptions to the law should be made in some cases?

8. What is the "riddle" mentioned in the last paragraph?

● WRITING TOPICS ●

1. This essay was written as an editorial and as such reflects the opinion of its writer. Write your own editorial expressing your view of the Gilbert case or of another mercy killing case you know of. Consider whether you think mercy killing is ever justified and, if so, under what circumstances it might be.

2. If you know of someone with Alzheimer's disease, describe the impact of that illness on the person who suffers from it and on the family members of that person. Or, if you do not know of anyone personally with Alzheimer's disease, do some library research and explain what the disease is and what its effect on humans are. Remember to document your sources and to give credit for any borrowed material.

3. Examine the issue of an individual's right to act according to conscience when the act would violate the law. Under what circumstances — aside from mercy killing — might such a dilemma occur? When might the issue of individual freedom take precedence over the law, or should the law always be obeyed?

NEITHER MORONS NOR IMBECILES NOR IDIOTS
In the Company of the Mentally Retarded

●

Sallie Tisdale

Sallie Tisdale is a writer and a part-time nurse. Among her publications are three books, The Sorcerer's Apprentice *(1986),* Harvest Moon *(1987), and* Lot's Wife: Salt and the Human Condition *(1988). Her essays have appeared frequently in* Harper's, *where the article from which the following excerpts are taken appeared in June 1990. The full article begins with a narrative of Tisdale's experience at a dance that concluded a convention of an organization called People First, whose membership is almost entirely mentally retarded, and of her visit to a Brooklyn housing facility for mentally retarded people. The remainder of the article, excerpted below, discusses the problems of defining mental retardation and the ways in which members of that population are able to find satisfaction in parenthood, work, and recreation.*

The subject of mental retardation is encumbered with conventional wisdom, small beliefs we cling to from childhood and large ideas that fuel the social machine. The main piece of fiction under which we labor, I think, is that we know what mental retardation is. We know that it exists: permanent, irreversible, tragic. Thousands of pages, dozens of definitions, have been written about retardation, but nothing comes close to defining it. And I can't write my own definition, either; when I try, I find myself relying on nothing more lucid than *difference from myself.* This is what drives the desire to define in the first place: These people are so unlike me, behave so unlike me, they must be something else altogether.

Less than a hundred years ago people we now call mentally retarded were labeled by researchers as morons, imbeciles, and idiots — each term referring to a different degree of defect — and were thought to be all of a type. They were considered incomplete humans, unable to feel pain, perhaps mad or possessed, and certainly dangerous. People called them the feebleminded, cretins, simpletons, dullards. Now we are to call them people-with-mental-retardation. I sometimes wonder what, left alone, the retarded would call themselves. And what would they call me? The word *retardation* only means delay, and in that sense it may be perfectly descriptive. It means the slowing down of something's course: A car's timing is retarded, and so is a flow of liquid, a tumor's growth. It is a vague and almost poetic word. And the rest — "mental" — is indefinable, a foggy reference to the life behind the eyes, impossible to measure and dangerous to judge.

The official definition of mental retardation today is one formulated by the American Association on Mental Retardation (AAMR). The AAMR carries out research, studies the results, asks for expert opinions. In its current form the definition of mental retardation has three parts: subnormal intellectual function, defined as an intelligence quotient (IQ) at least two standard deviations below the mean; poor adaptive behavior; and symptoms of retardation that appear during the developmental period. Based on the AAMR definition, between 2 and 3 percent of the population are retarded — five and a half to seven million people. This statistic remains fairly steady for reasons unclear. According to the AAMR, about 89 percent of this group are "mildly retarded." But here the plot begins to thicken.

There are two widely accepted categories of retardation: organic and   4 nonorganic. Organic retardation has more than 250 known causes, among them Down syndrome and other chromosomal disorders, metabolic imbalances, tumors, brain malformations, and trauma. But researchers in the field commonly hold that only about 20 percent of all the people called retarded have an organic problem.

The remaining 80 percent are affected by nonorganic retardation — retardation caused by, say, parental neglect or abuse, or by a baby's having eaten lead paint — and there is nothing physiologically wrong with them. Almost all the people classified as mildly retarded are considered to be nonorganically retarded. One of the more controversial questions in the field of mental retardation right now is whether the nonorganically retarded are — or should be labeled — retarded at all.

For years the measurement of one's IQ figured most significantly in our description of who is and who is not mentally retarded. IQ is a measurement of mental age divided by chronological age; a child of six who has the mental abilities of a six-year-old has an IQ of 100, the American mean. (About 50 percent of Americans are thought to have an IQ between 90 and 110.) An IQ of 70 is two standard deviations below the mean and is, therefore, the cutoff for defining retardation.

Because IQ tests are woefully inadequate — measuring a person's fund of information with little regard for the quality of one's mind or one's ability to learn — IQ as the primary measure of retardation has been slowly but surely disappearing. This has had a very real impact on a particular population — the enormous number of people called borderline, whose IQ scores hover between 70 and 85. In 1959 the two standard-deviations qualification was changed by the AAMR to one standard deviation. The number of retarded increased fivefold in one fell swoop; millions of people who until that moment had enjoyed official normality were reclassified as retarded. In 1973 the definition returned to two standard deviations, and all those people, in one stroke, became normal again.

I was skimming back issues of *The American Journal of Mental Deficiency*   8 not long ago when I found a story written in 1961 titled "A Provocative Case of Over-Achievement by a Mongoloid." The brief, scholarly article described a thirty-six-year-old man who had been diagnosed mongoloid at an early age and had lived his whole life with his mother. For the last years of her life the woman was an invalid, and her son was responsible for the household — he took care of housework, shopping, errands, finances, laundry, his own and her personal care. He also played the piano, read books and kept a journal, and made money by selling small homemade items in the neighborhood. The neighbors knew he was retarded, but no one seemed to care.

When his mother died he was committed to a "training school," where the author of the story found him. The man, called only E., was tested on entry and found to have an IQ of barely 28. The author seemed unwilling to admit that there might be something wrong with the test. If there is a lesson to be learned, he wrote, it is not to rely solely on IQ scores to predict outcomes. *If* there is a lesson. In other words, the test is not wrong in labeling the man profoundly retarded; it is E. who has been mistaken, who has "overachieved," as though he had gorged himself on skills. With the arid lack of narrative so common in these journals, the writer never reveals E.'s fate. I can't help but fear the obvious: that he never escaped the system he had until then so successfully confounded. He was, after all, profoundly retarded; his IQ made him so, and I imagine he was kept in the institution until he died.

The mental-retardation field is full of stories about retarded people who have gotten lost in the regular world for one reason or another and never been found again, so successfully did they *pretend* to be normal. The psychologist Robert Edgerton has followed a group of mentally retarded men who left an institution and entered the community as normal people more than twenty years ago; he finds them unusually optimistic in the face of adversity and no less able than their neighbors to get by. They are, he writes, hidden in "a cloak of competence," and he suggests that their unwillingness to be called retarded has kept them normal.

Most researchers in the field don't talk much at all about intelligence. Educators, for their part, talk about "delays." (One of the more consistent observations about the population called retarded is that they learn more slowly and tend to forget information more quickly than the rest of us.) A lot of people, especially those concerned with housing and employment, talk about "function." Experts refer to the mentally retarded who are able to care for themselves personally and socially as being "high function." Retarded people complimented by the accolade "high function" move in the world and take care of business in the same sorts of ways that you and I do. They are said to exhibit "adaptive behavior" as opposed to "adaptive failure."

One afternoon in San Francisco I was introduced to a middle-aged man 12 named Gary. Gary looks an awful lot like Humphrey Bogart, with a stubborn pugilist's face and a capacity for long, full silences. He will say nothing at all, then he will say much that isn't relevant, until he feels prepared to answer the question at hand. Gary was kept at home for many years, unused to the world, unskilled, a kind of Kaspar Hauser.

"I used to give Gary Coca-Colas, and he always put them in his bag with his other possessions," a recreational therapist who works with Gary told me. "And one day it dawned on me that maybe he can't open a Coca-Cola can. So I introduced him to the idea of prying open the cap, and he said, 'Oh!' and that world opened up, that problem was solved."

This therapist was going to drive me to where I was staying, and Gary home, after our talk, and Gary and I had to wait in a cold parking lot, after dark, for him to come and unlock the car doors. While we stood in the drizzle under the streetlights, Gary began to talk to himself. He wondered out loud where he would sit, where he *should* sit, whether he should put on his seat belt.

He shifted his weight from foot to foot, murmuring over and over, "I'll just ask him to repeat it." When we all got in the car Gary ran through his questions several times, until the therapist's patient, repetitive answers relieved him, and he settled back for the ride. So Gary — actually, by definition, an adaptive failure of magnificent proportions — makes his way in the world with constant, unshakable dignity.

●   ●   ●   ●

Beginning in the late nineteenth century and continuing for about sixty years, it was generally held that entire family lines were tainted by retardation and that it would be best — for society, for these families themselves — if family members were prevented from procreating. In 1927 Supreme Court Justice Oliver Wendell Holmes wrote the majority opinion in the case *Buck* v. *Bell*, a ruling in which the Court let stand a Virginia court decision ordering an institutionalized mentally retarded young woman to be sterilized. "She is the daughter of a feebleminded mother in the same institution, and the mother of an illegitimate feebleminded child," Holmes wrote. "We have seen more than once that the public welfare may call upon the best citizens for their lives. It would be strange if it could not call upon those who already sap the strength of the State for these lesser sacrifices. . . . Three generations of imbeciles are enough." Twenty years before, Indiana had passed a law permitting authorities to order compulsory sterilization (vasectomy, tubal ligation) for, among others, "idiots" and "imbeciles." Nor has such thinking disappeared altogether. In 1985 Canada allowed the hysterectomy of a mentally retarded ten-year-old girl, at her parents' request; the couple felt their daughter simply could not cope with the demands of menstruation. And in England as many as ninety sterilizations a year are performed on retarded teenagers.

No one knows how many retarded parents there are, but there are quite a few, and experts believe that the number is growing. To meet with retarded parents, I traveled to Los Angeles to learn about the SHARE/UCLA Parenting Program, one of the original intensive-education programs aimed specifically at retarded parents. The Parenting Program was designed by Dr. Alexander Tymchuk, a psychologist who teaches in the clinical psychiatry department at UCLA and who remains appalled at the lack of knowledge nationwide about retarded parents. Last year he wrote to dozens of private and governmental agencies in each state, trying to get a sense of how much the population of retarded parents has grown; the result, he said, was remarkable. Alaska reported one retarded parent; and Louisiana, Mississippi, and Alabama reported none at all.

The Parenting Program has several combination support-education groups in various neighborhoods of Los Angeles; I went to a Thursday morning class on a chilly October day at a community center in the mid-Wilshire area. I was early, but Wilma and Rashida were already at the center when I arrived. Wilma is a large black woman with a short, flattened head; her face is slightly squashed, like a bulldog's, and her voice is slow and lazy and soft. She stayed very near her daughter, a small girl wearing a very short cotton smock, with her kinky hair twisted into plastic barrettes. Rashida is Wilma's second child; neither Rashida nor her older sister is retarded. Wilma followed Rashida on an aimless toddler's path around the small, cement-floored room, with its small tables and chairs, its blackboard, its many posters of puppies and kittens.

Before long Delores, a Hispanic woman in her forties, arrived with her son Jesse. Delores also has an older, normal child. But Jesse is at least moderately retarded; he is a short, curly-haired boy, almost completely silent, with the characteristic features of Down syndrome: epicanthal folds, a protruding tongue, short fingers. He is four years old and still in diapers.

Two other mothers arrived, both quiet, well-dressed black women. (The 20 Parenting Program is mostly a project for retarded mothers.) Cynthia has two daughters, six and eight, both diagnosed as mildly retarded, and Sue has an eight-month-old infant who is normal. Last to arrive was Linda Andron, a social worker who administers the Parenting Program. A fast-talking, gregarious woman of middle age, she carried with her a giant plastic tub filled with puppets, dolls, toys, and art supplies. As Andron spread out paper and glue and precut teddy-bear silhouettes, she spoke to each child in turn, patting one on the head, chucking another's chin.

There is a weariness in Andron's voice. The mothers she works with are dogged by predictions of failure, by their own lack of education and training. (Education for the mentally retarded wasn't required by federal law until the early 1970s). It is especially difficult for Andron when one of the mothers in the program becomes pregnant: A maze of regulations restricts the advice she can give in such a situation, particularly the suggestion of an abortion. How, I wonder, would such a thing be put to a retarded woman, obvious as its advantages might at first appear? How does one advise her to consider an abortion — by pointing out how ill-prepared she is, how, well, *retarded* she is? Does one mention the possibility that the infant could be just like her?

I asked Andron if it was possible these mothers might be better parents because of their retardation.

"In some ways Delores is probably a better mother for Jesse than someone who has high expectations," she said. "He's just Jesse, that's her kid. She makes the other one do the homework, and she has people all through the building who help her. But Jesse's not any less worthwhile to her."

Part of the Thursday morning ritual is a walk to the grocery store. While 24 Andron returned to the children, helping them with an art project, Wilma, Sue, Delores, Cynthia, and I walked to the nearby 7-Eleven, where we bought cheese puffs, doughnuts, soft drinks, nachos with squirts of processed cheese and chili, and little bags of Fritos for the children. It was a desultory, languid hour, our conversation the same simple chat of any group of women with little in common but their children. On the walk back to the center I asked Delores about Jesse;

she described the day and night of his birth at length, but she never mentioned the fact that he is retarded. A while later, when I sat on a bench outside with Linda Andron, Delores walked by on the way to catch a taxi. Jesse gave Linda a hug, a vague smile, his eyes not quite meeting hers. Then he said his first words of the morning, "Bye-bye," and marched off to school.

That afternoon I drove to another neighborhood of Los Angeles, the industrial area called Culver City, to tour what is known as a sheltered workshop. Run by PAR (Production and Rehabilitation) Services, a division of the Exceptional Children's Foundation, the biggest agency for the retarded in Los Angeles, this particular workshop — PAR Westside — produces folding accordion files on a contract with the General Services Administration. It's a good contract, and the 100 employees start at minimum wage and can make up to six dollars per hour; the operation, though, is still running at a loss after three years of production.

In the front office of PAR Westside there is a series of neat cubicles for the secretarial staff, employee counselors, and supervisors. This is only a small part of a rambling building leading far back from the street, most of which is actual warehouse: cement floors, high open ceilings, fluorescent lights. Moving toward the rear, I saw several long counters, and along each counter were a dozen people on stools. Each person was sorting pencils into groups according to the shape and color of the erasers. At the front counter were the people who could count to two and sorted pairs; at the rear counter people could count to six, and they sorted by the half-dozen. I passed between counters, and in passing I crossed through uplifted faces and outstretched hands and greetings and queries of every kind. "Hello." "Halloo." "Name?" "Good day."

I chatted with a supervisor, a stout, radiant blond woman who became teary all at once when she mentioned a worker who had been promoted to the back room, out of her area. She missed him, she said, though he was only fifty yards away. A short bald man, leaning on a four-footed walker near the candy machines, planted himself in front of me and closed his eyes and held out one pale hand until I took it for a moment.

The file folders are made in the last room, a huge space thick with the smell 28 of hot glue and the huffing of hydraulics. Each step in the making of an accordion folder is done separately: The pieces of cardboard are scored in one place, folded in another, then labeled, glued, sorted, and so on. The center of the room is given over to four conveyor belts run at different speeds. Cardboard dividers labeled with different letters of the alphabet slide on the belts past the workers, who must find the correct letter and slip each divider into the correct slot of the folder. These employees are given a commission by the piece on top of their basic wage; they are trained on the slow belt and eventually graduate to faster speeds. The inspectors and supervisors are not retarded, but I was surprised to learn that a few of the line employees aren't either; because of another handicap or, in some cases, the inability to speak English, this is the best job they can find.

The trend in work for the retarded is toward something called supported employment, which takes place not in workshops but in the general sector. A job coach — paid by an agency like the Exceptional Children's Foundation, not the employer — first learns the necessary skill, then teaches it to the retarded employee on the job, staying beside the recruit as long as necessary. Employers who have tried it like supported employment, because the costs are low and the responsibility for training lies with the agency. The retarded are considered good workers, capable of productivity approaching 100 percent of their non-retarded counterparts, with lower absentee rates. The foundation is moving into supported employment slowly, unwilling, at present, to close the sheltered workshops run by PAR Services, which employ hundreds of people who are unlikely to be successful in other jobs. And all of these considerations pale next to the desire of the retarded to have work — to act in the world and be rewarded for the effort.

The Recreation Center for the Handicapped is a maze of buildings connected by corridors on a hill above the San Francisco Zoo. Ron Jones, forty-eight, with pale hair and a florid face, has been a specialist at the Rec Center for twelve years, teaching physical recreation and coaching a basketball team sanctioned by the Special Olympics. Jones says the Special Olympics officials aren't very fond of his team, because they aren't strong competitors in any conventional sense. With what he calls a "political attitude," he decided long ago that on *his* basketball team anyone could play and everyone could win. Every game, he fields between fifty and sixty players, divided into different squads by the color of their jerseys. There are almost as many women as men playing, and everyone is retarded; a few use crutches or wheelchairs, and a few are blind or deaf.

The Wildcats play a full and lusty season against a stunning array of opponents, including the San Francisco Police Department, the Salvation Army, a team made up of prisoners, and, once, the Chinese Consulate team. Ron Jones and the Wildcats are a cult legend of sorts in San Francisco, and I'd been wanting to play a game with them ever since I read *B-Ball*, Jones's memoir about the team. This was my chance, and I had recruited about a dozen people to be the Wildcats' first opponents of the season.

I arrived early for a pregame dinner in the cafeteria of the Rec Center and followed a step or two behind Jones as he entered the crowded room. A half-dozen people leapt from their seats to grasp his shoulder or slap him high-fives; almost everyone was wearing a headband labeled Wildcats.   32

At my table sat a man named Michael Rice, one of the main characters I knew from *B-Ball*. Michael is in his forties, a bear of a man with a lumpy, crooked face, shaggy hair, and a huge, deep laugh. He is one of the veteran players, a bit of a star. He seems to keep his mouth perpetually half-open, set to holler his agreement — or his derisive disagreement — with whatever you're about to say. Rice can't tell time. Clocks, watches, the analog concept — these mean nothing to him. But Michael Rice is never late; he runs his life and his days by the passage of buses along certain routes, by radio shows, by the regular schedules of people who do use watches. When Michael's aging parents die, Ron Jones and his wife will become his guardians.

After dinner I lay on the wooden stage at one end of the room and watched the crowd. They cleared their dishes, scraped their plates, carried milk cartons and bowls of leftover mashed potatoes back to the kitchen. There were no straight lines, no efficiency; people were grinning and stumbling into each other for hugs, to slap backs, and, again and again, to slap hands in the high-five. The room was full of people acting like they'd just won a grand prize, and I thought about how little etiquette there is among the retarded. One only needs not to be mean. Watching them, I was watching myself released.

The game was preceded by a rally and warm-up. One corner of the gym had been given over to a disc jockey, spinning and scratching at rap records while a full complement of cheerleaders — male and female staff in rally skirts, with pom-poms — practiced their routines. Squad after squad of players, in purple or red jerseys, took their places under the baskets, tripping through the time-honored routines of shoot and run, catch and pass.

I stood in the doorway, mentally reviewing the little I knew about basket- 36 ball. Ron Jones, a few yards away, was suddenly accosted by a pudgy-faced Chinese man wearing a red jersey. "Wha' team?" the man asked with urgency, pointing at the practice.

"*Our* team? We're the Wildcats."

"Wildcats?" the man asked again.

"Wildcats." Jones was definitive this time.

"Wildcats?" 40

"*Wildcats.*"

"Wildcats? Aww *right!*" And he threw up his hand for a high-five.

A short while later a man named Vincent joined me. We'd met at dinner. Vincent has a long, narrow face under a shock of brown hair. He shook my hand enthusiastically and for a long time.

"Can I be on your team?" he asked, and I couldn't imagine why not. So 44 Vincent defected from the Wildcats, with predictions of astonishing prowess, and in a moment of abandon he was joined by his friend Michelle. Michelle is a woman in her late twenties, short and heavy-chested, with a mouthful of crazy white teeth.

The half-dozen cheerleaders formed a tunnel of arms and pom-poms beneath one basket, and with a roar the Wildcats ran (stumbled, limped, rolled) through the tunnel and past their opponents, slapping hands. Midway through the line came a small pale man with almond eyes and a few brief strings of hair combed sideways. My hands were open for another high-five slap, but instead he grabbed my hand, turned it over, and delicately pressed his dry lips to it in a kiss.

The buzzer sounded and the game began. I was careful of the half-court line, careful to avoid the dreaded double dribble. A few minutes into the game, Jones, acting as referee and final authority, called time-out and required us to substitute players. Our starting five took seats, and we dispatched our other squad. A few moments later Jones called time again, and everyone stood there, waiting for an explanation. A young man with bent legs, in a purple jersey, wobbled slowly onto the court, dropped his crutches, and shot twice. Only when the ball fell short the second time did Jones whistle again and allow the players to move.

One of the fans on our side of the gym brushed the lint off his suit and joined the cheerleaders; another onlooker quietly opened a little suitcase and took out a trumpet. Jones was in and out of everything, dashing to and fro, whistling madly and switching players apparently at random. He's been known to bring a ringing phone onto the court, and a ladder; he's played with dogs, handcuffs, and bicycles. Last year Art Agnos, the mayor of San Francisco, played on a team fielded by State Assembly Speaker Willie Brown, and Jones gave Agnos a technical foul for the color of his shorts.

When a man in a wheelchair, pushed up and down the court by a staff   48 member, finally reached the basket with a ball in his hands, I stopped and stared at that high, high basket; but then a woman from the sidelines ran out and made a circle of her arms near his lap. He shot, and he hit. It wasn't competition anymore but play. It felt reckless, almost naughty; I was hiccuping with laughter. Then I was fouled with a bear hug from Michael Rice, and I had to turn around and shoot backward, over my head, with the whole room upside down and chanting.

Later, from nowhere, Michelle, sidling away from the other players, threw the ball with a wild two-handed shove. It fell through the net with a swish. Her jaw dropped and she clapped her hands to her cheeks, mouth wide with stupefied amazement, and the crowd of players surrounded her a moment to slap her back; then all the players on both teams ran in a stumbling ballet to the other end. All the players, that is, but Michelle; she stood transfixed by her own astonishing feat.

Just before the basketball game I was sitting with Jones in his little office, hearing the distant splash of swimmers in the therapy pool. A young man about to play his first game with the Wildcats stood just outside the door, looking in mournfully, waiting for the coach to tell him when to change his clothes. We had been talking about the qualities of retardation, and what it was, and what it meant to the rest of us: to the nonretarded.

"I think they offer something different from what I offer to the world," he said after a moment. "What do they give back to us? If they give back a sense of trust, and joy, and courage—well, these are things I'd think the world would be hungry for. Do you want miracles in your life? Are you going to get them anywhere else?"

● PERSONAL RESPONSE ●

What experiences have you had with mentally retarded people? What attitude do you take toward them? Do you hold any of the "small beliefs we cling to from childhood" that Tisdale refers to in paragraph 1?

● QUESTIONS FOR DISCUSSION ●

1. What do you think is Tisdale's central purpose in this essay? Does she argue for a redefinition of mental retardation? Is she just reporting on the position of the mentally

retarded in our society? Does she want "normal" people to see them differently from the way they are customarily viewed?

2. How does Tisdale's title reflect her attitude toward retarded people?

3. What is the "conventional wisdom" that "mental retardation is encumbered with" (paragraph 1)?

4. What is Tisdale's attitude toward the mental-health professionals who are responsible for defining mental retardation, both historically and now? Point out passages that support your answers.

5. How do the specific examples of people with retardation — Gary, Wilma, Delores, Michael Rice, for instance — help to balance the discussions of retardation in general?

6. Summarize the problems associated with defining mental retardation, according to Tisdale.

7. How is the issue of defining mental retardation different from the issue of what to call people who fit that definition? If you have read Nancy Mairs's "On Being a Cripple," in what way is the issue of what to call mentally retarded people related to what to call physically disabled people?

8. In what sense do you think Tisdale means that she "was watching [her]self released" (paragraph 34)?

• WRITING TOPICS •

1. In paragraph 10, Tisdale says that the psychologist Robert Edgerton suggests that the "unwillingness to be called retarded has kept them [people formally institutionalized who now live in the community] normal." Explain the extent to which you agree that refusing to be called something can actually prevent it from happening. Give examples of other labels that people could refuse to conform to.

2. Write an essay based on your own observations of attitudes toward the mentally retarded in your own community or in society at large. For instance, you might take into account agencies in your community that serve the retarded population, events such as the Special Olympics, or even portrayals of the mentally retarded on television shows.

3. If you know someone who has been categorized as retarded, describe that person's physical characteristics, personality, and daily life.

A FAMILY CONFRONTS MENTAL ILLNESS

●

MARY KAY BLAKELY

Mary Kay Blakely is a writer whose articles appear frequently in a variety of publications, including Ms. *and* Psychology Today. *She has written a book,* Wake Me When It's Over *(1989), from which the following excerpt was taken. In this excerpt, Blakely describes the wrenching mood swings of her manic-depressive brother, from "unhuman energy during his manic periods" to the "excruciating loneliness" of "his otherness" during his depressed periods.*

Francis Jude, my eldest brother, was brilliant and witty, the leading madman of my four eccentric siblings, and I miss him enormously. During his brief adult life, he suffered altogether eight nervous breakdowns, serving as many sentences — voluntary and not — in Chicago institutions. Whether his wild imagination caused the stunning chemical changes in his body or the other way around, he surged with unhuman energy during his manic periods, then was flattened for months with tremendous exhaustion. He committed suicide on Nov. 12, 1981.

The doctors' diagnosis was manic depression, but Frank thought of his illness as a spiritual fever. After his boyhood years as a Catholic seminarian, followed by an earnest search for God in the writings of Buddhist monks, Jewish rabbis, Protestant pastors, and, finally, Unitarian ministers, he'd formed a nonsectarian but wholly religious view of events. "We are all like bacteria in a banana," he once wrote after a manic episode, "each doing our own little thing, while the fruit is ripened for God's digestion." It was not unusual for Frank to see signs of God in a bunch of bananas — he saw God everywhere. At times he thought he was God Himself, infused with a euphoric rhythm inside his head he called "the beat, the beat, the beat."

Normally reserved and shy, he was charismatic and demonstrative when he was high. Frank ran for governor of Illinois once, on orders from above. He broke through security at the *Chicago Sun Times*, where he brought columnist Mike Royko the good news that he was destined to become Frank's campaign manager. Royko called my parents, and Frank spent the rest of his campaign at the Reed Mental Health Center.

Although I am an avowed agnostic myself, I thought Frank's spiritual 4 diagnosis was as credible as anything else. Nevertheless, I felt obliged to argue with him. During his first breakdown in 1967, when he was wired with electrodes and given shock treatments at Loretto Hospital in Chicago, he reported that he'd received messages directly from God Himself. The truth arrived in tremendous jolts, he said, just as he expected it would someday. I tried to help him unscramble his brain, pointing out the difference between electricity and divinity. It was machinery, not God, that sent the sizzling jolts through his mind, I explained.

"Truth doesn't fry your brain," I tried pointing out.

"Sometimes it *does*," he replied, wide-eyed, as surprised to report this revelation as I was to hear it. A look of sheer lucidity crossed his face, followed by sudden surprise and then vast confusion. It was a silent movie of the chaos inside his head — I could actually *watch* Frank losing his innocence. He shed a great quantity of that innocence in the shock-treatment room at Loretto Hospital, being electrified by truth.

The treatments halted his illness only temporarily. During subsequent breakdowns, he was studied and probed, tested and drugged, interviewed and examined by some of the most famous psychiatrists in Chicago, but no one could cure him. Attempts to stabilize his moods with lithium carbonate failed repeatedly, puzzling his physicians. Frank himself was amazed by the constant motion inside his mind. He said it felt like his head had been clapped between two powerful hands and was orbiting around a spinning discus thrower warming up for a mighty heave. He was anxious for the final thrust, releasing him from the dizzying spins into free flight.

I was one of Frank's main companions throughout his bouts of madness, when his mind rolled out to the ends of human passion. He would hear and see things I couldn't understand, and I spent countless hours arguing with him inside the wards of insane asylums. In polite company, they're referred to as mental health centers, but in the ravaged minds of the inmates, politeness was the first thing to go.

Frank would come back from his journeys into madness radically altered by what he had seen, and I understand now how much I relied on his expeditions. I was too much of a coward to let my own mind roll out full length, having witnessed the devastating price he paid.

His manic bouts were followed by long depressions, as he struggled to apply his dreams to ordinary life. The messages he believed so ardently during his seizures would melt doubt, and he felt his otherness with an excruciating loneliness. Paralyzed with indecision and fear, he would sleep through those months, sometimes for 20 hours at a time. The fantastic energy abandoned him, and he lifted his thin body out of bed as if it weighed 500 pounds. He described these terrible confrontations with his conscience as "*grand mal* seizures of despair." They were a regular stop on the circular course of his spiritual fevers.

In the spring of 1970, Frank was interned at the Illinois State Psychiatric Institute (ISPI) — it was his fourth breakdown, the most reckless one so far. It was our mother, Kay, who had arranged to get him into ISPI after reading a newspaper report about two psychiatrists from the University of Chicago who ran the experimental program. While it was still widely believed among psychiatrists then that bad mothering caused most mental problems, Dr. Herbert Y. Meltzer and Dr. Ronald Moline were among the pioneers who explored the possibility that manic depression was a result of a chemical imbalance.

Their early experiments turned up evidence of faulty genetic wiring, sug- 12
gesting that biology, not socialization, triggered the disease. They'd identified a
muscle enzyme that seemed to play a role in manic depression, and had been
given the ninth floor of ISPI to test their hypothesis. When Kay recognized her
son's symptoms in the report — the stunning physical changes Frank underwent
during his breakdowns — she scheduled an appointment, and Frank was ultimately admitted to the program.

Because the ISPI doctors were committed to a theory involving enzymes
and brain cells, they couldn't have been counting heavily on answers from
psychoanalysis. But because a cure was still unavailable through medicine, the
ISPI program included weekly doses of psychotherapy.

I hated the Thursday night sessions, when the patients and their families
were collectively grilled under the harsh fluorescent lights of the locked ward.
Maybe somewhere in the pasts of these humbled people there were cases of bad
mothering or absent fathering or emotional neglect — what family surviving the
'50s was exempt? — but I couldn't believe these human errors brought the
physical changes in Frank. I knew an unhappy childhood was not the problem. If
anything, my parents' unstoppable affection had postponed Frank's crisis. He
didn't have his first breakdown under their roof — it happened 240 miles away, at
Southern Illinois University the year he left home.

Each week Kay, my father Jerry, my brother Paul, and I joined the other
families with members impounded on ISPI's ninth floor for a rigorous interrogation of our pasts. My parents exempted Kevin and Gina, the two youngest
siblings, in an effort to spare them a direct confrontation with the terrifying look
of mental illness, even though they had witnessed Frank's bizarre behavior.
Whether obligation or tradition or just plain helplessness prompted this futile
treatment, the sessions were unproductive if not outright harmful. One week,
Jerry was questioned about his habit of shaking hands with his adult sons,
replacing the childhood hugs. The therapist on duty that night suggested our
father's formal handshakes had deprived Frank of his affectionate due. This was
ridiculous, Paul and I knew.

While my father tried to practice the emotional reserve required of his 16
generation of men, the disguise never completely covered him. I'd seen his eyes
fill up and his face become red repeatedly at baptisms and confirmations,
basketball games and high school plays. It was embarrassing to sit next to Jerry
when one of his children was on stage because invariably, unable to hold out for
the cover of final applause, he would pull out his handkerchief and alert the
audience to his severely clogged-up condition. There were plenty of crosses the
children of this complicated, emotional man had to bear during the John Wayne-
worshipping '50s, but being insufficiently loved was never one of them. Yet the
spring of 1970, a therapist unfamiliar with this history sent Jerry home in
despair. He spent the following months doubting himself, believing a dozen
more hugs might have saved his son from madness.

Few participants emerged from those evenings without confessing to some
charge, but the heaviest guilt was generally accepted by the mothers. During a

luckless search for signs of "over-mothering" or "dominance" or "aggression" in Kay one evening, the therapist appeared ready to move on to more promising candidates when he raised a question about "rejection." My mother remembered a night in 1949, when Frank was 3, that still caused her some regrets.

A pediatrician had applied bindings around Frank's head during a visit that afternoon, to flatten the ears a bit. As the bindings were applied I imagine the pediatrician caught my mother wincing. That wince appeared hundreds of times as her five offspring somersaulted through childhood — when I got my hand caught in the wringer of the washing machine or one of my brothers had his head stitched in the emergency room. She usually followed the wince with a pat of sympathy, a gesture of comfort.

The doctor, an authoritative man, disapproved of her soft-touch approach. He warned her of the dangers of coddling, especially coddling boys. There were lots of stories then about men whose lives were wrecked by homosexuality because their mothers kissed them too much.

Kay remembered being awake that whole night, listening to cries from the baby's room and wrestling with her urge to scoop him up and comfort him. It took tremendous discipline, but she accepted the punishment of the pediatrician's advice and resisted. She could still hear those cries, she told the therapist at ISPI 21 years later. She winced.

Perhaps that's when my brother may have felt rejected, she volunteered. How could he have known her longing to pick him up, to comfort him? How could he have known she was struggling to follow orders? Perceiving the fresh scent of guilt, the therapist probed deeper: Maybe she really did think he was homely — maybe she really was unconsciously rejecting him. My mother considered this suggestion for a moment. She looked across the room at my brother, then shook her head slowly. No, she said simply, without further explanation. Even ravaged by illness, even with something untamable coursing through him, Frank was clearly, electrically, a beautiful young man. My mother thought anybody looking at him could see that.

The weekend before Frank's suicide, he visited me in Fort Wayne, coming from Chicago by Greyhound. Over and over that weekend he told me how much he loved me. It was only later, when I went back over our long conversations, that I understood he was also saying goodbye. Ostensibly, he came to deliver a suitcase full of journal notes — jottings made at fever pitch — asking me to be his "translator." The structural ideas for his grand vision were all there, he thought, but lacked fluency. I accepted the sheaf of papers, fully aware that God might appear as an electric chair in the gospel according to Frank.

He, too, was a writer, but had abandoned very nearly all conventional forms in his rush to record gigantic thoughts. Some pages contained only a single sentence, no thoughts leading up to or away from it, like the solitary message of an obsessed placard carrier on the street. ("In the whitest light, the dancer becomes the dance," one page announced.) Frank's journal read like a series of baffling Zen koans, evidence of lunacy or brilliance.

Although it was painful to remember, I cherished that last visit together — it relieved any guilt I might have had about preventing his death. The flimsy gravity of human love cannot stop a man when he's in orbit with divine inspiration. He wasn't depressed that weekend — quite the opposite, in fact. He was riding the crest of a manic high, pacing about my quiet Fort Wayne neighborhood with frenetic energy.

I remember watching him through the kitchen window Saturday afternoon as he raked a month's accumulation of leaves with my sons. They filled a large tarp with leaves, then one or both of the kids would jump in and Frank would drag them to the curb. With a mighty heave, unexpectedly strong for his skinny, drug-shaken frame, he'd hoist the kids and leaves into the air.

The sound he emitted with each launch was a peculiar blend of karate yell and manic laugh, his voice undecided whether to expect pain or joy with the final thrust. Then he'd race the kids to the back of the yard and start all over, as if his life depended on filling the street with children and leaves. Long after the kids left the game, he was still filling the tarp.

Like the animated sorcerer's apprentice, he raked feverishly, piercing the night with howls of aching happiness. I stood at the window wondering what he thought he was hauling, to where. He was exceptionally tight-lipped about his plans that weekend. "It's one of those times when the irrational will become rational," he offered cryptically. "I'm in 'that magical moment when *is* becomes *if . . .*'" He caught himself and stopped, replacing the rest of e.e. cummings' poem with his quiet, lunatic grin. That smile was my personal legacy from Frank.

Sunday I drove Frank to the Greyhound station. Two nights later, Kay called 28 from Chicago. "Hello darling," she said softly, and I instantly raised both hands to the receiver. Kay saved "darling" for emergencies — her love was made of stronger stuff, herding five children through infancy and adolescence with exacting discipline.

"Are the children in bed?" she asked quietly. I sank into the chair next to the phone, a great ache swelling my throat, cutting off my air. I knew what she had to report. A letter from Frank had arrived that morning: "It was a beautiful letter," she said calmly, huskily, in a voice that had not yet fully recovered from an afternoon of tears. "It made us cry." She paused then, taking in an extra breath of air to hold her brief but heavy summary. "He thanked us for being his parents."

I knew his suicide was not an act of despair; in his own mind, he was committing an act of ultimate faith. It was a death from exhaustion, from the efforts of thinking and striving, and I was grateful he had finally reached the end of his pain.

His seemingly irrational decision did eventually become rational to me. When I re-read Frank's letters now, freed from the arrogant assumption that I could somehow save him, his brilliance and faith is more understandable to me. Frank thought of his life as "a divine, inscrutable prayer" and believed "my existence does not end with death." Though I'm still an agnostic, I'm inclined to accept his theory of immortality.

Since his permanent departure eight years ago, certain memories — a pile of 32 autumn leaves, a line of familiar poetry — will trigger a rush of recognition, and I feel the beat, the beat, the beat pumping through me. My own mind, stamped by his, reverberates with an eternal echo of love.

● PERSONAL RESPONSE ●

How do you think you would handle the wild mood swings of someone like Frank Blakely? What do you think of the way in which Blakely treated her brother?

● QUESTIONS FOR DISCUSSION ●

1. Blakely uses vivid, highly descriptive words, such as "stunning" and "surged" (paragraph 1), and figurative language, such as "It was a silent movie of chaos in his head" (paragraph 6). Find other examples of effective use of both literal and figurative language to convey sense experience.

2. What details do you think most forcefully describe Blakely's brother Frank?

3. Why do you think Blakely devotes so much space to the period in 1970 when Frank was institutionalized and the family participated in psychotherapy sessions?

4. Explain what Blakely means by "the John Wayne-worshipping '50s" (paragraph 16).

5. Summarize Blakely's feelings for her brother. What is her attitude toward his suicide?

6. What does Blakely mean when she says that she is "freed from the arrogant assumption that [she] could somehow save him" (paragraph 31)? What has freed her? Why is it an "arrogant assumption" to want to save her brother?

● WRITING TOPICS ●

1. Select one type of mental illness, such as schizophrenia, manic depression, or unipolar depression, and explain what it is and how it affects its victims.

2. If you personally know someone who is mentally ill, describe that person and your feelings for her or him. Include at least one extended account of an experience you have had together.

3. Describe an experience you have had with someone whose behavior or personality troubled you. How did you respond to the person and what did you learn from the experience?

USERS, LIKE ME
MEMBERSHIP IN THE CHURCH OF DRUGS

●

GAIL REGIER

Gail Regier teaches English at Auburn University. His short stories and essays have appeared in Harper's *and the* Atlantic, *among other publications. In the following essay, which appeared in the May 1989 issue of* Harper's, *Regier illustrates in vivid detail the fellowship he felt when he was once a member of "the martyred elite" who belonged to what he calls the Church of Drugs. "What we had in common," he writes, "was drugs. Getting high bound us together against outsiders, gathered us into a common purpose."*

Profiles of typical drug users, in the newspapers and on TV, obscure the fact that many users aren't typical. I used to do coke with a violinist who was the most sheltered woman I've ever known. My mushroom connection was a fifty-year-old school-bus driver. And one of my high-school buddies, who moved $1,000 worth of drugs a day in and out of his girlfriend's tattoo shop, would always extend credit to transients and welfare moms — debts he'd let slide after a while when they weren't paid.

It's easy to start thinking all users are media stereotypes: ghetto trash, neurotic child stars, mutinous suburban adolescents. Users, the media imagine, can't hold jobs or take care of their kids. Users rob liquor stores.

Real users, for all their chilly scorn of the straight world, buy into the same myths, but turn them inside out. The condescension becomes a kind of snobbery: we are different from the straight people, we are special, we are more free. We are spiritual adventurers. When I was twenty-four, which was not that long ago, my friends and I thought nothing was more hip than drugs, nothing more depraved, nothing more elemental. When we were messed up, we seemed to become exactly who we were, and what could be more dangerous and splendid? Other vices made our lives more complicated. Drugs made everything simple and pure.

Anyone who hangs around drugs learns not to think too much about all this, 4 learns to watch the bent spoon in the water glass.

Some of the users I knew were people with nothing left to lose. The rest of us were in it only a little for the money, more than a lot for the nights we would drive to one place after another, in and out of people's parties, looking for a connection. It was a kind of social life, and we weren't in any hurry.

What we had in common was drugs. Getting high bound us together against outsiders, gathered us into a common purpose. No one else understood us and we understood each other so well.

New Year's Eve 1979: We're riding around trying to cop some speed. My poet friend Brian° is driving and in the backseat is Guy, who is on probation and very uptight because we keep telling him the car is stolen. "You mothers are rounding me," he keeps saying. He doesn't believe us, but the game makes him real paranoid. We make some parties but the speed is always gone before we arrive, so we head for the truck stop where I used to work. The high-school kids who work there always have grass and pills. Their stuff is not so hot, but it's real cheap. Restaurant people have a high rate of casual use; the work's so menial you can't stand it without getting high.

The place is full of tired truck drivers and travelers with whiny kids. The hookers wear miniskirts and army jackets and all have colds. Our favorite waitress, Sherry, combines two parties to get us a booth. She's telling some truckers at the counter about her sexual problems with her husband. They tell her to wear leather panties and she sighs and says that doesn't work.

Fleetwood Mac songs shake the jukebox. Sherry slings us coffee and asks, What's the scam? Brian puts thumb and forefinger to his lips and mimes a toke from a joint. She goes back to the kitchen, and when she comes back tells us that Larry is holding. We take our coffee with us through the door marked AUTHO-RIZED PERSONNEL. Everybody in the kitchen is drunk. Two of the girls are playing the desert-island game: If you could have only two drugs for the rest of your life, what would they be? Sherry pours some cold duck from a bottle that was in the walk-in cooler.

There was a time when the rap here was all baseball and dates, but not anymore. Tonight the drizzle of abstractions is as vacuous as any graduate seminar. The kids say the owner gives them shit for coming to work stoned. They need their jobs but they know how they want to live. I tell them that the Church of Drugs has its own rituals and rules, and its members are a martyred elite. Brian tells Sherry about acid and stained glass. Guy tells the dishwasher how to tell if it's his starter or his alternator that's bad. The kids listen. They are impressed by us. They want to be like us.

Drug dealers on TV are vampires: oily, smooth, psychotic, sexy, human paradigms of the narcotics they sell. Larry is a skinny punk who is studying auto body at the vo-tech high school. Wearing a GMC cap and a long, stained apron, he stands behind a grease-blackened grill covered with steaks and bacon and skillets asizzle with eggs.

"Watch this shit," he tells another aproned kid, and motions to us to follow him. The kid protests that he'll get behind. Larry leads us back to the storeroom, past shelves of #10 cans and signs that read ALL DELIVERIES C.O.D. and ABSOLUTELY NO FIREARMS ALLOWED ON THESE PREMISES. He takes a baggie from his gym bag and shows us some speeders he says are pharmaceutical. The black capsules have the right markings on them, but they unscrew too easily and the bone-white powder inside isn't bitter enough. We tell him no thanks, but buy a joint from him for a dollar.

8

12

°[Author's note:] I have changed the names of those mentioned here for obvious reasons.

When I was selling drugs I made a lot of money, but I usually got stoned on the profits. It was black money and it seemed the highs I bought with it were free and therefore sweeter. I was a college dropout with a kid and a nervous wife. I worked as a cook in a Mexican café fifty hours a week and brought home $200. For that $200 I could buy half a kilo of sinsemilla, break it down into finger bags, and double my money. Selling meant I always had drugs — though we didn't that New Year's eve. Dealing, with its arcana of mirrors and scales, was a guild mystery, a secret, forbidden craft. It was a ticket to places I couldn't get to any other way. I got to know guys who drove Cadillacs and carried forged passports, guys who cooked acid and smack in basement labs, women who wore lots of rings and called every man Jones.

Brian and I smoke the joint on the back porch of the truck stop. The rain, we decide, is very righteous. Eighteen-wheelers grind and hiss their gaudy lights onto the interstate. Diane, a sloe-eyed, peach-skinned fifteen-year-old, comes out and vamps us for a couple of hits. I tell her about those cocaine nights when the room fills with snowflakes sifting down slow as if they were under water. She's kissing Brian and I've got my hand up her short skirt, but she refuses to get in the car with us.

Downtown by the hospital, we get in a confusion with some ambulance guys with their cherry top on. Bald tires skid on the wet pavement. Brian decides to let me drive. We stop at my house, where my wife is watching *Dick Clark's New Year's Rockin' Eve*. Her eyes are red from crying, but she tries to smile.

"Dan and Jan were here," she says. "Don't you remember we invited 16
them?"

I look in the refrigerator for wine. There isn't any.

"Brian and Guy are in the car," I say. "I've got to run them home."

"Then will you come back?"

"Come with us if you want." I know she won't. Our son's asleep upstairs. 20

"Don't get speed," she says.

"We're not."

"You get mean when you do speed."

I want to get wired. I head for the door. 24

We make the Steak N' Ale. In a real city there would be black guys pushing stuff on the sidewalk out front, but this is Springfield, Missouri, and we can't score. The manager, our connection, isn't around. At the bar we order shots of whiskey. The place is full of pretty girls, and even the ones who don't drink are drunk, but we're not looking for girls.

Guy says, "We should go see Casey." Casey is an old guy who sold black-market penicillin in post-war Europe. Brian doesn't know Casey but he knows he's expensive, and he fusses about that. But Guy and I are studying on how good Casey's crystal meth is and how Casey could get us a set of points so we could hit it.

On our way we boost three wine glasses and a bottle of Korbel from somebody's table. Sitting in the car, we drink to ourselves and the dying year. Brian wets his fingertip in the champagne and strokes it gently round and round the rim of his glass, making space noises rise from the crystal. We all do it, but then the noises turn spooky and we get paranoid. We drop the glasses out the window and drive.

Prudence is sitting on the front porch watching the rain. She kisses me and I taste her tongue. I introduce my friends and she kisses them. 28

"Casey's inside."

"Has he got meth?"

She shrugs. The business is Casey's gig. Prudence is twenty and has a cat named Lenin and a one-year-old baby. She's kept the job she had before she moved in with Casey: evening attendant at a laundry near the college. Her place is the cleanest in town. My buddies and I would drop in to wash some jeans and score a little pot, and end up hanging around all evening eating candy bars and flirting with Prudence.

On the weekends Prudence ran a perpetual carport sale, things she made 32 and stuff taken in barter from customers with cash-flow problems. Clothes and belt buckles, pipes and bottles, bootleg eight-tracks and cassettes with typed labels, old skin mags, car stereos and CB radios trailing cut wires.

The living room is brightly lit as always; Prudence leaves her pole lamps on twenty-four hours a day. Casey is sprawled among pillows on an old couch ripe with cigarette scars, culling sticks and seeds from some dope on the glass-topped coffee table. Framed beneath the glass are large-denomination bills from several South American countries. Casey's favorite objects litter the shelf below: brass pipes with small screw fittings, ceramic ashtrays from the commune at Ava, a rifle scope he uses to case visitors coming up the rutted driveway.

A candy dish holds pills — speckled birds and bootleg ludes coloring a base of Tylenol with codeine, bought over-the-counter in Canada. Casey offers us some, and I sift thumb and forefinger carefully through the pile and pick out two black beauties for tomorrow. Brian starts to take a handful and I sign him not to. Casey scarfs codeine the whole time we talk.

Prudence and I go to the kitchen to mix a fruit jar of gin and orange juice, stay there a little while to touch and neck. She has painted everything in the kitchen white, walls and floors and cabinets and fixtures, and in the glare of many bare bulbs the room is stark as a laboratory. White-painted plaster peels off the walls in loops and splinters. There are no dishes or pans; Prudence buys only things she can cook in her toaster oven.

Last time I was over, Casey went after Prudence with a ratchet wrench and I 36 had to talk him down. As we mix the drinks she tells me how she and Casey dropped acid together and now things are better. He's even starting to like the boy. I tell her how my four-year-old thinks acid is the best trick going, because when I'm tripping I play with him so much. We take baths together, drenching the floor with our bathtub games, while my wife sits on the toilet lid, watching us with her bright blue eyes.

On the floor, Lenin and the baby take turns peekabooing and pouncing. I'm surprised the baby isn't scared. I've changed my mind and dropped one of the beauties and I'm feeling edgy and fast and tricky. Lenin rubs himself against my ankles and I grow paranoid.

"You want to help me water the plants?" Prudence asks.

We climb the rungs nailed to the closet wall, push up the trapdoor, and crawl into the attic. Gro-lights illuminate twenty marijuana plants set in plastic tubs. Casey has run a hose up through the wall. I turn the water on and off for her as she crawls back and forth across the rafters on her hands and knees.

Downstairs, I can hear Brian on a rap. "Radiation will be the next great vice. They already use it with chemo to kill cancer. Soon they'll discover wavelengths that reproduce the effects of every known drug. The cops will be able to spot users easily 'cause we'll all be bald." 40

Prudence digs out a Mamas and Papas tape and plays "Straight Shooter." Casey tells us how some junkies will put off shooting-up until the craving starts, like getting real hungry before a steak dinner. I listen, but to me the addict world is as mythical as Oz. I've met junkies, but they were in town only accidentally and soon moved on to Kansas City or New Orleans. Like a symphony orchestra or a pro sports team, a junkie population needs a large urban center to support it.

Casey says that the word "heroin" is a corruption of the German word *heroisch*, meaning "powerful, even in small amounts." I cruise the bookshelf. A rogues' gallery: Henry Miller, Cocteau, Genet, de Sade's *Justine* in scarlet leather, *Story of O*. Casey explains a William Burroughs story he's just read, about a secret society dedicated to discovering the Flesh Tree described in an ancient Mayan codex. This is the rare and sacred plant from which human life originally derived. According to Burroughs, flesh is really a vegetable, and the human system of reproduction is a perversion of its true nature.

Casey talks very seriously about acquiring his own Tree of Flesh on his next trip to Mazatlán. He regards the story as journalism rather than parable — or seems to. We spend some time discussing how to care for the Tree of Flesh once Casey obtains it.

Guy asks Casey about the crystal meth. 44

"You don't want speed," I say. I'm feeling very articulate now. "What you want is a hit of junk." Guy shakes his head, but Brian looks thoughtful. "For ten minutes," I say, "you'll be as high as you ever thought you wanted to be. Then in half an hour you'll be as high as you *really* ever wanted to be."

"And then?" Guy says.

"You'll want *more*."

Inside the Church of Drugs, heroin users are an elite within the elite, saints of Instant Karma and Instant Death. Their stark games raise them to a place beyond the hype and chatter. 48

"When you shoot up," I tell them, "you're alone before the abyss. That's what shooting up is for."

The first time I shot up was the most frightened I've ever been. For me the fear was part of the high.

Guy and Brian have never done needles, but Brian is hard for it and helps me work Guy around. "We won't hit you in the vein," I assure him. "Just in muscle tissue, like a vaccination." We each give Casey a twenty. He drags an army-surplus ammo box from under the couch and rummages through it. Prudence puts the baby on the rug and goes to hunt up a needle.

When she returns with one, Casey measures out the heroin and I cook it in a   52
teaspoon dark with the flames of many lighters. When it's like molten silver,
Casey loads, taps bubbles out of the rig, and hits Guy in the shoulder before he
can change his mind. Brian thrusts his arm forward eagerly, his eyes ashimmer
with the romance of drugs, and I put the needle in him. They both vomit, the
way almost everybody does when they get their wings, then go serenely on the
nod. The baby is startled and then amused by their upheavals. We get them
settled and empty the bucket we had handy for them, then Casey and Prudence
hit each other. She has a glass of gin in one hand and breaks it on the coffee table
when the spasms hit her.

Last to do up, I take my time, pricking the point of the needle into the vein
of my inside forearm easing back a little before I push the trigger. Wisps of blood
claw up in the glass wand and a white light like a fist of thorns shoves everything
away.

Later we're stirring around again and starting to talk. The baby has been
crying for a while. Brian wipes the shards of broken glass off the coffee table
onto the rug in front of the baby, who quiets and reaches for these shiny new
toys.

After a few cuts the baby learns that broken glass can hurt him. He's crying
again. He tries to push the pieces away, but the splinters stick to his hands. He
rubs his small fists together and we all start laughing, we can't help it, he's so
cute. Prudence claps her hands and cheers on his efforts. He rubs his hands
against his face and the blood spots it like clown makeup. The baby cries so hard
he starts choking. It seems very funny. Then he starts gnawing at the slivers
between his fingers, and that is very funny too.

Casey gets straight first and washes the dried blood from the baby's face.   56
Guy can't walk and I help him outside into the cold air. Brian and Prudence are
messing around out by the car.

Casey comes out on the porch. His fingers are streaked with iodine. He
says, "Hey man."

I say Yeah.

Casey looks at Brian. "Don't bring him back here."

These days I'm a guy who goes six months or a year without smoking a joint.   60
I got out of drugs the way a lot of people do. One day I looked around and saw
that I was missing a lot of work, my nerves were bad, parties bored me, all my
friends were drugs. I quit selling and then I quit using. You know the story.

Prudence still lives in Springfield, in the same house north of the railroad
yards. Casey is gone but the carport sale continues. Her boy is ten, and maybe
there are some fine white scars at the corners of his mouth. Maybe they're just
my imagination.

When I quit drugs I thought the fighting in my marriage would stop. It
didn't. It wasn't the drugs my wife had always hated, it was the fellowship the
Church of Drugs provided. She still wants me home. I'm still not there.

One night last year when I didn't want to go home, I took a manic-
depressive writer on a 'shroom run to a stucco structure known as the House
With No Brains. Everyone there was younger than me. Some folks had heroin

and tried to missionary us into doing up. I just said no, but for weeks after that—
listen, this is important—for a long time after that, I thought about junk, talked
about it to people, started once to drive to the House but turned back. Every
time I picked up a spoon or struck a match, I thought about needle drugs, about
how clean and fine things could be.

● PERSONAL RESPONSE ●

How did you react to Regier's description of the drug scene he was once part of? What
impact did the scene with the baby and the broken glass have on you?

● QUESTIONS FOR DISCUSSION ●

1. How much do you think Regier assumes about his audience's knowledge of drugs?
2. What distinction does Regier draw between the media image of users and "real
   users"? How successfully do you think the examples of drug users he gives support his
   assertion about "real users"?
3. Explain what Regier means by the "Church of Drugs." How does his narrative account
   of New Year's Eve 1979 illustrate what he means?
4. Characterize Regier's relationship with his wife. What is the implication of the
   contrast between Regier's relationship with his fellow drug-users and his relationship
   with his wife?
5. What do the details about Casey and Prudence add to Regier's picture of the effect of
   drugs on interpersonal relationships in general?
6. How does the scene with the baby and the broken glass add to Regier's picture of the
   effect of drugs on behavior?
7. Why do you think Regier writes "Listen, this is important" (paragraph 63)? In what
   sense do you think he means that needle drugs could make things "clean and fine"
   (paragraph 63)?

● WRITING TOPICS ●

1. Write a narrative account of your own experience, or that of someone you know well,
   with drug use or abuse.
2. Explain the effects of drug use on your own family, group of friends, high school, or
   college.
3. Support or oppose the legalization of drugs. Consider possible benefits and drawbacks
   to their legalization.

AIDS AND THE SOCIAL CONTRACT

●

RICHARD GOLDSTEIN

Richard Goldstein is currently a senior editor and writer for The
Village Voice. *He is the author of* One in Seven: Drugs on Campus
(1966) and The Poetry of Rock *(1969). In the following article, which
appeared in December 1987 in* The Village Voice, *Goldstein writes
forcefully of the effects on AIDS victims of the stigma that surrounds
them and calls for the negotiation of a new social contract characterized
by "an expanded sense of equity — and empathy."*

T he first gay man I knew who died of AIDS did what no human being
with a mortal sphincter should have done — or so I told myself. The
second was an A-list achiever; he moved in "those circles" — no one
who would ever pick me up. So it went. Every time I heard about another death,
I would strain to find some basis for a distinction between the deceased and me:
He was a clone, a Crisco queen, a midnight sling artist. Then Nathan died of
AIDS, and Peter, and Ralph, to whom this piece is dedicated. When it moved in
on my friends, the epidemic shattered my presumption of immunity. I, too, was
vulnerable, and everything I thought and did about AIDS changed once I faced
that fact.

Something like this process is going on in what the media call the "general
public." There is a secret logic we apply to people with AIDS: they are sick
because they are the Other, and they are the Other because they belong to
groups that have always been stigmatized. Every now and then, we read about a
woman or child with AIDS, but usually, they are black — another invitation to
Otherness for the general public. The disease has brought all sorts of stigma to
the surface, and made the fears that any deviance conjures up seem hyper-real.
If anything, AIDS has made society less willing to confront those fears, because
they suddenly seem so useful as a way to distinguish between people — and
acts — that are "risky" or "safe." Rejecting partners who look like they run with
junkies or queers is a lot less threatening than mastering the art of condoms. We
would rather rely on stigma to protect us than on precautions that would force us
to acknowledge that AIDS is not only among us, but of us.

The hot topic in AIDS discussions right now is how efficiently HIV virus can
be transmitted during heterosexual intercourse. The medical answer is by no
means clear: About a third of the sex partners of infected IV drug users have
themselves become infected, but nearly all are women. To date, only six men in
New York City have acquired the virus during heterosexual intercourse.
Whether this ratio will change over time is anybody's guess. The point is that our
sense of who is vulnerable to AIDS is based not on conclusive information about
the disease, but on assumptions about its victims. Those who believe AIDS
could permeate society tend to see carriers as ordinary people who were

infected by specific practices. Any act that spreads the virus is potentially dangerous, regardless of its moral meaning. Those who are convinced the risk is low or nonexistent tend to see these acts, and the people who perform them, as isolated and perverse. Normal people don't do those things, and therefore, they will be spared. On the fringes of this scenario, AIDS is regarded as a natural process of eliminating the abominable.

Most of us are rationalists in the streets and moralists in the sheets. We look 4 back on the past, when people flocked to their churches in times of plague, with pity and contempt for those who thought piety would spare them. Yet we act as if only corrupt acts performed by corrupt people can transmit AIDS. What's more, we proceed as if the corrupt and the virtuous never meet in bed. In this incantation of immunity, I hear echoes of my own denial. Every gay man alive is Ishmael, with a tale to tell about the infinite capacity of human beings to deny what they cannot feel or see. But the stigma that surrounds homosexuality makes it hard for heterosexuals to act as if my witness applies to them. Few of my straight friends are compelled to ponder the question that has haunted me ever since I saw it plastered on a wall in Greenwich Village: "Why him and not me?"

That question must always be asked in regard to the sick, and it is never easy to answer. As Susan Sontag has observed, illness is made infinitely harder to bear by its affinity for metaphor. We pity the afflicted and simultaneously shun them, regardless of the actual danger they pose. In times of plague, the entire range of stigma is called into play in the service of public safety, and one is reminded that the word itself first entered our vocabulary as a description of the marks and signs of illness. For medieval Christians, lepers and victims of bubonic plague were literally *stigmatized*. This diagnosis persists in the contemporary notion that many illnesses — from cancer to ulcers — are expressions of a character flaw.

If the sick are often stigmatized, they are also, in many cases, dispensable. In the best of times, the temptation to ignore the vital interests of some patients is why we have an elaborate code of medical consent. But when plague strikes, we discover that there are no rights so inalienable that they cannot be subordinated to the greater good. Isolating the infected, which began with leprosy in the Middle Ages, soon became a standard public health measure, and once the concept of latent infection gained acceptance, the quarantine expanded to include anyone who might have been exposed. The pages of Defoe[1] are filled with the howls of those locked up in their homes — healthy people trapped with dying relatives or spouses. Finally, the entire city is stigmatized. Murder is not uncommon, as refugees wander the countryside in search of food and shelter. In the plague zone, all the amenities of death — the rituals of nursing, praying, and memorializing — are sacrificed to the imperatives of corpse disposal. Merrymaking is banned, and the stench of gunpowder and vinegar hangs in the air.

So far, our response to AIDS has been governed by the distinctly modern assumption that epidemics can be contained. The periodic demands to crack

---

[1] [Editor's note: Daniel Defoe, whose *Journal of the Plague Year* is a fictional account of the plague that swept Europe in the seventeenth century.]

down on commercial sex notwithstanding, very little has changed about the quality of public life in New York. The suffering of the afflicted, the fear and loathing of the well, are artfully privatized. Visitors would hardly know that this city is in the grip of a health emergency. Partly, this response reflects the fact that AIDS is a plague in slow motion, and we are witnessing a protracted period of latency with no real idea of how far the infection will extend. But our oblivious- ness also derives from the conviction that AIDS is a disease of deviants. This image persists because, in America, the virus did initially appear to single out groups — and acts — regarded as contaminating. Many illnesses transform their victims into a stigmatized class, but AIDS is the first epidemic to take stig- matized classes and make them victims. Not even syphilis was so precise.

Worse still, AIDS is demonstrably infectious. So carriers are marked both 8 by their Otherness and by the common humanity they are denied. They can infect anyone, though they themselves are infected because they are *not* just anyone. This paradox amplifies the fear and denial that always surround disease. AIDS is not just contagious; it is polluting. To catch this disease is to have your identity stolen; to be lowered, body and soul, into the pit of deviance. This is true even for an "innocent victim," since, once stigma attaches to an illness, it ceases to be about behavior. Anyone with AIDS becomes the Other. And since anyone can be otherized by this disease, deviance itself must be contagious. The most cherished components of personal identity can, irrationally and abruptly, be revoked. This may explain why, though a majority of Americans say they oppose discrimination against people with AIDS, 26 percent of those polled by Gallup last month still fear drinking from a glass or eating food prepared by an infected person. What people fear from casual contact is not so much the disease as its very real power to pollute.

Stigma is the reason an AIDS patient in North Carolina, being transferred from one hospital to another, arrived wrapped in a body bag with a small air tube protruding so he could breathe. Stigma is the reason a plane carrying demon- strators to the gay rights march on Washington was fumigated when the pas- sengers departed. Stigma is the reason a social worker in the Bronx must regularly visit a healthy child whose parents have succumbed to AIDS, because no neighbor will comb her hair. All these incidents occurred within the last year — while, the polls tell us, people are becoming more "enlightened" about AIDS. What people are becoming enlightened about is transmission modes, but the impact of stigma remains poorly understood.

It is rarely mentioned in discussions of AIDS prevention, though the fear of being stigmatized is often the reason infected people have sex without revealing the danger to their partners. It is seldom raised in discussions of testing, though stigma plays a part in determining who will be screened — and why people resist screening in the first place. Stigma has always been a factor in mass detentions; the incarceration of Japanese-Americans during World War II had everything to do with their Otherness. Yet, opponents of proposals to isolate AIDS carriers often argue their case on the less contentious grounds of cost efficiency. To acknowledge that so much of what we fear stems from a conviction that AIDS is a disease of people with "spoiled identities" (Erving Goffman's phrase), would threaten the validity of these categories. So liberals try to separate AIDS the infection from AIDS the stigma, as if, by skirting the issue, they can transcend it. But in fact an unexamined stigma is free to expand.

Because it is not an objective condition, but a relationship between the normal and the deviant, stigma ripples out from the reviled to include their families, their friends, their neighborhoods, even the cities where they congregate. Whole zip codes have been marked by some insurance companies as AIDS zones, and when rumors about a famous fashion designer circulated, the concern was whether people would still be seen in clothing that bears his name. The stigma of AIDS has the capacity to reinvigorate ancient stereotypes, not just about sexuality but about race and urbanity. And no city in America is more vulnerable to this conjunction of biases than New York. Half its AIDS cases are among IV drug users, most of them heterosexual and nonwhite. Unless a treatment is found, the death toll in East Harlem and Bed-Stuy will eventually approach what it is today in Kinshasa. As the boundaries of infection extend, more and more of us will live in fear of being stigmatized. And in the end, it won't matter who is actually vulnerable. The entire city will bear the brand of AIDS.

And its cost. By 1991, the state health department estimates, one in 10 hospital beds in the city will be occupied by AIDS patients. Some administrators think that figure will be more like one in four — a prospect that terrifies them, since the city's hospitals are already operating at 90 percent of capacity. Moreover, because so many AIDS patients in New York are IV users, they stay in the hospital longer than people with AIDS in other cities, and their infections are more expensive to treat. These patients are already putting an enormous strain on scarce medical resources. As the gap between supply and demand becomes acute, some form of triage could well emerge, along with violations of privacy, autonomy, and informed consent — concepts of medical ethics that were codified at the Nuremberg trials. The mounting despair of physicians in the face of demands that cannot be met from patients who cannot be saved is bound to affect the practice of medicine for all New Yorkers. The burnout is already leading to an exodus of medical residents and interns — as has often happened in cities besieged by plague.

But New York is only the focal point of an epidemic that will soon make its presence felt in every American city. A recent study sponsored by the Centers for Disease Control predicts that, by 1991, the bill for AIDS will be $8.5 billion in medical costs alone — more money than is spent on any group of patients except for victims of automobile accidents. By 1991, the "indirect costs," in productivity, of a disease that kills people in their prime will be more than $55 billion — 12 percent of the indirect cost of all illnesses. AIDS will be among the top 10 killers of Americans, and the leading killer of people between the ages of twenty-five and forty-four. "People don't seem to realize that, beyond compassion, there's a real self-interest in controlling AIDS, because we don't have the resources to handle this and all the other diseases," says medical ethicist Carol Levine, executive director of the Citizen's Commission on AIDS. "Everyone who gets sick will pay the price for thinking people can be separated."

Most of us still think AIDS is happening to someone else. It's not. AIDS is happening to some of us, and in some places, many of us. In the Bronx today, 6 percent of all women over 25 using a prenatal clinic, and 14 percent of all patients who had blood drawn in an emergency room, test positive for antibodies. Are they junkies? Are they faggots? Are they niggers? Are they us?

Where epidemics are concerned, the race, class, and sexuality of carriers has always played a major part in how they are cared for, and how dangerous they seem. Isolation, incarceration, the destruction of whole neighborhoods — all were public health measures practiced in this country, almost exclusively against poor, nonwhite, or sexually disreputable people. AIDS hysteria is a throwback to a politics of public health we thought we'd put behind us — the "purity crusade" that flourished in the early part of this century, constructing the reality of prohibition and the ideal of abstinence. It turns out that the hygiene police have been lying in wait for a crisis like this.

One has only to ponder the thundering silence in the Senate whenever   16
Jesse Helms rises to rail about "safe sodomy" to understand that this most social disease has occasioned a most political response. Every plan for prevention, every push for treatment and research funds, is guided by ideological assumptions, not just about the disease but about those who are vulnerable to it. The image of a person with AIDS determines who we think is guilty or innocent, where we fix blame for the epidemic, and whether we support a policy of education and volition or one of regulation and repression. As with all issues that arise from sexual politics, AIDS exhorts the right to fire and the left to platitudes. But beyond these reflexes, it taps our capacity for empathy, and so, AIDS transcends conventional divisions of left and right. *In These Times*, a socialist weekly with a profamily agenda, calls the president's program of routine testing, "by no means unreasonable." Nat Hentoff, an avowed advocate of minority rights, sees AIDS almost entirely as a threat to the majority. Some black activists regard the distribution of condoms as a "genocidal" act. In each case, one could argue that sexual conservatism is the driving force behind a paranoid agenda on AIDS. But C. Everett Koop, a reactionary on abortion, is a progressive on AIDS. Cardinal Kroll of Philadelphia may echo Vatican orthodoxy when he calls this epidemic "an act of vengeance against the sin of homosexuality," but the same tradition can encompass Sister Patrice, director of patient support services at Saint Vincent's, for whom AIDS is "an especially important time to live out reverence of the human being."

Where we place ourselves in relation to the stigma surrounding this disease determines what we think is necessary to protect ourselves; whether we think laws are needed to identify, and if necessary, isolate AIDS carriers; whether "innocent" people ought to take risks on their behalf. It isn't the extent of risk but its source that made a judge in California recently rule that a teacher of deaf children could be removed from the classroom because he carries HIV antibodies. It's the image of the carrier that makes physicians and cops insist on taking extraordinary precautions. In both these cases, people who might ordinarily place themselves in considerable peril shrink from the relatively minor danger posed by those who carry the HIV virus. In some cities, police who risk their lives in pursuit of criminals wear rubber gloves during a gay rights demonstration. At some hospitals, surgeons who run a high risk of contracting hepatitis (a blood-borne virus that infects twenty-five thousand health work-ers—and kills three hundred—every year) refuse to operate on people with HIV. There's not a single reported case of AIDS being transmitted in the op-erating room; only doctors and nurses who care for AIDS patients day after day, and lab technicians who are constantly exposed to live virus, have been infected in the line of duty. Nevertheless, Dr. Ronald M. Abel, who has emerged as a spokesman for surgeons refusing to operate on AIDS carriers, calls such "per-sonal, voluntary" decisions into question because they commit not only the physician but "dozens of operating-room assistants . . . to a high degree of risk." Though no policeman has ever been infected by a suspect, Phil Caruso, presi-dent of the Patrolmen's Benevolent Association, urges his members to "do whatever is necessary to protect your life and health in any police situation, be it a shootout or the handling of an AIDS sufferer, each of which is a potentially lethal proposition."

Carol Levine calls this refusal to deal with the relatively manageable hazards of AIDS "a disjunction of risk." She maintains that "what people are afraid of is not dying, but what happens before." A cop who is killed rescuing a baby from the ruins of a collapsed building becomes a hero. A doctor who risks his life to treat a victim of radiation poisoning, as happened recently in Brazil, makes the news-weeklies. But the HIV virus invests all its hosts with stigma. Doctors carrying AIDS have lost their practices; a policeman with AIDS could well imagine his peers abandoning him—and his family. Parents told that a classmate with AIDS poses no threat to their children might reason that, even if the children's safety is not at stake, their normalcy is. They may become bearers of a secondary stigma, shunned by other children even more insulated. And for what? "When you voluntarily assume a risk, it fits your self-image," says Levine. "But this is a risk you didn't bargain for—and it's being brought to you by people you're not crazy about—so it's perceived as unacceptable."

Though AIDS has been dehomosexualized in the popular imagination, its origins as a "gay plague" continue to haunt the afflicted—and prevent us from acknowledging that, on a global scale, most people with AIDS are heterosexuals and their children. "What's the hardest thing about getting AIDS?" goes the joke among gay men. "Convincing your mother that you're Haitian." This is a nasty gag about the hierarchy of stigma, but few Haitians would be amused. Each stigma feels like the ultimate injustice, and each oppression seems unique. But the odium attached to race and sexuality actually reflects a single process, whose function is to organize and validate the norm. Anyone can fall prey to such a beast—the "innocent victim" along with the defiled. The irony about health workers demanding that their patients be tested for AIDS antibodies is that it will surely lead to a demand that doctors and nurses take the test—with penalties inevitable for those infected.

I was surprised by the anxiety testing provokes in heterosexuals, until I 20 realized that nearly everyone I know has had a relationship with someone who might be infected. In any urban population, most people who take the test pass through a psychic rite that has less to do with fear of death than with the consequences of a positive result: guilt over the past, rage at the present, fear of the future. That fear must include not only the disease but disclosure — and the full range of rejection that might ensue. Yet it is seldom remarked that, for anyone in a vulnerable group, taking the test is an act of enormous courage. The only controversy is over whether such people should be forced to know their antibody status — and in this debate, the anguish of an AIDS "suspect" is easily subordinated to that great equalizer, the common good. Stigma determines whose interests are expendable. "You always assume the test will happen to someone else," says Levine. "Left to their own devices, most people don't want to know."

That may be wise. As *The New York Times* recently acknowledged, the potential for inaccuracy in the general population is high enough to make mass-testing a "treacherous paradox." Yet certain populations are expected to bear the uncertainty: soldiers, aliens applying for amnesty, Job Corps enrollees, and in some hospitals where state law permits, candidates for surgery. Just last month, at Jesse Helms's behest, the Senate voted to require all veterans' hospitals to "mandatorily offer" antibody testing — an interesting euphemism, since patients who refuse the offer would risk being treated like a person with AIDS. (Turning down the test is, in itself, a stigmatizing experience, because it implies that you have reason to suspect . . . you may have had sex with . . . or might even be . . . !) What these groups have in common is not the danger they might pose to others, but the fact that they depend on public institutions. In America, everyone who relies on the government must expect to forfeit some basic rights. As the debate over testing heats up — and it will, once AIDS enters the arena of presidential politics — we may see this psychodrama acted out on other populations stigmatized by their dependence, such as welfare recipients. An old adage must be dusted off in the current crisis: "If you prick us, do we not bleed?"

This is the classic response to bigotry. Yet it takes a leap of consciousness to see the connection between one stigma and another. Gay men and IV drug users face each other across a vast behavioral divide. But both cultures are based on behavior — indeed, an act of penetration — deemed illicit. Both deviate from the norms of ecstasy, and invest their deviance with enormous significance, using it to foster intimate bonds and a "lifestyle" with its own slang and gait. Both exist as distinct groups within every class, though the drug culture flourishes in the ghetto, as a gory symbol of its vulnerability, and gay culture is most militant in bourgeois society. Of course, shooting heroin has profound implications for one's health and security, while homosexuality, per se, does not. And the drug culture is a violent, haunted environment. But it *is* a culture, and though we need to keep its damage in mind, we also must wonder how much the antisocial behavior associated with IV use stems from stigma and from the stranglehold of dealers. Freed from both these sources of oppression, the IV user might emerge as a citizen, and we might have to think about what the word "junkie" really conveys.

"It seems that some real change in the cultural norms is going to be necessary," says Don Des Jarlais, a behavioral researcher at the State Division of

Substance Abuse Services. "Society will have to make a decision that the chance of spreading this virus is so great, and drug users play so crucial a part in that spread, that we cannot simply allow them to die of AIDS, or make a rule that they must stop using drugs in order *not* to die of AIDS."

Rescuing the IV user may involve some of the same techniques that have worked in the gay community. The sharing of needles must be understood in the same context as anal sex — as an ecstatic act that enhances social solidarity. "Within the subculture, the running partner becomes the substitute for family," Des Jarlais writes. "It would be considered a major insult to refuse to use one's partner's works ... [or] share one's own works. ... It would undermine the teamwork and synchronicity of intense experience that are the bases of the running-buddy relationship." One answer is to provide the IV equivalent of a condom: bleach kits or clean needles. Contrary to the assumption that drug users are oblivious to AIDS, Des Jarlais reports that the epidemic is "a topic of 'grave' concern among IV drug users" in several cities, and that they "want to learn how to protect themselves against exposure." Safe injection is as central to the humanistic AIDS agenda as safe sex.

Des Jarlais has observed much more ambivalence among drug users than among gay men about discussing AIDS prevention with their sexual partners. It may not be narcissism but fear of abandonment that stands in the way of candor. "Most IV users have their primary relationship with a non-drug-using partner," says Des Jarlais. The dependence for food, shelter, and money — not to mention emotional security — can be intense. "When you have a pair like that, there's no symmetricality of risk. To bring up the subject of AIDS points to the disparity in the relationship. Half the time, the partner using condoms gets abandoned by his female lover. So it's easier to practice safe sex with a casual partner than in a long-term relationship." Surveys have found the same phenomenon among gay men, but the likelihood that either partner could be carrying the virus makes mutual safety part of their bond.

Most gay men have other advantages — not just race and class, but organization. One has only to imagine what the response to AIDS would be like if the gay rights movement did not exist. There is no annual parade of drug users down Fifth Avenue, no press that circulates among them, and their advocacy organizations, such as ADAPT, are severely underfunded. This squad of former and current addicts tours the shooting galleries, dispensing condoms and clean needles. But they are hardly as effective as the *junkiebonden* (drug users' unions) of Holland, because in that country, the need to fight stigma with community is imbedded in both the legal and social service traditions. Organizing IV users may enable their culture to preserve its members by altering the rituals of risk, much as gay men have altered theirs. It may empower users to strike back at oppressive dealers and lobby for access to meaningful treatment. But funding this liberation means overcoming what Des Jarlais calls "an empathy barrier."

So far, the support system for people with AIDS has done more to break down this barrier than any church or public agency. About a quarter of the clients at Gay Men's Health Crisis are non-gay, and many groups for "body positives" (as carriers now call themselves) are integrated. But most gay men and IV users still cannot imagine that each other's identities might spring from a shared perspective. As Erving Goffman writes: "Persons with different stigmas are in an appreciably similar situation, and respond in an appreciably similar way." AIDS forces us to confront this commonality. The "innocent" black woman infected by her lover, the gay man whose class has always insulated him, the addict abandoned in a hospital ward—all were victims of stigma before they became victims of disease. And though they may live (and die) in utter contempt for each other's deviations from the norm, they are implicated in each other's fate. What happens to the prostitute can happen to the amateur; what they do to the junkie they can do to the fag.

In a hospital, everyone looks like the Other. An AIDS ward is no different, 28 except that, in a public hospital, it might be filled with black people. I walked through one such ward on assignment, trying not to look too hard at the flesh bundles in the beds. Finally, I took a long peek at a black woman in her late thirties, propped up on pillows, surrounded by tissues and magazines. She had the gaunt intensity that people in the late stages of AIDS often get, as if her entire being were confined to the eyes. I stopped seeing her race and sex, both of which are, in some sense, alien to me. Instead, I saw my lover. She resembled him, not as he was but as he might be if he ever got AIDS. I walked on quickly, struggling to fight the welling up of tears.

That night, I dreamt I was leaving my apartment for work. There was a corpse outside the door.

"Love," writes Martin Buber, "is responsibility of an I for a thou." In social terms, this suggests that the bond between citizens is essential to human development as the bond between lovers, or between parent and child. The social contract is a codification of that bond—an agreement to form a government that sustains us. There is a corollary obligation to protect each other, discharged through duties and limits on behavior which we accept as a fair price for the welfare of the community. Without this compact no individual can survive.

When a health crisis strikes, Buber's equation becomes demonstrable: the mutual obligation of the infected and the uninfected *is* the responsibility of an I for a thou. As we confront the limits of freedom, the ego becomes collectivized, and the community, an abstraction in ordinary times, becomes the tangible sum of its parts. An ethic of inclusiveness makes personal sacrifice not only bearable, but unremarkable. One simply does what is necessary, because, as Camus writes, "the only means of fighting a plague is common decency."

The gay community has gone through just such a process in the face of 32 AIDS. It has reshaped itself to care for its own, and changed behavior once regarded as the mark of liberation. But the boundaries of the gay social contract are tightly drawn, for obvious reasons. The common good has always been enforced at their expense. For homosexuals, "public health" has been a euphemism for stigma. They are among the usual suspects rounded up in panics over sexually transmitted disease. AIDS threatens to revive this tradition of hygiene pogroms on a much more devastating scale. William Buckley's suggestion that people with AIDS be tattooed on the forearm and buttocks to warn the uninfected shows how easily the technocratic imagination can conjure up what Goffman calls a "stigma symbol." Every now and then, someone hatches a gothic variation on Buckley's scheme; the urge to literally stigmatize the infected will not die. A newly published tome called *AIDS in America: Our Chances, Our Choices* recommends "discreet genital tattooing" — just outside the urethra for men, just inside the labia minora for women. Such proposals are always couched in the rhetoric of reason and equity, as if they would apply to anyone who happened to be infected. But in reality, they can only be enacted on people whose freedom is already precarious. IV users and prostitutes are eminently detainable, and the parole granted homosexuals can easily be revoked.

It's a mark of my generation to regard the social contract as fraught with bad faith. But AIDS can't be stopped without a compact among citizens, enforced by the government. It demands that we renegotiate the terms, infusing the contract with an expanded sense of equity — and empathy. "Our best weapon against AIDS," writes Dan Beauchamp, whose book, *The Health of the Republic,* will be published next year [1988 Temple University Press],

> would be a public health policy resting on the right to be different in funda-
> mental choices and the democratic community as 'one body' in matters of the
> common health. This new policy would mean the right of every individual to
> fundamental autonomy, as in abortion and sexual orientation, while viewing
> health and safety as a common good whose protection (through restrictions on
> liberty) promotes community and the common health.

Under a new social contract, we could talk about the limits on personal freedom in a time of plague; the need for vulnerable people to know their antibody status or act as if they are seropositive; the duty to protect your partners and inform others at risk. But saving lives also means setting limits on moralism: confronting the full range of human sexuality, including its expression in the erotics of shooting up; promoting the use of any implement — condoms, nee-dles — that slows the spread of AIDS (if anything, we will have to demand *better* implements); breaking down barriers of sexism that dispose women to infection and men to secrecy.

AIDS renders both the liberationist mentality and the moralistic world view obsolete. But so far, only the sexual revolution has been criticized — and in highly moralistic terms. The public health profession has beaten back the most savage proposals for dealing with AIDS, but it is neither powerful enough, nor militant enough, to stand up to political and social conservatism. Ethicists fill monographs with their vision of the social contract, while the usual bad bargain is forged by church and state. And the epidemic goes on, as sexually transmitted diseases always have — stoked by shame and secrecy.

That's the usual progressive objection to stigma. But in the age of AIDS, 36 social justice can't be promoted in purely pragmatic terms. It's too easy to imagine the majority protected by the erotic segregation that pervades American society. The danger is not that AIDS will wipe our species off the planet, but that it will wipe out people most of us already hate — and that is a moral as well as medical crisis. "My worst fear," says Beauchamp, "is not the concentration camps but a kind of paralysis, in which people will just be left to cope." As a professor of public health in Jesse Helms's home state, Beauchamp sees the epidemic not as an incarnation of the Holocaust (with which it is often wrongly compared), but as a "new civil war." The danger for him lies in "splitting off another chunk of the Republic," condemning millions of Americans to expendability. The wages of this sin is not only death, but "a kind of amnesia about who we are and who we want to be."

We are haunted by events that expose the gap between who we are and who we want to be. They may happen to other people, but they reveal us to ourselves. Hiroshima and Vietnam are watersheds in our culture because they were moral as well as military conflagrations. These two events shaped my generation. I believe AIDS will define the next.

● PERSONAL RESPONSE ●

Do you agree with Goldstein that a stigma surrounds AIDS victims? Have attitudes toward AIDS victims changed since the appearance of this article in 1987? What is your own attitude toward AIDS victims?

● QUESTIONS FOR DISCUSSION ●

1. What does Goldstein mean by the "incantation of immunity" and by his statement that "every gay man alive is Ishmael" (paragraph 4)?

2. What is the effect of the series of parallel sentences that conclude paragraph 14, beginning with "Are they junkies"? Why do you think Goldstein uses the words "faggots" and "niggers"?

3. How does Goldstein make effective use of the opinions of both those he agrees with and those he disagrees with?

4. What has been the effect on AIDS victims of the stigma against them, according to Goldstein?

5. According to Goldstein, what are the similarities and differences between homosexuals and drug addicts?

6. Explain in your own words what Goldstein means when he says that we must have a new social contract before AIDS can be stopped.

7. Do you think the comparison of the AIDS crisis with Hiroshima and Vietnam is an appropriate one? Explain your answer.

● WRITING TOPICS ●

1. Either agree or disagree with Goldstein's contention that AIDS victims are stigmatized in our society. In either case, give specific examples to support your own position.

2. Argue for or against the distribution of clean syringes to drug addicts.

3. Examine your own attitude toward AIDS and those who are its victims.

IF SHAKESPEARE HAD HAD A SISTER

●

Virginia Woolf

Virginia Woolf (1882–1941) was an essayist, journalist, and novelist. She was born in London to a wealthy and intellectual family, whose large library was the source of her education. Her highly acclaimed works include ten novels, six volumes of essays, and dozens of volumes of letters and diaries. Her novels include The Voyage Out *(1915),* Mrs. Dalloway *(1925), and* To The Lighthouse *(1927), while her collections of essays include* The Common Reader *(1925) and* A Room of One's Own *(1929). The selection below is excerpted from the third and the last of the six essays in* A Room of One's Own, *originally delivered as lectures at a women's college on the subject of women and fiction. The common theme of the series is that, because women have historically been denied both economic independence and private space and time in order to write, they have been excluded from the mainstream of intellectual and creative life.*

I t was disappointing not to have brought back in the evening some important statement, some authentic fact. Women are poorer than men because—this or that. Perhaps now it would be better to give up seeking for the truth, and receiving on one's head an avalanche of opinion hot as lava, discoloured as dish-water. It would be better to draw the curtains; to shut out distractions; to light the lamp; to narrow the enquiry and to ask the historian, who records not opinions but facts, to describe under what conditions women lived, not throughout the ages, but in England, say in the time of Elizabeth.

For it is a perennial puzzle why no woman wrote a word of that extraordinary literature when every other man, it seemed, was capable of song or sonnet. What were the conditions in which women lived, I asked myself; for fiction, imaginative work that is, is not dropped like a pebble upon the ground, as science may be; fiction is like a spider's web, attached ever so lightly perhaps, but still attached to life at all four corners. Often the attachment is scarcely perceptible; Shakespeare's plays, for instance, seem to hang there complete by themselves. But when the web is pulled askew, hooked up at the edge, torn in the middle, one remembers that these webs are not spun in midair by incorporeal creatures, but are the work of suffering human beings, and are attached to grossly material things, like health and money and the houses we live in.

I went, therefore, to the shelf where the histories stand and took down one of the latest, Professor Trevelyan's *History of England*. Once more I looked up Women, found "position of," and turned to the pages indicated. "Wife-beating," I read, "was a recognised right of man, and was practised without shame by high as well as low. . . . Similarly," the historian goes on, "the daughter who refused to marry the gentleman of her parents' choice was liable to be locked up, beaten and flung about the room, without any shock being inflicted on public opinion. Marriage was not an affair of personal affection, but of family avarice, particularly in the 'chivalrous' upper classes. . . . Betrothal often took place while one or both of the parties was in the cradle, and marriage when they were scarcely out of the nurses' charge." That was about 1470, soon after Chaucer's time. The next reference to the position of women is some two hundred years later, in the time of the Stuarts. "It was still the exception for women of the upper and middle class to choose their own husbands, and when the husband had been assigned, he was lord and master, so far at least as law and custom could make him. "Yet even so," Professor Trevelyan concludes, "neither Shakespeare's women nor those of authentic seventeenth-century memoirs, like the Verneys and the Hutchinsons, seem wanting in personality and character." Certainly, if we consider it, Cleopatra must have had a way with her; Lady Macbeth, one would suppose, had a will of her own; Rosalind, one might conclude, was an attractive girl. Professor Trevelyan is speaking no more than the truth when he remarks that Shakespeare's women do not seem wanting in personality and character. Not being a historian, one might go even further and say that women have burnt like beacons in all the works of all the poets from the beginning of time — Clytemnestra, Antigone, Cleopatra, Lady Macbeth, Phèdre, Cressida, Rosalind, Desdemona, the Duchess of Malfi, among the dramatists; then among the prose writers: Millamant, Clarissa, Becky Sharp, Anna Karenina, Emma Bovary, Madame De Guermantes — the names flock to mind, nor do they recall women "lacking in personality and character." Indeed, if woman had no existence save in the fiction written by men, one would imagine her a person of the utmost importance; very various; heroic and mean; splendid and sordid; infinitely beautiful and hideous in the extreme; as great as a man, some think even greater. But this is woman in fiction. In fact, as Professor Trevelyan points out, she was locked up, beaten and flung about the room.

A very queer, composite being thus emerges. Imaginatively she is of the highest importance; practically she is completely insignificant. She pervades poetry from cover to cover; she is all but absent from history. She dominates the lives of kings and conquerors in fiction; in fact she was the slave of any boy whose parents forced a ring upon her finger. Some of the most inspired words, some of the most profound thoughts in literature fall from her lips; in real life she could hardly read, could scarcely spell, and was the property of her husband. 4

It was certainly an odd monster that one made up by reading the historians first and the poets afterwards — a worm winged like an eagle; the spirit of life and beauty in a kitchen chopping up suet. But these monsters, however amusing to the imagination, have no existence in fact. What one must do to bring her to life was to think poetically and prosaically at one and the same moment, thus keeping in touch with fact — that she is Mrs. Martin, aged thirty-six, dressed in blue, wearing a black hat and brown shoes; but not losing sight of fiction either — that she is a vessel in which all sorts of spirits and forces are coursing and flashing perpetually. The moment, however, that one tries this method with the Elizabethan woman, one branch of illumination fails; one is held up by the scarcity of facts. One knows nothing detailed, nothing perfectly true and substantial about her. History scarcely mentions her. And I turned to Professor Trevelyan again to see what history meant to him. I found by looking at his chapter headings that it meant —

"The Manor Court and the Methods of Open-field Agriculture . . . The Cistercians and Sheep-farming . . . The Crusades . . . The University . . . The House of Commons . . . The Hundred Years' War . . . The Wars of the Roses . . . The Renaissance Scholars . . . The Dissolution of the Monasteries . . . Agrarian and Religious Strife . . . The Origin of English Sea-power . . . The Armada . . ." and so on. Occasionally an individual woman is mentioned, an Elizabeth, or a Mary; a queen or a great lady. But by no possible means could middle-class women with nothing but brains and character at their command have taken part in any one of the great movements which, brought together, constitute the historian's view of the past. Nor shall we find her in any collection of anecdotes. Aubrey hardly mentions her. She never writes her own life and scarcely keeps a diary; there are only a handful of her letters in existence. She left no plays or poems by which we can judge her. What one wants, I thought — and why does not some brilliant student at Newnham or Girton supply it? — is a mass of information; at what age did she marry; how many children had she as a rule; what was her house like; had she a room to herself; did she do the cooking; would she be likely to have a servant? All these facts lie somewhere, presumably, in parish registers and account books; the life of the average Elizabethan woman must be scattered about somewhere, could one collect it and make a book of it. It would be ambitious beyond my daring, I thought, looking about the shelves for books that were not there, to suggest to the students of those famous colleges that they should re-write history, though I own that it often seems a little queer as it is, unreal, lop-sided; but why should they not add a supplement to history? calling it, of course, by some inconspicuous name so that women might figure there without impropriety? For one often catches a glimpse of them in the lives of the great, whisking away into the background, concealing, I sometimes think, a wink, a laugh, perhaps a tear. And, after all, we have lives enough of Jane Austen; it scarcely seems necessary to consider again the influence of the tragedies of Joanna Baillie upon the poetry of Edgar Allan Poe; as for myself, I should not mind if the homes and haunts of Mary Russell Mitford were closed to the public for a century at least. But what I find deplorable, I continued, looking about the bookshelves again, is that nothing is known about women before the eighteenth century. I have no model in my mind to turn about this way and that. Here am I asking why women did not write poetry in the Elizabethan age, and I am not sure how they were educated; whether they were taught to write; whether they had sitting-rooms to themselves; how many women had children before they were twenty-one; what, in short, they did from eight in the morning till eight at night. They had no money evidently; according to Professor Trevelyan they were married whether they liked it or not before they were out of the nursery, at fifteen or sixteen very likely. It would have been extremely odd, even upon this showing, had one of them suddenly written the plays of Shakespeare, I concluded, and I thought of that old gentleman, who is dead now, but was a bishop, I think, who declared that it was impossible for any woman, past, present, or to come, to have the genius of Shakespeare. He wrote to the papers about it. He also told a lady who applied to him for information that cats do not as a matter of fact go to heaven, though they have, he added, souls of a sort. How much thinking those old gentlemen used to save one! How the borders of ignorance shrank back at their approach! Cats do not go to heaven. Women cannot write the plays of Shakespeare.

Be that as it may, I could not help thinking, as I looked at the works of Shakespeare on the shelf, that the bishop was right at least in this; it would have been impossible, completely and entirely, for any woman to have written the plays of Shakespeare in the age of Shakespeare. Let me imagine, since facts are so hard to come by, what would have happened had Shakespeare had a wonderfully gifted sister, called Judith, let us say. Shakespeare himself went, very probably — his mother was an heiress — to grammar school, where he may have learnt Latin — Ovid, Virgil and Horace — and the elements of grammar and logic. He was, it is well known, a wild boy who poached rabbits, perhaps shot a deer, and had, rather sooner than he should have done, to marry a woman in the neighbourhood who bore him a child rather quicker than was right. That escapade sent him to seek his fortune in London. He had, it seemed, a taste for the theatre; he began by holding horses at the stage door. Very soon he got work in the theatre, became a successful actor, and lived at the hub of the universe, meeting everybody, knowing everybody, practising his art on the boards, exercising his wits in the streets, and even getting access to the palace of the queen. Meanwhile his extraordinarily gifted sister, let us suppose, remained at home. She was as adventurous, as imaginative, as agog to see the world as he was. But she was not sent to school. She had no chance of learning grammar and logic, let alone of reading Horace and Virgil. She picked up a book now and then, one of her brother's perhaps, and read a few pages. But then her parents came in and told her to mend the stockings or mind the stew and not moon about with books and papers. They would have spoken sharply but kindly, for they were substantial people who knew the conditions of life for a woman and loved their daughter — indeed, more likely than not she was the apple of her father's eye. Perhaps she scribbled some pages up in an apple loft on the sly, but was careful to hide them or set fire to them. Soon, however, before she was out of her teens, she was to be betrothed to the son of a neighbouring wool-stapler. She cried out that marriage was hateful to her, and for that she was severely beaten by her father. Then he ceased to scold her. He begged her instead not to hurt him, not to shame him in this matter of her marriage. He would give her a chain of beads or a fine petticoat, he said; and there were tears in his eyes. How could she disobey him? How could she break his heart? The force of her own gift alone drove her to it. She made up a small parcel of her belongings, let herself down by a rope one summer's night and took the road to London. She was not seventeen. The birds that sang in the hedge were not more musical than she was. She had the quickest fancy, a gift like her brother's, for the tune of words. Like him, she had a taste for the theatre. She stood at the stage door; she wanted to act, she said. Men laughed in her face. The manager—a fat, loose-lipped man—guffawed. He bellowed something about poodles dancing and women acting—no woman, he said, could possibly be an actress. He hinted—you can imagine what. She could get no training in her craft. Could she even seek her dinner in a tavern or roam the streets at midnight? Yet her genius was for fiction and lusted to feed abundantly upon the lives of men and women and the study of their ways. At last—for she was very young, oddly like Shakespeare the poet in her face, with the same grey eyes and rounded brows—at last Nick Greene the actor-manager took pity on her; she found herself with child by that gentleman and so—who shall measure the heat and violence of the poet's heart when caught and tangled in a woman's body?—killed herself one winter's night and lies buried at some cross-roads where the omnibuses now stop outside the Elephant and Castle.

That, more or less, is how the story would run, I think, if a woman in 8 Shakespeare's day had had Shakespeare's genius. But for my part, I agree with the deceased bishop, if such he was—it is unthinkable that any woman in Shakespeare's day should have had Shakespeare's genius. For genius like Shakespeare's is not born among labouring, uneducated, servile people. It was not born in England among the Saxons and the Britons. It is not born today among the working classes. How, then, could it have been born among women whose work began, according to Professor Trevelyan, almost before they were out of the nursery, who were forced to it by their parents and held to it by all the power of law and custom? Yet genius of a sort must have existed among women as it must have existed among the working classes. Now and again an Emily Brontë or a Robert Burns blazes out and proves its presence. But certainly it never got itself on to paper. When, however, one reads of a witch being ducked, of a woman possessed by devils, of a wise woman selling herbs, or even of a very remarkable man who had a mother, then I think we are on the track of a lost novelist, a suppressed poet, of some mute and inglorious Jane Austen, some Emily Brontë who dashed her brains out on the moor or mopped and mowed about the highways crazed with the torture that her gift had put her to. Indeed, I would venture to guess that Anon, who wrote so many poems without signing them, was often a woman. It was a woman Edward Fitzgerald, I think, suggested who made the ballads and the folk-songs, crooning them to her children, beguiling her spinning with them, or the length of the winter's night.

This may be true or it may be false—who can say?—but what is true in it, so it seemed to me, reviewing the story of Shakespeare's sister as I had made it, is that any woman born with a great gift in the sixteenth century would certainly have gone crazed, shot herself, or ended her days in some lonely cottage outside the village, half witch, half wizard, feared and mocked at. For it needs little skill in psychology to be sure that a highly gifted girl who had tried to use her gift for poetry would have been so thwarted and hindered by other people, so tortured and pulled asunder by her own contrary instincts, that she must have lost her health and sanity to a certainty. No girl could have walked to London and stood at a stage door and forced her way into the presence of actor-managers without doing herself a violence and suffering an anguish which may have been irrational — for chastity may be a fetish invented by certain societies for unknown reasons — but were none the less inevitable. Chastity had then, it has even now, a religious importance in a woman's life, and has so wrapped itself round with nerves and instincts that to cut it free and bring it to the light of day demands courage of the rarest. To have lived a free life in London in the sixteenth century would have meant for a woman who was poet and playwright a nervous stress and dilemma which might well have killed her. Had she survived, whatever she had written would have been twisted and deformed, issuing from a strained and morbid imagination. And undoubtedly, I thought, looking at the shelf where there are no plays by women, her work would have gone unsigned. That refuge she would have sought certainly. It was the relic of the sense of chastity that dictated anonymity of women even so late as the nineteenth century. Currer Bell, George Eliot, George Sand, all the victims of inner strife as their writings prove, sought ineffectively to veil themselves by using the name of a man. Thus they did homage to the convention, which if not implanted by the other sex was liberally encouraged by them (the chief glory of a woman is not to be talked of, said Pericles, himself a much-talked-of man), that publicity in women is detestable. Anonymity runs in their blood. The desire to be veiled still possesses them. . . .

I told you in the course of this paper that Shakespeare had a sister; but do not look for her in Sir Sidney Lee's life of the poet. She died young — alas, she never wrote a word. She lies buried where the omnibuses now stop, opposite the Elephant and Castle. Now my belief is that this poet who never wrote a word and was buried at the crossroads still lives. She lives in you and in me, and in many other women who are not here tonight, for they are washing up the dishes and putting the children to bed. But she lives; for great poets do not die; they are continuing presences; they need only the opportunity to walk among us in the flesh. This opportunity, as I think, it is now coming within your power to give her. For my belief is that if we live another century or so — I am talking of the common life which is the real life and not of the little separate lives which we live as individuals — and have five hundred a year each of us and rooms of our own; if we have the habit of freedom and the courage to write exactly what we think; if we escape a little from the common sitting-room and see human beings not always in their relation to each other but in relation to reality; and the sky, too, and the trees or whatever it may be in themselves; if we look past Milton's bogey, for no human being should shut out the view; if we face the fact, for it is a fact, that there is no arm to cling to, but that we go alone and that our relation is to the world of reality and not only to the world of men and women, then the opportunity will come and the dead poet who was Shakespeare's sister will put on the body which she has so often laid down. Drawing her life from the lives of the unknown who were her forerunners, as her brother did before her, she will be born. As for her coming without that preparation, without that effort on our part, without that determination that when she is born again she shall find it possible to live and write her poetry, that we cannot expect, for that would be impossible. But I maintain that she would come if we worked for her, and that so to work, even in poverty and obscurity, is worth while.

● PERSONAL RESPONSE ●

What is your reaction to the story of Shakespeare's hypothetical sister? How convincing do you think it is? Explain your answer.

● QUESTIONS FOR DISCUSSION ●

1. How do you think Woolf's audience of college women in 1929 would have reacted to the story of Shakespeare's sister and to Woolf's challenge to them in the concluding paragraph? Would this essay still be appropriate to deliver as a lecture to an audience of college women today? Why or why not?

2. What is the tone of this essay? Does it seem bitter? Sad? Angry? Optimistic? Formulate your own assessment of the tone and find specific passages that support your answer.

3. Woolf frequently uses figurative language, especially metaphors and similes, to give life and color to her writing. In what ways is fiction "like a spider's web," (paragraph 2), for instance? Find other examples of such language.

4. What contrasts does Woolf find between the lives of fictional women and the lives of real women?

5. What is the point of Woolf's reference to a Mrs. Martin in paragraph 5?

6. How does Woolf use the references to Professor Trevelyan's *History of England* to justify her creation of a hypothetical sister for Shakespeare?

7. What are the "contrary instincts" that Woolf believes that women born with a gift in the sixteenth century would have been "tortured and pulled asunder by" (paragraph 9)?

8. Currer Bell, George Eliot, and George Sand (paragraph 9) were pseudonyms of Charlotte Brontë (1816–1855), Mary Ann Evans (1819–1880), and Amandine Aurore Lucie Dupin (1803–1876). How are those nineteenth-century women writers relevant to the point Woolf makes about talented sixteenth-century women?

● WRITING TOPICS ●

1. Explain whether or not you think Woolf's vision of the rebirth of Shakespeare's sister has been realized. That is, have the obstacles that historically lay in the paths of bright women been removed? If you think Woolf's vision has been realized, what has made it possible? If not, what obstacles still remain?

2. Woolf mentions Jane Austen and Emily Brontë as women writers who achieved recognition in a male-dominated field. Write an essay on a woman you know person-

ally or have read about who pioneered or became successful in a previously male-dominated field. Well-known examples include Amelia Earhart, Sally Ride, Sandra Day O'Connor, Geraldine Ferraro, and Barbara Walters, but there are scores more to choose from.

3. Select a profession or professions that have been largely female dominated and explain why men have been excluded and what has been done — or should be done — to break down the barriers.

LIVING ON THE OUTSIDE

●

ADDITIONAL WRITING SUGGESTIONS

1. Narrate your experience with a physical feature that was (or is) a source of embarrassment or anger to you.

2. Read about mental retardation in current periodicals and analyze contemporary attitudes toward mentally retarded people.

3. Explore the effects of widespread drug use on American society.

4. Argue for or against mandatory AIDS testing, taking into consideration such matters as individual rights, obligations to society, the conditions (if any) under which you think such testing should be mandatory and those under which it should be optional.

5. In paragraph 7 of his essay "AIDS and the Social Contract," Richard Goldstein observes that "many illnesses transform their victims into a stigmatized class." Select a group besides AIDS victims who are stigmatized by their illness and explain ways in which they are stigmatized.

6. In paragraph 6 of her essay "If Shakespeare Had Had a Sister," Virginia Woolf writes: "What one wants, I thought, . . . is a mass of information . . . [on] the life of the average Elizabethan woman." Do some library research on the subject of women's history to determine what has been done to find that "mass of information" and relate the results of your search. Would Woolf be pleased or disappointed by your findings?

7

CONFRONTING
PREJUDICE

PREJUDICE, CONFLICT, AND ETHNOVIOLENCE
A NATIONAL DILEMMA

●

JOAN C. WEISS

Joan C. Weiss is executive director of the National Institute Against Prejudice and Violence in Baltimore, Maryland. In its efforts to achieve its purpose of reducing prejudice and violence in our nation, the Institute monitors incidents of racial and ethnic violence and seeks ways to prevent such conflicts in the future. In the following 1989 article, reprinted from USA Today *Magazine, Weiss argues that, despite the civil-rights legislation of the 1960s, ours is still a highly segregated society.*

T he United States Constitution provides us with the tools we need to deal with racism," Pres. Reagan claimed in the spring of 1988 in a speech in which he compared human rights in the U.S. with those in the Soviet Union. While the Constitution is far-reaching and timeless beyond even the vision of its framers, providing us with a legal framework which enables us to attack many racist practices, laws do not solve problems. One of the great myths in this country is that civil rights were guaranteed with the passage of a few laws in the 1960's. Therefore, the logic proceeds, if people still are suffering the effects of racism, it is either because the laws are not being enforced adequately or because not enough time has passed. In other words, 25 years is a relatively short time and, in fact, strides have been made — we just need to be patient.

It is true that there is not adequate enforcement of civil and human rights statutes, and strides have been made. No one would argue with the fact that blacks and other minorities have entered mainstream America in a visible way. The number of black elected officials in this country is testimony to that, as are the number of minority-owned businesses, Jesse Jackson's candidacy, and a host of other measures one could choose.

However, it is easy to let these facts obscure reality. I recently participated in a conference in Jackson, Miss., sponsored by the U.S. Department of Housing and Urban Development in honor of the 20th anniversary of the passage of the Fair Housing Laws. After 20 years, according to the findings of a variety of recent studies, we continue to live in a highly segregated society.

Both institutionalized discrimination and individual prejudices are still at 4 work. Government policies virtually have eliminated low-income housing and, since minorities are disproportionately poor, the impact on them is devastating. Furthermore, minorities still are turned away from the rental of apartments and the purchase of homes. The methods of discrimination are just more subtle, more sophisticated than they used to be, so much so that black testers are sometimes unaware that prejudice has been at work until they see the test results.

The percentage of black high school graduates who go to college has declined since 1976, as has the proportion of blacks in graduate schools, which reached a new low in 1986. Housing and education are but two areas in which discrimination and prejudice are still problems.

Economic disparities between minorities and non-minorities persist, maintained by institutionalized discrimination. For example, 1986 figures indicate that poverty rates among blacks and Hispanics are nearly three times that for whites, according to a report by the Commission on Minority Participation in Education and American Life, which was formed by the American Council on Education and the Education Commission of the States. It adds that, "In education, employment, income, health, longevity and other basic measures of individual and social well-being, gaps persist—and in some cases are widening—between members of minority groups and the majority population."

Other factors compound the existing prejudice and discrimination, creating an environment ripe for intergroup tension. There has been a lack of planning with regard to the influx of immigrants, contributing to misunderstandings and conflict stemming from cultural differences among groups. We have seen a backlash to major social changes such as the women's and gay rights movement, as well as to the institution of affirmative action programs. The elimination of Federally funded social programs has sent an anti-authority message to the community. We also are affected by political and social events around the world. In this time of media satellites and instant news, we should understand fully what happens in South Africa, the Middle East, or Central America has a profound impact on intergroup relations in this country.

Bigotry Begets Violence

These factors have created fertile ground for violence motivated by bigotry. [8] There are extraordinary numbers of violent incidents based on someone's race, religion, ethnic background, and sexual orientation occurring around the country: harassment of victims day in and day out as they leave their homes; attacks on children as they go to school; bricks and gunshots through windows of homes, businesses, churches, and synagogues; crosses burned; death threats; racist graffiti; swastika paintings; arson; physical assaults; and murder. These acts of bigotry are happening in communities, schools, and workplaces all across the nation. No area is immune.

Nobody knows exactly how many crimes motivated by bigotry are committed because there is no accurate system of national data collection. We know from research at the National Institute Against Prejudice and Violence, however, that the problem is persistent, pervasive, and serious. Thousands of ethnoviolent incidents occur each year. In addition to the Institute's files, a number of other sources confirm the seriousness of this matter.

In Maryland, one of only eight states in the country with data collection legislation, between 350 and 500 incidents based on race, religion, and ethnicity were reported to the State Human Relations Commission each year from 1981 through 1986. The other states with data collection legislation—Connecticut, Illinois, Maine, Minnesota, Oklahoma, Pennsylvania, and Virginia—have not had their laws in effect long enough to have multi-year data available. However, the police in New York and Boston both have collected data for approximately eight years. The New York City police documented between 172 and 286 incidents each year from 1981 until 1986. Then, in 1987, in the wake of the Howard Beach racial attack, they documented 463 incidents. In Boston, the police department recorded over 2,700 incidents from 1978 through 1987.

Other sources include the Center for Democratic Renewal, which documented almost 3,000 incidents in the country from 1980 to 1987; the Anti-Defamation League of B'nai B'rith, which recorded 1,018 anti-Semitic incidents in 1987; and the National Gay and Lesbian Task Force, which documented over 7,000 instances of anti-gay violence in 1986. On the local level, human relations commissions in Montgomery County, Md., and Los Angeles County, Calif., as well as citizens' groups such as the North Carolinians Against Racist and Religious Violence, consistently have recorded dozens, sometimes hundreds, of incidents in their communities in the last few years. As high as the figures are, we know that they represent only a portion of the crimes that occur. Institute research findings show that one-third of victims never report their incidents to any official agency.

Campus violence has received considerable attention during the last two [12] years. In our study of violence on the University of Maryland's Baltimore County campus, we learned that one out of five minority students had been the victim of some form of harassment during the academic year. Based on accounts in the print media alone, the Institute recorded the occurrence of ethnoviolence at 155 different institutions of higher education between September, 1986, and May, 1988.

In addition, the white supremacist groups are alive and well. Though small in numbers, they have been responsible for a spate of violent crimes in recent years. Perhaps even more frightening are the youth groups which have sprung up. The Aryan Youth Movement and various Skinhead factions have been recruiting alienated teens and young adults, capturing their loyalty, playing on their fears, and fueling their anger until it erupts into violence, sometimes murder. However, too much attention to hate groups. They are our neighbors and our neighbors' children.

I'd like to share with you a few of the images in my head from interviewing victims as part of the data-gathering process for the Institute's seven-state study of the impact of incidents on victims.

- I'm listening to a middle-aged Laotian woman, talking through a translator, tell of being attacked at noon while walking to her English class. She
  never returned to school.

- I see the face of a young black father, his wife sitting next to him, his two-
  year-old son smiling, making friends with everyone in the room. The
  father is speaking fast and angrily about the repeated attacks on his home
  since he moved into a white neighborhood—trash on his lawn, windows
  broken arson, and death threats. He finally bought a gun. Quietly, he
  says, "I'm afraid of what I might do if I catch one of them. I'm damned if I
  don't protect my family and damned if I do. Either way, I'll lose with the
  system."

- I hear the voice of a 16-year-old son of an interracial couple, victims of
  harassment over a period of three years and, finally, a cross-burning. He
  says, wistfully, "My mom used to walk and talk to people. Now she's
  afraid. She just sits inside and reads all the time."

The effects of incidents on victims are traumatic and long lasting. They
experience fear and isolation, never knowing what future act awaits them. Their
sense of personal violation is similar to that of a rape victim. They lose sleep.
They fear for their lives and those of their children. Some change jobs. Some
move away from communities, looking for a safe place. They can not live in
peace.

WHAT CAN BE DONE?

A reporter came into my office recently to discuss what the National Institute 16
Against Prejudice and Violence does. After I briefly explained its programs, he
asked, "What is the solution to the problem? There has been violence based on
prejudice since the beginning of time. Do you really think you can do anything
which will make any difference?" On one level, his cynicism is understandable.
On another level, it is sad, because there *are* ways in which we can make a
difference, and believing otherwise means giving up and giving in.

The Institute has a multifaceted approach to the problem of violence
motivated by bigotry. We maintain a clearinghouse of information about incidents, as well as programs to prevent and respond to them. We publish a
newsletter, educational materials, and reports of our research. We have a
legislative manual of Federal and state civil and criminal remedies, and recently
published a report on bigotry and cable TV. The latest publication discusses the
legal and community issues involved in the use of cable television by racist and
anti-Semitic groups.

We provide consultation and technical assistance on preventing and handling incidents and responding to activities of the Ku Klux Klan, neo-Nazis, and
other hate groups. We have been asked for advice and assistance by the U.S.
Department of Housing and Urban Development, the U.S. Department of
Justice, state and local human relations commissions, and community groups.

We conduct original research on the causes and nature of incidents, their impact on victims, and the effectiveness of different methods of response. We are conducting research on ethnoviolence in the workplace and are about to embark on the first major national survey of victimization in the general population.

Our educational efforts include convening national and regional confer- 20 ences, conducting trainings and seminars, assisting educators in developing programs and curricular materials, and providing information to media.

Over the last few years, a variety of positive responses has emerged around the country. People of good will, responsible state and local agencies, and community organizations have formed coalitions and task forces. States have passed laws which proscribe activities of hate groups and increase penalties for hate crimes. The Institute increasingly has been asked to train community leaders, police officers, and human rights officials to identify, monitor, and respond to ethnoviolence. Victim assistance programs have been established, and a few creative criminal justice systems are utilizing alternative programs in the adjudication of crimes committed by juveniles.

The needed programs of prevention have been slower in coming, in part because we don't know enough about intervening in the direction of an individual's life to avert a course of violence, let alone violence motivated by prejudice. While we need more research in the area, we do know that intergroup relations and cross-cultural issues need to be addressed from the beginning of kindergarten through high school.

We also know that, until the economic disparities among different groups in our society are rectified and basic needs such as housing and employment are met, it will be impossible for us to deal effectively with intergroup tension. These needs create a barrier to educating youth, to dispelling the ignorance and fear and anger which erupt into violence.

We must educate public officials and citizens that ethnoviolence is not an 24 isolated phenomenon. Laws need to be passed. Law enforcement officials need to be trained. Victims need assistance and treatment. Curriculum materials need to be developed. Research needs to be done. We also must speak out — not to do so is to condone the pain and suffering which is going on all around us.

I shared all of these thoughts with the cynical reporter, but there is more. Underlying all that we do should be a commitment to social justice and human equality, and the realization that the inequities, injustice, and pain resulting from prejudice in our society hurt us all and sap the strength that we need as a nation to build a better future.

William Schwartz, a professor of social work, wrote of the importance of "lending a vision" to a group. In order to find solutions, we all must have a vision and lend it to those we meet in our communities, schools, and workplaces. This vision is one which gives rise to activism that changes what is. It is a vision that can see beyond the injustices of today to the possibility of a more just society tomorrow. Such a vision requires not only a depth of commitment to a set of ideals, but also the conviction that one's effort *can* make a difference and the belief that even small changes can be important.

BIGOTRY AND ETHNOVIOLENCE IN THE WORKPLACE

San Francisco, Calif. — A former employee of the Board of Public Utilities testified in Federal court that a one-time president and current member of the board had made disparaging remarks about black workers. When discussing giving employees a holiday on Martin Luther King, Jr.'s birthday, he had joked, "Shoot four more of them and give them a week off."

Fort Lauderdale, Fla. — "Nigger Squad" was spray-painted on the window of the Police Department's executive office, to which four black officers were assigned.

Annapolis, Md. — Alderman Carl Snowden, an outspoken black community leader, received hate mail at his City Hall office, including a photograph of a black man hanging from a tree with a caption warning Snowden of a similar fate.

Portland, Ore. — An employee of a transport company was harassed racially and fired. His supervisor called him a "fat Mexican," a "taco bender," a "wetback," and a "spic."

Seattle, Wash. — A black head janitor of an elementary school found dead animals, including a cat, opossum, squirrel, and raccoon, near her office.

Bensalem, Pa. — In a Federal court suit, a Jewish man claimed that a supervisor in the company where he worked made anti-Semitic remarks, including one in which he said the owner was "going to manufacture a special microwave oven just to put you in."

Lima, Ohio — A black foreman in a General Dynamics weapons plant found a burning cross suspended from one of his work cranes.

New York City — A white supervisor who supported black workers' demands for equal promotions received threatening letters addressed to "Race Traitor."

Chicago, Ill. — A U.S. District Court judge ruled that a black employee at an industrial tape plant was a victim of racial discrimination when, on separate occasions, he found a dead rat with its neck slit on his desk, oil in his shoes, worms near his lunch, and garbage on his desk.

Philadelphia, Pa. — The president of a branch of the NAACP found "Kill Niggers" scribbled on a doorjamb of his headquarters.

Cincinnati, Ohio — Dressed in mock Ku Klux Klan robes, a group of workers assaulted a black employee. They made a cross of paper, set it on fire, and attempted to put it between his legs.

● PERSONAL RESPONSE ●

What feelings did Weiss's descriptions of racism in our country evoke in you? What kinds of harassment or acts of violence have you witnessed? How did such incidents make you feel?

● QUESTIONS FOR DISCUSSION ●

1. What evidence does Weiss supply to support her argument that, despite the civil-rights legislation of the 1960s, ours is still a highly segregated society?

2. Describe the audience Weiss seems to have in mind. Do you think she anticipates an audience opposed to her viewpoint or one that will be sympathetic? Explain your answer.

3. Like many other writers, Weiss uses the strategy of illustrating generalizations with concrete examples, such as those in paragraph 14 which make vivid the "images in [her] head." Find at least two other places in which Weiss uses specific examples to support a generalization.

4. What evidence does Weiss provide to support her contention that "bigotry begets violence"?

5. Summarize the various approaches that the National Institute Against Prejudice and Violence has taken toward solving the problem of violence based on prejudice.

6. What actions does Weiss call for in order to deal with the problem of prejudice-motivated violence?

7. The section entitled "Bigotry and Ethnoviolence in the Workplace" was originally featured in a box following the conclusion of the article. Does setting this information off from the rest of the text seem a more effective strategy to you than including the examples in the body of the article? Why or why not?

● WRITING TOPICS ●

1. Narrate your first experience with prejudice, as either witness to it or victim of it. Describe in detail the incident and how it made you feel.

2. Offer a possible solution to the problem of bigotry and ethnoviolence in our nation.

3. Explore the personality of bigots. Are there particular characteristics, such as income, education, or geographical location, that bigots have in common? Under what circumstances does personal preference or opinion become prejudice?

COMPLEXION

●

Richard Rodriguez

Richard Rodriguez was born in San Francisco, the son of Mexican immigrants. He earned a B.A. and an M.A. at Stanford University and a Ph.D. in English from the University of California at Berkeley. A lecturer and a writer, he publishes frequently in such magazines as The American Scholar, Saturday Review, *and* Harper's. *In 1982, Rodriquez published* Hunger of Memory, *a collection of autobiographical essays in which he describes the conflicts and challenges of growing up in an immigrant household in America. The following excerpt is from a chapter of* Hunger of Memory *in which Rodriquez considers how skin color affects people's lives.*

Regarding my family, I see faces that do not closely resemble my own. Like some other Mexican families, my family suggests Mexico's confused colonial past. Gathered around a table, we appear to be from separate continents. My father's face recalls faces I have seen in France. His complexion is white—he does not tan; he does not burn. Over the years, his dark wavy hair has grayed handsomely. But with time his face has sagged to a perpetual sigh. My mother, whose surname is inexplicably Irish—Moran—has an olive complexion. People have frequently wondered if, perhaps, she is Italian or Portuguese. And, in fact, she looks as though she could be from southern Europe. My mother's face has not aged as quickly as the rest of her body; it remains smooth and glowing—a cool tan—which her gray hair cleanly accentuates. My older brother has inherited her good looks. When he was a boy people would tell him that he looked like Mario Lanza, and hearing it he would smile with dimpled assurance. He would come home from high school with girl friends who seemed to me glamorous (because they were) blonds. And during those years I envied him his skin that burned red and peeled like the skin of the *gringos.* His complexion never darkened like mine. My youngest sister is exotically pale, almost ashen. She is delicately featured, Near Eastern, people have said. Only my older sister has a complexion as dark as mine, though her facial features are much less harshly defined than my own. To many people meeting her, she seems (they say) Polynesian. I am the only one in the family whose face is severely cut to the line of ancient Indian ancestors. My face is mournfully long, in the classical Indian manner; my profile suggests one of those beak-nosed Mayan sculptures—the eaglelike face upturned, open-mouthed, against the deserted, primitive sky.

'We are Mexicans,' my mother and father would say, and taught their four children to say whenever we (often) were asked about our ancestry. My mother and father scorned those 'white' Mexican-Americans who tried to pass themselves off as Spanish. My parents would never have thought of denying their ancestry. I never denied it: My ancestry is Mexican, I told strangers mechanically. But I never forgot that only my older sister's complexion was as dark as mine.

My older sister never spoke to me about her complexion when she was a girl. But I guessed that she found her dark skin a burden. I knew that she suffered for being a 'nigger.' As she came home from grammar school, little boys came up behind her and pushed her down to the sidewalk. In high school, she struggled in the adolescent competition for boyfriends in a world of football games and proms, a world where her looks were plainly uncommon. In college, she was afraid and scornful when dark-skinned foreign students from countries like Turkey and India found her attractive. She revealed her fear of dark skin to me only in adulthood when, regarding her own three children, she quietly admitted relief that they were all light.

That is the kind of remark women in my family have often made before. As a   4
boy, I'd stay in the kitchen (never seeming to attract any notice), listening while my aunts spoke of their pleasure at having light children. (The men, some of whom were dark-skinned from years of working out of doors, would be in another part of the house.) It was the woman's spoken concern: the fear of having a dark-skinned son or daughter. Remedies were exchanged. One aunt prescribed to her sisters the elixir of large doses of castor oil during the last weeks of pregnancy. (The remedy risked an abortion.) Children born dark grew up to have their faces treated regularly with a mixture of egg white and lemon juice concentrate. (In my case, the solution never would take.) One Mexican-American friend of my mother's who regarded it a special blessing that she had a measure of English blood, spoke disparagingly of her husband, a construction worker, for being so dark. 'He doesn't take care of himself,' she complained. But the remark, I noticed, annoyed my mother, who sat tracing an invisible design with her finger on the tablecloth.

There was affection too and a kind of humor about these matters. With daring tenderness, one of my uncles would refer to his wife as *mi negra*. An aunt regularly called her dark child *mi feito* (my little ugly one), her smile only partially hidden as she bent down to dig her mouth under his ticklish chin. And at times relatives spoke scornfully of pale, white skin. A *gringo's* skin resembled *masa* — baker's dough — someone remarked. Everyone laughed. Voices chuckled over the fact that the *gringos* spent so many hours in summer sunning themselves. ('They need to get sun because they look like *los muertos*.')

I heard the laughing but remembered what the women had said, with unsmiling voices, concerning dark skin. Nothing I heard outside the house, regarding my skin, was so impressive to me.

In public I occasionally heard racial slurs. Complete strangers would yell out at me. A teenager drove past, shouting, 'Hey, Greaser! Hey, Pancho!' Over his shoulder I saw the giggling face of his girl friend. A boy pedaled by and announced matter-of-factly, 'I pee on dirty Mexicans.' Such remarks would be said so casually that I wouldn't quickly realize that they were being addressed to me. When I did, I would be paralyzed with embarrassment, unable to return the insult. (Those times I happened to be with white grammar school friends, *they* shouted back. Imbued with the mysterious kindness of children, my friends would never ask later why I hadn't yelled out in my own defense.)

In all, there could not have been more than a dozen incidents of name- 8 calling. That there were so few suggests that I was not a primary victim of racial abuse. But that, even today, I can clearly remember particular incidents is proof of their impact. Because of such incidents, I listened when my parents remarked that Mexicans were often mistreated in California border towns. And in Texas. I listened carefully when I heard that two of my cousins had been refused admittance to an 'all-white' swimming pool. And that an uncle had been told by some man to go back to Africa. I followed the progress of the southern black civil rights movement, which was gaining prominent notice in Sacramento's afternoon newspaper. But what most intrigued me was the connection between dark skin and poverty. Because I heard my mother speak so often about the relegation of dark people to menial labor, I considered the great victims of racism to be those who were poor and forced to do menial work. People like the farmworkers whose skin was dark from the sun.

After meeting a black grammar school friend of my sister's, I remember thinking that she wasn't really 'black.' What interested me was the fact that she wasn't poor. (Her well-dressed parents would come by after work to pick her up in a shiny green Oldsmobile.) By contrast, the garbage men who appeared every Friday morning seemed to me unmistakably black. (I didn't bother to ask my parents why Sacramento garbage men always were black. I thought I knew.) One morning I was in the backyard when a man opened the gate. He was an ugly, square-faced black man with popping red eyes, a pail slung over his shoulder. As he approached, I stood up. And in a voice that seemed to me very weak, I piped, 'Hi.' But the man paid me no heed. He strode past to the can by the garage. In a single broad movement, he overturned its contents into his larger pail. Our can came crashing down as he turned and left me watching, in awe.

'Pobres negros,' my mother remarked when she'd notice a headline in the paper about a civil rights demonstration in the South. 'How the gringos mistreat them.' In the same tone of voice she'd tell me about the mistreatment her brother endured years before. (After my grandfather's death, my grandmother had come to America with her son and five daughters.) 'My sisters, we were still all just teenagers. And since mi pápa was dead, my brother had to be the head of the family. He had to support us, to find work. But what skills did he have! Twenty years old. Pobre. He was tall, like your grandfather. And strong. He did construction work. "Construction!" The gringos kept him digging all day, doing the dirtiest jobs. And they would pay him next to nothing. Sometimes they promised him one salary and paid him less when he finished. But what could he do? Report them? We weren't citizens then. He didn't even know English. And he was dark. What chances could he have? As soon as we sisters got older, he went right back to Mexico. He hated this country. He looked so tired when he left. Already with a hunchback. Still in his twenties. But old-looking. No life for him here. Pobre.'

Dark skin was for my mother the most important symbol of a life of oppressive labor and poverty. But both my parents recognized other symbols as well.

My father noticed the feel of every hand he shook. (He'd smile some- 12 times — marvel more than scorn — remembering a man he'd met who had soft, uncalloused hands.)

My mother would grab a towel in the kitchen and rub my oily face sore when I came in from playing outside. 'Clean the *grasa* off of your face!' (*Greaser!*)

Symbols: When my older sister, then in high school, asked my mother if she could do light housework in the afternoons for a rich lady we knew, my mother was frightened by the idea. For several weeks she troubled over it before granting conditional permission: 'Just remember, you're not a maid. I don't want you wearing a uniform.' My father echoed the same warning. Walking with him past a hotel, I watched as he stared at a doorman dressed like a Beefeater. 'How can anyone let himself be dressed up like that? Like a clown. Don't you ever get a job where you have to put on a uniform.' In summertime neighbors would ask me if I wanted to earn extra money by mowing their lawns. Again and again my mother worried: 'Why did they ask *you*? Can't you find anything better?' Inevitably, she'd relent. She knew I needed the money. But I was instructed to work after dinner. ('When the sun's not so hot.') Even then, I'd have to wear a hat. *Un sombrero de* baseball.

(*Sombrero*. Watching gray cowboy movies, I'd brood over the meaning of the broad-rimmed hat — that troubling symbol — which comically distinguished a Mexican cowboy from real cowboys.)

From my father came no warnings concerning the sun. His fear was of dark 16 factory jobs. He remembered too well his first jobs when he came to this country, not intending to stay, just to earn money enough to sail on to Australia. (In Mexico he had heard too many stories of discrimination in *los Estados Unidos*. So it was Australia, that distant island-continent, that loomed in his imagination as his 'America.') The work my father found in San Francisco was work for the unskilled. A factory job. Then a cannery job. (He'd remember the noise and the heat.) Then a job at a warehouse. (He'd remember the dark stench of old urine.) At one place there were fistfights; at another a supervisor who hated Chinese and Mexicans. Nowhere a union.

His memory of himself in those years is held by those jobs. Never making money enough for passage to Australia; slowly giving up the plan of returning to school to resume his third-grade education — to become an engineer. My memory of him in those years, however, is lifted from photographs in the family album which show him on his honeymoon with my mother — the woman who had convinced him to stay in America. I have studied their photographs often, seeking to find in those figures some clear resemblance to the man and the woman I've known as my parents. But the youthful faces in the photos remain, behind dark glasses, shadowy figures anticipating my mother and father.

They are pictured on the grounds of the Coronado Hotel near San Diego, standing in the pale light of a winter afternoon. She is wearing slacks. Her hair falls seductively over one side of her face. He appears wearing a double-breasted suit, an unneeded raincoat draped over his arm. Another shows them standing together, solemnly staring ahead. Their shoulders barely are touching. There is to their pose an aristocratic formality, an elegant Latin hauteur.

The man in those pictures is the same man who was fascinated by Italian grand opera. I have never known just what my father saw in the spectacle, but he has told me that he would take my mother to the Opera House every Friday night — if he had money enough for orchestra seats. ('Why go to sit in the balcony?') On Sundays he'd don Italian silk scarves and a camel's hair coat to take his new wife to the polo matches in Golden Gate Park. But one weekend my father stopped going to the opera and polo matches. He would blame the change in his life on one job — a warehouse job, working for a large corporation which today advertises its products with the smiling faces of children. 'They made me an old man before my time,' he'd say to me many years later. Afterward, jobs got easier and cleaner. Eventually, in middle age, he got a job making false teeth. But his youth was spent at the warehouse. 'Everything changed,' his wife remembers. The dapper young man in the old photographs yielded to the man I saw after dinner: haggard, asleep on the sofa. During 'The Ed Sullivan Show' on Sunday nights, when Roberta Peters or Licia Albanese would appear on the tiny blue screen, his head would jerk up alert. He'd sit forward while the notes of Puccini sounded before him. ('Un bel dí.')

By the time they had a family, my parents no longer dressed in very fine clothes. Those symbols of great wealth and the reality of their lives too noisily clashed. No longer did they try to fit themselves, like paper-doll figures, behind trappings so foreign to their actual lives. My father no longer wore silk scarves or expensive wool suits. He sold his tuxedo to a second-hand store for five dollars. My mother sold her rabbit fur coat to the wife of a Spanish radio station disc jockey. ('It looks better on you than it does on me,' she kept telling the lady until the sale was completed.) I was six years old at the time, but I recall watching the transaction with complete understanding. The woman I knew as my mother was already physically unlike the woman in her honeymoon photos. My mother's hair was short. Her shoulders were thick from carrying children. Her fingers were swollen red, toughened by housecleaning. Already my mother would admit to foreseeing herself in her own mother, a woman grown old, bald and bowlegged, after a hard lifetime of working.

In their manner, both my parents continued to respect the symbols of what they considered to be upper-class life. Very early, they taught me the *propio* way of eating *como los ricos*. And I was carefully taught elaborate formulas of polite greeting and parting. The dark little boy would be invited by classmates to the rich houses on Forty-fourth and Forty-fifth streets. 'How do you do?' or 'I am very pleased to meet you,' I would say, bowing slightly to the amused mothers of classmates. 'Thank you very much for the dinner; it was very delicious.'

I made an impression. I intended to make an impression, to be invited back. (I soon realized that the trick was to get the mother or father to notice me.) From those early days began my association with rich people, my fascination with their secret. My mother worried. She warned me not to come home expecting to have the things my friends possessed. But she needn't have said anything. When I went to the big houses, I remembered that I was, at best, a visitor to the world I saw there. For that reason, I was an especially watchful guest. I was my parents' child. Things most middle-class children wouldn't trouble to notice, I studied. Remembered to see: the starched black and white uniform worn by the maid who opened the door; the Mexican gardeners — their complexions as dark as my own. (One gardener's face, glassed by sweat, looked up to see me going inside.)

'Take Richard upstairs and show him your electric train,' the mother said. But it was really the vast polished dining room table I'd come to appraise. Those nights when I was invited to stay for dinner, I'd notice that my friend's mother rang a small silver bell to tell the black woman when to bring in the food. The father, at his end of the table, ate while wearing his tie. When I was not required to speak, I'd skate the icy cut of crystal with my eye; my gaze would follow the golden threads etched onto the rim of china. With my mother's eyes I'd see my hostess's manicured nails and judge them to be marks of her leisure. Later, when my schoolmate's father would bid me goodnight, I would feel his soft fingers and palm when we shook hands. And turning to leave, I'd see my dark self, lit by chandelier light, in a tall hallway mirror.

● PERSONAL RESPONSE ●

What is your reaction to the name-calling incidents and other examples of discrimination that Rodriguez recounts? Were you ever the object of teasing or cruel remarks about a physical characteristic? If so, describe the experience.

● QUESTIONS FOR DISCUSSION ●

1. How would you describe Rodriguez's relationship with his family?

2. Rodriguez uses many Spanish words or phrases, often without translating them. If you do not know Spanish, did you have any difficulty determining the meanings of those words? Why do you think Rodriguez chose to use them?

3. Why do you think Rodriguez was so impressed by what the women in his family said about dark skin? What is Rodriguez's attitude toward his own skin color?

4. Locate and discuss the symbols that are important to Rodriguez's parents.

5. What connection does Rodriguez make between skin color and poverty?

6. What do the stories of their work experiences in America reveal about the lives of Rodriguez's uncle and father? What connection does Rodriguez draw between those experiences and the color of their skin?

7. What ideas from earlier in the essay do the concluding sentences refer to? What is the implication of Rodriguez's seeing "his dark self, lit by chandelier light"?

● WRITING TOPICS ●

1. Explore the effects of a particular physical characteristic — a prominent birth mark, skin color, racial background, birth defect, or the like — on your own life or the life of someone you know.

2. Portray two or three selected members of your family. What are their prominent personality traits and physical characteristics? Are they similar or different from one another? Try to give enough concrete details that your readers will be able to visualize each family member you describe.

3. Find an old photograph of your parents (or another couple from an older generation whom you know well) when they were newly wed and describe the picture. Consider the following questions: How do they look? What do they appear to be doing? What was the occasion for the photograph? What do you think they may have hoped for, and how have their lives turned out?

THE PSYCHOLOGICAL TERROR OF SEGREGATION

•

MARY E. MEBANE

*Mary E. Mebane was born in Durham, North Carolina, and has a B.A.
from North Carolina College at Durham and an M.A. and Ph.D. from
the University of North Carolina at Chapel Hill. She is a civil-rights
activist, a writer, and a teacher. Her books include* The Eloquence of
Protest *and two autobiographies,* Mary *(1981) and* Mary, the Wayfarer
(1983). In the following selection from Mary, *Mebane vividly conveys
one aspect of the experience of having been born into the last generation
before segregation became illegal, a "world without options," a world
characterized by psychological terrorism.*

H istorically, my lifetime is important because I was part of the last
generation born into a world of total legal segregation in the Southern
United States. When the Supreme Court outlawed segregation in the
public schools in 1954, I was twenty-one. When Congress passed the Civil
Rights Act of 1964, permitting blacks free access to public places, I was thirty-
one. The world I was born into had been segregated for a long time — so long, in
fact, that I never met anyone who had lived during the time when restrictive laws
were not in existence, although some people spoke of parents and others who
had lived during the "free" time. As far as anyone knew, the laws as they then
existed would stand forever. They were meant to — and did — create a world that
fixed black people at the bottom of society in all aspects of human life. It was a
world without options.

Most Americans have never had to live with terror. I had had to live with it
all my life — the psychological terror of segregation, in which there was a special
set of laws governing your movements. You violated them at your peril, for you
knew that if you broke one of them, knowingly or not, physical terror was just
around the corner, in the form of policemen and jails, and in some cases and
places white vigilante mobs formed for the exclusive purpose of keeping blacks
in line.

It was Saturday morning, like any Saturday morning in dozens of Southern
towns.

The town had a washed look. The street sweepers had been busy since six 4
o'clock. Now, at eight, they were still slowly moving down the streets, white
trucks with clouds of water coming from underneath the swelled tubular sides.
Unwary motorists sometimes got a windowful of water as a truck passed by. As it
moved on, it left in its wake a clear stream running in the gutters or splashed on
the wheels of parked cars.

Homeowners, bent over industriously in the morning sun, were out pushing
lawn mowers. The sun was bright, but it wasn't too hot. It was morning and it was

May. Most of the mowers were glad that it was finally getting warm enough to go outside.

Traffic was brisk. Country people were coming into town early with their produce; clerks and service workers were getting to the job before the stores opened at ten o'clock. Though the big stores would not be open for another hour or so, the grocery stores, banks, open-air markets, dinettes, were already open and filling with staff and customers.

Everybody was moving toward the heart of Durham's downtown, which waited to receive them rather complacently, little knowing that in a decade the shopping centers far from the center of downtown Durham would create a ghost town in the midst of the busiest blocks on Main Street.

Some moved by car, and some moved by bus. The more affluent used cars,   8 leaving the buses mainly to the poor, black and white, though there were some businesspeople who avoided the trouble of trying to find a parking place downtown by riding the bus.

I didn't mind taking the bus on Saturday. It wasn't so crowded. At night or on Saturday or Sunday was the best time. If there were plenty of seats, the blacks didn't have to worry about being asked to move so that a white person could sit down. And the knot of hatred and fear didn't come into my stomach.

I knew the stop that was the safety point, both going and coming. Leaving town, it was the Little Five Points, about five or six blocks north of the main downtown section. That was the last stop at which four or five people might get on. After that stop, the driver could sometimes pass two or three stops without taking on or letting off a passenger. So the number of seats on the bus usually remained constant on the trip from town to Braggtown. The nearer the bus got to the end of the line, the more I relaxed. For if a white passenger got on near the end of the line, often to catch the return trip back and avoid having to stand in the sun at the bus stop until the bus turned around, he or she would usually stand if there were not seats in the white section, and the driver would say nothing, knowing that the end of the line was near and that the standee would get a seat in a few minutes.

On the trip to town, the Mangum Street A&P was the last point at which the driver picked up more passengers than he let off. These people, though they were just a few blocks from the downtown section, preferred to ride the bus downtown. Those getting on at the A&P were usually on their way to work at the Duke University Hospital—past the downtown section, through a residential neighborhood, and then past the university, before they got to Duke Hospital.

So whether the driver discharged more passengers than he took on near the   12 A&P on Mangum was of great importance. For if he took on more passengers than got off, it meant that some of the newcomers would have to stand. And if they were white, the driver was going to have to ask a black passenger to move so that a white passenger could sit down. Most of the drivers had a rule of thumb, though. By custom the seats behind the exit door had become "colored" seats, and no matter how many whites stood up, anyone sitting behind the exit door knew that he or she wouldn't have to move.

The disputed seat, though, was the one directly opposite the exit door. It was "no-man's-land." White people sat there, and black people sat there. It all depended on whose section was full. If the back section was full, the next black passenger who got on sat in the no-man's-land seat; but if the white section filled up, a white person would take the seat. Another thing about the white people: they could sit anywhere they chose, even in the "colored" section. Only the black passengers had to obey segregation laws.

On this Saturday morning Esther and I set out for town for our music lesson. We were going on our weekly big adventure, all the way across town, through the white downtown, then across the railroad tracks, then through the "colored" downtown, a section of run-down dingy shops, through some fading high-class black neighborhoods, past North Carolina College, to Mrs. Shearin's house.

We walked the two miles from Wildwood to the bus line. Though it was a warm day, in the early morning there was dew on the grass and the air still had the night's softness. So we walked along and talked and looked back constantly, hoping someone we knew would stop and pick us up.

I looked back furtively, for in one of the few instances that I remembered 16 my father criticizing me severely, it was for looking back. One day when I was walking from town he had passed in his old truck. I had been looking back and had seen him. "Don't look back," he had said. "People will think that you want them to pick you up." Though he said "people," I knew he meant men — not the men he knew, who lived in the black community, but the black men who were not part of the community, and all of the white men. To be picked up meant that something bad would happen to me. Still, two miles is a long walk and I occasionally joined Esther in looking back to see if anyone we knew was coming.

Esther and I got to the bus and sat on one of the long seats at the back that faced each other. There were three such long seats — one on each side of the bus and a third long seat at the very back that faced the front. I liked to sit on a long seat facing the side because then I didn't have to look at the expressions on the faces of the whites when they put their tokens in and looked at the blacks sitting in the back of the bus. Often I studied my music, looking down and practicing the fingering. I looked up at each stop to see who was getting on and to check on the seating pattern. The seating pattern didn't really bother me that day until the bus started to get unusually full for a Saturday morning. I wondered what was happening, where all these people were coming from. They got on and got on until the white section was almost full and the black section was full.

There was a black man in a blue windbreaker and a gray porkpie hat sitting in no-man's-land, and my stomach tightened. I wondered what would happen. I had never been on a bus on which a black person was asked to give a seat to a white person when there was no other seat empty. Usually, though, I had seen a black person automatically get up and move to an empty seat farther back. But this morning the only empty seat was beside a black person sitting in no-man's-land.

The bus stopped at Little Five Points and one black got off. A young white man was getting on. I tensed. What would happen now? Would the driver ask the black man to get up and move to the empty seat farther back? The white man had a businessman air about him: suit, shirt, tie, polished brown shoes. He saw the empty seat in the "colored" section and after just a little hesitation went to it, put his briefcase down, and sat with his feet crossed. I relaxed a little when the bus pulled off without the driver saying anything. Evidently he hadn't seen what had happened, or since he was just a few stops from Main Street, he figured the mass exodus there would solve all the problems. Still, I was afraid of a scene.

The next stop was an open-air fruit stand just after Little Five Points, and 20 here another white man got on. Where would he sit? The only available seat was beside the black man. Would he stand the few stops to Main Street or would the driver make the black man move? The whole colored section tensed, but nobody said anything. I looked at Esther, who looked apprehensive. I looked at the other men and women, who studiously avoided my eyes and everybody else's as well, as they maintained a steady gaze at a far-distant land.

Just one woman caught my eye; I had noticed her before, and I had been ashamed of her. She was a stringy little black woman. She could have been forty; she could have been fifty. She looked as if she were a hard drinker. Flat black face with tight features. She was dressed with great insouciance in a tight boy's sweater with horizontal lines running across her flat chest. It pulled down over a nondescript skirt. Laced-up shoes, socks, and a head rag completed her outfit. She looked tense.

The white man who had just gotten on the bus walked to the seat in no-man's-land and stood there. He wouldn't sit down, just stood there. Two adult males, living in the most highly industrialized, most technologically advanced nation in the world, a nation that had devastated two other industrial giants in World War II and had flirted with taking on China in Korea. Both these men, either of whom could have fought for the United States in Germany or Korea, faced each other in mutual rage and hostility. The white one wanted to sit down, but he was going to exert his authority and force the black one to get up first. I watched the driver in the rearview mirror. He was about the same age as the antagonists. The driver wasn't looking for trouble, either.

"Say there, buddy, how about moving back," the driver said, meanwhile driving his bus just as fast as he could. The whole bus froze — whites at the front, blacks at the rear. They didn't want to believe what was happening was really happening.

The seated black man said nothing. The standing white man said nothing. 24

"Say, buddy, did you hear me? What about moving on back." The driver was scared to death. I could tell that.

"These is the niggers' seats!" the little lady in the strange outfit started screaming. I jumped. I had to shift my attention from the driver to the frieze of the black man seated and white man standing to the articulate little woman who had joined in the fray.

"The government gave us these seats! These is the niggers' seats." I was startled at her statement and her tone. "The president said that these are the niggers' seats!" I expected her to start fighting at any moment.

Evidently the bus driver did, too, because he was driving faster and faster. I 28 believe that he forgot he was driving a bus and wanted desperately to pull to the side of the street and get out and run.

"I'm going to take you down to the station, buddy," the driver said.

The white man with the briefcase and the polished brown shoes who had taken a seat in the "colored" section looked as though he might die of embarrassment at any moment.

As scared and upset as I was, I didn't miss a thing.

By that time we had come to the stop before Main Street, and the black 32 passenger rose to get off.

"You're not getting off, buddy. I'm going to take you downtown." The driver kept driving as he talked and seemed to be trying to get downtown as fast as he could.

"These are the niggers' seats! The government plainly said these are the niggers' seats!" screamed the little woman in rage.

I was embarrassed at the use of the word "nigger" but I was proud of the lady. I was also proud of the man who wouldn't get up.

The bus driver was afraid, trying to hold on to his job but plainly not willing 36 to get into a row with the blacks.

The bus seemed to be going a hundred miles an hour and everybody was anxious to get off, though only the lady and the driver were saying anything.

The black man stood at the exit door; the driver drove right past the A&P stop. I was terrified. I was sure that the bus was going to the police station to put the black man in jail. The little woman had her hands on her hips and she never stopped yelling. The bus driver kept driving as fast as he could.

Then, somewhere in the back of his mind, he decided to forget the whole thing. The next stop was Main Street, and when he got there, in what seemed to be a flash of lightning, he flung both doors open wide. He and his black antagonist looked at each other in the rearview mirror; in a second the windbreaker and porkpie hat were gone. The little woman was standing, preaching to the whole bus about the government's gift of these seats to the blacks; the man with the brown shoes practically fell out of the door in his hurry; and Esther and I followed the hurrying footsteps.

We walked about three doors down the block, then caught a bus to the 40 black neighborhood. Here we sat on one of the two long seats facing each other, directly behind the driver. It was the custom. Since this bus had a route from a black neighborhood to the downtown section and back, passing through no white residential areas, blacks could sit where they chose. One minute we had been on a bus in which violence was threatened over a seat near the exit door; the next minute we were sitting in the very front behind the driver.

The people who devised this system thought that it was going to last forever.

● PERSONAL RESPONSE ●

How did you respond to each of these people on the bus with Mebane: the antagonists, the bus driver, the outspoken little woman, and the rest of the passengers? How do you think you would have acted had you been on that bus?

● QUESTIONS FOR DISCUSSION ●

1. Why do you think Mebane goes into such detail in paragraphs 3–8 to describe the activities of the townspeople on the Saturday morning of the bus incident? How does that setting contrast with what happens on the bus?

2. Why do you think Mebane mentions that in a decade downtown Durham would become a ghost town (paragraph 7)?

3. How well does the incident on the bus dramatize the psychological terror of segregation? Point out specific details that you think are particularly effective for conveying that terror.

4. What other kind of psychological terror does paragraph 16 reveal that Mebane had to live with?

5. What is Mebane's purpose in paragraph 22, when she first describes the confrontation between the two antagonists? To what degree do you think their conflict is about power and control as well as rage and hostility?

6. How does Mebane's attitude toward the "stringy little black woman" change as a result of the incident on the bus? How does she feel about the other key players in this scene, that is, the two men involved in the conflict and the bus driver?

7. How do the other passengers, both black and white, respond to the conflict between the two antagonists?

8. Why do you think Mebane ended as she did? What is the effect of that final sentence?

● WRITING TOPICS ●

1. Narrate your own experience of being in the company of two people in conflict. Provide details about the setting for the incident, the reason for the conflict, your own response to it, and the outcome.

2. If you have witnessed or been party to racial conflict, narrate your experience.

3. Define psychological terror of a type different from what Mebane writes of in her essay, dramatizing what the term means through a vivid, extended illustration.

JUST WALK ON BY
A BLACK MAN PONDERS HIS POWER TO ALTER PUBLIC SPACE

———————————————— ● ————————————————

BRENT STAPLES

Brent Staples holds a Ph.D. in psychology from the University of Chicago. After working at a variety of newspapers, including the Chicago Sun-Times, he became an editorial editor with the New York Times Book Review in 1985. He is currently an assistant editor of the Metropolitan section of the New York Times. The essay reprinted below, which appeared in Ms. in 1986, describes how Staples first learned that, largely because of his skin color, there are limitations on the places he is free to go.

My first victim was a woman—white, well dressed, probably in her early twenties. I came upon her late one evening on a deserted street in Hyde Park, a relatively affluent neighborhood in an otherwise mean, impoverished section of Chicago. As I swung onto the avenue behind her, there seemed to be a discreet, uninflammatory distance between us. Not so. She cast back a worried glance. To her, the youngish black man—a broad six feet two inches with a beard and billowing hair, both hands shoved into the pockets of a bulky military jacket—seemed menacingly close. After a few more quick glimpses, she picked up her pace and was soon running in earnest. Within seconds she disappeared into a cross street.

That was more than a decade ago. I was twenty-two years old, a graduate student newly arrived at the University of Chicago. It was in the echo of that terrified woman's footfalls that I first began to know the unwieldy inheritance I'd come into—the ability to alter public space in ugly ways. It was clear that she thought herself the quarry of a mugger, a rapist, or worse. Suffering a bout of insomnia, however, I was stalking sleep, not defenseless wayfarers. As a softy who is scarcely able to take a knife to a raw chicken—let alone hold it to a person's throat—I was surprised, embarrassed, and dismayed all at once. Her flight made me feel like an accomplice in tyranny. It also made it clear that I was indistinguishable from the muggers who occasionally seeped into the area from the surrounding ghetto. That first encounter, and those that followed, signified that a vast, unnerving gulf lay between nighttime pedestrians—particularly women—and me. And I soon gathered that being perceived as dangerous is a hazard in itself. I only needed to turn a corner into a dicey situation, or crowd some frightened, armed person in a foyer somewhere, or make an errant move after being pulled over by a policeman. Where fear and weapons meet—and they often do in urban America—there is always the possibility of death.

In that first year, my first away from my hometown, I was to become thoroughly familiar with the language of fear. At dark, shadowy intersections in Chicago, I could cross in front of a car stopped at a traffic light and elicit the *thunk, thunk, thunk, thunk* of the driver—black, white, male, or female— hammering down the door locks. On less traveled streets after dark, I grew accustomed to but never comfortable with people who crossed to the other side of the street rather than pass me. Then there were the standard unpleasantries with police, doormen, bouncers, cab drivers, and others whose business it is to screen out troublesome individuals *before* there is any nastiness.

I moved to New York nearly two years ago and I have remained an avid night 4 walker. In central Manhattan, the near-constant crowd cover minimizes tense one-on-one street encounters. Elsewhere—visiting friends in SoHo, where sidewalks are narrow and tightly spaced buildings shut out the sky—things can get very taut indeed.

Black men have a firm place in New York mugging literature. Norman Podhoretz in his famed (or infamous) 1963 essay, "My Negro Problem—And Ours," recalls growing up in terror of black males; they "were tougher than we were, more ruthless," he writes—and as an adult on the Upper West Side of Manhattan, he continues, he cannot constrain his nervousness when he meets black men on certain streets. Similarly, a decade later, the essayist and novelist Edward Hoagland extols a New York where once "Negro bitterness bore down mainly on other Negroes." Where some see mere panhandlers, Hoagland sees "a mugger who is clearly screwing up his nerve to do more than just *ask* for money." But Hoagland has "the New Yorker's quick-hunch posture for broken-field maneuvering," and the bad guy swerves away.

I often witness that "hunch posture," from women after dark on the warrenlike streets of Brooklyn where I live. They seem to set their faces on neutral and, with their purse straps strung across their chests bandolier style, they forge ahead as though bracing themselves against being tackled. I understand, of course, that the danger they perceive is not a hallucination. Women are particularly vulnerable to street violence, and young black males are drastically overrepresented among the perpetrators of that violence. Yet these truths are no solace against the kind of alienation that comes of being ever the suspect, against being set apart, a fearsome entity with whom pedestrians avoid making eye contact.

It is not altogether clear to me how I reached the ripe old age of twenty-two without being conscious of the lethality nighttime pedestrians attributed to me. Perhaps it was because in Chester, Pennsylvania, the small, angry industrial town where I came of age in the 1960s, I was scarcely noticeable against a backdrop of gang warfare, street knifings, and murders. I grew up one of the good boys, had perhaps a half-dozen fist fights. In retrospect, my shyness of combat has clear sources.

Many things go into the making of a young thug. One of those things is the 8 consummation of the male romance with the power to intimidate. An infant discovers that random flailings send the baby bottle flying out of the crib and crashing to the floor. Delighted, the joyful babe repeats those motions again and again, seeking to duplicate the feat. Just so, I recall the points at which some of my boyhood friends were finally seduced by the perception of themselves as tough guys. When a mark cowered and surrendered his money without resistance, myth and reality merged — and paid off. It is, after all, only manly to embrace the power to frighten and intimidate. We, as men, are not supposed to give an inch of our lane on the highway; we are to seize the fighter's edge in work and in play and even in love; we are to be valiant in the face of hostile forces.

Unfortunately, poor and powerless young men seem to take all this nonsense literally. As a boy, I saw countless tough guys locked away; I have since buried several, too. They were babies, really — a teenage cousin, a brother of twenty-two, a childhood friend in his mid-twenties — all gone down in episodes of bravado played out in the streets. I came to doubt the virtues of intimidation early on. I chose, perhaps even unconsciously, to remain a shadow — timid, but a survivor.

The fearsomeness mistakenly attributed to me in public places often has a perilous flavor. The most frightening of these confusions occurred in the late 1970s and early 1980s when I worked as a journalist in Chicago. One day, rushing into the office of a magazine I was writing for with a deadline story in hand, I was mistaken for a burglar. The office manager called security and, with an ad hoc posse, pursued me through the labyrinthine halls, nearly to my editor's door. I had no way of proving who I was. I could only move briskly toward the company of someone who knew me.

Another time I was on assignment for a local paper and killing time before an interview. I entered a jewelry store on the city's affluent Near North Side. The proprietor excused herself and returned with an enormous red Doberman pinscher straining at the end of a leash. She stood, the dog extended toward me, silent to my questions, her eyes bulging nearly out of her head. I took a cursory look around, nodded, and bade her good night. Relatively speaking, however, I never fared as badly as another black male journalist. He went to nearby Waukegan, Illinois, a couple of summers ago to work on a story about a murderer who was born there. Mistaking the reporter for the killer, police hauled him from his car at gunpoint and but for his press credentials would probably have tried to book him. Such episodes are not uncommon. Black men trade tales like this all the time.

In "My Negro Problem — And Ours," Podhoretz writes that the hatred he [12] feels for blacks makes itself known to him through a variety of avenues — one being his discomfort with that "special brand of paranoid touchiness" to which he says blacks are prone. No doubt he is speaking here of black men. In time, I learned to smother the rage I felt at so often being taken for a criminal. Not to do so would surely have led to madness — via that special "paranoid touchiness" that so annoyed Podhoretz at the time he wrote the essay.

I began to take precautions to make myself less threatening. I move about with care, particularly late in the evening. I give a wide berth to nervous people on subway platforms during the wee hours, particularly when I have exchanged business clothes for jeans. If I happen to be entering a building behind some people who appear skittish, I may walk by, letting them clear the lobby before I return, so as not to seem to be following them. I have been calm and extremely congenial on those rare occasions when I've been pulled over by the police.

And on late-evening constitutionals along streets less traveled by, I employ what has proved to be an excellent tension-reducing measure: I whistle melodies from Beethoven and Vivaldi and the more popular classical composers. Even steely New Yorkers hunching toward nighttime destinations seem to relax, and occasionally they even join in the tune. Virtually everybody seems to sense that a mugger wouldn't be warbling bright, sunny selections from Vivaldi's *Four Seasons*. It is my equivalent of the cowbell that hikers wear when they know they are in bear country.

● PERSONAL RESPONSE ●

How do you feel about Staples' decision to change his own behavior in public in order to accommodate other people's fear of him? Would you be willing to do the same? Why or why not?

● QUESTIONS FOR DISCUSSION ●

1. Why does Staples use the word "victim" in his opening paragraph? In what sense is that white woman a "victim"? Who else might be considered a victim? Is Staples himself a victim? Explain your answer.

2. How is Staples able to "alter public space in ugly ways" (paragraph 2)? What do you think he means by "ugly"?

3. How does Staples feel about his effect on other people? Is he angry? sympathetic? outraged? Does he consider their fear unfair or irrational? Find specific passages to support your answer.

4. What does Staples mean by "the language of fear" (paragraph 3)?

5. In paragraphs 8 and 9, Staples explains a definition of manhood that he chose early in life not to embrace. What is that definition and why did he reject it?

6. What is Staples' image of himself? How does it differ from the image that others have of him?

7. Is Staples' experience entirely a racial issue? If not, what else accounts for the fear he elicits from other people?

8. Read Mary Mebane's "The Psychological Terror of Segregation" and discuss the connections you see between that essay and this one.

● WRITING TOPICS ●

1. Staples' point of view is that of a black man who is frightening to many people, particularly white women, as illustrated vividly in his opening paragraph. Explore possible reasons for the apprehension of the woman in paragraph 1 and the actions she took in response to it.

2. If you have ever unintentionally frightened someone, narrate what happened and explain how it made you feel. Or, if you have been in the position of the "victim" Staples describes, narrate that experience and discuss reasons for your own behavior.

3. Consider the extent to which fear or perceived danger has the power to control or alter behavior. Select a specific situation or condition — AIDS, nuclear power plants, an outbreak of a contagious disease, an increase in assaults on campus — and explain in detail how it controls or changes behavior.

CARRIE BUCK'S DAUGHTER

●

STEPHEN JAY GOULD

Stephen Jay Gould was born in New York City, attended Antioch College, and earned a Ph.D. in paleontology from Columbia University. A faculty member of Harvard University since 1967, Gould teaches biology, geology, and the history of science. He is also a prolific writer, noted for his ability to describe scientific phenomena in easily understood lay terms. A contributor of over one hundred articles to scientific journals, Gould also writes a monthly column for Natural History *magazine. Many of those essays have been collected in* Ever Since Darwin *(1978),* The Panda's Thumb *(1980),* Hen's Teeth and Horse's Toes *(1983), and* The Flamingo's Smile: Reflections in Natural History *(1985). He has also written* The Mismeasure of Man *(1981). In "Carrie Buck's Daughter," reprinted from* The Flamingo's Smile, *Gould presents evidence that a Supreme Court decision supporting compulsory sterilization of mentally retarded women was based on "a patent falsehood" and that the central figure in the case was not mentally deficient. Instead, Carrie Buck was the victim of prejudice.*

T he Lord really put it on the line in his preface to that prototype of all prescription, the Ten Commandments:

> . . . for I, the Lord thy God, am a jealous God, visiting the iniquity of the fathers upon the children unto the third and fourth generation of them that hate me (Exod. 20:5).

The terror of this statement lies in its patent unfairness — its promise to punish guiltless offspring for the misdeeds of their distant forebears.

A different form of guilt by genealogical association attempts to remove this stigma of injustice by denying a cherished premise of Western thought — human free will. If off-spring are tainted not simply by the deeds of their parents but by a material form of evil transferred directly by biological inheritance, then "the iniquity of the fathers" becomes a signal or warning for probable misbehavior of their sons. Thus Plato, while denying that children should suffer directly for the crimes of their parents, nonetheless defended the banishment of a personally guiltless man whose father, grandfather, and great-grandfather had all been condemned to death.

It is, perhaps merely coincidental that both Jehovah and Plato chose three generations as their criterion for establishing different forms of guilt by association. Yet we maintain a strong folk, or vernacular, tradition for viewing triple occurrences as minimal evidence of regularity. Bad things, we are told, come in threes. Two may represent an accidental association; three is a pattern. Perhaps, then, we should not wonder that our own century's most famous pronounce-

4

ment of blood guilt employed the same criterion — Oliver Wendell Holmes's defense of compulsory sterilization in Virginia (Supreme Court decision of 1927 in *Buck* v. *Bell*): "three generations of imbeciles are enough."

Restrictions upon immigration, with national quotas set to discriminate against those deemed mentally unfit by early versions of IQ testing, marked the greatest triumph of the American eugenics movement — the flawed hereditarian doctrine, so popular earlier in our century and by no means extinct today, that attempted to "improve" our human stock by preventing the propagation of those deemed biologically unfit and encouraging procreation among the supposedly worthy. But the movement to enact and enforce laws for compulsory "eugenic" sterilization had an impact and success scarcely less pronounced. If we could debar the shiftless and the stupid from our shores, we might also prevent the propagation of those similarly afflicted but already here.

The movement for compulsory sterilization began in earnest during the 1890s, abetted by two major factors — the rise of eugenics as an influential political movement and the perfection of safe and simple operations (vasectomy for men and salpingectomy, the cutting and tying of Fallopian tubes, for women) to replace castration and other socially unacceptable forms of mutilation. Indiana passed the first sterilization act based on eugenic principles in 1907 (a few states had previously mandated castration as a punitive measure for certain sexual crimes, although such laws were rarely enforced and usually overturned by judicial review). Like so many others to follow, it provided for sterilization of afflicted people residing in the state's "care," either as inmates of mental hospitals and homes for the feebleminded or as inhabitants of prisons. Sterilization could be imposed upon those judged insane, idiotic, imbecilic, or moronic, and upon convicted rapists or criminals when recommended by a board of experts.

By the 1930s, more than thirty states had passed similar laws, often with an expanded list of so-called hereditary defects, including alcoholism and drug addiction in some states, and even blindness and deafness in others. These laws were continually challenged and rarely enforced in most states; only California and Virginia applied them zealously. By January 1935, some 20,000 forced "eugenic" sterilizations had been performed in the United States, nearly half in California.

No organization crusaded more vociferously and successfully for these laws [8] than the Eugenics Record Office, the semiofficial arm and repository of data for the eugenics movement in America. Harry Laughlin, superintendent of the Eugenics Record Office, dedicated most of his career to a tireless campaign of writing and lobbying for eugenic sterilization. He hoped, thereby, to eliminate in two generations the genes of what he called the "submerged tenth" — "the most worthless one-tenth of our present population." He proposed a "model sterilization law" in 1922, designed

to prevent the procreation of persons socially inadequate from defective inheritance, by authorizing and providing for eugenical sterilization of certain potential parents carrying degenerate hereditary qualities.

This model bill became the prototype for most laws passed in America, although few states cast their net as widely as Laughlin advised. (Laughlin's categories encompassed "blind, including those with seriously impaired vision; deaf, including those with seriously impaired hearing; and dependent, including orphans, ne'er-do-wells, the homeless, tramps, and paupers.") Laughlin's suggestions were better heeded in Nazi Germany, where his model act inspired the infamous and stringently enforced *Erbgesundheitsrecht*, leading by the eve of World War II to the sterilization of some 375,000 people, most for "congenital feeblemindedness," but including nearly 4,000 for blindness and deafness.

The campaign for forced eugenic sterilization in America reached its climax and height of respectability in 1927, when the Supreme Court, by an 8–1 vote, upheld the Virginia sterilization bill in *Buck* v. *Bell*. Oliver Wendell Holmes, then in his mid-eighties and the most celebrated jurist in America, wrote the majority opinion with his customary verve and power of style. It included the notorious paragraph, with its chilling tag line, cited ever since as the quintessential statement of eugenic principles. Remembering with pride his own distant experiences as an infantryman in the Civil War, Holmes wrote:

> We have seen more than once that the public welfare may call upon the best citizens for their lives. It would be strange if it could not call upon those who already sap the strength of the state for these lesser sacrifices. . . . It is better for all the world, if instead of waiting to execute degenerate offspring for crime, or to let them starve for their imbecility, society can prevent those who are manifestly unfit from continuing their kind. The principle that sustains compulsory vaccination is broad enough to cover cutting the Fallopian tubes. Three generations of imbeciles are enough.

Who, then, were the famous "three generations of imbeciles," and why should they still compel our interest?

When the state of Virginia passed its compulsory sterilization law in 1924, [12] Carrie Buck, an eighteen-year-old white woman, lived as an involuntary resident at the State Colony for Epileptics and Feeble-Minded. As the first person selected for sterilization under the new act, Carrie Buck became the focus for a constitutional challenge launched, in part, by conservative Virginia Christians who held, according to eugenical "modernists," antiquated views about individual preferences and "benevolent" state power. (Simplistic political labels do not apply in this case, and rarely in general for that matter. We usually regard eugenics as a conservative movement and its most vocal critics as members of the left. This alignment has generally held in our own decade. But eugenics, touted in its day as the latest in scientific modernism, attracted many liberals and numbered among its most vociferous critics groups often labeled as reactionary and antiscientific. If any political lesson emerges from these shifting allegiances, we might consider the true inalienability of certain human rights.)

But why was Carrie Buck in the State Colony and why was she selected? Oliver Wendell Holmes upheld her choice as judicious in the opening lines of his 1927 opinion.

> Carrie Buck is a feeble-minded white woman who was committed to the State
> Colony. . . . She is the daughter of a feeble-minded mother in the same
> institution, and the mother of an illegitimate feeble-minded child.

In short, inheritance stood as the crucial issue (indeed as the driving force
behind all eugenics). For if measured mental deficiency arose from malnourishment, either of body or mind, and not from tainted genes, then how could
sterilization be justified? If decent food, upbringing, medical care, and education might make a worthy citizen of Carrie Buck's daughter, how could the State
of Virginia justify the severing of Carrie's Fallopian tubes against her will? (Some
forms of mental deficiency are passed by inheritance in family lines, but most
are not—a scarcely surprising conclusion when we consider the thousand
shocks that beset us all during our lives, from abnormalities in embryonic
growth to traumas of birth, malnourishment, rejection, and poverty. In any case,
no fair-minded person today would credit Laughlin's social criteria for the
identification of hereditary deficiency—ne'er-do-wells, the homeless, tramps,
and paupers—although we shall soon see that Carrie Buck was committed on
these grounds.)

When Carrie Buck's case emerged as the crucial test of Virginia's law, the
chief honchos of eugenics understood that the time had come to put up or shut
up on the crucial issue of inheritance. Thus, the Eugenics Record Office sent
Arthur H. Estabrook, their crack fieldworker, to Virginia for a "scientific" study
of the case. Harry Laughlin himself provided a deposition, and his brief for
inheritance was presented at the local trial that affirmed Virginia's law and later
worked its way to the Supreme Court as *Buck v. Bell.*

Laughlin made two major points to the court. First, that Carrie Buck and 16
her mother, Emma Buck, were feeble-minded by the Stanford–Binet test of IQ,
then in its own infancy. Carrie scored a mental age of nine years, Emma of seven
years and eleven months. (These figures ranked them technically as "imbeciles"
by definitions of the day, hence Holmes's later choice of words—though his
infamous line is often misquoted as "three generations of idiots." Imbeciles
displayed a mental age of six to nine years; idiots performed worse, morons
better, to round out the old nomenclature of mental deficiency.) Second, that
most feeblemindedness resides ineluctably in the genes, and that Carrie Buck
surely belonged with this majority. Laughlin reported:

> Generally feeble-mindedness is caused by the inheritance of degenerate quali-
> ties; but sometimes it might be caused by environmental factors which are not
> hereditary. In the case given, the evidence points strongly toward the feeble-
> mindedness and moral delinquency of Carrie Buck being due, primarily, to
> inheritance and not to environment.

Carrie Buck's daughter was then, and has always been, the pivotal figure of
this painful case. I noted in beginning this essay that we tend (often at our peril)
to regard two as potential accident and three as an established pattern. The
supposed imbecility of Emma and Carrie might have been an unfortunate
coincidence, but the diagnosis of similar deficiency for Vivian Buck (made by a
social worker, as we shall see, when Vivian was but six months old) tipped the

balance in Laughlin's favor and led Holmes to declare the Buck lineage inherently corrupt by deficient heredity. Vivian sealed the pattern—*three* generations of imbeciles are enough. Besides, had Carrie not given illegitimate birth to Vivian, the issue (in both senses) would never have emerged.

Oliver Wendell Holmes viewed his work with pride. The man so renowned for his principle of judicial restraint, who had proclaimed that freedom must not be curtailed without "clear and present danger"—without the equivalent of falsely yelling "fire" in a crowded theater—wrote of his judgment in *Buck* v. *Bell*: "I felt that I was getting near the first principle of real reform."

And so *Buck* v. *Bell* remained for fifty years, a footnote to a moment of American history perhaps best forgotten. Then, in 1980, it reemerged to prick our collective conscience, when Dr. K. Ray Nelson, then director of the Lynchburg Hospital where Carrie Buck had been sterilized, researched the records of his institution and discovered that more than 4,000 sterilizations had been performed, the last as late as 1972. He also found Carrie Buck, alive and well near Charlottesville, and her sister Doris, covertly sterilized under the same law (she was told that her operation was for appendicitis), and now, with fierce dignity, dejected and bitter because she had wanted a child more than anything else in her life and had finally, in her old age, learned why she had never conceived.

As scholars and reporters visited Carrie Buck and her sister, what a few   20 experts had known all along became abundantly clear to everyone. Carrie Buck was a woman of obviously normal intelligence. For example, Paul A. Lombardo of the School of Law at the University of Virginia, and a leading scholar of *Buck* v. *Bell*, wrote in a letter to me:

> As for Carrie, when I met her she was reading newspapers daily and joining a more literate friend to assist at regular bouts with the crossword puzzles. She was not a sophisticated woman, and lacked social graces, but mental health professionals who examined her in later life confirmed my impressions that she was neither mentally ill nor retarded.

On what evidence, then, was Carrie Buck consigned to the State Colony for Epileptics and Feeble-Minded on January 23, 1924? I have seen the text of her commitment hearing; it is, to say the least, cursory and contradictory. Beyond the bald and undocumented say-so of her foster parents, and her own brief appearance before a commission of two doctors and a justice of the peace, no evidence was presented. Even the crude and early Stanford–Binet test, so fatally flawed as a measure of innate worth (see my book *The Mismeasure of Man*, although the evidence of Carrie's own case suffices) but at least clothed with the aura of quantitative respectability, had not yet been applied.

When we understand why Carrie Buck was committed in January 1924, we can finally comprehend the hidden meaning of her case and its message for us today. The silent key, again as from the first, is her daughter Vivian, born on March 28, 1924, and then but an evident bump on her belly. Carrie Buck was one of several illegitimate children borne by her mother, Emma. She grew up with foster parents, J. T. and Alice Dobbs, and continued to live with them as an adult, helping out with chores around the house. She was raped by a relative of her foster parents, then blamed for the resulting pregnancy. Almost surely, she was (as they used to say) committed to hide her shame (and her rapist's identity), not because enlightened science had just discovered her true mental status. In short, she was sent away to have her baby. Her case never was about mental deficiency; Carrie Buck was persecuted for supposed sexual immorality and social deviance. The annals of her trial and hearing reek with the contempt of the well-off and well-bred for poor people of "loose morals." Who really cared whether Vivian was a baby of normal intelligence; she was the illegitimate child of an illegitimate woman. Two generations of bastards are enough. Harry Laughlin began his "family history" of the Bucks by writing: "These people belong to the shiftless, ignorant and worthless class of anti-social whites of the South."

We know little of Emma Buck and her life, but we have no more reason to suspect her than her daughter Carrie of true mental deficiency. Their supposed deviance was social and sexual; the charge of imbecility was a cover-up, Mr. Justice Holmes notwithstanding.

We come then to the crux of the case, Carrie's daughter, Vivian. What 24 evidence was ever adduced for her mental deficiency? This and only this: At the original trial in late 1924, when Vivian Buck was seven months old, a Miss Wilhelm, social worker for the Red Cross, appeared before the court. She began by stating honestly the true reason for Carrie Buck's commitment:

> Mr. Dobbs, who had charge of the girl, had taken her when a small child, had reported to Miss Duke [the temporary secretary of Public Welfare for Albemarle County] that the girl was pregnant and that he wanted to have her committed somewhere — to have her sent to some institution.

Miss Wilhelm then rendered her judgment of Vivian Buck by comparing her with the normal granddaughter of Mrs. Dobbs, born just three days earlier:

> It is difficult to judge probabilities of a child as young as that, but it seems to me not quite a normal baby. In its appearance — I should say that perhaps my knowledge of the mother may prejudice me in that regard, but I saw the child at the same time as Mrs. Dobbs' daughter's baby, which is only three days older than this one, and there is a very decided difference in the development of the babies. That was about two weeks ago. There is a look about it that is not quite normal, but just what it is, I can't tell.

This short testimony, and nothing else, formed all the evidence for the crucial third generation of imbeciles. Cross-examination revealed that neither Vivian nor the Dobbs grandchild could walk or talk, and that "Mrs. Dobbs' daughter's baby is a very responsive baby. When you play with it or try to attract its attention — it is a baby that you can play with. The other baby is not. It seems very apathetic and not responsive." Miss Wilhelm then urged Carrie Buck's sterilization: "I think," she said, "it would at least prevent the propagation of her kind." Several years later, Miss Wilhelm denied that she had ever examined Vivian or deemed the child feebleminded.

Unfortunately, Vivian died at age eight of "enteric colitis" (as recorded on her death certificate), an ambiguous diagnosis that could mean many things but may well indicate that she fell victim to one of the preventable childhood diseases of poverty (a grim reminder of the real subject in *Buck* v. *Bell*). She is therefore mute as a witness in our reassessment of her famous case.

When *Buck* v. *Bell* resurfaced in 1980, it immediately struck me that Vivian's case was crucial and that evidence for the mental status of a child who died at age eight might best be found in report cards. I have therefore been trying to track down Vivian Buck's school records for the past four years and have finally succeeded. (They were supplied to me by Dr. Paul A. Lombardo, who also sent other documents, including Miss Wilhelm's testimony, and spent several hours answering my questions by mail and Lord knows how much time playing successful detective in re Vivian's school records. I have never met Dr. Lombardo; he did all this work for kindness, collegiality, and love of the game of knowledge, not for expected reward or even requested acknowledgment. In a profession — academics — so often marred by pettiness and silly squabbling over meaningless priorities, this generosity must be recorded and celebrated as a sign of how things can and should be.)

Vivian Buck was adopted by the Dobbs family, who had raised (but later sent away) her mother, Carrie. As Vivian Alice Elaine Dobbs, she attended the Venable Public Elementary School of Charlottesville for four terms, from September 1930 until May 1932, a month before her death. She was a perfectly normal, quite average student, neither particularly outstanding nor much troubled. In those days before grade inflation, when C meant "good, 81–87" (as defined on her report card) rather than barely scraping by, Vivian Dobbs received A's and B's for deportment and C's for all academic subjects but mathematics (which was always difficult for her, and where she scored D) during her first term in Grade 1A, from September 1930 to January 1931. She improved during her second term in 1B, meriting an A in deportment, C in mathematics, and B in all other academic subjects; she was placed on the honor roll in April 1931. Promoted to 2A, she had trouble during the fall term of 1931, failing mathematics and spelling but receiving A in deportment, B in reading, and C in writing and English. She was "retained in 2A" for the next term — or "left back" as we used to say, and scarcely a sign of imbecility as I remember all my buddies who suffered a similar fate. In any case, she again did well in her final term, with B in deportment, reading, and spelling, and C in writing, English, and mathematics during her last month in school. This daughter of "lewd and immoral" women excelled in deportment and performed adequately, although not brilliantly, in her academic subjects.

In short, we can only agree with the conclusion that Dr. Lombardo has reached in his research on *Buck* v. *Bell* — there were no imbeciles, not a one, among the three generations of Bucks. I don't know that such correction of cruel but forgotten errors of history counts for much, but I find it both symbolic and satisfying to learn that forced eugenic sterilization, a procedure of such dubious morality, earned its official justification (and won its most quoted line of rhetoric) on a patent falsehood.

Carrie Buck died last year. By a quirk of fate, and not by memory or design, she was buried just a few steps from her only daughter's grave. In the umpteenth and ultimate verse of a favorite old ballad, a rose and a brier—the sweet and the bitter—emerge from the tombs of Barbara Allen and her lover, twining about each other in the union of death. May Carrie and Vivian, victims in different ways and in the flower of youth, rest together in peace.

● PERSONAL RESPONSE ●

Explain your reaction to the fate of Carrie Buck.

● QUESTIONS FOR DISCUSSION ●

1. How does Gould connect the opening quotation from Exodus to the Carrie Buck case?

2. What connections does Gould draw between the eugenics movement in the United States and the practices carried out in Nazi Germany in the period before World War II?

3. Summarize the circumstances surrounding the *Buck* v. *Bell* case. What were the issues involved in it? What arguments were made in favor of compulsory sterilization? What was it that convinced eight of the Supreme Court justices to uphold the practice, according to the opinion of Oliver Wendell Holmes?

4. Where does Gould allow his own opinions toward the Carrie Buck case to surface? Does that subjectivity add to or detract from his purpose in this essay?

5. What evidence does Gould supply to support his belief that Carrie Buck was the victim of prejudice and shame and that she was not mentally deficient?

6. What evidence does Gould present to demonstrate that Carrie Buck's daughter, Vivian, could not have been mentally deficient?

7. What is the "message for us today" of the Carrie Buck case (paragraph 22)?

● WRITING TOPICS ●

1. Although the case of *Buck* v. *Bell* was decided almost 70 years ago, the issues it raises about the conflict between the rights of individuals and the law are similar to those of some contemporary social problems. Demonstrate connections between the Carrie Buck case and a current social issue such as AIDS, the rights of terminally ill patients to die, or parental consent in the case of teenage abortion.

2. Argue your own position on a contemporary social issue or problem.

3. Trace the series of events that led to a specific action or result, as Gould does with the events that led to the *Buck* v. *Bell* Supreme Court decision.

BARBARA PIERRE

●

WILLIAM LEAST HEAT MOON

William Least Heat Moon earned critical acclaim with the publication of Blue Highways: A Journey into America *(1982), a record of his travels throughout the country on America's back roads and of his conversations with the people he met on that journey (see Chapter 4). In this excerpt from* Blue Highways, *Heat Moon records his conversation with Barbara Pierre, a woman he met in St. Martinville, Louisiana, who provides a provocative viewpoint on prejudice and the status of race relations in our country.*

Because of a broken sealed-beam headlight and Zatarain's Creole Mustard, an excellent native mustard, I met Barbara Pierre. I had just come out of Dugas' grocery with four jars of Zatarain's, and we almost collided on the sidewalk. She said, "You're not from St. Martinville, are you? You can't be."

"I'm from Missouri."

"What in the world are you doing here? Got a little Huck Finn in you?"

"Just followed the bayou. Now I'm looking for the Ford agency."   4

"Coincidences. I work there. I'll show you the way."

She was a secretary at the agency and took classes at the University of Southwestern Louisiana in Lafayette when she could. I asked about St. Martinville, but she had to start working before we could say much.

"Here's an idea," she said. "Come by at noon and we can have lunch at my place. I live in the project on the other side of the bayou."

I picked her up at twelve. She asked about the trip, especially about Selma   8 and how things were as I saw them. "A white man griped about changes, and a black said there weren't enough changes to gripe about."

"That's us too. What we want is slow coming — if it's coming at all. Older blacks here are scared of whites and won't do much for change if it means risk. Others don't care as long as everything gets smothered over with politeness by whites. Young blacks see the hypocrisy — even when it's not there. But too many of them are juked on drugs, and that's where some of this town wants us."

"Don't any whites here try to help?"

"A few, but if a white starts helping too much, they get cut off or shut down by the others and end up paying almost the price we do. Sure, we got good whites — when they're not scared out of showing sympathy."

On Margaret Street, she pointed to her apartment in a small one-story brick 12 building. Standard federal housing. As we went to the door, a shadowy face watched from behind a chintz curtain in another apartment.

"See that? Could be the start of bad news," she said.

"Maybe I should leave. I don't want to cause trouble for you."

"Too late. Besides, I live my own life here. I won't be pushed. But it'll come back in some little way. Smart remark, snub. One old white lady kicks me at the library. Swings her feet under the table because she doesn't want my kind in there. I could break her in two, she's so frail. She'll be kicking like a heifer if she gets wind of this."

Barbara Pierre's apartment was a tidy place but for books on the sofa. "You can see I still use the library even with the nuisances. The kicking bitch hides books I return so I get overdue notices and have to go prove I turned the book in. I explain what's going on, but nothing changes. Simplest thing is trouble."

"That's what I heard in Selma."

"I'm not alone, but sometimes it seems like a conspiracy. Especially in little towns. Gossip and bigotry—that's the blood and guts."

"Was that person who just looked out the window white?"

"Are you crazy? Nobody on this end of Margaret Street is white. That's what I mean about us blacks not working together. Half this town is black, and we've only got one elected black official. Excuse my language, but for all the good he does this side of the bayou, he's one useless black mofo."

"Why don't you do something? I mean you personally."

"I do. And when I do, I get both sides coming down on me. Including my own family. Everywhere I go, sooner or later, I'm in the courtroom. Duplicity! That's my burning pot. I've torn up more than one court of law."

We sat down at her small table. A copy of *Catch-22* lay open.

"Something that happened a few years ago keeps coming back on me. When I was living in Norristown, outside Philadelphia, I gained a lot of weight and went to a doctor. She gave me some diet pills but never explained they were basically speed, and I developed a minor drug problem. I went to the hospital and the nuns said if I didn't sign certain papers they couldn't admit me. So I signed and they put me in a psychiatric ward. Took two hellish weeks to prove I didn't belong there. God, it's easy to get somebody adjudicated crazy."

"Adjudicated?"

"You don't know the word, or you didn't think I knew it?"

"It's the right word. Go on."

"So now, because I tried to lose thirty pounds, people do a job on my personality. But if I shut up long enough, things quiet down. Still, it's the old pattern: any nigger you can't control is crazy."

As we ate our sandwiches and drank Barq's rootbeer, she asked whether I had been through Natchitoches. I said I hadn't.

"They used to have a statue up there on the main street. Called the 'Good Darkie Statue.' It was an old black man, slouched shoulders, big possum-eating smile. Tipping his hat. Few years ago, blacks made them take it down. Whites couldn't understand. Couldn't see the duplicity in that statue—duplicity on *both* sides. God almighty! I'll promise them one thing: ain't gonna be no more gentle darkies croonin' down on the levee."

I smiled at her mammy imitation, but she shook her head. "In the sixties I wanted that statue blown to bits. It's stored in Baton Rouge now at LSU, but they put it in the wrong building. Ought to be in the capitol reminding people. Preserve it so nobody forgets. Forgives, okay—but not forgets."

"Were things bad when you were a child?" 32

"Strange thing. I was born here in 'forty-one and grew up here, but I don't remember prejudice. My childhood was warm and happy—especially when I was reading. Maybe I was too young to see. I don't know. I go on about the town, but I love it. I've put my time in the cities—New Orleans, Philly. Your worst Southern cracker is better than a Northern liberal, when it comes to duplicity anyway, because you know right off where the cracker crumbles. With a Northerner, you don't know until it counts, and that's when you get a job done on yourself."

"I'd rather see a person shut up about his prejudices."

"You haven't been deceived. Take my job. I was pleased to get it. Thought it was a breakthrough for me and other blacks here. Been there three weeks, and next Wednesday is my last day."

"What happened?" 36

"Duplicity's what happened. White man in the shop developed a bad back, so they moved him inside. His seniority gets my job. I see the plot—somebody in the company got pressured to get rid of me."

"Are you going to leave town?"

"I'm staying. That's my point. I'll take St. Martinville over what I've seen of other places. I'm staying here to build a life for myself and my son. I'll get married again. Put things together." She got up and went to the window. "I don't know, maybe I'm too hard on the town. In an underhanded way, things work here—mostly because old blacks know how to get along with whites. So they're good darkies? They own their own homes. They don't live in a rat-ass ghetto. There's contentment. Roots versus disorder." She stopped abruptly and smiled. "Even German soldiers they put in the POW camp here to work the cane fields wanted to stay on."

We cleared the table and went to the front room. A wall plaque: 40

OH LORD, HELP ME THIS DAY
TO KEEP MY BIG MOUTH SHUT.

On a bookshelf by the window was the two-volume microprint edition of the *Oxford English Dictionary*, the one sold with a magnifying glass.

"I love it," she said. "Book-of-the-Month Club special. Seventeen-fifty. Haven't finished paying for it though."

"Is it the only one in town?"

"Doubt it. We got brains here. After the aristocracy left Paris during the French Revolution, a lot of them settled in St. Martinville, and we got known as *Le Petit Paris*. Can you believe this little place was a cultural center only second to New Orleans? Town started slipping when the railroad put the bayou steamers out of business, but the church is proof of what we had."

"When you finish the college courses, what then?" 44

"I'd like to teach elementary school. If I can't teach, I want to be a teacher's aide. But—here's a big 'but'—if I can make a living, I'll write books for children. We need black women writing, and my courses are in journalism and French. Whatever happens, I hope they don't waste my intelligence."

She went to wash up. I pulled out one of her books: *El Señor Presidente* by Guatemalan novelist Miguel Asturias. At page eighty-five she had underlined two sentences: "The chief thing is to gain time. We must be patient."

On the way back to the agency, she said, "I'll tell you something that took me a long time to figure out—but I know how to end race problems."

"Is this a joke?"   48

"Might as well be. Find a way to make people get bored with hating instead of helping. Simple." She laughed. "That's what it boils down to."

● PERSONAL RESPONSE ●

How are attitudes toward minorities in your hometown similar to or different from the attitudes Barbara Pierre attributes to the people of St. Martinville?

● QUESTIONS FOR DISCUSSION ●

1. Why do you think Heat Moon devotes a section of his book, *Blue Highways*, to Barbara Pierre? That is, what do you think it is about her that reveals something of the American character?

2. What are race relations like in St. Martinville, according to Pierre?

3. What does Pierre mean by the word "duplicity"? How does the "Good Darkie statue" in Natchitoches illustrate what she means by that word? Where else does she illustrate what the word means?

4. Why do you think Heat Moon comments on Pierre's use of the word "adjudicated"?

5. What does Pierre mean by her comparison of "Southern cracker" and "Northern liberal" (paragraph 33)?

6. Notice the details of Pierre's apartment that Heat Moon selects to include in his account of their conversation. What does each of the following reveal about Barbara Pierre: *Catch-22* (paragraph 23), the wall plaque (paragraph 40), the *Oxford English Dictionary* (paragraph 40), and *El Señor Presidente* (paragraph 46)?

7. What do you think Pierre means by "roots versus disorder" (paragraph 39)?

8. Explain what you understand Pierre to mean by her solution to end race problems (paragraph 49).

● WRITING TOPICS ●

1. Narrate a personal experience you have had as the victim of prejudice for any reason — your sex, your class, your race, your status as student, or your difference from others around you.

2. Characterize your hometown or a particular neighborhood on the basis of its acceptance or rejection of cultural, ethnic, or racial diversity.

3. Interview someone you know on the subject of prejudice. Then write an essay about the interview in which you rely on dialogue and careful selection of detail to convey both the personality and the experiences of the person you interviewed.

I BECAME HER TARGET

●

ROGER WILKINS

Roger Wilkins is a senior fellow at the Institute for Policy Studies in Washington, D.C., and chairperson of the Pulitzer Prize Board. In the following essay, which first appeared in Newsday *in 1987, Wilkins narrates how his eighth-grade history teacher not only helped him gain self-confidence but also, in one memorable incident, broke down the barriers between him and his classmates that had been created by ignorance and stereotypes.*

My favorite teacher's name was "Dead-Eye" Bean. Her real name was Dorothy. She taught American history to eighth graders in the junior high section of Creston, the high school that served the north end of Grand Rapids, Mich. It was the fall of 1944. Franklin D. Roosevelt was president; American troops were battling their way across France; Joe DiMaggio was still in the service; the Montgomery bus boycott was more than a decade away, and I was a 12-year-old black newcomer in a school that was otherwise all white.

My mother, who had been a widow in New York, had married my stepfather, a Grand Rapids physician, the year before, and he had bought the best house he could afford for his new family. The problem for our new neighbors was that their neighborhood had previously been pristine (in their terms) and they were ignorant about black people. The prevailing wisdom in the neighborhood was that we were spoiling it and that we ought to go back where we belonged (or alternatively, ought not intrude where we were not wanted). There was a lot of angry talk among the adults, but nothing much came of it.

But some of the kids, those first few weeks, were quite nasty. They threw stones at me, chased me home when I was on foot and spat on my bike seat when I was in class. For a time, I was a pretty lonely, friendless and sometimes frightened kid. I was just transplanted from Harlem, and here in Grand Rapids, the dominant culture was speaking to me insistently.

I can see now that those youngsters were bullying and culturally disadvan-   4
taged. I knew then that they were bigoted, but the culture spoke to me more powerfully than my mind and I felt ashamed for being different—a nonstandard person.

I now know that Dorothy Bean understood most of that and deplored it. So things began to change when I walked into her classroom. She was a pleasant-looking single woman, who looked old and wrinkled to me at the time, but who was probably about 40.

Whereas my other teachers approached the problem of easing in their new black pupil by ignoring him for the first few weeks, Miss Bean went right at me.

On the morning after having read our first assignment, she asked me the first question. I later came to know that in Grand Rapids, she was viewed as a very liberal person who believed, among other things, that Negroes were equal.

I gulped and answered her question and the follow-up. They weren't brilliant answers, but they did establish the facts that I had read the assignment and that I could speak English. Later in the hour, when one of my classmates had bungled an answer, Miss Bean came back to me with a question that required me to clean up the girl's mess and established me as a smart person.

Thus, the teacher began to give me human dimensions, though not perfect ones for an eighth grader. It was somewhat better to be an incipient teachers' pet than merely a dark presence in the back of the room onto whose silent form my classmates could fit all the stereotypes they carried in their heads.

A few days later, Miss Bean became the first teacher ever to require me to think. She asked my opinion about something Jefferson had done. In those days, all my opinions were derivative. I was for Roosevelt because my parents were and I was for the Yankees because my older buddy from Harlem was a Yankee fan. Besides, we didn't have opinions about historical figures like Jefferson. Like our high school building or old Mayor Welch, he just was.

After I had stared at her for a few seconds, she said: "Well, should he have bought Louisiana or not?"

"I guess so," I replied tentatively.

"Why?" she shot back.

Why! What kind of question was that, I groused silently. But I ventured an answer. Day after day, she kept doing that to me, and my answers became stronger and more confident. She was the first teacher to give me the sense that thinking was part of education and that I could form opinions that had some value.

Her final service to me came on a day when my mind was wandering and I was idly digging my pencil into the writing surface on the arm of my chair. Miss Bean impulsively threw a hunk of gum eraser at me. By amazing chance, it hit my hand and sent the pencil flying. She gasped, and I crept mortified after my pencil as the class roared. That was the ice breaker.

Afterward, kids came up to me to laugh about "Old Dead-Eye Bean." The incident became a legend, and I, a part of that story, became a person to talk to.

So that's how I became just another kid in school and Dorothy Bean became "Old Dead-Eye."

● PERSONAL RESPONSE ●

To what extent do you agree with Wilkins that prejudice comes in part from the stereotypes children are taught? Who teaches children stereotypes? What can be done to prevent or undo stereotyping?

● QUESTIONS FOR DISCUSSION ●

1. What does Wilkins imply is the connection between prejudice and ignorance?
2. What purpose is served by the references to Franklin D. Roosevelt, Joe DiMaggio, and the Montgomery bus boycott (paragraph 1)?
3. Wilkins narrates the events leading up to the incident of the eraser throwing in chronological order, but he also includes his perception of those events as an adult. Where does he shift to his adult perception? What purpose is served by doing so?
4. Explain what Wilkins means when he writes that "the dominant culture was speaking to me insistently" (paragraph 3). What effect did that insistent "speaking" have on the young Wilkins?
5. What does Wilkins mean when he says that the youngsters who bullied him were "culturally disadvantaged" (paragraph 4)?
6. In what ways did Dorothy Bean give Wilkins "human dimensions" (paragraph 8)? What were those dimensions?
7. Why does Wilkins call the eraser-throwing incident Miss Bean's "final service" (paragraph 14) to him?

● WRITING TOPICS ●

1. Explain how a teacher influenced you to see yourself differently, gain self-confidence, or solve difficulties you were having.
2. Narrate an incident from your childhood in which other children were cruel or bullying to you, including your perception of the incident at the time and your perception of the incident now. Can you account for the other children's treatment of you? Do you feel differently about it now, looking back from the perspective of adulthood?
3. Read Alice Walker's essay "Beauty: When the Other Dancer Is the Self" in Chapter 6 and then compare her essay with Wilkins' essay. How are the two essays similar? How do they differ?

HOW IT FEELS TO BE COLORED ME

●

ZORA NEALE HURSTON

Zora Neale Hurston (1903–1960) was born in the small all-black town of Eatonville, Florida, and educated at Howard University, Barnard College, and Columbia University. Barnard's only black student, she received a degree in anthropology in 1928. After gathering material in her hometown of Eatonville, Hurston edited a collection of black folklore, Mules and Men *(1935). She went on to write short stories, drama, essays and novels, of which* Their Eyes Were Watching God *(1937) is perhaps her best known. Her autobiography,* Dust Tracks on a Road, *was published in 1942. "How It Feels to Be Colored Me," published in* The World Tomorrow *in 1928 and written with the zest and indomitable spirit of the young Hurston, is a powerful tribute to her sense of cosmic importance and her refusal to accept prejudice and concepts of racial superiority or inferiority.*

I am colored but I offer nothing in the way of extenuating circumstances except the fact that I am the only Negro in the United States whose grandfather on the mother's side was *not* an Indian chief.

I remember the very day that I became colored. Up to my thirteenth year I lived in the little Negro town of Eatonville, Florida. It is exclusively a colored town. The only white people I knew passed through the town going to or coming from Orlando. The native whites rode dusty horses, the Northern tourists chugged down the sandy village road in automobiles. The town knew the Southerners and never stopped cane chewing when they passed. But the Northerners were something else again. They were peered at cautiously from behind curtains by the timid. The more venturesome would come out on the porch to watch them go past and got just as much pleasure out of the tourists as the tourists got out of the village.

The front porch might seem a daring place for the rest of the town, but it was a gallery seat for me. My favorite place was atop the gate-post. Proscenium box for a born first-nighter. Not only did I enjoy the show, but I didn't mind the actors knowing that I liked it. I usually spoke to them in passing. I'd wave at them and when they returned my salute, I would say something like this: "Howdy-do-well-I-thank-you-where-you-goin'?" Usually automobile or the horse paused at this, and after a queer exchange of compliments, I would probably "go a piece of the way" with them, as we say in farthest Florida. If one of my family happened to come to the front in time to see me, of course negotiations would be rudely broken off. But even so, it is clear that I was the first "welcome-to-our-state" Floridian, and I hope the Miami Chamber of Commerce will please take notice.

During this period, white people differed from colored to me only in that they rode through town and never lived there. They liked to hear me "speak 4 pieces" and sing and wanted to see me dance the parse-me-la, and gave me generously of their small silver for doing these things, which seemed strange to me for I wanted to do them so much that I needed bribing to stop. Only they didn't know it. The colored people gave no dimes. They deplored any joyful tendencies in me, but I was their Zora nevertheless. I belonged to them, to the nearby hotels, to the county — everybody's Zora.

But changes came in the family when I was thirteen, and I was sent to school in Jacksonville. I left Eatonville, the town of the oleanders, as Zora. When I disembarked from the river-boat at Jacksonville, she was no more. It seemed that I had suffered a sea change. I was not Zora of Orange County any more. I was now a little colored girl. I found it out in certain ways. In my heart as well as in the mirror, I became a fast brown — warranted not to rub nor run.

But I am not tragically colored. There is no great sorrow dammed up in my soul, nor lurking behind my eyes. I do not mind at all. I do not belong to the sobbing school of Negrohood who hold that nature somehow has given them a lowdown dirty deal and whose feelings are all hurt about it. Even in the helter-skelter skirmish that is my life, I have seen that the world is to the strong regardless of a little pigmentation more or less. No, I do not weep at the world — I am too busy sharpening my oyster knife.

Someone is always at my elbow reminding me that I am the granddaughter of slaves. It fails to register depression with me. Slavery is sixty years in the past. The operation was successful and the patient is doing well, thank you. The terrible struggle that made me an American out of a potential slave said, "On the line!" The Reconstruction said "Get set!"; and the generation before said "Go!" I am off to a flying start and I must not halt in the stretch to look behind and weep. Slavery is the price I paid for civilization, and the choice was not with me. It is a bully adventure and worth all that I have paid through my ancestors for it. No one on earth ever had a greater chance for glory. The world to be won and nothing to be lost. It is thrilling to think — to know that for any act of mine, I shall get twice as much praise or twice as much blame. It is quite exciting to hold the center of the national stage, with the spectators not knowing whether to laugh or to weep.

The position of my white neighbor is much more difficult. No brown specter pulls up a chair beside me when I sit down to eat. No dark ghost thrusts its leg against mine in bed. The game of keeping what one has is never so exciting as the game of getting. ⁸

I do not always feel colored. Even now I often achieve the unconscious Zora of Eatonville before the Hegira. I feel most colored when I am thrown against a sharp white background.

For instance at Barnard. "Beside the waters of the Hudson" I feel my race. Among the thousand white persons, I am a dark rock surged upon, and overswept, but through it all, I remain myself. When covered by the waters, I am; and the ebb but reveals me again.

Sometimes it is the other way around. A white person is set down in our midst, but the contrast is just as sharp for me. For instance, when I sit in the drafty basement that is The New World Cabaret with a white person, my color comes. We enter chatting about any little nothing that we have in common and are seated by the jazz waiters. In the abrupt way that jazz orchestras have, this one plunges into a number. It loses no time in circumlocutions, but gets right down to business. It constricts the thorax and splits the heart with its tempo and narcotic harmonies. This orchestra grows rambunctious, rears on its hind legs and attacks the tonal veil with primitive fury, rending it, clawing it until it breaks through to the jungle beyond. I follow those heathen — follow them exultingly. I dance wildly inside myself; I yell within, I whoop; I shake my assegai above my head, I hurl it true to the mark *yeeeeooww!* I am in the jungle and living in the jungle way. My face is painted red and yellow and my body is painted blue. My pulse is throbbing like a war drum. I want to slaughter something — give pain, give death to what, I do not know. But the piece ends. The men of the orchestra wipe their lips and rest their fingers. I creep back slowly to the veneer we call civilization with the last tone and find the white friend sitting motionless in his seat, smoking calmly.

"Good music they have here," he remarks, drumming the table with his 12 fingertips.

Music. The great blobs of purple and red emotion have not touched him. He has only heard what I felt. He is far away and I see him but dimly across the ocean and the continent that have fallen between us. He is so pale with his whiteness then and I am *so* colored.

At certain times I have no race, I am *me*. When I set my hat at a certain angle and saunter down Seventh Avenue, Harlem City, feeling as snooty as the lions in front of the Forty-Second Street Library, for instance. So far as my feelings are concerned, Peggy Hopkins Joyce on the Boule Mich with her gorgeous raiment, stately carriage, knees knocking together in a most aristocratic manner, has nothing on me. The cosmic Zora emerges. I belong to no race nor time. I am the eternal feminine with its string of beads.

I have no separate feeling about being an American citizen and colored. I am merely a fragment of the Great Soul that surges within the boundaries. My country, right or wrong.

Sometimes, I feel discriminated against, but it does not make me angry. It 16 merely astonishes me. How *can* any deny themselves the pleasure of my company? It's beyond me.

But in the main, I feel like a brown bag of miscellany propped against a wall. Against a wall in company with other bags, white, red and yellow. Pour out the contents, and there is discovered a jumble of small things priceless and worthless. A first-water diamond, an empty spool, bits of broken glass, lengths of string, a key to a door long since crumbled away, a rusty knife-blade, old shoes saved for a road that never was and never will be, a nail bent under the weight of things too heavy for any nail, a dried flower or two still a little fragrant. In your hand is the brown bag. On the ground before you is the jumble it held — so much like the jumble in the bags, could they be emptied, that all might be dumped in a single heap and the bags refilled without altering the content of any greatly. A bit of colored glass more or less would not matter. Perhaps that is how the Great Stuffer of Bags filled them in the first place — who knows?

● PERSONAL RESPONSE ●

How do you feel about Hurston's assessment of being black in white America? What is your reaction to her comment that "the game of keeping what one has is never so exciting as the game of getting" (paragraph 8)?

● QUESTIONS FOR DISCUSSION ●

1. In one word, characterize Hurston's tone in this essay and then, for class discussion, see how many of your classmates came up with the same or a synonymous word. What passages in particular express this tone?

2. Why do you think Hurston does not tell the details about how she "became colored" on her trip from Eatonville to Jacksonville? Why are the details of that trip not important to the purpose of her essay?

3. Hurston makes liberal use of vivid similes and metaphors, beginning in paragraph 3 with the theater metaphor and ending with the extended comparison of humans to variously colored bags. What does Hurston mean in paragraph 6 when she says she is "busy sharpening [her] oyster knife"? Find other comparisons that you believe are particularly expressive and explain their meanings.

4. Hurston makes some references to people, things, and events that she assumes her readers will recognize. Because the essay was written in 1928, however, you may not know that Peggy Hopkins Joyce (paragraph 14) was an American beauty and fashion-setter of the 1920s. The Boule Mich (paragraph 14) is the Boulevard Saint-Michel, a fashionable street in Paris, and an assegai (paragraph 11) is a light spear used by tribesmen in southern Africa. What are "the terrible struggle" and the "Reconstruction" Hurston refers to in paragraph 7? What is the Hegira (paragraph 9)?

5. Explain what Hurston means in paragraph 8 when she says that her white neighbor is in a worse position than she is.

6. What does Hurston mean when she refers to herself as "the Cosmic Zora" (paragraph 14)?

7. How important does Hurston think skin color is?

8. What does Hurston believe is truly important about each human being?

● WRITING TOPICS ●

1. If you can remember a single event or time when you became aware of some aspect of yourself that you had not previously realized, narrate an account of what happened and describe how your view of yourself changed.

2. Write an essay addressed to Zora Neale Hurston in which you explain to her what race relations are like in our country now.

3. Read Richard Rodriguez's "Complexion" in this chapter and compare and/or contrast that essay with this one in terms of the writers' attitudes toward skin color, the importance they place on it, how they view its effect on people's lives, and any other points you wish to consider.

CONFRONTING PREJUDICE

—————————————— • ——————————————

ADDITIONAL WRITING SUGGESTIONS

1. Define prejudice by using specific examples or illustrations to dramatize its meaning.

2. Narrate an experience in which you were very much aware of your difference—in skin color, political beliefs, religious beliefs, or some other noticeable way—from others around you. Explain the situation, how you differed from others, and how you felt about the experience.

3. Narrate a personal experience with being the victim of name-calling or other verbal abuse. What were the circumstances of the incident? How did you respond to it? How did you feel afterwards?

4. Explore why some people hold prejudices against other people whose skin color, religion, nationality, or the like is different from their own.

5. Interview people who lived through the 1950s and 1960s about what they remember of segregation and the civil-rights movement and write an essay reporting what you learn.

6. Explore the question of whether or not segregation is a thing of the past, taking into consideration other kinds of prejudice besides racial. See, for instance, Richard Goldstein's essay "AIDS and the Social Contract" in Chapter 6.

7. Show the effects of one kind of prejudice—racial, religious, sexual, or the like—on a person or a group of people.

8

REPRESSION

AND

FREEDOM

THE LOST GENERATION

●

DORINDA ELLIOTT

Dorinda Elliott is Beijing bureau chief for Newsweek. *In the following article, published in* The New Republic *in April 1990, Elliott reports on the ways in which China's college and university students manage to keep their prodemocracy spirit alive despite government repression.*

The pseudonym he chooses is George—for George Bush, whom he thanks for preserving Sino–U.S. relations. Unlike Chinese students in the United States, many Beijing students worry that noisy U.S. protests against China's repressive policies could backfire, perhaps leading to a ban on overseas studies. George, a graduate student at China's Technology University, is a product of Deng Xiaoping's open-door policy. He likes to wear a Princeton T-shirt that an American friend gave him. He prefers the Beatles and Hemingway to *The East Is Red* and the works of Mao. George's hope in life is to go to the United States to study.

Last spring, when thousands of students started marching to Tiananmen Square, George thought there was little hope for a successful popular rebellion. But by May 4, the seventieth anniversary of China's first democracy protests, he was swept up by the huge numbers. Wearing his Princeton T-shirt, he sat with his classmates singing Russian revolutionary songs. His department's Party leader even joined in. There was an exhilarating sense that through the people's sheer willpower, China might really become a more open and democratic country.

After Tiananmen Square, George, like other students, wrote a report supporting the crackdown for his school's Communist Party leaders. "It made me sick," he says, "but I had to do it." One of his classmates was crushed by an armored personnel carrier. Another was just released from the hospital after recovering from a gunshot wound. But nobody mentions that night to him, or asks about his experiences. "What's the point in getting things stirred up?" says George. "We've learned no student movement means anything here."

With the help of a propaganda book called *56 Terrifying Days*, each student 4 wrote a required account of his activities for each day of the movement. Students were given three chances to report everything they did; if the third version was still unacceptable, they would get black marks in their Party files. Those files, called "*dangan*," follow citizens for life: black marks mean a bad job, even possible banishment to farflung, undeveloped parts of the country after graduation. But unlike former political campaigns, this time nobody rats on friends; nobody even mentions that their Party leader was in the square. He stands at the front of the classroom praising the students for their restraint. "Nobody went to the square," he says. "Your attitude was correct."

The authorities have imposed a mind-numbing program of political indoctrination. On top of the usual required heavy dose of politics — including history of the Communist Party, Marxist philosophy, history of the Chinese revolution — the weekly political study session includes lectures and small group discussions on the "quelling of the counterrevolutionary rebellion." In recent years, as Deng policies stressed pragmatism and economic efficiency, politics courses had become less and less important. Now students must score well in them if they want to get assigned good jobs by the state.

Though students are forced to publicly renounce the movement, they find ways of resisting. When George's department Party chief showed students a propaganda movie about the Nationalist era, students hooted and cheered when Chiang Kai-shek, supposed to represent the epitome of evil, conceded to a dialogue with demonstrating students, then used only water cannon to disperse the crowd. Qinghua University, China's most prestigious science institute, also showed students propaganda films with the hope of inculcating a bit of the spirit of hard work and plain living that the Communist revolutionaries lived by in the Yanan guerrilla base some fifty years ago. Instead, the students started cheering when a Nationalist soldier in one old film began beating a Communist agent.

In discussion groups each student is expected to explain why the government was right to smash the student movement. To avoid having to speak, one group of students at Beijing University cleverly asked the blue Mao-suited Party cadre running the discussion to reread the speech being discussed — so they could catch each important point, they said. But most students play the game, mouthing the lines they read in *People's Daily.* "We have to speak," says Xiao Zhang (a pseudonym). "Otherwise the leaders will say we have ghosts in our hearts — that there's something wrong with our thinking."

Xiao Zhang and his classmates endure a bleak nightly routine. Wearing five or six layers of clothing, they trudge across campus through biting winter winds to study in a bare, unheated classroom. By nine they return to their dorm rooms, off an unlit hallway. Their cluttered, filthy concrete cubicles are just big enough for four bunk beds and a table. Cigarette butts and squashed food litter the floor. At 10:30 students receive a fifteen-minute warning; clutching tin pails, they rush to wash their faces and feet. Because there is no hot water in the dorm, it's far too cold to take showers every day. At 10:45 authorities pull the switch. There is no more electricity in the building for the night.

But students don't accept authority as readily as they once did. "Lights out is when the dorms come to life," says Xiao Zhang. "Everyone pulls out their shortwave radios and the rooms buzz with talk of the latest changes in Eastern Europe." When Voice of America reported that Nicolae Ceausescu had fallen, he and his friends threw bottles out their windows in celebration. It was a bold act. Since the words for little bottle, "*xiao ping,*" are a homonym for Deng Xiaoping's name, the message was clear to all who heard the glass tinkling on the frozen ground outside. The university's Party leaders subsequently posted warnings in dorms that announced: "Anybody who breaks bottles will be dealt with severely."

Eastern Europe has provided a spark of hope for China's demoralized students. But nervous campus authorities have stepped up surveillance, and students know that tens of thousands of troops are still poised at the edge of the city. Late last year three students at Qinghua University killed themselves, jumping out the windows of their dorm buildings. Two others have tried. Terrified that the deaths might stir up protests again, university authorities quickly spread the word that the suicides were love-related. But one student chose October 1, China's National Day, to jump, suggesting he had a desperate political message to deliver. Xiao Zhang says glumly, "It will be ten years before we can have any freedom again. I have no real hope anymore."

Beijing University, the traditional heart of China's democracy movement, has been labeled a "disaster area" by Party leaders because of the deep-seated resistance to Party propaganda. Following Ceausescu's downfall, students posted a handscrawled "big-character poster," or *dazibao,* describing him as a lost dog looking for the other three dogs named after China's top leaders. "If anybody finds these dogs," the sarcastic poster said, "please call 890634." The number represented the date of the June massacre. The university's president was replaced by a conservative economist, Wu Shuqing, who led a witch-hunt to root out rebellious students and, more important, teachers who had participated in the movement.

One young teacher, who calls herself Susan to avoid identification on the phone, was under investigation for some eight months after June. At irregular intervals, she was called in to sit across the table from three teachers from her department, all Party members, answering their stern questions as if she were a criminal. At first she denied that she had participated in pro-democracy ac- tivities — until one day one of her questioners produced evidence the she had attended a meeting of young teachers supporting the students. "We cannot protect you," the teacher said angrily. "If you confess, the Party will be lenient." Her worst "crime," she assumes, was talking occasionally to foreigners about what she saw on campus. In China, that could be called treason. So far Susan has not been punished; but she worries that authorities are watching her carefully and that she still could be fired. 12

A new educational policy is restricting study in the West. The State Educa- tion Commission in February issued a regulation requiring graduates to "serve the country" for five years before being allowed to study overseas. Universities last year began sharply limiting the number of students who could take the TOEFL English proficiency test needed to enter most U.S. schools. This year George's school announced that graduate students cannot take it at all unless they have relatives overseas. To discourage students from wasting days lining up for the limited chances to take the test, Qinghua University officials didn't announce the place of registration. Panicked students lined up anyway in random spots around the university. The final announcement sparked a chaotic stampede from all over campus. One of the students who recently jumped to his death carried a notebook with the words "TOEFL, TOEFL, TOEFL. CONFI- DENCE, CONFIDENCE, CONFIDENCE" etched on the cover.

● PERSONAL RESPONSE ●

How do you think you would react to living in an environment as repressive as that of the Chinese students Elliott writes about?

● QUESTIONS FOR DISCUSSION ●

1. Why do you think Elliott focuses on the student George in her opening paragraphs? Where else does she use the example of specific individuals? What is gained by using extended examples of a few people in an essay that is about almost all students and teachers in Chinese colleges and universities?

2. What details are especially effective in conveying the sharp contrast between the exhilaration of students during the spring rallies with the atmosphere in their schools after the rebellion?

3. In paragraph 8, Elliott gives many details to make vivid the "bleak nightly routine" of students. Where else does Elliott provide concrete details to develop or illustrate general statements?

4. What were the effects on Chinese students of the crushed prodemocracy student rebellion?

5. In what ways have students in China continued to express their rebellion?

6. Explain the title of this essay. In what way(s) are these students members of "the lost generation"?

● WRITING TOPICS ●

1. Narrate an incident in which you and/or your friends rebelled against authority.

2. Using your own experience, contrast life as an American college student with life as a student as Elliott describes it.

3. Identify what you believe were restrictions on your freedom in high school or which you see as restrictions now in your college or university.

TEN-DAY WONDER

●

Thomas Omestad

Thomas Omestad is an associate editor of Foreign Policy. *During the November 1989 protests in Czechoslovakia, he met with opposition and government leaders in Prague. The essay below, published in the December 1989 issue of* The New Republic, *is Omestad's analysis of how the dissidents were able to turn their marginal protest movement into an enormous mass movement. In just ten days, antigovernment factions accomplished what they had been trying to do for decades, bring down Czechoslovakia's oppressive Communist government.*

The enormous mass movement that has essentially overthrown Czechoslovak communism rose up with amazing speed. By the last week in November millions of people had participated in demonstrations across the country. Yet as recently as October 28 — Czechoslovakia's independence day — dissidents could bring only 10,000 people into the streets. These brave souls had scarcely unfurled their pro-democracy banners before truncheon-wielding police were chasing them through Prague's winding Gothic lanes. Three weeks later throngs of hundreds of thousands of people were routine in Wenceslas Square. In a matter of days they brought down the Communist leadership and dispatched the Party toward permanent oblivion.

The long-suffering dissident community deserves much of the credit for the dramatic turnaround. But news reports have largely overlooked the role played by the students. Hundreds of students from Charles University and other Prague colleges were clubbed by police at a November 17 march marking the 50th anniversary of the Nazi murder of Czech student demonstrators in 1939. The regime's decision to knock heads was a monumental blunder. Milos Jakes, the Communist Party boss, hoped it would frighten the students back into apathy. But the dramatic liberalizations in the Soviet Union, Poland, Hungary, and especially East Germany had primed the Czechoslovak public for rapid change, as had hints of intensifying Soviet pressure on the hard-line Czechoslovak regime to reform. The zeal with which security forces bloodied unarmed students shocked Czechoslovaks more than any other event since Soviet tanks rolled over the Prague Spring reforms 21 years ago. It shattered the passivity that had long frustrated dissident organizers. "This is the start of the finish of this government," one man shouted prophetically during the violence.

The awful parallel between the regime's violence against student demonstrators and that of the Nazis exactly 50 years earlier created an immensely powerful emotional rallying point. The next day young Praguers were mobilizing for a student strike, calling for mass protests and a nationwide work stoppage, and fanning out across the capital with handbills. It was the students who finally cast off the legacy of timidity and fear left by the Prague Spring, and who bridged the considerable gap dividing oppositionists from the public.

The snap founding of Civic Forum, the new umbrella opposition group, just two days after the police beatings signaled clearly that members of the disparate activist community had at last pulled together. They had emerged from a period of soul-searching over strategy with a will to seize the moment and an unsuspected mastery of coalition politics. "Now it isn't a small, foolish group of so-called dissidents," said Civic Forum's leader, Vaclav Havel. "We are at the time of a real beginning of a real opposition movement in this country."

From then on Civic Forum rode a tidal wave of popular discontent. In little more than a week, the democracy movement was transformed from a motley band of dissidents into an organized opposition — and more. "We're no longer the opposition," Michael Horacek, a spokesman, proclaimed during the stunningly successful general strike on November 27. "They [the Communists] are the opposition." In a region where history, seemingly frozen for four decades, now moves with unnatural rapidity, the evolution of the Czechoslovak opposition movement has broken all records. In ten days it achieved what Poland's Solidarity took nine years to extract: a commitment by Communists accustomed to jailing their critics to abandon the Party's monopoly on power.

When the wave of protests hit on November 17, activists were mulling over their past and future. Their principal achievement, as veteran dissident Jiri Dienstbier said, had been preserving the moral will to resist: "We are passing a small candle through the darkness." The movement's major failing had been its inability to spark protests across Czechoslovak society. The massive demonstrations in East Germany seemed to cause only ripples in Czechoslovakia. As long as the "socialist certainties" of sausage and beer remained in ample supply, the conventional analysis held, the complacent Czechs and Slovaks would not join their East German neighbors in the streets. "In my opinion this society is completely destroyed," Ivan Lamper, an editor of a samizdat political magazine, lamented to me before the first mass rallies. "People want democracy but they don't want to pay for it." Dissidents bemoaned the lack of a central opposition organization and of an alternative political program. And they didn't seem to be closing the gap between the largely Prague-based intelligentsia, which guides the opposition, and the rest of Czechoslovakia's 15 million people. Many of Solidarity's leaders built their legitimacy as representatives through years of close contact with the masses. But the writers, artists, actors, and journalists of Czechoslovakia's opposition functioned mainly as a moral beacon for a demoralized society. As practical politicians, they were a bit inept.

Of course, marginalizing the opposition had been precisely the aim of the government's relentless campaign of harassment, jailings, and surveillance. It usually refused to acknowledge the opposition's existence. When it did, the dissidents were branded as creations of the Western media and human rights groups. Members of the Communist Party who had joined en masse to participate in the Prague Spring reforms had been purged en masse after the 1968 Warsaw Pact invasion. They and other oppositionists who emerged later found themselves stoking coal, cleaning latrines, and the like. Their children encountered mysterious difficulties getting admitted to college. Their telephones and apartments were bugged. They lived under the constant threat of interrogation, searches, and jail. Police were assigned to them like case workers. Fear of such punishments limited the number of Czechoslovaks willing to join up with the intellectuals. Not surprisingly, the independent groups had to concentrate more on mere survival than on developing a political program.

Both the problems and the strengths of the opposition were exemplified by Havel, the country's best-known dissident. A slight, soft-spoken playwright of enormous personal courage, Havel spent five years in prison, where he nearly died of illness. His plays have been banned in Czechoslovakia. His prominence as an artist and his persistence against the state made him the symbol of dissent. Yet all along Havel was more a spokesman of conscience than a potential political leader. "I do not intend to take for myself the role of professional politician. I have never had that ambition," he said even as Civic Forum was formed. Some of Havel's fellow dissidents, though not questioning his pre-eminence in the movement, have pushed him to act boldly. They criticized him sharply for advising the country's young people to avoid a pro-democracy rally in August after the government hinted that it could turn into another Tiananmen Square massacre. "Vaclav Havel is a man of good heart, a humanitarian," Petra Uhl, a prominent and often-jailed dissident, told the *Washington Post* two months later. "The problem is he does not support any concrete political program. He is an intellectual to such a high degree that I don't think he will be able to pursue one."

Through the mid-1980s the sole preserve of open opposition was Charter 77, the renowned human rights manifesto signed by Havel and hundreds of others. The candle was being kept aflame, but just barely. But in the last two years the arrival of a younger generation of students and workers began recharging the movement. Free of their elders' defeatism, they acted out of frustration with the authorities' refusal to accept Gorbachev-era freedoms. They rejected the unwritten social compact by which the Communists filled store shelves in exchange for sullen acceptance of the regime's stifling orthodoxy. The new generation coalesced in more than 30 new groups and began to link up with the older dissidents. A group called the Czech Children, made up of activists in their 20s, joined in demonstrations for political freedoms and environmental protection. The John Lennon Peace Club grew out of an informal group advocating independent cultural activity and respect for human rights. And the pranksterish Society for a Merrier Present, armed with truncheons made of cucumbers and salami, staged mock police assaults on demonstrators in Prague. Some of the merry policemen later ate their truncheons.

Independent activism spread in other directions. Widely circulated petitions called for the release of jailed dissidents and an open discussion of 1968. Demand grew for samizdat publications. Thousands of Slovaks flocked to Catholic pilgrimages with anti-Communist undertones. Former associates of Alexander Dubček, the ousted father of the Prague Spring's "socialism with a human face," formed Obroda, a self-described "club for socialist restructuring." Dubček himself emerged from his partly self-imposed isolation as a low-level

8

forestry bureaucrat in Bratislava, calling for a Czechoslovak *perestroika* in interviews with foreign newspapers, on Leningrad TV, and on the Voice of America.

Finally, Havel became the publicly recognized leader of the opposition. Intent on making an example of him, the regime staged a harsh show trial in February for his role in pro-democracy demonstrations the previous month. Yet the Communists' vitriolic media campaign against him unwittingly heightened Havel's celebrity status. A covertly made tape recording of a secret speech by Jakes revealed that he felt Havel's jailing had been a tactical error; Jakes suggested instead that police target less prominent dissidents whose incarceration would draw little notice abroad.

From its inception, Civic Forum's role has been — to use Havel's favorite characterization — improvised. The Forum made a set of specific demands that those Communist leaders tied to the Warsaw Pact intervention step down, that an independent investigation of the November 17 police brutality be launched, and that political prisoners be freed. After the first mass protest, Forum representatives opened talks with the more reformist — and opportunistic — prime minister, Ladislav Adamec, securing from him a pledge against further police or army intervention. Havel initially declined to urge people into the streets; that call came from students. Yet one day later he was encouraging a vast crowd in Wenceslas Square to keep up the pressure on the government. Any lingering hesitation to act had been overwhelmed by the revolution from below. The Forum's "improvisation" was taking its cue from the action in the streets, not from the cooler deliberations of the Prague intellectuals. 12

Yet as the mass demonstrations continued, Civic Forum's organizational skills radically improved. It was increasingly able to channel, if not control, the public outpouring. From its makeshift headquarters in the basement of the Magic Lantern Theater, it organized the later protests and led the general strike. Just as significant, it was able to halt the mass rallies after the strike in order to conduct power-sharing talks in a calmer atmosphere. It won the grudging recognition of the new Communist Party chief, Karel Urbanek, who replaced Jakes on November 25, as a legitimate negotiating partner. And the once-reluctant Havel, who still longs to return to the theater, seemed to find his voice — and to accept his political role — in the week-long national catharsis at Wenceslas Square.

Havel and other opposition leaders originally conceived of Civic Forum as a Czechoslovak version of East Germany's largest opposition group, New Forum. It was to be neither a political party nor an alternative government. Just the same, Civic Forum quickly found itself pushed beyond negotiating the terms of a dialogue with the government to conducting one. Then the Forum abruptly decided to act as a political party, much like Solidarity did in Polish elections earlier this year. Forum leaders announced that they would endorse candidates to run against Communists next year, when Czechoslovakia holds its first free elections since the postwar Communist takeover. Even with the Civic Forum's shortcomings — above all its lack of workers' representatives — no other group was in a position to use the people's power in the streets to wrest concessions from the government. Civic Forum leaders now see their group as a watchdog over the transition to democracy.

The Czechoslovaks' disgust with communism is so pervasive that even the Party soon accepted the need for a transitional coalition government with non-Communists. It had become clear even to the Communists that their monopoly on power was now untenable. The goal of a coalition government, from the Forum's perspective, will be to secure fair, multiparty elections and constitutional guarantees of free speech, a free press, and freedom of association. After next year's elections the Forum may dissolve itself and let traditional political parties do their work.

Some of those parties are already coming into focus. The Socialist Party, 16 long a toady in the Communist-run National Front, switched sides and backed Civic Forum; it could become an electoral force of its own. The Democratic Initiative, an opposition group founded in 1987, is stepping forward as a Western-style liberal party. Non-collectivized farmers are planning to launch a party. And Communist reformers have formed a group called the Democratic Forum, which could conceivably break away from the Communist Party. Other parties will undoubtedly crowd into the field in the coming weeks.

In the interim, the Forum will have to decide what its role will be. It must also develop a consensus program of starter reforms. (Wisely, opting out of the Warsaw Pact is emphatically not one of them.) And there is the immediate question of who will serve in a coalition government. Although the Forum was not insisting that its members be named to a coalition Cabinet, it was claiming a de facto veto power over those appointed. It promptly exercised that veto when Adamec, apparently restrained by remaining Communist Party conservatives, tried to weasel out of his promise to share power with non-Communists. On December 3 he announced a new Cabinet, in which only five of 21 posts were transferred to non-Communists and 13 of the ministers had served in the previous Cabinet. The opposition called another mass demonstration and threatened a second general strike unless the Cabinet was recast to reflect the Communists' loss of influence. Another improvisation. Havel and Civic Forum will undoubtedly be making many more of them through this exhilarating season of the Prague Fall.

● PERSONAL RESPONSE ●

At what point do you think you would forget the intimidation of an oppressive government and risk everything, even your life, to achieve freedom?

● QUESTIONS FOR DISCUSSION ●

1. According to Omestad, why had the dissident movement in Czechoslovakia failed to gain widespread popular support before the November revolution?

2. How had the Communist government controlled dissidents and kept them marginalized?

3. What contrasts does Omestad draw between the revolution in Czechoslovakia and Poland's Solidarity movement?

4. Omestad attributes some of the success of the November revolution in Czechoslovakia to students. How were students instrumental?

5. Discuss the historical context of this essay by identifying the references in paragraph 2 to "the dramatic liberalizations in the Soviet Union, Poland, Hungary, and especially East Germany."

6. What was the Tiananmen Square massacre (paragraph 8)?

7. What was the process by which the Civic Forum became a significant factor both during and following the revolution?

● WRITING TOPICS ●

1. Define what you think freedom means to the Czechoslovakians who revolted.

2. Select one specific revolution you have read about and explain a major reason for the revolution.

3. Select one specific revolution you have read about and explain one, two, or several effects of that revolution.

EXODUS FROM TYRANNY

●

H. JOACHIM MAITRE

H. Joachim Maitre is dean of the College of Communication at Boston University. In 1953, he participated in the battles against Soviet troops who had occupied Berlin and in November of that year fled East Germany to the West. In this January 1990 Reader's Digest article, Maitre uses a combination of subjective personal memories with objective political analysis to explain why the best and brightest East Germans fled to the West and how their exodus led to the destruction of the Berlin Wall.

They were the refugees of autumn. Some came with only the clothes on their backs, others with the few possessions they could carry. Some traveled alone, some with babies in their arms and small children in tow. Never before had the expression "voting with their feet" been given such vivid substance.

It was a flood of East German refugees to the West in 1961 that caused the communist government to build the infamous Berlin Wall. And in a delicious symmetry of history, it was East German refugees streaming to the West this past fall who tore that stolid government apart and forced The Wall open.

I was not surprised that these young East Germans should flee when they found the door to freedom slightly open. After all, hundreds of thousands before them had risked — and sometimes lost — their lives to escape while the door was bolted. By 1961, when The Wall went up, East Germans found themselves behind a sullen barrier of masonry, mines and machine guns. So they crawled west under barbed wire, dodging searchlights and watchdogs. They dug tunnels, swam rivers, flew out in homemade balloons, smashed through in crazy, makeshift armored trucks.

The attempts and escapes were so numerous and commonplace as to be almost trite. Even we who had made "the crossing" paid scant attention. But no one could ignore this mass exodus. It began in May, when Hungary started to dismantle its section of the Iron Curtain. East Germans by the thousands headed down through Czechoslovakia to Hungary, all hoping to cross into Austria. Daunted by their sheer numbers, Hungary finally let them go in September. When the hardline Czech government sealed its Hungarian border, East Germans en route to Hungary sought asylum at the West German embassy in Prague.

I studied the faces of these people who had crossed into Austria or who looked out from the crowded West German embassy compound in Prague. To see such desperation, anxiety and finally tearful relief on these well-fed faces was the most damning possible indictment of East Germany. Wasn't this the foremost economy in the Soviet bloc? Wasn't this where German

4

industriousness and discipline had managed to make even communism work? Yet a couple from Potsdam, both of them teachers and making a comfortable living, bolted west because, as they explained, "everything soon will shatter in our country."

Actually, everything had shattered long ago. It had shattered in the very presumption of Stalin that the human spirit could be coldly manipulated for the needs of the state. His puppet leaders had festooned the fraud with promises and dubbed it the German Democratic Republic. Those who bought it—the ruthless, the power-bent—became the state and to hell with the rest of us.

I was a boy. I did not grasp the meaning of freedom fully enough to realize it had been destroyed. But I learned quickly. As a member of the Free German Youth (the "Vanguard of Socialism"), I had been ordered to literally drag an old, sick couple from their home so they would register to vote for the communists in the "democratic" elections of 1951. This was not right, I told my superiors. I refused to obey.

I was expelled from the organization. The group's chairman—a man clearly on his way up in the system—stiffly shook my hand at my trial. He made it clear that dismissal from the prestigious youth group meant the end of any hope for a real career in the new Germany. But he held forth the chance that I could redeem myself by a life of "socialist production" as a menial worker. He was a young former roofer from the Saarland named Erich Honecker.

And so one day in June 1953, caught up in the rage sweeping a starving and oppressed Berlin, I found myself in the battles with Soviet occupation troops, and in brash, boyish anger cursed and threw cobblestones at the T-34 tanks that roamed the streets to protect the new order.

There was noise and shouting and death in the air. Only later did it dawn on me that it was the hope of freedom which had died—and freedom was everything. Then, as soon as I could, I got out, slipping past the border guards to West Germany at a little town called Tiefenbrunn early in November.

I remembered that day as I read of these new refugees, as I saw them on the television news, smiling deliriously from train windows in railroad stations at Hof and Giessen, greeted by crowds with tears streaming down their faces.

These people were well-dressed by Eastern European standards, and well-educated. Some were attorneys, doctors, professors. Many were craftsmen, skilled factory workers and bosses; store clerks, secretaries, butchers, shopkeepers, accountants. They were in fact the communist state's people of promise and potential, most of them between the ages of 20 and 40.

For years, many of them had tried to believe that the price of socialist progress was censored and confiscated mail, and the monitoring of their "social habits" by the Stasi, the state security police. And as the government of my former youth leader, Erich Honecker, proved ever more stern and doctrinaire, they had resigned themselves to fashioning some kind of nest in the spreading branches of the state bureaucracy.

Others held the hope that they, too, might join those old men of the ruling elite who drove Western cars and enjoyed every luxury in the privacy of their estates within a walled compound near the Berlin suburb of Wandlitz ("Vol-vograd," workers derisively called it).

They had taken great pains to play the game. They had joined the blue-shirted Young Pioneers at age six, and the Free German Youth at 14. They had won medals for their mastery of Marx and Lenin and joined the Society for German-Soviet Friendship.

But an awful irony was everywhere at hand. Their country was indeed the 16 model Stalinist state envisioned when it was founded, and it had "progressed" accordingly. The government boasted about the standard of living. After all, they didn't have to stand in line for toilet paper like the people in Moscow.

But being "better off" than the rest of the family of communist police states with their sham economies didn't count for much. Citizens of the "First Workers' and Peasants' State on German Soil" looked with envy at friends or neighbors fortunate enough to receive clothes, food and consumer goods from relatives in the West. Some grasped that these "care packages" were emblematic of the staggering billions of dollars a year in West German trade and aid that kept their inefficient, centrally planned economy afloat. The routine affluence they saw on West German television seemed scarcely believable.

They had to wait ten or 15 years to buy a car, usually a wretchedly built Trabant. They saw about them a crumbling highway system; ancient railroad rolling stock on poorly maintained tracks; drab, shoddy buildings.

These material things were only symptoms. We Germans have a profound sense of order and of the importance of *Heimat*, home, which has endured far worse than mere shabbiness or hardship. There was a far deeper reason that these people forfeited everything and embraced instead the uncertain status of refugees: *the realization that human beings are overqualified to live in a communist state*. These bright, young East Germans had seen the future, and it did not work.

I remembered that during the Berlin uprising of 1953, playwright Bertolt 20 Brecht had scribbled in his notebook: "The government had lost all trust in its people. . . . Would it not be simpler for the government to dissolve the people and choose another?" These *were* the new people of East Germany, and they had lost any trust that their government would ever tire of its fraud upon them.

I had sensed early that I could not build a life on the premise the state knew best how I should live. It was easy for me to leave. I had nothing to lose. But these new refugees had everything to lose. In the thrall of communism their only solace was their possessions, honors, a niche in the system, whatever they might win by obedience and accommodation. It was no small thing to give them up; no small thing for them to teach us again the needed lesson that comfort and security are no substitutes for liberty. It would be wrong to describe these people as disillusioned. Prisoners, even if relatively well cared for, hold few illusions about prison. These refugees, tossing their East German money out of train windows at the border, were eminent realists. They left behind houses and apartments that had cost them dearly in routine payoffs and years on waiting lists. They left their highly prized automobiles, keys in the ignition, on the streets of Prague.

They had no idea, of course, that they were the vanguard of an exodus that would change history; no idea that their desire to be free was the tremor that would shake East Germany to its foundation. By October 18, as embarrassment grew over the hemorrhage of the country's very lifeblood, Erich Honecker was deposed by the East German Politburo. By November 8, most of the Politburo itself had resigned. Honecker's successor, Egon Krenz, tried desperately to restore order to a government that had been the grim symbol of order in Eastern Europe.

An eerie atmosphere descended on the country. Stores closed for lack of clerks. Trains were left without engineers; factories without skilled workers; villages without bakers, doctors, teachers, ambulance drivers. The next day, November 9, the unthinkable happened. The East German government announced that its citizens were free to pass directly into West Germany. The Wall had come down.

In the ecstatic celebrations that followed, I could not forget those refugees   24 of autumn, and the escapees before them. *They* had brought this about. They had shocked their rulers into reality by fashioning a unique and courageous plebiscite on democracy. They triumphed because they were willing to abandon everything *für Freiheit* — for freedom.

● PERSONAL RESPONSE ●

Under what circumstances would you be willing to leave your job, your home, and your car to go to a new country with absolutely no guarantees about what lies ahead for you there?

● QUESTIONS FOR DISCUSSION ●

1. Who is Maitre more interested in here, the newly liberated East Germans or those who fled before the Wall came down? Why do they interest him more than the others?

2. What does Maitre mean by "delicious symmetry" (paragraph 2) and "sullen barrier" (paragraph 3)? Find other examples of vivid language, colorful metaphors and similes, or other effective word choice.

3. What does the fact that Maitre himself fled East Germany add to the essay?

4. What is the "awful irony" Maitre refers to in paragraph 16?

5. Explain what Maitre means when he writes, "Never before had the expression 'voting with their feet' been given such vivid substance" (paragraph 1).

6. What examples of the tyranny of communist rule does Maitre provide?

7. Trace the series of events in 1989 that led to the November 9 announcement that the Berlin Wall would come down.

● WRITING TOPICS ●

1. Drawing on your own knowledge or on library research, write an essay on the Berlin Wall. Select a particular focus, such as why it was erected, what its impact on Germany was, dramatic attempts to escape across it, or the events surrounding its destruction.

2. Speculate on what it must have been like to live under the East German regime.

3. If you or someone you know has had personal experience with escaping from an oppressive regime, narrate the circumstances of the escape.

FROM NICHOLAS II TO GORBACHEV
A Family's Survival Amid Soviet Antisemitism

●

David Remnick

David Remnick is a Washington Post *foreign service correspondent. The following essay, which appeared in* The Washington Post Weekly Edition *in May 1990, features the last remaining survivor of the Doctors' Plot, one of the many attempts to purge Jews from the Soviet Union. In it, Remnick covers the experiences with antisemitism of four generations of Soviet Jews.*

An exodus has begun. A people that once seemed destined for oblivion is getting visas for a new life. But Yakov Rappaport, the only remaining survivor of Stalin's final attempt at a purge of Soviet Jews, says he will not join the new wave out. His time is past.

Half-ignored in the great storm of the Gorbachev Revolution, the "Jews of Silence" are leaving the Soviet Union: 100,000 last year went to Israel and the West; hundreds of thousands more wait for permission and tickets. Sitting at a scarred table set with old china and a pot of steaming tea, Rappaport wishes them all well, all his friends, his colleagues, his granddaughter, Vika.

"I'm 91 years old. It's too late for me," he says in his apartment off the Leningrad Highway. "I'll stay on here. I'll be buried here. What have I got left to give to Israel?"

Thirty-seven years ago Joseph Stalin ordered the arrest of a group of 4 prominent doctors, most of them Jewish, claiming they were poisoning the Kremlin leaders and covering up their intrigues. Stalin's murderous paranoia was ready to soar once more.

The Great Teacher of the Peoples gave personal instructions to the investigator: "If you do not obtain confessions from the doctors we will shorten you by a head!" Most historians agree that had Stalin not died in March 1953, he would have ordered the execution of the physicians arrested in "The Doctors' Plot," possibly as a prelude to a nationwide deportation and purge of the Soviet Jews.

"I thought I was finished, a dead man," Rappaport says. "But they let me out of jail one day, for no reason at all it seemed. I couldn't understand what had happened until I came home and my wife told me that Stalin was dead. It was just dumb luck, for me — and probably for hundreds of thousands of other Jews."

Just after Mikhail Gorbachev's speech two years ago calling for historians to fill in the "blank spots" of the Soviet past, both Yakov and his daughter, Natalya, a renowned chemist, published their memoirs of the Doctors' Plot.

Those two pieces, printed in literary journals with circulations in the millions, were among the first articles on the crimes of Stalinism, and the very first major works published here for decades on the theme of Soviet antisemitism.

"We took a walk in the forbidden zone," Natalya says as she pours out the   8
tea. "It was awfully lonely."

Father and daughter are devoted to one another in an easy, undramatic way. At the table their stories, even their sentences, elide into a single line of thought and memory. After a few hours it becomes clear that their family narrative is nothing less than the Jewish experience in the Soviet Union in this century. "There is a whole age behind these eyes," Yakov says. "From Nicholas II to Gorbachev."

Natalya smiles and puts her hand over her father's knobby wrist. There is great love between them, but there is a tension as well. "I've wanted to emigrate since the '60s, but my parents refused to go," Natalya says.

"They were afraid, and I couldn't persuade them. They decided it was too late for them and that they should die here. My mother is gone now. I cherish her memory and I love my father very much. But still, I cannot forgive them this."

As he hears this, the fingers on Yakov Rappaport's left hand tremble slightly.   12
He says nothing, just stares at the teapot and lets it pass. He had heard this before. When Natalya begins to speak of the rise of antisemitic groups such as Pamyat and of fears that a worsening economy will lead some people to turn on the old familiar scapegoat, Yakov shakes his head. "I've seen this before," he says. "I'm not afraid."

Just days before, Vika, the youngest generation of the Rappaport family and a theatrical designer of audacity and ambition, left for Jerusalem. At 24, Vika is cynical about Gorbachev's *glasnost*, but she is also its child. Where her mother and grandfather were always hesitant to talk with strangers about their fears and histories, Vika is blunt, ironic, fearless. Before she left, she said this:

"I'm not scared of the latest wave of antisemitism. They are pathetic people and they will always be around. I'm leaving because I cannot stand it here any longer: the rules, the psychology, the gray sameness of everything. If I stay here, I will suffocate. Unless a brick were to fall on my head, I could predict every moment of my life here until I die. I want to have children one day but I will not have them here. I will miss everyone, but I am gone."

Weekend mornings sometimes, Yakov Rappaport looks out his apartment window at the Pamyat punks in black T-shirts carrying placards around the All Saints' Church: "Zhids Out!" "Down With the Judeo-Masonic Conspiracy!"

"I have seen this before too," Rappaport says.   16

He grew up in the Crimean city of Simferopol on the Black Sea. His father, Lev, taught Russian and mathematics at a local school. Yakov Rappaport's first memory is of a pogrom in 1905.

"I was 6 years old. We were having a science lesson when the Cossacks rushed in. The school was destroyed. I remember the globes were smashed, there was broken glass everywhere, and my father was badly injured. The police brought the bodies to the morgue, and my father along with them because they thought he was dead. One of our friends saw my father there, only by chance, and they could hear him moaning. He was unconscious, covered with blood. His fingers and hands had been broken by the truncheons. He had tried to guard his face, so they just broke the arms. It took months for him to heal.

"This friend of ours tried to drag my father through a gate to a cab. The school principal was there and he was shouting, 'Go away, you Jew!' When my father finally returned to the school weeks later, the other teachers shunned him. They would not speak to him, and he finally had to leave the school. This is what was first imprinted on my memory as a child."

As a boy, Rappaport also was terrified by the 1911 Beilis case in the Ukraine, 20
which was set off when police in Kiev found the corpse of a 13-year-old Russian boy. What followed was a kind of mass hysteria, after the boy's mother, a prostitute, accused the Jews of murdering her son to use his blood for a ritual — a 'Blood Accusation' rooted in antisemitic folklore in the Ukraine. The czarist government arrested a Jewish factory worker, Mendel Beilis.

"It was an accusation against all Jews, not just Beilis," Rappaport says. "In our school, about half the class believed the accusations, and half did not." But the jury, made up of mostly illiterate Ukrainian peasants, rejected the Blood Accusation and set Beilis free.

And so it went, from one year to the next in Rappaport's life. There were attacks on the Jews in schools and in the courts. Discrimination, life-threatening and petty, touched every facet of ordinary life. Jewish students like Rappaport even had to pay extra fees to study in the schools. "My family was never religious, but my whole life in the czarist times let me know who I was," Rappaport says.

A keen student of natural science, Rappaport set off to study medicine in Petrograd, the city of the czars that would soon be the city of revolution. Petrograd was outside the Pale of Settlement where Jews were made to live, but for some reason the university let him study there. "All in all, I think the czars were somehow more liberal than the Bolsheviks were." Rappaport arrived in 1915 and rented the corner of someone's room.

Those years were for him a mix of medicine and revolt. After mornings in 24
class and autopsy rooms, he sat in the galleries of the Duma, the Russian legislature, listening to the sentiment gather against the czar. Later, he says, he stood on the street and watched the newly arrived Lenin preach workers' revolution from the apartment balcony of the city's richest ballerina. Soon there were food riots and student protests.

"When the first — the February — revolution took place and the czar fell, I was there," Rappaport remembers. "I was armed with a rifle and a pistol. Together with the workers I helped arrest the czarist ministers. It was a real bourgeois revolution. . . . We thought we would have a constitutional state, like in France and other parts of Western Europe. I don't think that was a naive hope."

Rappaport was studying and working in the Crimea in the autumn of 1917, when Lenin's Bolsheviks took control of the government. "Parliamentary creti- nism," Lenin declared the parliament, and set about instituting a one-party autocracy.

Rappaport became a prominent pathologist. He got into trouble in the late 1930s when, as the head of the admissions committee at a medical institute in Moscow, he would not discriminate against the children of the "enemies of the state"—those who had been arrested or shot for no reason by Stalin's secret police.

Rappaport guessed that he himself had avoided arrest and execution in the camps only because the country could ill afford to wipe out all its best doctors. 28

"But the truth is I really don't know why I got through the Purges," he says. "Fortune?"

During the Battle of Stalingrad in 1943, the pivotal point in the war for the Soviet Union, Rappaport finally gave in and became a party member—"for patriotic, not political reasons." Until then, Rappaport had refused membership even though it might have hastened his advancement in the scientific world—"I was never a Bolshevik and never wanted to be." But now he joined, he says, because "at that time the party was the only force that held the country together.

"What I will always remember is the interview I had at party headquarters. The first thing they asked me was, 'What is Zionism? What do you think of it?'

"I was angry with this, but I answered: 'Zionism is the national liberation movement of Jews aimed at the organization of their own territorial state.' 32

"They were stunned. They said, 'A liberation movement?'"

One day when Natalya Rappaport was 14, the doorbell rang. One of the family's closest friends, Myron Vovci, a physician, already had been arrested, and the newspapers and radio had begun a crude propaganda campaign against the "devils in white coats," the Jewish "doctor-murderers."

"There were rumors that, for the sake of 'protecting' the others—the 'innocent' Jews—from the mass hatred, camps were being set up for them in Siberia. All of them would be sent there soon," Natalya writes in "Memory Is Also a Kind of Medicine." "The question of how to execute the criminals was widely discussed. Informed circles in my class contended that they would be hanged in Red Square. Many were worried whether the execution would be open to the public or only to those with special permission. Someone consoled the disappointed: 'Don't worry. Surely they will film it.' And I only dreamed about Vovci on the gallows."

Now, the secret police had come for Yakov Rappaport. The agents rifled 36 through every drawer and book, noting a few volumes of Freud as evidence for the ritual court protocols. During the search, one of the agents cut his finger. Terrified that Natalya's mother would poison him with contaminated iodine, he refused treatment: "They phoned somewhere for a car," Natalya recalls, "and the suffering one was taken away—most likely to a special clinic where his scratch would be treated by a trusted, dependable Russian surgeon."

The arrest in February 1953 was, for Natalya, what the 1905 pogrom in Simferopol had been for her father—the pivotal memory of what it means to be a Jew in a hostile place. "Stalin is a bastard and a criminal," Natalya's mother told her, "but never say this to anyone. Do you understand?"

Natalya's friends scorned her, stared at her in class. The children in the courtyard mocked her, telling her that her father had taken pus from cancerous corpses and rubbed it into the skin of healthy people. They hurled rotten tomatoes, stones and dead mice at her. The police confiscated all money, bonds and bank passbooks. Natalya's mother sold the family's copies of Tolstoy, Pushkin and Hugo to buy bread and milk. A sickly child, Natalya lay awake nights wondering when the police would come for her mother too.

She was sure her father had been killed. (After all, why had the prison authorities said that it was no longer "necessary" to deliver food parcels to the jail?) But just three days after Stalin's death in March, there was a phone call, a stark male voice: "I am calling at the request of the professor. The professor asked me to tell you that he is healthy, feels fine and is concerned about his family. What should I tell him?"

While the rest of the nation mourned the death of the Great Leader, the 40 family began its celebration, and on April 4 Yakov Rappaport returned from Moscow's Lefortovo Prison. Before coming up to the apartment he called from a phone downstairs: "I didn't want them to have a heart attack at the sight of me," he says.

Every year since, the survivors of the Doctors' Plot gathered for a party on that day as an anniversary of freedom. They celebrated survival. "Now there is only me," Rappaport says. "My family and I, we celebrate alone."

Yakov Rappaport came home a grateful man. When his wife died in the early '70s, he met a widow at the funeral, and for years the two have lived together — "in sin," Natalya adds with a smile.

Even now it is hard for Yakov to find much fault with Nikita Khrushchev — "not after he freed hundreds of thousands of people and gave them back their good name."

But for Natalya, now in her fifties, the Doctors' Plot was a divide between 44 childhood and adulthood, innocence and alienation. The end of the purge meant freedom for her father, but a different quality of mind and trust for the daughter:

"I began to see all the lies around me. I began to have a double life, one outside of my circle when I had to be careful what I did and said, and one inside my circle of family and friends when I could have my own thoughts, my real life, the times when I could be myself.

"My attitude toward people had changed. There were so many who had betrayed us, people I never would have suspected. I stopped trusting people. And I began to understand — really understand — that I was Jewish. I understood that to be Jewish was to be persecuted. Years passed until I understood that, and maybe I don't have a full understanding even now. After all, I am deprived of Jewish history, Jewish culture, Jewish language."

State antisemitism has followed Natalya Rappaport throughout her life and career as a specialist in chemical polymers. After graduation she and the rest of her Jewish classmates were sent off to work in a lowly factory while others got institute jobs. Eventually she won a spot at a prestigious institute, but she was told she could not advance very far.

"I don't have anything against you or your abilities, Natalya Yakovna, but 48 there are just too many Jews in your department," said one of the institute chiefs.

"The regional Communist Party committee is already angry with your lab boss for hiring too many Jews. Do you want him to have any further problems?"

In 1978, she watched with astonishment as a somewhat less deadly version of the Doctors' Plot was played out at her father's institute. Local authorities received an anonymous "tip" that Russian patients were dying while Jewish patients were being cured. The letters charged the Jewish doctors at the institute with carrying out Nazi-like experiments on the Russians and covering up the crimes.

"Instead of throwing the accusations in the garbage, the authorities made a thorough investigation," Natalya says. "Can you imagine? Ancient history all over again. And guess what? It turns out that there had been no experiments after all."

Natalya was stymied in her attempts to leave the country for Israel or the United States. Israelis promised her an immediate post at the Weizmann Institute, but she could not persuade her parents to move. And her husband, Volodya, was also hesitant. "He is a very indecisive man," she says now. "This issue almost broke up our marriage. I think my life would have been different in Israel. As a scientist I could have worked as far as my talents could bring me. Here I am trapped, kept in a cage."

She was determined that her daughter, Vika, would learn to live and think 52 like a free woman. At first, when the little girl came home humming and singing the Bolshevik hymns she had been taught in school, Natalya was furious.

"I told her to shut up, but she loved those songs," Natalya says. "When I tried to counter the lies she was being told in school and I told her to look around at the real life around her, she started crying and shouting, defending what she was told in the second and third grade. She was struggling for the sake of these beautiful lies."

But as she grew older, Vika grew more aware, began to understand the deep contradictions between the history of her own grandfather and the textbooks at school.

"By the time I was 13 I already knew that I could no longer live here," Vika said. "I was still in the Soviet Union, but I knew it was temporary. Just by thinking that way it set me free."

On the night of Vika's departure, she and her mother drove around the 56 neighborhood in their tiny orange Lada. Natalya glanced in the rear-view mirror and noticed they were being followed. Natalya pulled into the local police station and said, "What the hell is going on? Why are you having me followed?"

"It's for your own protection," the police captain said. Natalya was furious, but her daughter smiled, as if in justification. That night, Vika flew to Budapest, and then switched planes for Ben Gurion Airport in Tel Aviv. She is living now in Jerusalem and looking for work in the theater.

With her father here and her daughter in Israel, Natalya admits she feels like a "woman in the middle." She does everything she can to avoid the inevitable question of her father's death, and it is hard to ask her to think ahead. But the subject is never very distant from her mind.

"I know what you are thinking," she says. "And the answer is yes. When he is gone, I will be gone too."

● PERSONAL RESPONSE ●

What is your reaction to Rappaport's refusal to leave the Soviet Union? Given the same circumstances, which position do you think you would hold, that of Rappaport, his daughter Natalya, or his granddaughter Vika? Explain your answer.

● QUESTIONS FOR DISCUSSION ●

1. How well do you think Remnick has illustrated the contrasting views of Rappaport and his daughter?
2. What details indicate the close relationship between Yakov and Natalya Rappaport, despite their differing views on leaving the Soviet Union?
3. How does Vika differ from both her mother and her grandfather?
4. Find examples of Remnick's use of anecdotes or brief stories in his account of both Yakov and Natalya's experiences with antisemitism. What do these brief narratives add to the essay?
5. Explain what Yakov Rappaport means when he says "There is a whole age behind these eyes" (paragraph 9).
6. How did the Doctors' Plot change Natalya Rappaport?
7. How well do you think Remnick has dramatized "what it means to be a Jew in a hostile place" (paragraph 37)? Explain your answer.

● WRITING TOPICS ●

1. If you have witnessed or experienced antisemitism, narrate the incident.
2. Explain how you believe you would react to living in a country where you were persecuted for your beliefs.
3. Compare or contrast the kind of repression Remnick describes here with that described in any of the first three essays in this chapter.

MYSTERY IN A SOVIET LIBRARY

●

Victor Zaslavsky

Victor Zaslavsky is a professor of sociology at Memorial University of Newfoundland, Canada. He emigrated there from the Soviet Union, where he had taught at the University of Leningrad. The editor of the twentieth-century Russian literature series published in Sellerio, Italy, Zaslavsky has published short stories in English, Italian, and Russian, as well as the books The Neo-Stalinist State: Class, Ethnicity and Consensus in Soviet Society *(1982) and, with Robert J. Brym,* Soviet-Jewish Emigration and Soviet Nationality Policy *(1983). In the following essay published in the* Partisan Review *in 1988, Zaslavsky explains something of "the capricious library-access hierarchy of the Soviet Union" and what happened to him when he discovered the identity of his mysterious study-table partner in the limited-access reading room of the Central Public Library.*

American libraries suffer from what Stalin would have called a "peasant leveling mentality." Simply anyone can walk in, go to the stacks and choose a book . . . simple as buying a piece of cheese. I suspect that these computerized cemeteries impart no respect whatever toward books, but rather depress readers. The will to write, to add yet another tome to the multitudes standing on the shelves, is completely dissipated. Soviet libraries are very different . . .

And I know what I miss in American libraries. It is that in many of them the traditions of Western individualism are obeyed to such an extent that the tables are big enough for only one reader. For this reason alone, I never would have had the chance to share a table at the Central Public Library with a certain reader registered under the surname Carrasco, whose real identity aroused in me an obsessive curiosity.

It was an opportunity arrived at after years spent traversing the capricious library-access hierarchy of the Soviet Union. When I was just ten years old, my school's head librarian noticed my love for books and co-opted me onto the Library Council. The council's first memorable act was purging books. Immediately after the war, textbooks were scarce, and my school received two hundred history textbooks printed in the mid-1930s. To purge the old edition of "the enemies of the people," we would open to page 181 and spill ink on the portraits of Marshals Tukhachevsky and Blucher.

The store of books in the school library was meager, textbooks excepted, and I read quickly. The librarian wrote me a recommendation for the district library for grown-ups. The district library was subject to almost military discipline. Books could be signed out three at a time and exchanged no sooner than three days later. The library had a catalogue but it was out of bounds. To sign out a book the reader had to name the author; if he could not, which was usually the case, he had to mention at least what kind of book he wanted. "Something about love," the women quickly said. The men often hemmed and hawed, their hands aflutter.

When I entered the university, I reached a new height. The student library was a department of the Central Public Library, which, despite its name, was open only to scientific researchers. It was not open to the man in the street either—a student pass was required. This was a real library with a large catalogue and specialized reading rooms. Books could not be signed out—a great defect, as the number of students seeking admittance easily exceeded the number of seats. One had to show up at seven o'clock in the morning and queue for an hour and a half. Those who arrived later waited even longer, until one of the early birds, done for the day, left a place.

After graduating I was finally granted the precious right to study in the Central Public Library. A "research pass" for the main reading room was required, and a university diploma was a prerequisite. It was the Olympus of libraries: millions of volumes, a gigantic collection of manuscripts accumulating over the centuries, even Voltaire's private book collection.

To avoid confusion, the readers were divided into three categories. The first and certainly most numerous had the right of access to "common reading rooms." These were homey and quiet. The walls supported heavy prerevolutionary shelves, so that the truly essential references were always at hand. The forty-five volumes of Lenin's *Collected Works* (fourth edition), in brown covers, went nicely with the three score light brown volumes of Marx and Engels, while the cool primness of the fifty-five blue volumes of Lenin's *Full Collected Works* (fifth edition) harmonized well with three dozen more assorted Lenin volumes in dull red. The modesty of the classics clashed with the vanity of the rather temporary guests: the thick volumes of current Politburo members' speeches with their fashionable glossy, gold-stamped covers, looking *nouveau riche* and even opulently gangsterlike among the aristocracy of spirit. The common reading rooms are chronically overcrowded; the latecomers line the walls, marking time by leafing through the *Manifesto* or *What Is to Be Done?*

Reading rooms for professors and academicians are another thing altogether. Although the same brown-blue volumes populate the shelves and the tables are graced by the same green lampshades, there is always space for more among the famous linguists and literature specialists. There sits Vladimir Propp, past victim of the anti-cosmopolitan campaign, forever stiff with fear. Victor Shklovsky steps in like an old wrestler, pushing through invisible opponents. The common and professional reading rooms merge in the corridors, the smoking room, and the marble staircase, where open-mouthed graduate students peck at the crumbs of wisdom dropped by their supervisors.

The upper grade of readers inhabits a different realm still, having access to "restricted reading rooms"—"*spetskhran*" in Russian, or "spets" for short. Spets house the books defined as anti-Soviet and that require of their readers a greater political maturity. By definition, all of these should have been published after 1917, but there are also prerevolutionary works of authors who managed to write an anti-Soviet something even before the revolution. The majority of Western editions, except for technical and pure science texts, are found in the *spetskhran*.

To gain entrance into the spets one first obtains a supporting letter from a reputable research institute or university, signed by its troika of director, party secretary, and chairman of the trade union committee. But the decisive information characterizing the candidate's political maturity arrives through the invisible network that links the spets to the departments responsible for state security in every respectable organization. The supporting letter should contain the subject of the proposed research, lest the spets librarian hand out books on unrelated topics. Hence, those coveting the spets try to formulate their topics in the vaguest of terms. Almost everyone admitted to the spets examines all-encompassing topics, such as "culture and personality," "criticism of bourgeois ideology," and the like.

The *spetskhran* is located in Room 88. I would enter the spets trembling and proffer my internal passport and pass to the guard with a shaking hand, trying to appear exactly like the photographs in my documents. I trembled openly, for I knew the guards took pleasure in that. It was easy, as I really was afraid: what if the guard should detect my political immaturity, notice my moral infirmity, or simply observe in my eyes the desire that he and his organization go to hell? To my good fortune, the guards had not yet learned to read minds.

The spets room had space for no more than a hundred at a time, but it was never full. Apparently, politically mature researchers were as hard to come by in the city as ripe pineapples in its vegetable stores. To the newcomer the most striking aspect of Room 88 was the high shelves on the walls, crammed not with the habitual blue-brown volumes promising the last word on every subject, but with endless rows of bright covers — the cry of advertising, the chaos of the ideas market. The forbidden fruit could be plucked directly from the shelves. A strange feeling would grip me, a mixture of confusion, elation, and, most of all, the stupefaction of freedom.

The elation passed fairly quickly when it turned out that in the spets freedom took the form of Engels's "recognition of necessity." Almost any book could be chosen, but it had to be registered in the reader's personal selection sheet. It was easy to see that from time to time the overseeing organization would peruse the books selected by a given reader over a year or two and draw certain inferences about his interests and progress in his studies. If the reader felt the need to keep his interests to himself, great care had to be taken to conceal it. The simplest tactic was to select as many books as possible, so that the true choices were buried by the mountain of books registered as ballast. But the method could backfire if a perusal of his choices led the organization to draw spurious conclusions by fabricating connections between the chosen books — and sometimes to bring charges against the reader.

Somehow the atmosphere in the spets was always tense. The readers did not speak to each other, even if they were acquaintances. People sat two to a table in their assigned seats, and even if they shared a table for years they never exchanged words or recognized each other. Each guarded his own secret, and when they left Room 88 it was as if their secrets ran along on a leash.

I got hold of a comfortable table by a window with a view onto Nevsky Prospekt, where a worried humanity could be observed queuing with shopping bags at the famous Eliseev food store. For a full year I had the table to myself and, having grown accustomed to solitude, was almost offended when one day a neighbor materialized. He carried at least two dozen books, embracing the stack like a bundle of firewood. He loaded the books onto his half of the table and apparently wanted to give me a friendly nod but cut himself short, understanding the impropriety of such a greeting. In response I shifted my chair slightly to the left. The exchange was the utmost in politeness given the circumstances: we acknowledged each other's existence in a place where people should not notice each other.

My neighbor showed up almost every day and came to interest me more and more. He was without distinguishing marks: simply a tall, broad-shouldered man, about sixty, with a stubborn chin. A Ukrainian, perhaps. Obviously he had been strong but had gained weight from lack of exercise. Then again, all the habitués of the spets gained weight at that age: there could not have been too many athletes in such a place. He dressed in Western style, but that was no rarity in the spets either. Nonetheless, my neighbor was markedly different from a typical spets reader, and it took me a while to realize why. Usually the *spetskhran* customer tried to shrink, hide, disappear. We all prayed for invisibility, wished to be forgotten, so that nothing threatened our fragile right to read forbidden literature. My neighbor, however, had some sort of inner confidence. He did not seem afraid to lose the precious privilege, nor did he appear to revel in his unique status. Even more surprising was his way of reading. An ordinary reader always remembered he was not alone and hence kept up an expression of distaste or boredom no matter how gripping the book—as if he were being forced to read or to chew on a lemon. It was our disagreeable profession, after all, that compelled us to read Western propaganda rather than join the rest of the populace and rejoice in optimistic Soviet literature. My neighbor, for his part, was obviously and completely captivated by his reading; he read and repeated to himself, he smiled and smirked. Once, when he stepped out for a moment, I could not help breaking the sacred rules of the spets; quickly, thieflike, I riffled through his pile of books. The opened one turned out to be *L'Affaire Toulaev* by Victor Serge—neither the book nor the author meant anything to me. But his other books struck me. They were by Trotsky or about him, and almost all of them in French or Spanish. Even more amazingly, my neighbor disdained concealing his interest. In 1950, during a search of the apartment of the father of one of my friends, they found Trotsky's *Literature and Revolution*. At the closed trial the prosecutor stated that "with every page the accused took another step toward betrayal of the fatherland." The accused cried with joy after being sentenced to twenty-five years—he had expected the firing squad. And my neighbor, he read Trotsky as if it were the most ordinary thing! The only explanation was that he belonged to the dying breed of "anti-Trotskyist propagandists." But they all worked at an institution that was privy to special sources of information and had no need to visit the spets.

The urge to find out about my neighbor grew daily. To inquire directly was out of the question, but to wait for a lucky accident to give away his name could take years. Still, I had some special sources of my own. Natasha, my "almost sister," worked in the library. She was not my sister, but ever since I had had a brief affair with her older sister — for whom I pined hopelessly for a long time — we had been trusting and devoted friends. The youngest Ph.D. in the library, she was the head of a department and a person of influence. But even she had trouble finding out the name. The first flash of information was puzzling. He was registered under the surname of Carrasco. "But that's Cervantes," I said, surprised. "Remember, he had a character named Carrasco?" "A pseudonym, maybe," Natasha guessed. Her curiosity was also aroused.

Several days later Natasha called me and said that she would come around in half an hour. I knew from her voice that something had happened. "I cracked it!" she blurted out in the doorway and then whispered: "It's Ramon Mercader." "Who?" I did not understand. "Ramon Mercader!" And she added in my ear, "The guy who killed Trotsky. But, for God's sake, don't tell anyone. We'll both be jailed. And in different cells, at that."

I asked around a bit and scraped some "facts" together, although they were all based on rumors. They said Mercader spent twenty years in a Mexican prison. They said that for "exemplary success in an important governmental mission, Stalin made Mercader a Hero of the Soviet Union and that all those years the Gold Star awaited Mercader in a safe deposit box. He did not get much out of it. Mercader returned during the Khrushchev years, not a good time for him. Although the victims of the 1930s show trials had not been rehabilitated, the condemnations of Trotsky as a Gestapo agent and Bukharin as a Nazi spy were also out of fashion. The word of the day was to "forget and never mention!" Thus, Mercader was sent to Prague. They said that he later came to sympathize with Dubček and the Prague Spring and had to be shipped back to the Soviet Union. Now he shuttled back and forth between Moscow and Leningrad — more accurately, between two *spetskhrans*, supposedly writing memoirs.

From that day on, I could not work in the spets. I bombarded my neighbor 20 with questions: "Is it true that you're the very same Mercader? Why did you take the name Carrasco? Do you mean Trotsky was insane, a new Don Quixote? Do your children know who you are? And how do you feel now, thirty years after the murder of Leon Davidovich?" Of course, all of these questions resounded only in my mind. A direct question could end badly for me and for Natasha. But I could no longer sit quietly in my seat nor read nor concentrate. I exchanged books needlessly. I stepped out into the smoking room — although I did not smoke. All the while I kept up an imaginary dialogue with Mercader. It was a sort of curse.

Mercader took no notice of my agitation or, indeed, my presence. But he had a hard time reading as well. He obviously conducted his own endless dialogue with Trotsky or, perhaps with the authors of books about Trotsky. He argued, he accused, he defended himself . . . Sometimes he would pace back and forth in the corridor or jump up clenching his fists. Did he feel he was squeezing the icepick's handle, about to strike? Could those tales about a victim's ghost pursuing the murderer be true?

Knowing and not being able to tell is torture. I could no longer work at the same table as Mercader, but I was reluctant, even afraid to change my seat in Room 88. Thus, I trudged through the common reading rooms, greeted friends, talked about everything except what was on my mind, generally wasted time. I was so disturbed by the persistent internal dialogue that I lost all sense of caution. And I was swiftly punished.

If to gain access to the spets was like winning a lottery, to lose it through carelessness was like losing the winning ticket. It happened so rarely that the story is worth telling. Once, lost in indecision, I was walking through the library and ran into an old pal who had the strangest job in the world. He was a translator of nonexistent poetry from Central Asian languages. His clients were poets from Central Asia, or sometimes from Caucasian republics, who absolutely had to publish in Russian. If a translation then appeared in a central journal, the poet was showered with goodies: membership in the Union of Writers, well-paid book contracts with local publishing houses, official positions, power. The creative process went like this. The poet explained in less than lapidary Russian prose what poem he would write if only he could. My friend nodded approvingly and took notes. Only a few days later he would read to the poet a flowing stream of verse in which Soviet rule triumphed over the desert and the happy Kirghiz (Kazakh, or any other Central Asian person) wrote a song about his newfound happiness. The central journals had a quota for ethnic minorities: sooner or later they published my friend's poems, for he was, after all, a talented versifier. My friend sincerely admired his clients. "What vitality!" he would exclaim. "Under a different regime these people would play the stock market or join the Mafia. Here they become poets and join the Union of Writers. Such characters won't lose out in any place."

The translations commanded a princely reward. Grapes and aromatic melons, Armenian cognac thirty years old, and Turkoman carpets—all on top of the honorarium. However, there were also a few real poets who published real books—occasionally good books—and then the work took a serious turn. My friend maintained a group of Central Asian language specialists who made literal translations and got paid by the line. This threw up another obstacle. Several copies of the text were needed, but transcription of Central Asian texts was painful and expensive. The library owned a Xerox machine, but it was guarded like a bank vault. Two trusted comrades—the head of the copying department and the Xerox operator—kept the two different keys to the machine, and both had to be inserted in the appropriate slots for the machine to function. A reader was entitled to ten pages of copy a day. Worse, to copy these ten pages one needed the approval of the department head, who knew no foreign languages, certainly no Central Asian ones. Thus, there arose the classic Catch-22: for permission to make the copies necessary for the translation, one had first to present the translation itself. My friend removed this obstacle by those same gifts of the grateful South; a good part of them found their way to those responsible for the Xerox machine.

That unfortunate day I met my friend as he mournfully lugged a whole heap of poetry to the Xerox room. Delighted to see me, he begged my help with the Xeroxing. "Two's company," he convinced me and promised to reward me with a copy of a small book of my choice. The temptation was great: for a long time I had coveted a collection of Mandelstam's poetry, *The Stone*, not to be found for any money. But surely in the end I agreed because Mercader made my life a misery and I was ready for anything to avoid returning to Room 88. Later Natasha reproached me for my complete loss of sanity and self-control. Everyone knew that the extraordinary powers of the copying department bred intrigue and denunciations by the envious. Whatever the cause, as we approached the end of our Xeroxing several inspectors barged in — surely alerted by a tip — and found us in the act: a copy of Mandelstam, a load of copies of poems in unknown languages; and no permit to use the Xerox machine.

The consequences were horrifying. A report arrived at my institute detailing my "breaking of library rules." To wit: "illegal use of Xerox machine . . . serious infraction against instructions concerning *spetskhran* materials — attempted bribery of library staff . . ." There were other paragraphs that now escape my memory. Altogether they certainly amounted to less than "treason" but sounded worse than, say, "armed robbery." As the head of the first department brusquely told me: "Lucky they were dusty poems, or else off to Siberia for you." I did not lose my job but was demoted and lost not only my access to the spets but also the use of the entire library.

I did begin a new ascent to the spets, but then my emigration made it all meaningless. In those years I completely lost sight of Ramon Mercader. Rumor had it that he contracted cancer and was allowed to die in Cuba. I would like to know what his gravestone says: Carrasco, Mercader, or, simply, the man who killed Trotsky. And did he ever finish those memoirs?

● PERSONAL RESPONSE ●

What is your reaction to Zaslavsky's descriptions of the processes for admission to the various libraries he used in the Soviet Union?

● QUESTIONS FOR DISCUSSION ●

1. Do you think that Zaslavsky really believes that American libraries "suffer," that the multitudes of readily available books "depress readers" (paragraph 1)? How does his account of the process of obtaining access to libraries in the Soviet Union help you understand his tone in that paragraph?

2. Zaslavsky's language is richly detailed with vivid images, as in the sentence beginning "The modesty of the classics clashed . . ." in paragraph 7. Find other passages that you think are particularly descriptive and explain why they are effective.

3. To fully appreciate Zaslavsky's essay, you should have some understanding of the political history of the Soviet Union. If you do not already know, use whatever resources you have available to identify these people, things, or events: Lenin, Marx, and Engels (paragraph 7), the politburo (paragraph 7), the 1917 Revolution (paragraph 9), Trotsky (paragraph 16), and Stalin and Khrushchev (paragraph 19).

4. What does Zaslavsky mean by "the stupefaction of freedom" (paragraph 12)?

5. In the course of his narrative, Zaslavsky reveals some things about life in general in the Soviet Union during the period he is recounting, from his offhand reference to the difficulties of getting ripe fruit (paragraph 12) to his chilling account of the fate of his friend's father (paragraph 16). Where else does he give such details? What picture emerges of daily life in the Soviet Union during this period?

6. How does Zaslavsky build suspense as he describes his growing intrigue with the "mysterious" man who shares his reading table in Room 88?

7. How did the discovery of the mystery man's identity lead to Zaslavsky's demotion and loss of library privileges?

● WRITING TOPICS ●

1. Zaslavsky writes, "Knowing and not being able to tell is torture" (paragraph 22). If you have ever been in a position of knowing something you could not tell, describe how you felt about being in that position and tell the results of the experience.

2. If you have visited a foreign country, compare and contrast that country with your own, focusing on several significant features rather than on a number of general ones.

3. Describe your own encounters with bureaucratic red tape.

CINDERELLA'S STEPSISTERS

●

TONI MORRISON

Toni Morrison is widely acclaimed as one of the best writers in Amer-
ica. After earning her master's degree from Cornell University in 1955,
she taught English until she became an editor for Random House in
1968. Since then she has taught classes in black literature and fiction
writing at Yale and Barnard, but her chief occupation is writing. Her
novels include The Bluest Eye *(1970),* Song of Solomon *(1977), which*
won the National Book Award, Tar Baby *(1981), and* Beloved *(1988),*
which won the Pulitzer Prize for fiction. In "Cinderella's Stepsisters,"
which was originally delivered as a commencement address at Barnard
College and subsequently adapted for the September 1979 issue of Ms.
magazine, Morrison warns her audience against becoming oppressors
of other women and urges them to draw on their nurturing sides when
making decisions that affect the wellbeing of others.

Let me begin by taking you back a little. Back before the days at college. To nursery school, probably, to a once-upon-a-time time when you first heard, or read, or, I suspect, even saw "Cinderella." Because it is Cinderella that I want to talk about; because it is Cinderella who causes me a feeling of urgency. What is unsettling about that fairy tale is that it is essentially the story of household—a world, if you please—of women gathered together and held together in order to abuse another woman. There is, of course, a rather vague absent father and a nick-of-time prince with a foot fetish. But neither has much personality. And there are the surrogate "mothers," of course (god- and step-), who contribute both to Cinderella's grief and to her release and happiness. But it is her stepsisters who interest me. How crippling it must have been for those young girls to grow up with a mother, to watch and imitate that mother, enslaving another girl.

I am curious about their fortunes after the story ends. For contrary to recent adaptations, the stepsisters were not ugly, clumsy, stupid girls with outsize feet. The Grimm collection describes them as "beautiful and fair in appearance." When we are introduced to them they are beautiful, elegant, women of status, and clearly women of power. Having watched and participated in the violent dominion of another woman, will they be any less cruel when it comes their turn to enslave other children, or even when they are required to take care of their own mother?

It is not a wholly medieval problem. It is quite a contemporary one: feminine power when directed at other women has historically been wielded in what has been described as a "masculine" manner. Soon you will be in a position to do the very same thing. Whatever your background—rich or poor—whatever the history of education in your family—five generations or one—you have taken advantage of what has been available to you at Barnard and you will therefore have both the economic and social status of the stepsisters *and* you will have their power.

I want not to *ask* you but to *tell* you not to participate in the oppression of 4 your sisters. Mothers who abuse their children are women, and another woman, not an agency, has to be willing to stay their hands. Mothers who set fire to school buses are women, and another woman, not an agency, has to tell them to stay their hands. Women who stop the promotion of other women in careers are women, and another woman must come to the victim's aid. Social and welfare workers who humiliate their clients may be women, and other women colleagues have to deflect their anger.

I am alarmed by the violence that women do to each other: professional violence, competitive violence, emotional violence. I am alarmed by the willingness of women to enslave other women. I am alarmed by a growing absence of decency on the killing floor of professional women's worlds. You are the women who will take your place in the world where *you* can decide who shall flourish and who shall wither; you will make distinctions between the deserving poor and the undeserving poor; where you can yourself determine which life is expendable and which is indispensable. Since you will have the power to do it, you may also be persuaded that you have the right to do it. As educated women the distinction between the two is first-order business.

I am suggesting that we pay as much attention to our nurturing sensibilities as to our ambition. You are moving in the direction of freedom and the function of freedom is to free somebody else. You are moving toward self-fulfillment, and the consequences of that fulfillment should be to discover that there is something just as important as you are and that just-as-important thing may be Cinderella—or your stepsister.

In your rainbow journey toward the realization of personal goals, don't make choices based only on your security and your safety. Nothing is safe. That is not to say that anything ever was, or that anything worth achieving ever should be. Things of value seldom are. It is not safe to have a child. It is not safe to challenge the status quo. It is not safe to choose work that has not been done before. Or to do old work in a new way. There will always be someone there to stop you. But in pursuing your highest ambitions, don't let your personal safety diminish the safety of your stepsister. In wielding the power that is deservedly yours, don't permit it to enslave your stepsisters. Let your might and your power emanate from that place in you that is nurturing and caring.

Women's rights is not only an abstraction, a cause; it is also a personal affair. 8 It is not only about "us"; it is also about me and you. Just the two of us.

● PERSONAL RESPONSE ●

Do your own observations support Morrison's that women with power tend to abuse it, particularly when other women are affected? Do men abuse power?

● QUESTIONS FOR DISCUSSION ●

1. Barnard is a women's college in New York City. How much do you think Morrison's speech is shaped by the fact that the graduating class she was addressing was entirely female?

2. What clues are there that this was originally a speech? What changes do you think Morrison would have made had she written it for the magazine originally?

3. Why do the stepsisters in "Cinderella" interest Morrison more than the other characters in the story?

4. What does Morrison mean by power that is wielded "in what has been described as a 'masculine' manner" (paragraph 3)? What is a "masculine manner"?

5. What examples of "the violence that women do to each other" (paragraph 5) does Morrison give?

6. Explain what Morrison means by the distinction between having the power and having the right to make decisions that "enslave other women" (paragraph 5).

7. What does Morrison suggest women do to avoid oppressing and doing violence to other women?

8. In what way is women's rights "not only about 'us' [but also] about me and you. Just the two of us" (paragraph 8)?

● WRITING TOPICS ●

1. Taking Morrison's comments as a starting point, contrast the "feminine" way of using power with the "masculine" way. Or, argue that there is no difference between the ways in which men use power and the ways in which women use it.

2. Explain the distinction between having power to abuse others and feeling that you have the right to use that power. Use specific examples of situations that would dramatize the difference.

3. Illustrate what Morrison means when she says that "the function of freedom is to free somebody else" (paragraph 6).

ABOLISH AMERICAN APARTHEID

●

Jonathan Freedman

Jonathan Freedman is an opinion columnist and editorial writer whose work appears on the Los Angeles Times *Op-Ed page and the* New York Times *editorial page. He has published a volume of short fiction,* The Man Who'd Bounce the World *(1979), and is currently writing a book on poverty in America. An editorial writer for the* San Diego Union Tribune *from 1981 to 1990, he was awarded the Pulitzer Prize in Distinguished Editorial Writing in 1987 for his series advocating human rights for undocumented immigrants. The following editorial from that series draws an analogy between the treatment of illegal aliens in America and the treatment of blacks in South Africa.*

They live in polluted squatter camps. They toil in factories by day, but at night they are hunted like animals. They produce the crops, but they are not permitted to own the land. They serve in homes but sleep in shacks. They have no rights, no representation in government, no freedom of speech in a land which is a democracy. If they are passive and do their work, they are tolerated by the white elite. But if they protest, they are fired and returned to their homelands. Periodically the owners of the land become appalled by the squatters and bulldoze the camps. Their children, born far from their homelands, are strangers in the new land and strangers in their fathers' land. Generations live in a separate society, serving the main society, but denied its rights and privileges.

These victims of apartheid are not thousands of miles away in South Africa, but here in America—in San Diego. We call them illegal aliens, but their status and their living conditions are not that different from the blacks of Soweto.

Americans are justly incensed by the horrors of apartheid in South Africa. But students protesting against apartheid at the University of California at San Diego are blind to the system of illegal alien farm labor in San Diego County. Concerned Americans raising money to boycott South Africa are unaware that the waiters and busboys serving them at fund-raisers are illegal aliens. The joggers who eat fresh strawberries at the roadside avert their heads from the field workers stooping in the sun, who live in the squatter camps of California.

South African apartheid is evil, a system which dooms that land to despair 4 and bloodshed. But South Africa is at least honest about its separate and unequal society. America is not. An estimated 6 million to 12 million illegal aliens live in this country, picking our crops, working in our sweatshops, an invisible minority.

Yes, many are better off economically than their brothers in their distant villages. So also the blacks in Soweto are better off than those in the impoverished homelands. But the illegal aliens are not free. They live in constant fear of being caught in the wrong place and deported. They cannot, in many places, go to a bus station or eat in a restaurant without being detected and deported.

And yet they are working for the benefit of employers who know they are illegal, know they have no rights, and exploit them.

Many Americans want to disinvest from firms doing business with South Africa. But we do not disinvest from farms and factories and restaurants and hotels that hire illegal aliens in America. We maintain a system by which it is legal to hire illegal aliens but illegal for them to work here, a system equal in hypocrisy to the pass laws of South Africa.

Americans look the other way when dealing with their own system of   8
apartheid. And Congress, by its repeated deadlock, has ratified the system of illegal immigration and illegal labor. Some sing of the virtues of illegal labor for the United States economy. They resemble the Afrikaaner apologists for apartheid who turn up at newspapers, arguing the justice of their system, or their predecessors in the American South, the gentlemanly apologists for that benign, Bible-recognized institution, slavery.

Apartheid is racist wherever it exists. It is inhuman in South Africa and inhuman in southern California. It destroys the moral fabric of our society and leaves a legacy of discrimination and suffering.

But we are blind to it. We point our finger at the South Africans and feel self-satisfied at our enlightened society. While the waiters bring us fresh strawberries picked by illegal aliens living in ravines and hootches. Here. Today.

We have no direct power to halt apartheid in South Africa. But we can and must stop illegal immigration and exploitation here. We must make it illegal for employers to hire illegal aliens. We must offer amnesty to aliens, to bring them out of hiding. We must abolish apartheid in America.

● PERSONAL RESPONSE ●

Freedman uses a typical strategy of argumentation, the analogy, to convince his readers that his position is a valid one. How convincing do you find Freedman's central comparison? Explain your answer.

● QUESTIONS FOR DISCUSSION ●

1. Why does Freedman not say who "they" are until paragraph 2?
2. What purpose is served by Freedman's use of "they" and "we"?
3. What ironies does Freedman see in the protests of Americans against South Africa's apartheid system?
4. Find all of the parallels Freedman draws between the position of illegal aliens in America and that of blacks in South Africa. Are all of the parallels convincing?
5. What effect do you think Freedman wants to achieve in paragraph 10 with the series of fragments beginning "While the waiters bring . . ."?
6. How convincing do you find the solutions Freedman offers in his final paragraph?

● WRITING TOPICS ●

1. Identify another group of people who are treated in a manner similar to that of illegal aliens in southern California and write your own editorial on the subject.

2. Write a letter to the editor in which you either agree or disagree with Freedman's views.

3. Argue for or against the special treatments received by the members of a specific group of people, such as the homeless, AIDS victims, or ethnic minorities. If appropriate, use analogy as a primary means of development.

THE DECLARATION OF INDEPENDENCE

●

THOMAS JEFFERSON

*Thomas Jefferson (1743–1826) was one of the most influential states-
men in the formation of the new republic of the United States of
America. A lawyer who graduated from William and Mary College,
Jefferson was elected to the Virginia House of Burgesses, was elected
governor of Virginia, and became a delegate to the Continental Congress in 1775. After the Revolutionary War, Jefferson served as secretary of state under Washington, as vice-president under John Adams,
and then as third president of the United States. Although several other
men helped write the Declaration of Independence and although it was
amended by the Continental Congress before its adoption on July 4,
1776, Jefferson was the chief author of the document. Its classic logical
process and direct, forceful language are characteristic of Jefferson's
writing style.*

When in the course of human events, it becomes necessary for one people
to dissolve the political bands which have connected them with another, and to assume among the Powers of the earth, the separate and
equal station to which the Laws of Nature and of Nature's God entitle them, a
decent respect to the opinions of mankind requires that they should declare the
causes which impel them to the separation.

We hold these truths to be self-evident, that all men are created equal, that
they are endowed by their Creator with certain unalienable Rights, that among
these are Life, Liberty, and the pursuit of Happiness. That to secure these
rights, Governments are instituted among Men, deriving their just powers from
the consent of the governed. That whenever any Form of Government becomes
destructive of these ends, it is the Right of the People to alter or to abolish it, and
to institute a new Government, laying its foundation on such principles and
organizing its powers in such form, as to them shall seem most likely to effect
their Safety and Happiness. Prudence, indeed, will dictate that Governments
long established should not be changed for light and transient causes; and
accordingly all experience hath shown that mankind are more disposed to suffer,
while evils are sufferable, than to right themselves by abolishing the forms to
which they are accustomed. But when a long train of abuses and usurpations
pursuing invariably the same Object evinces a design to reduce them under
absolute Despotism, it is their right, it is their duty, to throw off such government, and to provide new Guards for their future security. Such has been the
patient sufferance of these Colonies; and such is now the necessity which
constrains them to alter their former Systems of Government. The history of the
present King of Great Britain is a history of repeated injuries and usurpations,

all having in direct object the establishment of an absolute Tyranny over these States. To prove this, let Facts be submitted to a candid world.

He has refused his Assent to Laws, the most wholesome and necessary for the public good.

He has forbidden his Governors to pass Laws of immediate and pressing 4 importance, unless suspended in their operation till his Assent should be obtained; and when so suspended, he has utterly neglected to attend to them.

He has refused to pass other Laws for the accommodation of large districts of people, unless those people would relinquish the right of Representation in the Legislature, a right inestimable to them and formidable to tyrants only.

He has called together legislative bodies at places unusual, uncomfortable, and distant from the depository of their Public Records, for the sole purpose of fatiguing them into compliance with his measures.

He has dissolved Representative Houses repeatedly, for opposing with manly firmness his invasions on the rights of the people.

He has refused for a long time, after such dissolutions, to cause others to be 8 elected; whereby the Legislative Powers, incapable of Annihilation, have returned to the People at large for their exercise; the State remaining in the mean time exposed to all the dangers of invasion from without, and convulsions within.

He has endeavored to prevent the population of these States; for that purpose obstructing the Laws of Naturalization of Foreigners; refusing to pass others to encourage their migration hither, and raising the conditions of new Appropriations of Lands.

He has obstructed the Administration of Justice, by refusing his Assent to Laws for establishing Judiciary Powers.

He has made Judges dependent on his Will alone, for the tenure of their offices, and the amount and payment of their salaries.

He has erected a multitude of New Offices, and sent hither swarms of 12 Officers to harass our People, and eat out their substance.

He has kept among us, in time of peace, Standing Armies without the consent of our Legislature.

He has affected to render the Military independent of and superior to the Civil Power.

He has combined with others to subject us to jurisdictions foreign to our constitution, and unacknowledged by our laws; giving his Assent to their acts of pretended Legislation:

For quartering large bodies of armed troops among us: 16

For protecting them, by a mock Trial, from Punishment for any Murders which they should commit on the Inhabitants of these States:

For cutting off our Trade with all parts of the world:

For imposing Taxes on us without our Consent:

For depriving us in many cases, of the benefits of Trial by Jury: 20

For transporting us beyond Seas to be tried for pretended offenses:

For abolishing the free System of English Laws in a Neighbouring Province, establishing therein an Arbitrary government, and enlarging its boundaries so as to render it at once an example and fit instrument for introducing the same absolute rule into these Colonies:

For taking away our Charters, abolishing our most valuable Laws, and altering fundamentally the Forms of our Governments:

For suspending our own Legislatures, and declaring themselves invested 24 with Power to legislate for us in all cases whatsoever.

He has abdicated Government here, by declaring us out of his Protection and waging War against us.

He has plundered our seas, ravaged our Coasts, burnt our towns and destroyed the Lives of our people.

He is at this time transporting large Armies of foreign Mercenaries to compleat the works of death, desolation and tyranny, already begun with circumstances of Cruelty & perfidy scarcely paralleled in the most barbarous ages, and totally unworthy the Head of a civilized nation.

He has constrained our fellow Citizens taken Captive on the high Seas to 28 bear Arms against their Country, to become the executioners of their friends and Brethren, or to fall themselves by their Hands.

He has excited domestic insurrections amongst us, and has endeavored to bring on the inhabitants of our frontiers, the merciless Indian Savages, whose known rule of warfare, is an undistinguished destruction of all ages, sexes and conditions.

In every stage of these Oppressions We Have Petitioned for Redress in the most humble terms: Our repeated petitions have been answered only by repeated injury. A Prince, whose character is thus marked by every act which may define a Tyrant, is unfit to be the ruler of a free People.

Nor have We been wanting in attention to our British brethren. We have warned them from time to time of attempts by their legislature to extend an unwarrantable jurisdiction over us. We have reminded them of the circumstances of our emigration and settlement here. We have appealed to their native justice and magnanimity and we have conjured them by the ties of our common kindred to disavow these usurpations, which would inevitably interrupt our connections and correspondence. They too have been deaf to the voice of justice and of consanguinity. We must, therefore, acquiesce in the necessity, which denounces our Separation, and hold them, as we hold the rest of mankind, Enemies in War, in Peace Friends.

We, therefore, the Representatives of the United States of America, in 32 General Congress, Assembled, appealing to the Supreme Judge of the world for the rectitude of our intentions, do, in the Name, and by Authority of the good People of these Colonies, solemnly publish and declare, That these United Colonies are, and of Right ought to be, Free and Independent States; that they are Absolved from all Allegiance to the British Crown, and that all political connection between them and the State of Great Britain, is and ought to be totally dissolved; and that as Free and Independent States, they have full power to levy War, conclude Peace, contract Alliances, establish Commerce, and to do all other Acts and Things which Independent States may of right do. And for the support of this Declaration, with a firm reliance on the protection of Divine Providence, we mutually pledge to each other our lives, our Fortunes and our sacred Honor.

● PERSONAL RESPONSE ●

Although most of the draft that Jefferson and his co-authors presented to the Continental Congress was accepted, the Congress made some amendments before it was adopted. One notable amendment was the deletion of a lengthy, fierce condemnation of the slave trade. Why do you think delegates to the Congress wanted that section removed before they would sign the document? What passages or words would drafters of a similar document today omit or change? Explain your answer.

● QUESTIONS FOR DISCUSSION ●

1. What are the premises upon which the argument of the Declaration of Independence is based?
2. What conclusion are readers of this document expected to reach?
3. In what way are the truths listed in paragraph 2 "self-evident"?
4. What evidence does Jefferson supply to support his argument?
5. Why do you suppose Jefferson felt confident of his audience's agreement with his position?
6. Once he has established the sound logic of his argument, Jefferson uses emotionally charged language to appeal to the patriotic feelings of the colonists and thus strengthen his ability to convince them. Examples of such language are "most wholesome and necessary for the public good" in paragraph 3, "forbidden" and "utterly neglected" in paragraph 4, and "refused" in paragraph 5. Find other examples of Jefferson's appeal to emotions.

● WRITING TOPICS ●

1. Jefferson argues that "Life, Liberty, and the pursuit of Happiness" are among the "unalienable Rights" humans are entitled to. Select one additional human or civil right, perhaps drawing from the subjects discussed in other chapters of this book, and argue that it is "unalienable."
2. Another of Jefferson's "self-evident" truths is that "all men [and women] are created equal." Argue for or against this assumption.
3. Identify a specific kind of practice, policy, or custom at any level (parental, local, state, federal, or foreign) that you feel is despotic and argue for its abolition.

REPRESSION AND FREEDOM

●

ADDITIONAL WRITING SUGGESTIONS

1. Define either repression or freedom by using an extended example of an experience or situation that you feel best exemplifies the meaning of that word.

2. Compare and/or contrast a particular movement in the United States, such as civil rights, gay rights, or women's liberation, with liberation movements in another country.

3. Read some recent periodicals and then trace the events leading to the revolutions in any of the countries referred to in Omestad's article—Hungary, Poland, East Germany, or the Soviet Union.

4. Focusing on a specific country, discuss the means by which a government is able to keep its people oppressed.

5. Analyze some specific aspect of the system of apartheid in South Africa: what the system is, how it benefits those in power, what its effect is on those oppressed by it, how those in power maintain it, or what those oppressed by it are doing to end it. You might also consider writing a profile of one of the key figures in the anti-apartheid movement.

PERMISSIONS AND ACKNOWLEDGMENTS

———————————————— ● ————————————————

For permission to use the selections reprinted in this book, the author is grateful to the following publishers and copyright holders:

JENNIFER CRICHTON   For "Who Shall I Be?" by Jennifer Crichton. First published in *Ms*. Magazine in 1984. Reprinted by permission of the author.

THE PUTNAM PUBLISHING GROUP   For "A Textbook Pregnancy" by Perri Klass. Reprinted by permission of *The Putnam Publishing Group* from *A Not Entirely Benign Procedure* by Perri Klass. Copyright © 1987 by Perri Klass.

WILLIAM MORROW AND COMPANY, INC.   For "Deems" from *The Good Times* by Russell Baker. Copyright © 1989 William Morrow & Co., Inc. Reprinted by permission of the publisher.

PARADE   For "The Teacher Who Changed My Life" by Nicholas Gage. First published in *Parade*, December 17, 1989. Reprinted with permission from Parade, copyright © 1989.

THE NEW YORK TIMES   For "One Man's Kids" by Daniel Meier from *About Men* column in *The New York Times Magazine*, November 1, 1987. Copyright © 1987 by The New York Times Company. Reprinted by permission.

JOE QUEENAN   For "I Married an Accountant" by Joe Queenan. First published in *Newsweek*, November 14, 1988. Reprinted with permission of the author and *Newsweek*.

Ms. MAGAZINE   For "Chinese Puzzle" by Grace Ming-Yee Wai. First published in *Ms*. Magazine, July, 1988. Copyright © 1988, *Ms*. Magazine. Reprinted with permission of the author and *Ms*. magazine.

FABER AND FABER LIMITED   For "Thinking as a Hobby" an essay in *Holiday* magazine, 1961. Copyright © William Golding 1961. Reprinted by permission of Sir William Golding and Faber and Faber Ltd.

TIME   For "The Decline of Neatness" by Norman Cousins. Published in *Time*, April 2, 1990. Copyright © 1990 The Time Inc. Magazine Company. Reprinted by permission.

SUSAN OHANIAN   For "Ruffles and Flourishes" by Susan Ohanian, from *Atlantic* 260 (September 1987): 20–22. Reprinted by permission of the author.

THE WASHINGTON POST COMPANY   For "Training for Real Life" and "It's Failure, Not Success" by Ellen Goodman. Copyright © 1987, The Boston Globe Newspaper Company/The Washington Post Writers Group. Reprinted with permission.

HARPER & ROW   For "Living Like Weasels" from *Teaching A Stone To Talk* by Annie Dillard. Copyright © 1982 by Annie Dillard. Reprinted by permission of Harper & Row, Publisher, Inc.

RANDOM HOUSE, INC.   For "On Excellence" from *Metaphor and Memory* by Cynthia Ozick. Copyright © 1989 by Cynthia Ozick. Reprinted by permission of Alfred A. Knopf, Inc.

THE NEW YORK TIMES   For "Values Which Are Simply There" by Sue Halpern from *The New York Times Magazine*, May 20, 1990. Copyright © 1990 by the New York Times Company. Reprinted by permission.

ROBERT SCHOLES   For "Teach Ethics and Values in School" by Robert Scholes. Published in *The Philadelphia Inquirer*, June 24, 1989. Reprinted by permission of Robert Scholes.

HARPER'S MAGAZINE   For "Think About It" by Frank Conroy. Copyright © 1988 by *Harper's* magazine. All rights reserved. Reprinted from the November issue by special permission.

HARCOURT BRACE JOVANOVICH, INC.   For "Shooting an Elephant" by George Orwell from his volume *Shooting An Elephant and Other Essays*. Copyright © 1950 by Sonia Brownell Orwell and renewed 1978 by Sonia Orwell, reprinted by permission of Harcourt Brace Jovanovich, Inc.

DAVE BARRY   For "Designer Genes: An Immodest Proposal for Sexual Realignment" by Dave Barry. First published in *Ms.* magazine, September 1985. Reprinted by permission of the author.

M.O.M. MAGAZINE   For "How We Named Our Baby" by Sarah Pattee. First published in *Mothers and Other Midwives* magazine, Spring 1989. Reprinted with permission of *M.O.M* magazine.

THE UNIVERSITY OF GEORGIA PRESS   For "The Miracle Chicken" from *Maps to Anywhere* by Bernard Cooper. Copyright © 1990 by Bernard Cooper. Used by permission of the University of Georgia Press.

THE NEW YORK TIMES   For "The Androgynous Man" by Noel Perrin from *The New York Times Magazine*, February 5, 1984. Copyright © 1984 by The New York Times Company. Reprinted by permission.

THE NEW YORK TIMES   For "Alone Together: The Unromantic Generation" by Bruce Weber from *The New York Times Magazine*, April 5, 1987. Copyright © 1987 by The New York Times Company. Reprinted by permission.

ANNIE ROIPHE   For "Why Marriages Fail" by Anne Roiphe. Published in *Family Weekly*, February 27, 1983. Reprinted by permission of the author.

NORTH POINT PRESS   For "Men and Women in Search of Common Ground" excerpted from *Home Economics*, copyright © 1987 by Wendell Berry. Reprinted by permission of North Point Press.

ROBERT NEMIROFF   For "In Defense of the Equality of *Men*" by Lorraine Hansberry. Copyright © 1985 by Robert Nemiroff. All rights reserved. Reprinted by permission of Robert Nemiroff.

DAVID MORRIS   For "Rootlessness Undermines Our Economy as Well as the Quality of Our Lives" by David Morris. First published in *Utne Reader*, May/June 1990. Reprinted with permission of the author.

WILLIAM MORROW   For "Kids in the Mall: Growing Up Controlled" from *The Malling of America* by William Severini Kowinski. Copyright © 1985 by William Severini Kowinski. Reprinted by permission of William Morrow & Co.

TIME   For "Slow Descent into Hell" by Jon D. Hull. Published in *Time*, February 2, 1987. Copyright © 1987 Time Inc. Reprinted by permission.

THE GEORGIA REVIEW   For "From Outside, In." Originally appeared in *The Georgia Review*, Volume XLI, No. 2 (Summer 1987), © 1987 by the University of Georgia. © 1987 by Barbara Mellix. Reprinted by permission of Barbara Mellix and *The Georgia Review*.

LITTLE, BROWN AND COMPANY   For Part 3, Chapter 13 and Part 1, Chapters 1, 2, 3, and 14 from *Blue Highways: A Journey Into America* by William Least Heat Moon. Copyright © 1982 by William Least Heat Moon. Reprinted by permission of Little, Brown and Company.

MACMILLAN PUBLISHING COMPANY "Borders" is reprinted with permission of Charles Scribner's Sons, an imprint of Macmillan Publishing Company, from *Crossing Open Ground* by Barry Lopez. Copyright © 1981, 1988 Barry Holstun Lopez. (First appeard in *Country Journal*, Sept. 1981.)

E. P. DUTTON For "Just Married" from *The Solace of Open Spaces* by Gretel Ehrlich. Copyright © 1985 by Gretel Ehrlich. Reprinted by permission of the publisher, Viking Penguin, a division of Penguin Books USA Inc.

HARCOURT BRACE JOVANOVICH, INC. For "My Wood" from *Abinger Harvest*, copyright © 1936 and renewed 1964 by E. M. Forster, reprinted by permission of Harcourt Brace Jovanovich, Inc.

THE NEW YORK TIMES For "Two Varieties of Killers" from "Hers" (column) by Ellen Currie. Published in *The New York Times*, August 21, 1986. Copyright © 1986 by The New York Times Company. Reprinted by permission.

LADIES' HOME JOURNAL For "The War Against Women" by Carol Lynn Mithers which appeared in the October 1989 issues of *Ladies' Home Journal* magazine. Copyright © 1989, Meredith Corporation. All rights reserved. Reprinted from *Ladies' Home Journal* magazine.

CARYL RIVERS For "Rock Lyrics and Violence Against Women" by Caryl Rivers. Published in *Boston Globe*, 1985. Reprinted by permission of the author.

PARENTS' MUSIC RESOURCE CENTER For "My Turn: Some Reasons for Wilding" by Tipper Gore and Susan A. Baker. Published in *Newsweek*, May 29, 1989. Reprinted by permission of Parents' Music Resource Center.

THE NEW YORK TIMES For "Public & Private: Old Enough to Kill" by Anna Quindlen from *The New York Times*, April 1, 1990. Copyright © 1990 by The New York Times Company. Reprinted by permission.

THE NEW REPUBLIC For "Guns 'Я' Us" by Matthew Maranz. Published in *The New Republic*, January 23, 1989. Reprinted by permission of *The New Republic*, © 1989, The New Republic, Inc.

GAIL BUCHALTER For "Why I Bought a Gun" by Gail Buchalter. First published in *Parade* magazine in 1988. Reprinted by permission of the author.

HARPER & ROW For excerpt from *Stride Toward Freedom* by Martin Luther King, Jr. Copyright © 1958 by Martin Luther King, Jr., renewed © 1986 by Coretta Scott King, Dexter King, Martin Luther King III, Yolanda King, and Bernice King. Reprinted by permission of HarperCollins Publishers.

HARCOURT BRACE JOVANOVICH, INC. For "Beauty: When the Other Dancer is the Self" from *In Search of Our Mothers' Gardens*, copyright © 1983 by Alice Walker, reprinted by permission of Harcourt Brace Jovanovich, Inc.

THE UNIVERSITY OF ARIZONA PRESS For "On Being a Cripple" from *Plaintext* by Nancy Mairs. Copyright © 1986 the University of Arizona Press. Reprinted by permission of the publisher.

TIME For "The Quality of Mercy Killing" by Roger Rosenblatt. Published in *Time*, August 26, 1985. Copyright © 1985 Time Inc. Reprinted by permission.

HARPER'S MAGAZINE For "Neither Morons Nor Imbeciles Nor Idiots; In the Company of the Mentally Retarded" by Sallie Tisdale. Copyright © 1990 by *Harper's Magazine*. All rights reserved. Reprinted from the June issue by special permission.

RANDOM HOUSE, INC. For "A Family Confronts Mental Illness" from *Wake Me When It's Over* by Mary Kay Blakely. Copyright © 1989 by Mary Kay Blakely. Reprinted by permission of Times Books, a division of Random House, Inc.

HARPER'S MAGAZINE   For "Users Like Me: Membership in the Church of Drugs" by Gail Regier. Copyright © 1989 by *Harper's Magazine*. All rights reserved. Reprinted from the May issue by special permission.

THE VILLAGE VOICE   For "AIDS and the Social Contract" by Richard Goldstein. Published in *The Village Voice*, December 19, 1987. Reprinted by permission of the author and *The Village Voice*.

HARCOURT BRACE JOVANOVICH, INC.   For "Shakespeare's Sister" from *A Room of One's Own* by Virginia Woolf, copyright 1929 by Harcourt Brace Jovanovich, Inc. and renewed 1957 by Leonard Woolf, reprinted by permission of the publisher.

SOCIETY FOR THE ADVANCEMENT OF EDUCATION   For "Prejudice, Conflict, and Ethnoviolence" by Joan C. Weiss reprinted from *USA Today Magazine*, May 1989. Copyright © 1989 by the Society for the Advancement of Education.

DAVID R. GODINE PUBLISHER INCORPORATED   For "Complexion" from *Hunger of Memory* by Richard Rodriguez. Copyright © 1982 by Richard Rodriguez. Reprinted by permission of David R. Godine, Publisher.

E. P. DUTTON   For Chapter 18 from *Mary* by Mary Mebane. Copyright © 1981 by Mary Elizabeth Mebane. Reprinted by permission of the publisher, Viking Penguin, a division of Penguin Books USA Inc.

BRENT STAPLES   For "Just Walk On By" by Brent Staples. First published in *Ms.* magazine, September 1986. Reprinted with permission of the author.

W. W. NORTON & COMPANY, INC.   For "Carrie Buck's Daughter" reprinted from *The Flamingo's Smile: Reflections in Natural History*, by Stephen Jay Gould, by permission of W. W. Norton and Company, Inc. Copyright © 1985 by Stephen Jay Gould.

ROGER WILKINS   For "I Became Her Target" by Roger Wilkins. Published in *Newsday*, September 9, 1987. Reprinted with permission of the author.

CLIFFORD J. HURSTON   For "How It Feels To Be Colored Me" by Zora Neale Hurston. First published in *The World Tomorrow* in 1928. Permission provided by the Estate of Zora Neale Hurston.

NEW REPUBLIC   For "The Lost Generation" by Dorinda Elliot. First published in *The New Republic*, April 9, 1990. Reprinted by permission of *The New Republic*, © 1990, The New Republic, Inc.

NEW REPUBLIC   For "Ten-Day Wonder" by Thomas Omestad. Published in *The New Republic*, December 25, 1984. Reprinted by permission of *The New Republic*, © 1984, The New Republic, Inc.

H. JOACHIM MAITRE   For "Exodus From Tyranny" from *Freedom on the March* II by H. Joachim Maitre. First published in *Reader's Digest*, January 1990. Reprinted with permission of the author and from the January 1990 *Reader's Digest*.

THE WASHINGTON POST   For "From Nicholas II to Gorbachev, a Family's Survival Amid Soviet Antisemitism" by David Remnick. Published in *The Washington Post*, May 21, 1990. Copyright © 1990, The Washington Post. Reprinted with permission.

VICTOR ZASLAVSKY   For "Mystery in a Soviet Library" by Victor Zaslavsky. First published in *Partisan Review*, vol. 55, no. 1, 1988. Copyright © 1988 by Partisan Review Inc. Reprinted with permission of the author.

TONI MORRISON   For "Cinderella's Stepsisters" by Toni Morrison. First published in *Ms.* magazine, September 1979. Copyright © Toni Morrison. Reprinted with permission of the author.

JOHNATHAN FREEDMAN   For "Abolish American Apartheid" by Johnathan Freedman. First published in the *San Diego Union Tribune*, May 9, 1985. Reprinted with permission of the author.